Dublin Burial Grounds & Graveyards

By the same author

James Joyce's Dublin Houses and Nora Barnacle's Galway
City of Dublin
A Literary Guide to Dublin

This publication has received support from the Heritage Council
under the 2001 Publications Grant Scheme.

Dublin Burial Grounds
& Graveyards

Vivien Igoe

Photographs by
Paddy Tutty

WOLFHOUND PRESS

Published in 2001 by
Wolfhound Press Ltd
68 Mountjoy Square
Dublin 1, Ireland
Tel: (353-1) 874 0354
Fax: (353-1) 872 0207

British Library Cataloguing in Publication Data
A catalogue record for this book is available from the British Library.

ISBN 0-86327-872-8

5 4 3 2 1

Maps of Glasnevin and Mount Jerome Cemeteries: Michael Gleeson
Map of Dean's Grange Cemetery: Eilish Young
Cover Design: Graham Thew Design
Cover Image: Paddy Tutty
Typesetting and book design: Wolfhound Press
Printed and bound by MPG Books Ltd., Bodmin, Cornwall

CONTENTS

LIST OF ILLUSTRATIONS

ACKNOWLEDGEMENTS

Special thanks are due to the following people for their assistance and courtesy, Brendan O'Donoghue, Director, National Library of Ireland and the staff of the National Library; Mary Kelleher, Librarian, and the staff of the Royal Dublin Society Library; Dr Raymond Refausse, Librarian, and Dr Susan Hood, of the Representative Church Body Library; Beatrice Doran, Librarian, and Mary O'Doherty, of the Royal College of Surgeons in Ireland, and Gregory O'Connor, Archivist, the National Archives.

I would also like to thank Matthew Quigley and David Walsh, Dean's Grange Cemetery; John Kinahan and Mervyn Colville, Glasnevin Cemetery; Lucy Lynam, Mount Jerome Cemetery; Gloria O'Neill, Ballybough Burial Ground; Henry Morris, Grangegorman Military Cemetery; Father Herman, CP, Mount Argus and Sheila Crowley from St Mary's Pro-Cathedral, all of whom provided help in various ways.

For some points of information I would like to thank the following: Dr Benedict Kiely, James Boys, Mona Brase, Ciara Byrne, Patrick Casey, Leo Collins, Brian Coleman, Brendan Crowe, Bob Cudmore, Dr John Fleetwood, Bill Fitzroy, Joseph C. Gallagher, the Revd Mark Gardner, Arthur Garrett, Grania Gilroy, Dr John Goodbody, Professor Conal Hooper, Joe Langtry, Mary McQuillan, Elizabeth Morgan, Dominick Murphy, Anne Nolan, Tony O'Doherty, Father Fergus O'Donoghue, SJ, Bernie O'Donoghue, Aidan O'Hanlon, Father John O'Keeffe, OFM, Tim O'Neill, Danny Parkinson, Trevor Plowman, Letitia Pollard, Barbara Roe, Helen Rutledge, Mark Rutledge, Glenn Thompson, Thomas A. Veale, Pat Walsh, Jed Walsh and Finola Watchorn.

I would like to thank Leo Collins for his assistance in sourcing old Dublin maps.

For the photography in this book, much appreciation and thanks goes to Paddy Tutty for his extraordinary patience through the many months of work in various climatic conditions. He spent many hours with his cameras, between climbing over walls, sitting on kerbstones, cleaning graves, and waiting for the rain to cease or the clouds to pass, to take the wonderful photographs of the many monuments and gravestones.

My thanks must also go to my husband Michael for his help and support throughout.

A Note on the Maps

The maps of Glasnevin and Mount Jerome Cemeteries were drawn by Michael Gleeson. The map of Dean's Grange Cemetery was drawn by Eilish Young.

For more detailed information on streets and roads, the reader may find it helpful to consult the Ordnance Survey Street Map of Dublin.

In loving memory of my father

Laurence J. Veale

Introduction

Graveyards form an important part of our national heritage and have a universal interest and appeal. In Dublin City and county there are a variety of burial grounds, which unravel our Nation's past and form a historical resource of prime importance. There are over 200 burial grounds in Dublin City and county, 72 of which are included in this book. This number comprises churchyards, graveyards and some churches which contain vaults. The graveyards also include denominations such as Quaker, Jewish, Moravian, and Huguenot.

The Irish weather has worked on some of the memorial stones with detrimental effect leaving many of the older ones illegible. Fortunately in some cases, many of the inscriptions were recorded before this happened. A number of the older headstones give an insight into the local history and crafts carried out in a particular area. They indicate the occupation or trade of the individual interred. In some cases, a large number of children are named on a family gravestone. They often predeceased their parents, which illustrates the social conditions prevalent at the time.

Many of the cemeteries provide the amenity of a park with a wide range of both native and foreign trees. Both the common and the Irish yew trees are synonymous with the landscape of our graveyards. The yew tree was venerated by the Celts, and the Druids believed it to be immortal. They have extraordinarily long lives, some being more than a thousand years old. It is said that the roots of the yew were charged with the thoughts of the dead, which their branches in turn, scattered to the winds.

The purpose of this book is to act as a guide and to provide the reader with information on some of the old burial grounds within Dublin City and a small selection in the county of Dublin, many of which date from early Christian times. A selection of the people who are buried in them is included – many of whom influenced the course of history by their contribution in various fields.

The geographic area covered comprises Dublin City and its outskirts, stretching in an arc from Howth on the north side, to the sixth century monastic site in Killiney on the south side. Due to space limitations, choices had to be made, and the ones chosen are all within reach of the city by the DART or bus. Naturally, there are omissions and these include the large number of medieval churches with their burial grounds in north County Dublin. However, there is a reference section at the end of the book, which lists the cemeteries not included.

There was quite a large concentration of small churches with graveyards contained within a relatively small area of the old city. Some of these no longer remain due to redevelopment of an area or changes in the street structure. These include a couple of Pre-Viking churches which represent two of Dublin's most ancient parishes of St Bride's on Bride Street and St Michael-Le-Pole off Ship Street which is the only Dublin churchyard known to have contained a round tower. It was badly damaged by a storm in 1775 and demolished the following year. The church of St John the Evangelist in Fishamble Street was demolished in 1884 due to the Corporation's plan to link Christchurch Place with Dame Street. The parish records pertaining to St John's are one of the most important collections of parish records held in the custody of the Representative Church Body Library which is the principal repository for over 800 Church of Ireland parish registers. St Peter's in Aungier Street, built on the site of an older church is also gone.

A few churches which had churchyards attached are no longer used as places of worship and some have been transformed into commercial ventures. These include St Mary's in Mary Street, St James's in James's Street, St Paul's in North King Street, St Andrew's in Suffolk Street, which now serves as Dublin's main Tourist Office, and St Michael and John's in Lower Exchange Street, which is now the venue for *The Dublin Viking Adventure*.

However, some old churches with churchyards in the city are still in use such as St Michan's, St Werburgh's and St Audoen's, which has the distinction of serving its parishioners on a continuous basis for over eight hundred years.

Some former city churchyards are now used as car parks. These include St Anne's in Dawson Street, St Mark's in Pearse Street, St Andrew's in Suffolk Street and St Paul's in North King Street. Other churchyards have been landscaped and are now public parks such as St Kevin's in Camden Row, St Catherine's in Thomas Street, St Audoen's in Cornmarket, St Mary's in Mary Street, and Little St George's in Hill Street. The Cabbage Garden is also a park. In all these places, there are still some memorials to be seen.

Inevitably, with the conversion of these churchyards into parks, many of the old memorials, which were a visual record of the past and the work of Dublin's craftsmen, have disappeared. This denudes the burial ground of an essential part of its written heritage, which was carved in stone. These inscribed headstones, which provided valuable personal and historical information, were a medium of record, which is now a lost heritage to a whole area or locality.

A number of churches in County Dublin with adjoining burial grounds date back to the early Christian period such as St Mobhi's (Glasnevin), St Fintan's (Clonkeen), St Brigid's, (Stillorgan), St Nahi's (Taney), Kilgobbin, Killiney, Kilternan, Tully, Whitechurch, Kilbarrack and Raheny. There are strong links with the past and the early days of the Christian church in Ireland which can be seen in the decorated old stone slabs and crosses found in some of these churches such as Tully, Kilgobbin and Killiney. The churchyard at Rathmichael contains the stump of a round tower.

In pre-Christian times, families buried their dead wherever they wished to do so, on a mountain, in a bog or nearer to home. In the early Christian period, ordinary people buried their dead outside the walls of their villages or towns in special places set aside specifically for that purpose. These places were not connected with churches and were know as cemeteries, which means dormitories or sleeping places.

Before 1538 there was no law in existence which required parish records to be kept. Hence, before that date it is difficult to ascertain where burials took place.

Later, the churches had churchyards attached, which were used for burials. Church vaults were also used. Within the city, Dublin was fairly compact and densely populated and these churchyards became so overcrowded that it caused a serious health hazard to the public. As a result, a law was passed whereby all further burials could only take place in locations outside the walls of towns and cities. The *Burial Act of 1855* was the start of the development of cemeteries in Britain and Ireland.

At the time of the Reformation, the old Catholic burial grounds passed into Protestant hands. As a result, Roman Catholics possessed no cemeteries to bury their dead. Burials could only take place in Protestant churchyards. This meant that the parson received substantially increased revenue and tithes from people to whom he did not administer. The burial fees were known to be excessively exorbitant. This annoyed Irish Catholics countrywide and was compounded by a rule forbidding the Catholic burial service in cemeteries under Protestant control. Sometimes, a small piece of earth was placed in the coffin of a Catholic and the prayers scheduled to be said at the graveside were recited before the cortege left the house or place where the person had died.

St James's, along with Bully's Acre in Kilmainham and St Kevin's in Camden Row, were the burial grounds most used by Catholics during penal times. A number of unpleasant incidents took place during funerals at St James's and St Kevin's churchyards which are included in later chapters.

It was because of this and the order issued by the archbishop of Dublin, Dr William Magee, who opposed Catholic Emancipation 'that the burial service in any of the churchyards within his jurisdiction should not be read by a Roman Catholic clergyman' that Daniel O'Connell organised a meeting of the Catholic Association on 1 November 1823.

O'Connell urged that the only means by which the Catholics could get rid of such injustices which had occurred would be 'to form an association for the purchase of ground, to serve as an asylum where their bones could be deposited, with the forms of Christian burial, without fear of insult, and where the Irish Catholics might enjoy the exercise of a religious ceremony of which they only, of the whole Christian world, were deprived'. A committee was formed with O'Connell as chairman.

As a result, the non-denominational cemetery in Goldenbridge was established in 1827. On 15 October 1829, six months after the Act of Catholic Emancipation had been passed, the new site at

Goldenbridge was blessed. Land was then acquired for a non-denominational cemetery in Glasnevin, which was opened in February 1832.

Mount Jerome Cemetery opened in 1836. This was the main cemetery on the south side for members of the Protestant faith. There were possibly a few Catholic burials here from time to time as an article entitled *A Ramble in Our Cemeteries* published in 1859 states that interments of Roman Catholics frequently took place. These increased in the 1920s when there was an industrial dispute at Glasnevin Cemetery.

The *Burial Act of 1855* resulted in the closure of many of the older churchyards within the city and county of Dublin due to overcrowding. In 1861, the Board of Guardians of Rathdown bought land in Dean's Grange for the purpose of creating a new cemetery. Dean's Grange, the largest cemetery in south county Dublin was opened in 1865. In 1964, it was extended to include Shanganagh Cemetery, which is situated just beyond Shankill.

Dublin Burial Grounds & Graveyards

Arbour Hill Cemetery and the Croppies' Acre

Situation: The Croppies' Acre is between Benburb Street and Wolfe Tone Quay.
Arbour Hill Cemetery is off Arbour Hill
Period in use: 1704–1920s
Bus Nos (from city centre): 25, 26, 79 or 90 to Heuston Station (Cross at Heuston Bridge)

The area around Arbour Hill was partially owned by Christ Church Cathedral in the Middle Ages and was used for the storage of corn, hence the name Cnoc an Arbhair (corn hill). A gallows once overlooked the hill, which was used as a place of execution. Robin Hood's famous lieutenant, Little John who settled in the area, is said to have ended his days here.

It has associations with two burial grounds, the Croppies' Acre and Arbour Hill Cemetery. Collins Barracks (formerly the Royal Barracks) is situated between both of them.

This district is associated with many historical and blood curdling events, in particular the 1798 revolutionary period when a number of Croppies were massacred by the yeomen under the orders of Cornwallis, the Lord Lieutenant. In a letter to the Duke of Portland he wrote 'any man in a brown coat who was found within seven miles of the field of action was butchered without discrimination'. Cartloads of mutilated bodies were brought into the city and dumped on the pavement of Barrack Street (now Benburb Street) where they were displayed covered in blood and dirt. These, together with the Croppies who were executed at Arbour Hill, are interred in a field known as The Croppies' Acre that runs alongside Wolfe Tone Quay. Situated south of Benburb Street, this was part of the land that extended in front of the barracks down to the Liffey.

This has now been designated the 1798 Croppies' Acre Memorial Park and incorporates many features connected with 1798 such as the Croppies, Wolfe Tone, the connection with France and the Tree of Liberty. It is beautifully landscaped with large slabs of granite in a chequer-board pattern set into the grass. A stepping stone pathway winds its way between the stones and leads to an area of Contemplation. Here there is an unusual water feature. Water, which is the symbol of life and healing, is used here to show the birth of freedom and democracy in Ireland. This area, which is partially enclosed by two ascending stone walls, contains Seamus Heaney's beautiful and evocative poem, 'Requiem for the Croppies'. This is inscribed on the inner face of the south wall with the associated barley motifs and the *United Irishmen's Catechism.*

The graves, which are unmarked, contain the remains of Matthew Wolfe Tone, a brother of Theobold Wolfe Tone and Bartholomew Teeling who accompanied Wolfe Tone to France and served a campaign under Hoche. He was captured after the surrender at Ballinamuck and was tried by court-martial at the Royal Barracks, sentenced to death and executed at Arbour Hill on 24 September 1798. It was said 'neither the intimation of his fate, nor the near approach of it, produced on him any diminution of courage. With firm step and unchanged countenance he walked from the prison to the place of execution, and conversed with an unaffected ease while the dreadful apparatus was preparing.' His remains, with those of many other executed persons, were thrown into what was then known as 'The Croppies' Hole'.

Wolfe Tone, who died in the Provost's Prison in 1798, is commemorated with a memorial in the Croppies' Acre Memorial Park. The Office of Public Works manages the park and its landscape maintenance is provided by Dúchas.

OPENING TIMES:
MON–SAT 10.00 A.M.–5.00 P.M.
SUN 12 NOON–5.00 P.M.

Directly behind the Croppies' Acre Memorial Park is Collins Barracks, which was formerly the Royal Barracks. Designed by Thomas Burgh, it was built in 1701. In April 1997, the army officially vacated the barracks and it now houses the new National Museum of the Decorative Arts. Directly behind this is Arbour Hill Cemetery.

In 1848, the detention barracks and church at Arbour Hill were constructed. At that time, the grounds were enclosed and divided out into three areas or plots. The first one directly behind the church was the garrison cemetery.

The burials in this cemetery comprise mainly British military personnel and their families. Two examples are as follows:

Sacred to the memory of | Corp William Jackson | of the 13th Light Dragoons | who departed this life | 16th April 1859 aged 24 years.

He served through the whole of the Crimean campaign | This tribute of respect is erected by his brother | Non-Commissioned Officers.

And an altar type tomb bears the inscription:

Major General | Sir Guy Campbell Bart, C.B. Colonel of the 3rd West India Regiment | and in Command of the | Western District | of Ireland | Died Jany 27th 1840 | aged 64 years.

I will lay down in peace and take my rest | For it is thou Lord only makest me dwell in safety.

[1] THE GARDEN OF REMEMBRANCE, ARBOUR HILL.

[2] The 1798 Croppies' Memorial Park.

Most of the headstones in the garrison cemetery were cleared and placed around the boundary wall where they afford interesting reading for the military historian. The area they formerly occupied is now a neatly manicured lawn.

The second plot to the north of this was used as a school playground for the two small schools once situated within the grounds. Adjoining the school playground but separated by a high wall was the third plot, which was the exercise yard for prisoners. These two sections were amalgamated and form a large space along with the beautifully laid-out Garden of Remembrance. The garden, which contains the remains of the executed leaders of the 1916 Rising, comprises a lawn area with a wide variety of trees which includes a row of poplars, a wide sweeping chestnut, copper beech, sycamore, lime, yew, mountain ash, cherry, laburnum and silver birch.

The executions of the fourteen leaders of the Rising were carried out at dawn in the grey high-walled stone-breaker's yard in Kilmainham Gaol between the 3 and 12 May 1916. With the exception of James Connolly, all of the leaders were confined at Richmond Barracks in Inchicore where they were court-martialled and sentenced to death. They were then transported to Kilmainham Gaol the day before their execution.

On 3 May 1916 in the north-east corner of the exercise yard in Arbour Hill, a grave was prepared for the interment of the executed leaders whose remains were transported from Kilmainham Gaol by a horse-drawn vehicle. Details concerning the order of their interments were kept and a numbered brick was placed at the head of each of the fourteen men in sequence of their burial. Their remains were covered with quicklime.

The seven signatories of the Proclamation of the Irish Republic included Patrick Pearse, the poet and writer born in 1879 in Great Brunswick Street (now Pearse Street) and executed on 3 May; Thomas Clarke, the first signatory of the Proclamation, who was born in 1857 on the Isle of Wight and executed on 3 May; Seán MacDiarmada, born in 1884 in Co. Leitrim and executed on 12 May; Thomas MacDonagh, the poet born in Cloughjordan, Co. Tipperary in 1878 and executed 3 May; Eamonn Ceannt, born in 1881 in Ballymore, Co. Galway and executed 7 May; James Connolly, trade union organiser, born in 1868 in Edinburgh and executed on 9 May and Joseph Plunkett, the poet, born in Dublin in 1887. Plunkett had married Grace Gifford, the artist, in the Catholic chapel of the Gaol on 3 May, just hours before his execution.

Others who were executed in 1916 at Kilmainham Gaol and are buried here include Major John MacBride, born in 1865 in Westport, Co. Mayo and executed on 5 May. He married Maud Gonne in 1903 by whom he had one son, Seán MacBride; William Pearse, born in 1881 and executed on 4 May. He was the younger brother of Patrick Pearse; Seán Heuston, born in 1891 in Dublin, and executed on 8 May;

Michael O'Hanrahan, born in New Ross in 1877 and executed the 4 May; Edward Daly, born in Limerick and executed on the 4 May and Con Colbert born near Newcastle, Co. Limerick in 1896 and executed on 8 May.

These burials are now set in the Garden of Remembrance in an oblong green sward with a limestone kerb around it in which the names of those interred are engraved both in Irish and in English. A curved wall serves as a backdrop. In the centre of the wall is a gold cross and on either side of the cross the Proclamation of the Republic is engraved both in Irish and in English. The inscription was designed and engraved by the late Michael Biggs.

President John F. Kennedy laid a wreath at the memorial on this hallowed ground on 28 June 1963 and in April 1966, President Eamon de Valera unveiled a plaque with the names of all those who had died.

OPENING TIMES:

APRIL–OCTOBER: MON–FRI 8.30 A.M.–7.00 P.M.

OCTOBER–APRIL: MON–FRI 8.30 A.M.–5.00 P.M. SAT & SUN ALL YEAR: 11.00 A.M.–5.00 P.M.

LEFT: [3] JOSEPH MARY PLUNKETT (1887–1916).

Ballybough (Jewish Burial Ground)

Situation: 65 Fairview Strand, Dublin 3

Period in use: c. 1718–1908

Bus Nos (from city centre): 31, 31B, 32, 32B

Ballybough, which is situated just over a mile from the city centre, derives its name from Baile Bocht meaning 'the town of the poor'. The district was near the city and in close proximity to the sea and was an advantageous landing place for overseas invaders. Up until just over a century ago it was always considered a foreign quarter and particularly so in the seventeenth and eighteenth centuries. The Quakers, who first came to Ireland in 1654, settled in this area for a time, as did the Huguenots when they first came to Dublin circa 1698.

The earliest Jews who arrived to Ireland in any significant number were of Spanish and Portuguese origin. Manual Pereira, who arrived in Dublin with his brother in 1662, established a synagogue in Crane Lane, off Dame Street. Around the year 1718 they too settled in the Ballybough area in a place known as Annadale north of the river Tolka. Annadale, which is situated off Phillipsburgh Avenue, is now a housing scheme.

The site for the first Jewish burial ground in Dublin was acquired in 1718. Chichester Philips of Drumcondra Castle, the owner of the plot in Fairview Strand, leased it on 28 October 1718. It is in close proximity to Annadale. On 17 August 1748, the London congregation bought it as a leasehold property for the term of one thousand years at the nominal rent of one peppercorn. They also paid for the wall enclosing the burial ground which measures 'half a rood and five perches' or approximately 2,500 square metres.

A description of the burial ground is given in a book entitled *Excursions Through Ireland* (author unknown) printed in 1816:

> On the road leading to Ballybough there is a Jew's cemetery, a piece of ground enclosed by a high wall and planted with shrubs and trees. Here appear a few tombstones inscribed with Hebrew characters: and they were formerly much more numerous until stolen to be converted into hearthstones and to other purposes.

It continues:

> A Jew paying a visit a short time ago to a Christian friend in the vicinity of Ballybough Bridge found him in the act of repairing his house. Examining the improvements he perceived near the fireplace a stone with a Hebrew inscription intimating to the astonished Israelite that the body of his father was buried in the chimney.

25

[4] THE TOMB OF ALDERMAN LEWIS HARRIS (1812–76) IN BALLYBOUGH CEMETERY.

The man in question was Solomon Cohen, who died in Dublin before 1816 and whose tombstone was discovered by his son in a house close to the graveyard.

In 1857 a small caretaker's house, now a listed building, was erected. It replaced a hut built in 1798 by the Cohen family. The small tablet on front of the house states 'Built in the year 5618'. It proves confusing to passers-by but this is the Jewish calendar corresponding to the year 1857. The burial ground is directly behind this unusual building.

The graves, which number 148, are inscribed in both the English and Hebrew languages. They are easily located, as the graveyard is small, neat and well kept. Two large trees, a chestnut and a sycamore provide shade. The inscriptions on some of the memorials are now illegible. In many cases, the inscription states where the person interred was born, or lived formerly, and also the Jewish calendar month of death. Below are a few examples:

Joseph Rosenburg, son of Pesach. Native of Gorsd, Poland. d. 24th Nisan, 5625 (20/4/1865) aged 25.

Nathan Symons of Hamburgh, native of Amsterdam d. 15th May, 5605 (1845). Aged 39.

David Rosenthal, native of Hanover. d. 22nd Kislev, 5630 (1869)

Isaac Isaacs, son of Abraham. Late of Falmouth, d. Jan. 22nd, 1847: 5th Shevat, 5607.

Sarah, wife of Henry de Groot of Rotterdam. d. 18th Tammuz, 5631 (1871). Aged 81.

Samuel Stavenhagen, son of GersHond. 28th Tishrei, 1889. Aged 80. Both natives of Germany.

Many of the older memorials were removed from the burial ground, which resulted in the loss of much information. Only one memorial now remains from the eighteenth century. This is towards the west wall and is situated between rows I and II. It stands alone in what was once a row and marks the burial place of Jacob Wills who was born in France in 1701 and died in Dublin in 1777. He traded as a jeweller at Essex Quay from 1769 to 1772. On his retirement, his grandson Isaac Isaacs succeeded him in the business. His gravestone bears the following inscription:

Jacob Wills d. 17th Adar 11, 5537(1777), aged 76.

An inscription in Hebrew follows this. (Jacob son of Johannan Weil, known as Jacob Frenchman).

Moses Jacob Cowan who died on 16 February 1748 was born in Polish Prussia in 1683. A dwarf, he was obviously a very talented acrobat and was known for his surprising performances in balancing and other feats, appearing at the New Wells at Clerkenwell in 1746 and at Sadlier's Wells. He did not live permanently in Dublin as he belonged to a travelling show, which was on tour. His funeral by all accounts proved a great attraction to passers-by as the hearse was followed on foot by members of his travelling show, together with his friends of the Jewish community. The gravestone of Jacob Cowan is now missing and his grave is unmarked but thought to be in the same row as that of Jacob Wills.

Jacob Phillips, a well-known chocolate maker from Crane Lane who died on 13 January 1748 is believed to be buried in this same row. He settled in Dublin in the early 1700s and was lay head of the Jewish community in 1746.

Lewis Harris, a former alderman of the city of Dublin, is interred in Row V from the west wall. He has a fine tomb, which bears the following inscription:

Lewis Harris, Alderman of the city of Dublin. d. 11th Ab: Aug. 1st, 5636(1876). Aged 64. His family revered him. His fellow citizens honoured him.

Sadly, Alderman Harris died the day before he was due to be made Lord Mayor of Dublin. He lived at 1 Royal Marine Terrace, Bray, in County Wicklow. Every Jew in Dublin attended his funeral, together with aldermen, lawyers, physicians and clergy. His second wife, Juliette, is interred beside him, rather than in the same grave. A second body is never interred in the same grave. This is an act of veneration not possible in other burial places due to larger communities and restrictions on available space.

Their son Herbert Wormser Harris, who is interred close by, died quite young. His inscription reads:

Herbert Wormser Harris. Science scholar and Senior Moderator, B.A.T.C.D. d. 1st May, 5640 (1880), in his 22nd year.

Juliette's second son Ernest Wormser Harris who died aged eighty-six on 26 April 1946 is buried nearby. He was President of the Dublin Hebrew Congregation, Hon Solicitor and Life Vice-President. He married Maud Jeanette daughter of Herman Boas of Belfast

Among the interesting features in this burial ground are the memorials commemorating the Cohen family, which are all located in the same section. Carved clearly on the top of each of the Cohen head-stones is a pair of hands. This indicates that they were descendants of the Cohens who were priests of Israel. The hands are shown as blessing the people. The family were black-lead pencil makers who carried on their business at 8 Charlemont Bridge and later in Charlemont Street. One of them, Abraham Cohen who died at his residence in Charlemont Street on 20 January 1854, had amassed quite a fortune from his production of halfpenny pencils and left £45,000 of an estate.

There is a curious double headstone, the left side of which is blank and the right side of which commemorates Solomon Levenston who was born in 1830 in Glasgow and died on 3 October 1887. There is a story relating to the blank side. It was preserved for his wife Kate Lipman of London, who was alleged to be of the family of Sir Joseph Lyons (1848–1917) of the well-known catering firm. She died in April 1916 during the first week of the Rebellion. Sadly, it was not possible to transfer her remains across the city to Ballybough and she was interred at Beth Olam, Dolphin's Barn.

A small plaque on the east wall bears the inscription 'To our beloved sister Dinah Minnie' set up by an American solicitor about 1932.

Few burials have taken place in Ballybough since the opening of Beth Olam in 1883. The more recent took place in the years 1901, 1908, 1946 and 1958, which was the last one. This was the interment of

[5] THE HEBREW AND ENGLISH INSCRIPTION ON THE GRAVESTONE OF TSERNA RACHEL COHEN WHO DIED ON '28TH DAY OF KISLAV 5658, AGED 73 YEARS'. (BALLYBOUGH)

Maud Jeanette Boas (Mrs Ernest Wormser Harris) who was buried beside her father Herman Boas (1827–1917). This was the last burial for those holding burial rights. The cemetery is now closed.

The members of the Jewish community interred at Ballybough represent many trades and professions. Few descendants of the people interred in this burial ground are still in Ireland.

There are two other Jewish cemeteries in Dublin. These include the Beth Olam (Orthodox), Aughavangh Road, Crumlin which opened in 1883 and Woodtown (Progressive Congregation), Rathfarnham which opened in the spring of 1953.

The Ballybough burial ground is under the care of the Dublin Jewish Board of Guardians.

The Irish Jewish Museum at 3/4 Walworth Road, off Victoria Street contains material relating to the history of the Jews in Ireland.

BULLY'S ACRE AND KILMAINHAM BURIAL GROUNDS (3)

SITUATION: THE ROYAL HOSPITAL KILMAINHAM, DUBLIN 8

ENTRANCE BY MILITARY ROAD, KILMAINHAM, EIGHT MINUTES WALK FROM HEUSTON STATION

PERIOD IN USE: FROM MEDIEVAL TIMES TO 1832

BUS NOS (FROM CITY CENTRE): 68, 69, 78A, 79, 123 AND 90 (DART FEEDER BUS FROM CONNOLLY AND TARA STREET STATIONS TO HEUSTON)

The burial grounds are closed to the public pending completion of restoration work. However, access may be gained with special permission from the Office of Public Works.

A brief outline of the Kilmainham site and the Royal Hospital is given below, as many people associated with it since the time of St Maigneann are interred in one of the three the burial grounds in the complex.

Less than two miles west of Dublin City centre is the finest seventeenth-century and earliest surviving public building in Ireland – The Royal Hospital Kilmainham. The story of the historic site on which the hospital now stands dates back to 606 AD when St Maigneann founded a church here which gave the Gaelic name, Cill Maigneann, or Kilmainham as it is known today. The only reminder of these monastic days is the remains of a tenth-century decorated granite cross shaft which is possibly the remains of the boundary cross or 'termon' associated with St Maigneann's church which may be seen in Bully's Acre.

In 1174, after the Norman invasion, Richard, Earl of Pembroke, who was known as Strongbow, founded his Priory for the Knights Hospitallers or Knights of St John of Jerusalem. These knights offered hospitality to pilgrims and cared for the poor and wretched. They carried on their work until the time of the Reformation of King Henry VIII, when the monasteries were suppressed in 1540.

The Viceroy then occupied the vacated lands and Priory which was known as 'The Castle at Kilmainham.' The only depiction of this Priory is on the *Down Survey Map of Kilmainham Parish*, drawn by Robert Girdler in 1655.

In 1680, James Butler, Duke of Ormonde, who was viceroy at the time, petitioned Charles II to have a hospital built in Ireland for pensioner soldiers. Ormonde had got his inspiration from Les Invalides; a hospital built in Paris in 1670 by Louis XIV. In a charter, Charles directed that the hospital be built near

30

the city of Dublin and for this purpose he was granted sixty-four acres of land, formerly belonging to the Priory of St John. Ormonde laid the foundation stone on 29 April 1680. William Robinson, who was surveyor general in Ireland, designed the building, which was classical in layout and continental in style.

The first men were admitted to Kilmainham in 1684 and by March 1686, twenty men were on the hospital roll. The earliest casualties from the Battle of the Boyne were treated at the hospital in 1690 under the care of Patrick Dun, the first medical officer to the Hospital and the personal physician of the Duke of Ormonde.

The pensioners at Kilmainham came from different parts of England and Ireland, and had fought in places such as the Crimea, India, Afghanistan and Waterloo. Many were badly wounded and some had no family to look after them. They found a place of refuge at the Royal Hospital, where they were fed, clothed and received medical attention.

During the time of the 1916 Rising, 2,500 British troops from various regiments occupied Kilmainham, a building that could accommodate at most 400 pensioner soldiers. Although not directly attacked, the building was under constant fire. In 1922, the Royal Hospital was handed over to the Irish Free State. In the late 1920s, when the building ceased to function for the purpose for which it was built, the remaining pensioners were transferred to the Royal Hospital in Chelsea. It was used by the Garda Síochána and later as a storage area for the National Museum of Ireland. It gradually fell into disrepair and in 1980, exactly 300 years after Ormonde had laid the foundation stone, restoration of the building commenced. It was opened to the public as the National Centre for Culture and the Arts in 1985 and in May 1991 it was designated as the Irish Museum of Modern Art.

BULLY'S ACRE

This is reputedly the oldest burial ground in Dublin. Encompassing 3.7 acres, Bully's Acre was also known as the Hospital Fields. It was in use from the time of St Maigneann up to the year of the great cholera epidemic in 1832 when it was closed to the general public.

Covering this time span, the burial ground would contain the remains of monks, knights, princes, illustrious chiefs, warriors, executed criminals, and ordinary Dublin citizens. Only about seventy gravestones now remain ranging in date from 1764 to 1832. In 1832 the burial ground was closed to the public due to overcrowding. Asiatic cholera had reached Ireland and thousands fell victim to the disease. Within ten days, five hundred burials took place at Bully's Acre. Dalton in the History of County Dublin states that during the six months that the cholera raged in Dublin, 3,200 burials were made in Bully's Acre.

31

Some decades ago Bully's Acre was planted with trees. The place was tidied up and levelled out, when (it is said) many of the flat slabs and sunken headstones were covered over with soil and completely buried. The majority of those buried in Bully's Acre were poor, so their graves are left unmarked. It was popular with them because burials could be performed without charge. Traders, merchants and many better-off citizens were also buried here being attracted to the holy ground associated with the monastery.

According to tradition, Brian Ború camped here before the Battle of Clontarf in 1014 where he defeated the Danes. Tradition also claims that following the battle, the bodies of his slain son Murrough, and grandson Turlough, were interred near the ancient cross, the shaft of which still remains to the left of the main gate into the burial ground

The body of Robert Emmet was buried in Bully's Acre. He was executed on 20 September outside St Catherine's church on Thomas Street after his failed rebellion in 1803. His body was removed from Thomas Street in a common cart, first to Newgate and then to Kilmainham Gaol, where it was left for some hours in the vestibule until arrangements were made for its interment. Interestingly, while Emmet's body was at the Gaol, permission was granted to a Dublin gentleman to take a plaster cast of the face of the deceased.

In 1836 George Dunn, the gaoler of Kilmainham confirmed that the body was conveyed to the gaol and placed in the outer entry of the prison, with orders that if it was not claimed immediately by friends of Emmet, it was to be interred in Bully's Acre. Dunn stated that the remains were buried beside the grave of Felix Rourke, near the right hand corner of the burial ground, next to the avenue of the Royal Hospital and at no great distance from the former entrance which is now built up. Dunn further confirmed that soon after the burial the remains of Emmet were removed from Bully's Acre with great privacy and buried somewhere in Dublin. Despite various searches, the location still remains a mystery.

Dan Donnelly, the famous Dublin born boxer who died aged fifty in 1820 is also buried here. It was reported in the *Dublin Penny Journal* (1832) that he was interred in Murrough's grave, which is adjacent to the tenth-century cross shaft to the left of the entrance gate. Five years earlier, he defeated George Cooper, the

[6] THE DECORATED GRANITE CROSS SHAFT IN BULLY'S ACRE WHICH MAY ORIGINALLY HAVE BEEN THE 'TERMON' OR BOUNDARY CROSS OF ST MAIGNEANN'S CHURCH.

English champion boxer on the Curragh in Co. Kildare. A monument in Donnelly's Hollow near Newbridge, Co. Kildare, marks the venue of the fight. It takes the form of a stone surrounded by railings. The railings represent the ring made by the spectators and the stone is the spot where Donnelly and Cooper fought.

In Bully's Acre there is no trace now of the memorial that was erected over Donnelly, which took the form of an altar-tomb. This was engraved with details from his career and the various successes, which he had in the boxing ring. It was thought that some guardsmen who were on duty in Kilmainham destroyed it at nightfall. As a result, the regiment became so unpopular with the citizens of Dublin that it was removed to other quarters within a short time. Poor Dan Donnelly did not lie at rest for long!

Shortly after his burial his body was resurrected and being such a hero there was understandably a public outcry. His remains were of special interest for medical research as he was over six feet in height and his arms were the longest in the history of pugilism! He could button his knee breeches without even stooping! One arm was dismembered from the rest of his body and put on display in a pub named the Hideout in Kilcullen, Co. Kildare, and was on display there until recently.

The first gravestone inside the gate at Bully's Acre is inscribed:

IHS with cross and heart. *Here lieth the body of Mr Phillip Reilly | of Pill Lane, starch manufacturer, who departed this life Apr 23rd 1786 aged 33 years. | Also his father, mother and their (sic) | grandchildren. Erected by Mrs Mary Rile wife of the above Phillip.*

A headstone close to the ancient cross shaft with some parts of it now quite illegible, reads:

This stone was Erected by Con O'Neill | in Memory of his Brother Phelix O | Neill who Departed this Life Octr | the 8th 1764 Aged 36 years.

Close to this is a now illegible narrow slab, which reads:

Heare lyeth | the body of | James Reilly | who depd | This life Nov ; ye 19th 1785 | adg. 80. |

Many locals are interred here, such as James Harrington. His gravestone, which is near the entrance gate, is sited just beneath an ash tree. There is an IHS with cross and heart engraved on the top of the stone, which reads:

Here lyeth the body of James | Harrington of Boe Bridge who departed this life the 22 Febr | 1786 aged 39 years. Also here lyeth 5 of his children. May | the Lord have mercy on their souls Amen. This is erected by his disconsolate widow Ann Harrington.

And just beyond the ancient cross shaft is a memorial erected by Joseph Flanagan for his family, which reads:

Memento Mori. This stone was erected by | Joseph Flanagan of Thomas | Street, starch manufacturer, in | memory of his father and mother, | brothers and sisters, and 4 of his | children who died young. RIP Amen.

Another local living near the Royal Hospital grounds has a memorial stone on which IHS is carved beneath a heart with a chalice on either side. It reads:

Memento Mori. | This stone was erected by Honor | McDermott of Bridgefoot Street | in memory of her beloved husband Bartholomew McDermott | who departed | this life April the 5th 1815 aged 56 years. | Also her two sons, John McDermott who departed this life May | the 4th 18(?) 4 aged 19 years | Patrick McDermott who departed this life February the | 4th aged 26 years, | and five of her children who died young. Here also lieth the above named | Mrs Honor McDermott who departed this life April 5th 1826 aged 64 years. | RIP Amen.

From early times, at midsummer each year, large and unruly crowds gathered to celebrate the feast of St John at the nearby St John's Well. [St John's pattern was held on 24 June]. This caused havoc in Bully's Acre and the nearby Holy Well of St John, but following legal proceedings and rioting in 1764 said to have been led by the notorious Liberty Boys, the public right of access had to be maintained.

At times unusual and even strange events took place in these hallowed grounds. During the eighteenth and nineteenth centuries, it was known to be a great haunt of bodysnatchers, resurrectionists or sack-'em-up men who sold the bodies to doctors or surgeons in both Dublin and England for dissection. Bully's Acre seems to have been within a prime target area as it was within easy reach of the Dublin medical schools. Also, it was not all that well-guarded as can be seen from this report in 1830 in *The Lancet*:

An abundant supply is obtained for all the Dublin Schools from the burying ground known as the Bully's Acre. There is no watch on this ground and subjects are to be got with great facility. The price this season is £1.5s.0d. Last season they were to be had for ten shillings.

The pensioner soldiers at the Royal Hospital kept an eye on the place, as several of their fellow pensioners were buried in the section to the north of Bully's Acre. There are many stories about brawls and altercations, some quite gruesome, others amusing. In November 1825 a sentinel captured a well-known resurrectionist named Thomas Tuite who was a regular supplier to four surgeons. He had in his possession five bodies. When searched, his pockets were found to contain an abundance of teeth. He claimed that these were from old people and were not very good, but that pure white wholesome teeth were worth £1 a set, while bodies might only get ten shillings! He was given a gaol sentence of six months.

Another incident at Bully's Acre involved Dr Peter Harkan from a private medical school in Dawson Street, which was run by Sir Philip Crampton. One night Harkan, accompanied by some students, led a raid on Bully's Acre. The group encountered a watchman and scurried over a nearby wall, except Harkan who waited until his students were clear. He then made a run for the wall but, when he was halfway over it, the watchman grabbed hold of his leg. Meanwhile the students at the other side were pulling his arms to heave Harkan over safely to their side. The students who outnumbered the watchman won the contest but the unfortunate Harkan never fully recovered from his ordeal of being constantly pulled backwards and forwards over a rough wall. His untimely death a few years later was related to this incident.

Adjacent to Bully's Acre there are two interesting military cemeteries. These include The Privates' Burial Ground, which adjoins the northern end of Bully's Acre and The Officers' Burial Ground, which is separated from Bully's Acre by the long straight western avenue.

THE PRIVATES'/ IN-PENSIONERS' BURIAL GROUND (THE RHK)

This is where the remains of old soldiers or the in-pensioners of the Hospital are interred. Access to this is through Bully's Acre. Proceed through the main gateway and continue straight down the pathway through the second gate. The in-pensioners' burial ground is divided by a wall into two parts. This first section is the oldest and covers the period from December 1880 to May 1905. Little remains of any gravestones in this section. Formerly numbered shamrocks, which are now missing, marked the majority of mounds.

There is a stone plaque inserted on the south wall beside the pathway, which reads:

Within the precincts of this cemetery have been laid | To rest the remains of 334 in pensioners who have died | In the Royal Hospital Kilmainham their names regiments | and dates of decease will be found inscribed on brass | tablets in the respective chapels of the Institution.

The three brass plaques that adorn the wall outside the door of the deconsecrated chapel of the Royal Hospital contain details on the 334 pensioners.

Section one also contains four larger gravestones. One of the four is illegible. Another is fairly recent and commemorates those interred in Bully's Acre who were exhumed due to road widening and reburied in this section. It reads:

This stone was erected | By Dublin Corporation | To Honour those unknown | Persons who were interred | In the nearby Bully's Acre | In the Distant past | And whose remains were | respectfully exhumed | And reinterred beneath | This spot in 1991. Go nDéana Dia Trócaire ar a n-anam

Two of them refer to pensioners. The inscriptions read:

Peter Ruthven, died 30th March 1904 aged 71 years,
Erected by his son.

and

George Harrison
Late Colour Sergeant 2nd West Riding Regt.
Died 8th June 1902
Aged 40 years

Buried here was Joseph Binns of the Royal Sappers and Miners. He was admitted to the Royal Hospital in July 1878 and died there on 24 January 1881, at the age of 84. He served in the Peninsular War and was present at the blockade of Pampeluna, the siege and storming of San Sebastian and blockade of Bayonne. He was wounded on 31 August 1813 at San Sebastian and received the Peninsular medal.

In an unmarked grave is Pensioner Christopher Hanlon of the 13th Hussars who died at the Royal Hospital on 15 February 1890, aged 63. He was awarded three good conduct badges. He served in the Crimean war and was present at Balaclava and Sebastopol.

Was engaged in the charge of the Light Brigade; severely wounded in the neck by a lance, and taken prisoner of war; had a horse shot under him and rifle bullet passed through his clothing across his breast and passed out through his bridle arm.

Section 2, which contains twenty-one rows of graves, spans the period from June 1905 to February 1931. The number of In-Pensioners buried here is 309.

OPPOSITE PAGE: [7] PRIVATE ROBERT MONEYPENNY, 8TH HUSSARS, WHO RODE AT BALACLAVA IN 1854.

Just inside the entrance, there is a row of memorials to some young British soldiers who were killed in 1916. The inscriptions read:

Sacred | To the memory of | C.Q.M.S Coyle D.C.M. | 3rd Royal Irish Rifles. | Killed in action in Dublin 30th April 1916. | Erected by his Brother Comrades. | Also in memory of | Rfn. C Duggan 3rd Royal Irish Rifles | and | Pte. Leen 5th Royal Irish Lancers. | R.I.P. | Death Divides. But memory clings.

5617 Private | J.H. Bradford | Notts and Derby Regiment | 5th May 1916 age 19

3493 Lance Cpl | T.H. Chapman | Notts and Derby Regiment | 27th April, 1916 .

8379 Private | H.Phillips | Royal Irish Regiment | 25th April 1916 age 23 + Greater Love hath no man.

4643 Private | A.Warner | Notts and Derby Regiment | 27th April 1916 age 19 + Dearly loved.

In a shady corner of this cemetery lie the remains of pensioner Robert Moneypenny, who was born in the parish of St Peter's in Drogheda, Co. Louth.

Aged nineteen, the blue-eyed, brown-haired Moneypenny, five foot seven inches tall, enlisted at Dublin on 18 March 1846. He embarked for the Crimea aboard the H.T. *Echunga* on 15 May 1854. He fought in the Crimea and rode in the charge of the Light Brigade at Balaclava in October 1854. He was awarded the Distinguished Conduct Medal for 'praiseworthy and gallant service throughout the campaign.' He was discharged from Dundalk Barracks in October 1856 'on the reduction of the Regiment' and because he was no longer thought to be effective. He had served ten years and a hundred and sixty days.

On 1 October 1878, he was admitted as an In-Pensioner to the Royal Hospital, where he died on 8 April 1906 just before his eightieth birthday. His small white marble gravestone is inscribed:

Private Robert Moneypenny. 8th Hussars. (Rode at Balaclava)Died 8.1.06

The Dowager Countess Wolsley presented a portrait of Moneypenny to the Royal Hospital Kilmainham on 28 April 1919, but its whereabouts are unknown.

Many of the Kilmainham pensioners interred in this burial ground were awarded medals for bravery and for their efforts in the battlefields at the Crimea [Alma, Inkerman and Sebastopol] Waterloo, India, the Peninsula and elsewhere. All of these medals where originally displayed in cases in the Great Hall at the Royal Hospital when the pensioners were in residence. There is now only a small selection of them on view in the heritage orientation space which was created recently by the Office of Public Works and Dúchas. This is located to the right of the reception area in the building.

THE OFFICERS' BURIAL GROUND

The West Avenue leading up to the Royal Hospital separates the Officers' Burial Ground from Bully's Acre. It was used for the deceased officers, staff and some of the inmates of the hospital. It contains circa sixty-seven memorials, many of which are almost illegible. In this area is the oldest legible headstone recorded. It is rudely cut in relief on a small brown flat stone, and is well hidden under a bush. It is inscribed:

Heare Liet | H the body of | Hive [Hugh?]Hackett | And Elizabet | H Hacket wh | o died in the | Yeare 1652.

The oldest legible military grave, which is of great interest, reads:

Here Lieth | the body of | Corporal William Proby | who died 28th | July 1700.

Proby was a veteran of Ormonde's wars, having served as a musketeer in the battle of Baggotrath and having been wounded while serving under Schombert at the Battle of the Boyne in 1690. He was among one of the earliest inmates at the Royal Hospital.

Another early memorial is that of Lt David Buchanan, the inscription of which is now illegible. The Buchanan coat of arms of a lion rampant within a border charged with fleurs-de-lis is cut at the top of a large square headstone, which is inscribed:

Here Lyeth the body of | Lieut David Buchanan who | Dyed the 13 day of Novemr | 1720 in ye 85 years of his age | And Livd[sic]13 years[..mo.]N | This in ye Royal Hospi[ ]

The Blackburne family who were casualties from the sinking of the HMS Leinster by German torpedoes on 10 October 1918 are also interred here.

To the glory of God | and the beloved memory of | Lt Col Charles Blackburne DSO, | 5th Dragoon Guards, | born 20th May 1876, | and of Charles Betram (Peter) his son | born 3rd Sep 1911 | who are both buried here. | Also of Beatrice Audrey his daughter, | born 24th June 1907. | All of whom lost their lives in the sinking of HMS Leinster by a German submarine 10th October 1918.

Members of the Royal Hospital staff included a chaplain whose grave consists of a low-railed enclosure:

Sacred to the memory of the Rev George Hare, chaplain for 32 years to the Royal Hospital, died 21 May 1882 aged 82 years.

39

Medical staff interred here includes William Carte whose grave is enclosed in a railed area. It reads:

In loving memory | of | William Carte, | staff surgeon, JP, FRCSI, | physician and surgeon to the Royal Hospital | for 41 years, | died 24th April 1899 aged 69 years. | He served in 28th Regiment during Crimean War, | medal, 2 clasps, Turkish medal, subsequently in 4th Light Dragoons. | Also in memory of Mary his first wife | died 28th January 1859, and following children: Thomas died April 1859 aged 3 months, | Ellen died 29th June 1865 aged 9 years. | William Alexander, surgeon major, died 26th April 1900 aged 42, buried at sea. | Children of 2nd wife: | Ellen Alexandra died 6th January 1873 aged 5 months | Sydney George died 13th September 1892 aged 26. | Francis Lindesay, surgeon captain, served in Egypt and India and Chin Lushai Expedition | 1889–1890, medal and clasp, died at Allahabad | 2nd April 1894 aged 31 years. | Also in memory of Annie, | second wife of the above named | William Carte, who died 6th Aug 1913. 'Thy will be done.'

Another surgeon was George Renny (1757–1848) who is buried here together with members of his family.

Sacred to the memory of | Mrs Renny, | the beloved wife of Dr Renny, | who departed this life on | the 7th of January 1828 aged 58 years. | Also here are deposited the remains of | George Renny, | son of Doctor Renny, | who died on the 29th September 1914 | in his 21st year. And of | Mrs Anne Renny, aunt of the above | Mrs Renny, who died on the 24th December 1824 | aged 88 years. Likewise the remains of | William Renny Esqre, | born 28th November 1802, | died 7th October 1840. | And of George Renny Esqre MD, | born August 18th 1757, | died November 11th 1848.

George Renny, a Scotsman, studied medicine at Edinburgh University. In November 1783 he was appointed to the Royal Hospital Kilmainham. It was due to him that a board was formed at Dublin Castle to investigate the causes and epidemics which devastated the country at the time.

Renny served for a time as Governor to the nearby Foundlings' Hospital in James's Street and also of Cork Street Fever Hospital. During his journeys from the Royal Hospital to Cork Street he became aware of the lack of water available to the poor in the area and succeeded in having forty street fountains erected with water supplied by the Grand Canal. He tended cholera victims in the Royal Hospital during the cholera epidemic in 1832.

Dr Renny was a tall broad-shouldered man who always wore a blue, long-tailed coat furnished with brass buttons. He resided in the Deputy Master's house, which overlooks the formal gardens in the grounds of the Royal Hospital. He dined early, after which he invariably took a walk (weather permitting) to the entrance of the Hospital and back, usually with his hands clasped behind his back. This performance he repeated twice or trice, but he was never known to take a fourth turn! Dr Renny retired in February 1848 aged ninety-one and died the following November.

A small stone obelisk in a railed enclosure marks the burial place of a child with the sad little epitaph 'Lov'd child, adieu'. The child was Georgina Vivian who died aged eleven years in 1835 [?]. She was the daughter of Lieut-General Sir R. Hussey Vivian who was Master of the Royal Hospital for four years from 1831.

Two former adjutants of the Royal Hospital whose graves are side by side are Major George Farmer and Captain William Strickland McGill. McGill of the seventy-ninth Cameron Highlanders served in the campaigns of the Crimea and Indian Mutiny. He was adjutant at the Royal Hospital for eighteen years where he died on 2 November 1886. Farmer, of the 4th (Queen's Own) Hussars, served as adjutant for ten years and died in office at the Royal Hospital on 4 October 1891 aged fifty-one years.

The three burial grounds at Kilmainham are under the care of the Office of Public Works.

[8] THE GRAVESTONE OF LT DAVID BUCHANAN WHO DIED AT THE ROYAL HOSPITAL ON 13 NOVEMBER 1720 IN HIS 85TH YEAR. THE BUCHANAN COAT OF ARMS IS INSCRIBED ON THE STONE.

Cabbage Garden and Huguenot Burial Ground

Situation: Cathedral Lane off Kevin Street Lower, Dublin 8

Period in use: 1666–1878

Situated close to city centre

The entrance to this cemetery, which is now a small park, is at the end of Cathedral Lane. It lies to the south of St Patrick's Cathedral and is known as the 'Cabbage Garden' graveyard. There is a Huguenot burial plot integrated into the Cabbage Garden. Roger Kendrick, the City Surveyor, surveyed both these burial grounds in 1754. The Cabbage Garden was also known to be a favourite burial place with the Wesleyans.

There are two theories about how it got the unusual name of the 'Cabbage Garden.' The first is that it had some association with the Capuchins and that cabbage was a corruption of the word Capuchin. However there are no existing records to show that the Capuchins were associated with this plot. The other theory is that the area was formerly used as a garden plot to grow cabbages for Oliver Cromwell's soldiers. The latter theory would therefore seem the more acceptable.

At the time, most of the land lying south of Upper Kevin Street, as far as the present South Circular Road, was laid out in various plots which were used as vegetable gardens. The minute books of the Dean and Chapter of St Patrick's contains numerous references to them giving the names of the owners, such as the 'Chancellor's Gardens', 'Alderman Tighe's Orchard', 'Mr Forte's Garden', 'Mr Kinshelagh's Garden', 'Mr John Cormack's Garden' and 'Fernley's Gardens' to name but a few.

When Cromwell and his troops and horses arrived in Dublin they required accommodation. Cromwell was provided with a large house, which was situated on the corner of nearby Werburgh Street and Castle Street. The Wide Street Commissioners were later to demolish this in 1812. Down the hill, St Patrick's Cathedral provided ample room to stable the horses and the troops were accommodated elsewhere in the vicinity. Cromwell's soldiers had a fondness for cabbage, which apparently was unavailable in Ireland at that time. So they rented land from Philip Fernley in which the vegetables were grown. The name 'Cabbage Garden' still exists today for this plot of land, and this is where the cemetery is now sited.

In Monck Mason's *History of St Patrick's Cathedral* there are numerous references to the Cabbage Garden. A mandate dated 14 March 1666 from the Lord Lieutenant and Privy Council prompted the Dean and Chapter of St Kevin's to grant three stangs of grounds to the parish of St Nicholas Without for the interment of the parishioners of the Close.

Adjacent to St Patrick's Cathedral there was a graveyard from very early times. By the time of the early seventeenth century it began to get overcrowded. It was known as the Vicar's Bawn or the Old Churchyard to distinguish it from the nearby Cabbage Garden, which served the parish of St Nicholas Without.

After the revocation of the *Edict of Nantes*, a number of Huguenots came to Ireland. Those who came to Dublin settled around the Liberties of St Patrick and the Liberty of the Earl of Meath, where the wool and other city trades were carried on.

Through the permission of the Archbishop of Dublin, the Lady Chapel at St Patrick's Cathedral had been granted to the French Conformists as a place of worship, which they used from 1666 until 1816. With the influx of Huguenots in the 1690s, a chapel of ease was established in St Mary's Abbey in Capel Street. The French Non-Conformists had chapels in Lucy Lane (now Chancery Place) and in Peter Street.

There were four Huguenot burial grounds in Dublin, one of which was included in the Cabbage Garden (See also Merrion Row, St Luke and St Nicholas Without, and Peter Street).

In 1681, the Huguenots were leased a narrow strip of land in the Cabbage Garden by the Archbishop of Dublin, which they used as a burial ground until 1858. The area measured one hundred and fifty foot long by thirty foot wide at one end and thirty-eight feet wide at the other. The entrance was through a gateway on the right-hand side of the Cabbage Garden from which it was divided by a high wall. This was the first Huguenot burial ground for the Conformist Congregation. They were granted this land on condition that they enclosed the ground with an adequate stone or brick wall and provided a decent gate. They had to maintain it in good repair on a lease from the Churchwardens of St Patrick's Cathedral at twelve pence a year.

The cobble-stoned approach to this cemetery has altered from its original state and the main carriage drive has completely vanished.

There are Huguenot names associated with various trades on the memorials. It was remarked that, if all the inscriptions were transcribed from the memorials here, it would make a comprehensive Directory of the merchants and tradesmen of the Liberties.

As the Cabbage Garden has been converted into a park, the memorials have been moved from their original locations and now line the boundary walls. Many of the Huguenot gravestones are missing and some are badly chipped, broken and damaged. Some of the inscriptions are still legible. These include the surnames of Allenet, Anthony, Clamouse, Lapierre, Pineau, and Servin Vareilles. Other Huguenot families who were interred here include the Allens, Beauchamps, Belsonne, Chaigneaus, De L'Isles, De Moulins, Favières, Girots, Lanauzes, Langlois, Ligoniers, Maignor, Mathurins, Martinets, Rambauts, Racines, St Germains, Saurins and Pellisiers.

Among the notable Huguenots were the La Touche family. David Digues des Rompières La Touche who was born near Blois in France in 1671 joined Caillemotte's Huguenot Regiment and served with King William at the Battle of the Boyne in 1690. At the conclusion of the war, the regiment was disbanded in Dublin and La Touche established a silk, poplin and cambric business in High Street. He was elected as a member of the Trinity Guild of Merchants, which controlled most of the commerce in Dublin. Other Huguenots passing through Dublin entrusted their money and valuables to him. Together with another weaver, Nathaniel Kane, he established a bank, which in 1722 moved to Castle Street, where it stood until the nineteenth century. This famous La Touche Bank was the precursor for the Bank of Ireland. La Touche is commemorated by two portraits in the Bank of Ireland headquarters in Baggot Street. On 17 October 1745 he died suddenly in the Chapel of the Castle Yard where he worshiped each morning. His cortège took him passed St Patrick's Cathedral where, on 5 July 1699 in the Lady Chapel, he had married Mademoiselle Judith Biard, a Dutch woman who died in 1713 aged thirty-one. His son, also named David, died at his home at Bellevue, Co. Wicklow in 1785 and was buried with his father in the Cabbage Garden (see also Whitechurch new). The La Touche memorial, like many others in this burial ground is unfortunately now missing.

The *Dublin Evening Telegraph* of 19 February 1898 published some inscriptions from memorials in the Cabbage Garden which make intriguing reading such as the inscription below of two young lovers, Annie Major and John Lyons. They were aged 17 and 24 respectively at the time of Annie's death in 1784. Fourteen years later John was buried in the same grave.

Underneath Lyeth the remains of Mr John Lyons who | Departed this life February 7, in the 38th year of his | Age. 1798.

Here also lieth his much lamented friend Miss Annie | Major who departed this life in the 17th year of her | Age the 15th day of October 1784.

It was not age that tottered to this grave, | But blooming & in youthful prime, | Here dropped the beauty nature gave, | And here will slumber to the end of time.

An eminent historian and antiquary, the Revd Edward Ledwich, who was Vicar of Aghaboe, erected a vault to the Ledwich family. The inscription on a large horizontal stone, originally on granite supports, bore a long inscription, an extract from which follows:

THE CEMETERY OF THE LEDWICH FAMILY. This family, | so named from Lanwyche, in Shropshire, removed | to the Palatinate of Chester, and from thence came | with DE BURGO, ancestor of the CLANRICKARDS, to Ireland | about 1280. The De Burgos conferred on them large | possessions in Westmeath and Longford, where they | were Barons Palatines, as appears by Camden's Annals | at the end of his 'Britannia.' A branch settled near | Drogheda. The last of it was COLONEL LEDWICH, who | suffered the misfortunes of James 11. His son Edward | was bred to the leather trade, and followed it extensively | in Patrick Street in this city. He had by his wife, | ELIZA ARTHUR three sons, Edward, Dean of Kildare | and Prebendary of Christ Church; | John, who followed his father's business in the same street. JOHN LEDWICH, | before mentioned was born, 27th Novr, 1714, and died | 22 May 1794. He left by his wife ELIZA DAVIS, two | children, LETTICE, wife of the Revd. James Whitelaw, Vicar of St Catherine's, Dublin; and EDWARD, Vicar, | of Aghaboe, in the Queen's County, at whose sole | expense this memorial of his ancestors who lie here | interred has been made.

[9] MEMORIAL STONES, MANY BEARING HUGUENOT NAMES, IN THE CABBAGE GARDEN PARK, FORMERLY THE CABBAGE GARDEN CEMETERY, CATHEDRAL LANE, DUBLIN 8.

A number of religious figures with the name Morgan are also interred here:

Here lieth the Body of the Revd ALLEN MORGAN late | Prebendary of St Audoens Dublin who Departed this | life September ye 28th 1763 Aged 58.

Here lie the bodies of the Very Revd ALLEN MORGAN | Dean of Killaloe, who died Augst 7th 1830. Aged 69. | And | John G. Morgan Esqre, Nephew of the above and Son of | the late Revd H MORGAN, Prebendary of Leighlin died | Janry 9th 1869. Aged 67.

A father's tribute to his daughter is on the following inscription:

This stone was erected by William Dycear in memory | of his beloved daughter, Mary Dycear who departed | This life June 19th 1814 aged 17 years. | The voyage of life's end, | The mortal affliction is past, | The age that in heaven she'll spend, | Forever and ever shall last

There is a rather picturesque little bridge over the Grand Canal at Mount Street Upper named Huband Bridge. It was named after Joseph Huband who was a director of the Grand Canal Company in 1791. Members of his family are interred here. Edward Evans copied the inscriptions, which were on a large horizontal stone, supported by four pillars, in 1898. The inscription reads:

This stone hath been placed here An. Dom. 1797 by Joseph Huband, Grandson of Edmund next under | named, in the place of a stone much decayed | and broken whereon were the two next following inscrip | tions:-

This stone and Burial Place belongeth to Mr Edmund | HUBAND and his Posterity An. Dom. 1690. Here lie | Sixteen of his children.

The above named EDMUND HUBAND died An. Dom. 1719 | and was buried in a Vault under the Church of the | Parish of St Luke.

Here lieth EDMUND HUBAND son of the above named | EDMUND HUBAND and father of Joshua Huband Joseph | Huband which Edmund, Father of Joshua and Joseph died An. Dom. 1757.

The Cabbage Garden was closed for burials in 1878, although some did take place after that date. The park is now under the care of Dublin Corporation.

CARRICKBRENNAN CHURCHYARD

SITUATION: CARRICKBRENNAN ROAD, MONKSTOWN, CO. DUBLIN

PERIOD IN USE: UNKNOWN

BUS NOS (FROM CITY CENTRE): 7, 7A OR 8 TO MONKSTOWN

Carrickbrennan Churchyard in the maritime parish of Monkstown is situated five miles south east of the city. Coming from Monkstown village, the entrance is through a small gate in the wall on the left-hand side before reaching the roundabout on Carrickbrennan Road.

The churchyard, enclosed by a wall, is on the site of a medieval monastery which was dedicated to St Mochonna, a sixth-century Bishop of Holmpatrick in Skerries. The monks were Cistercian and were regulated by the chapter of St Mary's Abbey. Over time, the church became ruinous, and in 1668 it was replaced by another church built by Edward Corker. It is the ruins of this church which stands in the graveyard today. In the early nineteenth century, some structural work was carried out to create a watchman's house to deter the body snatchers that were prevalent at that time. The vault below served as housing for the watchman's dogs.

The imposing ruin of Monkstown Castle, on the far side of the roundabout, is on the site of the original castle. It was built in the thirteenth or fourteenth century by the same Cistercian monks of the Abbey of St Mary's in Dublin. The main tower dates from the fifteenth or sixteenth century, with the western portion of the tower added later. In the sixteenth century, the castle was granted to Sir John Travers for his services to the Crown. Later owners included the Eustaces, Sir Henry Wallop and Henry Cheevers. In the Cromwellian period, General Edmund Ludlow took over the castle. However, after the restoration it was returned to the Cheevers who later sold it to Archbishop Boyle. In the nineteenth century, it was badly damaged. Some of the people associated with Monkstown Castle were interred in the old graveyard in Monkstown. These included Henry Cheevers who died in 1640 and Sir John Travers who died on 16 May 1652.

In the early 1900s Monkstown was described as

being delightfully situated on the south side of the bay in Dublin. The rural portion embraces some of the rich and varied landscapes; innumerable seats and villas encircled in demesnes, or adorned with shrubberies and gardens abound, other residences in beautiful terraces, front the sea.

[10] THE MEMORIAL TO CAPT. BOYD, AND THE FIVE CREW MEMBERS OF THE *HMS AJAX* WHO LOST THEIR LIVES ON 9 FEBRUARY 1861.

Being a maritime parish, the old churchyard with its yew-lined walks has a number of interesting and unusual memorials pertaining to our marine heritage. It contains the remains a number of seafaring people. Some of them lived and died in the parish; others lost their lives at sea. Three major sea disasters, two that happened on the same night, occurred in the area in the nineteenth century. These included the shipwrecks of the *Rochedale*, the *Prince of Wales* and the *HMS Ajax*.

On Wednesday 18 November 1807 the *Rochedale* of Liverpool, along with the *Prince of Wales* and other transports, sailed from the Pigeonhouse Harbour in Dublin. On board the *Rochedale* was the staff of the 97th regiment numbering two hundred and sixty five. These included part of the 97th, or Queen's Germans and men from the Irish militia of the south Cork and Mayo regiments who had volunteered for Foreign Service. The ship ran into the most atrocious weather of sleet and snow accompanied by a strong easterly gale. The following day she was observed labouring in turbulent seas in the bay, hoisting blue lights and repeatedly firing guns as signals of distress.

Several anchors were thrown from the *Rochedale*, which just dragged and then snapped. The weather was so bad that no help could reach her. Gradually she was swept along past Sandycove, the old pier in Dún Laoghaire, and finally she struck the sharp jagged rocks under the Martello Tower at Seapoint. It was just half a mile from where the *Prince of Wales* was wrecked.

Ironically, the *Rochedale* was so close to the shore that a twelve-foot plank would have reached the quarter-deck from it. But the weather was so ferocious and the night so dark that the passengers on board were unaware of their proximity to the land.

No one escaped alive from the *Rochedale* which comprised one major(Gormocan), two lieutenants (Long and Power), one ensign, eight sergeants, nine corporals, one hundred and seventy-three rank and file, forty-two women and twenty-nine children. Most of the victims were interred in Carrickbrennan churchyard.

There is a memorial stone to Major Charles Gormocan, near the entrance and a mound and a memorial stone to the officers and soldiers of the 97th regiment with the following inscription:

Sacred | To the memory of the | Non commissioned officers and | Private soldiers belonging to his Majesty's | 97th Regiment of foot who were | Unfortunately shipwrecked on this coast | in the Rochedale Transport and perished | On the night of the 19th November 1807 | In commemoration of the distinguished | Gallantry of this Corps and the important | Services they had rendered to their King | and Country this record has been | Placed on their Tomb | by order of General the | Earl of Harrington | Commander of the Forces in Ireland.

On 9 February 1861, the coastguard vessel, the *Ajax* came to grief in a blizzard and its crew of six perished. Captain John McNeil Boyd and his coastguards were on their way to help rescue the crew of the brigantine *Neptune*, which was on the rocks off the east pier in Dún Laoghaire. An enormous wave swept them into the sea. The bodies of five of the men were recovered but Capt. Boyd's body was not recovered until about two weeks after the event. Members of the Royal St George's Yacht Club erected a monument to Captain Boyd on the East Pier in Dún Laoghaire. It is in the form of an obelisk.

Captain Boyd is buried in the churchyard of St Patrick's Cathedral where he is commemorated by a monument. The five members of his crew are interred in Carrickbrennan where they are commemorated with an unusual marble monument on which is carved a sea rescue, surmounted by a small lighthouse. The memorial is inscribed on both sides. The first side reads:

In memory of Capt. JOHN MCNEIL BOYD R.N. | JOHN CURRY leading seaman THOMAS MURRAY Able Seaman | JOHN RUSSELL ordinary seaman, JOHN JOHNSON ordinary seaman, | ALEXANDER FORSYTH ordinary seaman | of H.M.S. Ajax | who lost their lives | on the outside of the East Pier | at Kingstown | in Noble efforts to rescue the crew | of the wrecked brig. Neptune | during a fearful gale from | the E.N.E . on 9th Feb.1861.

The reverse side reads:

To commemorate the death of | six brave sailors of H.M.S. Ajax | this monument is raised | The Providence of God ordered that they should die | not on board their ship | defending their country | but as Christian men | seeking to save their perishing brethren | They glorified God | Whose waves went over them | By a death not unmeet | for sailors of Christian Britain. Greater love hath no many than this, that a man lay down his life for his friends. John.15.13.

Erected by COMMODORE | HASTINGS R.YELVERTON C.B. | Controller-general | of the Coast guard | The officers & ship's company (including tenders) of H.M.S. AJAX | & the officers & men of Kingstown | district of coast guard.

Interestingly, it was as a result of these major sea disasters with the loss of so many lives that led to an asylum harbour being built in Dublin Bay. In 1817 the Lord Lieutenant laid the foundation stone of

Dún Laoghaire Harbour. This helped the area prosper and it was further improved by the opening of the Dublin to Kingstown railway line in 1834.

Some other mariners interred here are commemorated with memorials, on which are inscribed the following:

Sacred to the memory of Richard Nicel aged 29 years Captain of the Main Top of H.M.S. Frigate Gragon who was accidentally drowned on 26 Dec. 1848

WILLIAM H. TILTMAN Quartermaster H.M.S. Pallas, who was drowned at Kingstown Harbour on the night of 5 May 1870 aged 34 years.

A Welshman Thomas Garratt is commemorated with a sandstone gravestone.

Sacred to the memory of Capt. | THOMAS GARRATT of Flint | in Wales. Died at sea | July 21 1849 in the 38th year | of his life. | His death was much lamented.

In rare cases it specifies on a gravestone the cause of death:

In memory of Frederick Harvey McCausland. Born in Russia 18th February 1818. Died at Monkstown of the smallpox, April 1885.

Two of the older memorials include people from the city:

This stone and burial place belong to Willm. Hall of the Coombe. Here lieth the body of John Hall of Dunlary father of above Wm. who died 3 October 1750 aged 58.

Daniel Dickenson late of the City of Dublin Merchant died 5 May 1777 after 60 years as a Citizen, Husband, Parent and Friend.

The great great grandson of Ulick Burke, who fell at Aughrim on 12 July 1691 is interred here. He was William H. Burke, late Commander of H.M. Cruiser Kite, a native of Glenarm, Co. Antrim, who died at Kingstown on 11 December 1859 aged seventy-two.

Joseph Holt (1762–1826), who died in Kingstown after his return from Australia, is buried here. An insurgent and son of a prosperous Protestant farmer in Wexford, he figured prominently in the Rebellion of the United Irishmen. In June 1798 at the battle of Ballyellis near Carnew, he gained a complete victory over the government forces. At one time he had 13,000 men under his command. After the collapse of the Rising, he escaped capture for a number of months but surrendered and was sentenced and transported to Botany Bay in New South Wales, Australia. He worked hard, bought some land and prospered but decided in 1812 to return to Ireland. On his return journey, he was shipwrecked on Eagle Island, but eventually arrived back to Dublin via Rio de Janeiro and Liverpool in April 1814. He started a business as a publican, which failed financially. He sold out and retired to Kingstown where he died on 16 May 1826.

The inscription on Holt's gravestone had been partly obliterated by weathering. It reads:

Joseph Holt, late of Kingstown, who departed this life on 6th May 1826 aged 64 years. Also his wife Esther, who died the 24th June 1827 aged 70. Erected by their son Joshua of Sidney, also their daughter Marianne, relict of Mr Shaw.

Just beside it is a small memorial stone, which reads:

To Commemorate | The heroic part played by | Joseph Holt | in the 1798 Rebellion | In Wicklow, Wexford and Meath. | Erected by the National Graves Association | 1994.

[11] THE WEATHERED GRAVESTONE OF JOSEPH HOLT. BESIDE IT IS THE MEMORIAL STONE ERECTED IN 1994 BY THE NATIONAL GRAVES ASSOCIATION.

The memorial to Charles Haliday (1789–1826), the antiquary who died in Monkstown on 14 September 1866 is inserted into the wall at the corner of the bottom left-hand side. He wrote on the history of Dublin and published *Scandinavian Kingdom of Dublin* (1881). His collection of books was left to the Royal Irish Academy.

There are quite a number of military people buried here. Among them is Captain Patrick Dyone (1812–1874) whose gravestone records that he fought in the Afghan Campaign of 1839–1842. He served with the 17th Queen's Lancers, which later became the 17th/21st Lancers.

On entering the gate to the cemetery, the second monument on the right-hand side is enclosed by a chain. This is the grave of Hugh Pollock, which also contains a memorial to his son H. Trevor Pollock, an officer with the Royal Bengal Army.

Sir William Betham (1779–1853) who succeeded Sir Chichester Fortescue as Ulster King at Arms in 1813 was born in Stradbrook in Suffolk. He inherited his interest in genealogy from his father. He devoted his life to collecting genealogical records and heraldic documentation on Irish families. Betham's memorial, which is the first headstone on the left inside the gate, has a cast-iron monument, and is an interesting example of the monumental art of the Victorian era. It is inscribed:

In memory of | Sir WILLIAM BETHAM | Knight | Ulster King of arms | of all Ireland | born 22nd May 1779 | Died 26th October 1853 | and | Elizabeth his wife | Died 30th Dec 1856.

Credit is due to the members of the Carrickbrennan Graveyard Restoration Project who carried out work on the graveyard in the mid 1980s. The area was cleared of weeds and dangerous trees were removed. The boundary walls were fixed and headstones which had fallen were repaired and reset and the ironwork surrounding the graves was restored.

Besides the existing old English yew tree and Irish yews which line the pathways, some new trees were planted. These include a bhoton pine (pinus wallichiaha) and a dawn redwood which was planted by Denis O'Conor Don, the historian and President of the Dún Laoghaire Historical Society. Various plants were donated and now this old churchyard is ablaze with colour in the spring with flowering shrubs such as ribes, forsythia, and hebes with clumps of daffodils and primroses interspersed.

Carrickbrennan Churchyard is under the care of the Corporation of Dún Laoghaire.

Castle Avenue
(St John the Baptist) Churchyard

Situation: Castle Avenue, Clontarf, Dublin 3

Period in use: c. 1700. Closed except to those with burial rights

Bus Nos (from city centre): 29a, 31 & 130; (from Clontarf Dart Station): 103, 104

The church and churchyard of St John the Baptist is situated on the left-hand side of Castle Avenue and adjoins the grounds of Clontarf Castle. It is approximately two and a half miles from the city centre.

The Clontarf area is of historical interest as it was here that Brian Ború fought the great battle on Good Friday 1014, which ended Danish power in Ireland.

Originally the area from Clontarf Road to the Castle gate occupied the centre of the township. In former times the principal lands of the parish, which were richly wooded and finely cultivated, appear to have been occupied by a religious house founded in 550 and erected into a commandery of the Knights Templar in the reign of Henry 11. On the suppression of that order, it became a preceptory of the Knights Hospitallers of St John of Jerusalem and was one of the main appendages of the Priory at Kilmainham.

Eventually, it came into the possession of Admiral Vernon, when the Crown conferred the land on him. It later passed on to J.E.V. Vernon. The Castle, one of the first within the English Pale, was taken down in 1835 and the present one was built on the site.

It is interesting to note that some of the lovely leafy avenues in the area are named after old families associated with the vicinity such as Vernon Avenue. Haddon Road, which adjoins the Castle, is named after Haddon Hall the historic Derbyshire estate, which was acquired by the Vernons. Sir George Vernon of Haddon in the sixteenth century was a man of immense wealth. His daughter, Dorothy eloped and married Sir John Manners, ancestor of the Duke of Rutland. The romantic circumstances of their marriage are commemorated in Haddon Hall.

The church dedicated to St John the Baptist occupies the site of the ancient monastery and was rebuilt in 1609. It contained a number of noteworthy monuments, though some important ones are now gone. With the unroofing of the church, a number of monuments were left exposed to the elements.

One of these included a monument commemorating Charles Bourchier of Northamptonshire who died in 1716. His memorial unfortunately was broken in an attempt to remove it. It bore the following inscription, which gives a lot of historical information on his family:

Near this place is inter'd Charles Bourchier, Esq, of
Northamptonshire. He died on the 18th day of May 1716, in the 52nd
year of his age; and Barbara, his wife, eldest daughter of
Richard Harrison, Esqr of Balls, in Hertfordshire, who died the
27th day of Decemr 1719, in the 51st year of her age. They
came into Ireland after the Revolution with the Honble Genl
Villiers, father to the present Earl of Grandison, and Uncle to
the aforesaid Barbara. They left 2 sons and five daughters,
vizt the Honble Richard Bourchier, Esq, now Governor of
Bombay in the East Indies; the Reverend Edward M. Bourchier,
of Hertford; and Mary, Barbara, Catherine, Anna Maria, and
Arrabella. Barbara was married to Richd Prittie, Esqr, of
Tipperary; Catherine, to William Yarner, grandson to
Sir Abraham Yarner, Anna Maria, to the Right Honble Lord
Ward, of Himley, in Staffordshire; Arrabella died unmarried.
Their virtues are so well known as to render eulogies unnecessary.
Mary, their eldest daughter, erected this monument to their memory.
Anno Domini MDCCLVIII

The churchyard contains some unusual memorials such as the family vault of the Vernons, tombs of the Dawsons of Dawson Grove in Co. Monaghan, MacCauslands of Omagh, Rochforts, Armstrongs, a slab to Sarah Hadsor, 1751, John Cavanagh, 1767, and Archibald Douglas, son of General Douglas, 1787.

At the eastern gable of the church there is a monument commemorating John Kilpatrick, who represented the borough of Granard in the Irish Parliament. He also distinguished himself at Plassey in Bengal, India. Also of military interest is the memorial to Henry O'Dell, which reads:

Major Henry E. O'Dell died 18th Sept 1864
Aged 74 years. He served with the 5th Regiment
Of Foot in the Peninsular War, and received
the War Medal and nine clasps —

This monument is erected by his youngest

daughter and her husband, the Revd J. Pratt, Rector of Clontarf.

A flat white marble stone commemorates the popular local doctor. It reads:

DOCTOR WILLIAM FAUSETT T.C.D., M.R.C.S.I.

Moville, died Novr 29th, 1880, aged 69

years, for 43 years the beloved physician

of Clontarf.

On the north side of the old church and nearly in line with the east gable is a flat stone, which commemorates Maria Lady Burdett, who died on 5 July 1816 aged thirty-five years. She was the wife of Sir William Bagenal Burdett Bart

On the left-hand side of the pathway is the grave of Lord Ardilaun's private secretary, Walter Keating.

The churchyard is under the care of Dublin Corporation, Environmental Health Department.

[12] THE CHURCH OF ST JOHN THE BAPTIST, CLONTARF.

CHALONER'S CORNER, TRINITY COLLEGE

SITUATION: TRINITY COLLEGE GROUNDS

PERIOD IN USE: FROM EARLY 1600S

SITUATED IN CITY CENTRE

Trinity College, which was founded in 1591 by Queen Elizabeth I on land which had belonged to the Augustinian priory of All Hallows, has what must be the smallest cemetery in the whole of Dublin city. It is tucked away in a quiet shady little corner up a small path, which is situated between the Chapel and the Dining Hall. To get there, proceed through the main entrance of Trinity College to Front Square and turn left to the chapel.

Chaloner's Corner is called after Dr Luke Chaloner, the first provost of Trinity College who died in 1613. The area is almost triangular shaped with two of the sides bounded by the back corner of the chapel walls. The remaining boundary consists of a black railing and entry is by a small gate. There are four memorials on the walls. These include one to F.S.L. Lyons, a former provost of the College, which reads:

Here rest the ashes | of | Francis Stewart Leland Lyons | FELLOW AND PROVOST OF THIS COLLEGE | Sometime Professor of Modern History | in the University of Kent at Canterbury | and Master of Eliot College | Renowned as a scholar | esteemed as a teacher | beloved as a man | Born 11 November 1923; died 21 September 1983.

Lyons was born in Derry and was the author of a number of books including *John Dillon: A Biography* (1968); *Ireland since the Famine* (1971) and *Charles Stewart Parnell* (1977).

Another wall memorial commemorates D.A. Webb:

In memory of | DAVID ALLARDICE WEBB | Fellow of the College, 1949 and Senior Fellow, 1978 | Botanist, Zoologist, Naturalist, Teacher and College Historian. | Professor of Plant Biology (1950–1965), Botany (1954–1965), and Systematic Botany(1966–1994) | A much loved servant and resident of the college for over fifty years. | Born 12 August 1912; died 26 September 1994.

A wall memorial to George Browne (Provost, 1695) is unfortunately now quite illegible due to weathering.

[13] CHALONER'S CORNER IN TRINITY COLLEGE, THE SMALLEST CEMETERY IN DUBLIN.

Chaloner's memorial tomb, originally alabaster-topped, is the most prominent in this little burial ground. It bears the following inscription:

RUCAE CHALONER | QUI INTER PRIMOS SOCIOS COLLEGII SS TRINITATIS | A REGINA ELIZABETHA CONSTITUTUS FUIT | AD 1592. | OBIIT DIE 27 APRILIS AD 1613.

The remaining three memorials consist of flat slabs on the ground and commemorate the following College Provosts: *FRANCISCI ANDREWS, LLD, RICARDI BALDWIN S.T.P.* and *GULIELMI TEMPLE LLD.*

Small narrow stone steps lead from the burial ground down into the vaults underneath the chapel. The original college chapel was replaced in 1684. This chapel is referred to as the old chapel. The Bishop of Kildare consecrated the present chapel in 1798.

A number of Provosts and Fellows are buried under the old chapel although some of their memorials have now been removed to the little burial ground as stated below. Among them are included:

Lucas Chaloner was the first Provost and died 1613. His memorial was removed and is now in the cemetery behind the church; William Temple, Provost 1609 (Died 1627); Anthony Martin, Provost 1645 (Died 1650); Thomas Seale, Provost 1660 (Died 1676); George Brown, Provost 1695 (Died 1699). His memorial is now in the cemetery; Robert Huntingdon, Provost 1683 (Died 1701); Richard Baldwin, Provost 1717 (Died 1758) His memorial is now in the cemetery; John Stearne MD, Fellow 1660 (Died 1669). He was a founder member of the College of Physicians in Dublin and its first President; Francis Andrews, Provost 1748 (Died 1774). His memorial is now in the cemetery.

John Temple, Fellow 1618. He was the son of the Provost William Temple. He is noted for his work entitled *History of the Irish Rebellion of 1641, together with the Barbarous Cruelties and Bloody Massacres that ensued thereupon*. This book was first published in 1646 and went through several editions. In 1648 he was appointed Commissioner of the Great Seal of Ireland and in 1653 a Commissioner of Forfeited estates. He died on 14 November 1677 and was buried beside his father. Two of his sons who were born in England included Sir William Temple, the statesman and friend and patron of Jonathan Swift, and Sir John Temple, Speaker of the Irish House of Commons, who was father of the first Viscount Palmerston.

A number of Provosts and Bishops are interred in the crypt under the vestibule and these include:

Richard Murray, Provost in 1795 (Died 1799); William Newcome, Archbishop of Armagh (Died 1800); Matthew Young, Bishop of Clonfert (Died 1800); John Brinkley, Bishop of Cloyne (Died 1835); Thomas Elrington, Bishop of Ferns (Died 1835); George Hall, Bishop of Dromore (Died 1811); Dr John Law, Bishop of Elphin (Died 1810).

Some of those interred in the vault under the Ante chapel at the eastern end include:

Francis Sadleir, Provost 1837 (Died 1851); Richard McDonnell (Died 1867); Charles W. Wall, Vice-Provost (Died 1862); Samuel Kyle, Bishop of Cork, Provost 1820; Henry Wray, Vice-Provost (Died 1847); Thomas Prior, Vice-Provost (Died 1843); Stephen Sandes, Bishop of Killaloe (Died 1842); Francis Hodgkinson, Vice-Provost (Died 1840); Bartholomew Lloyd, Provost 1831 (Died 1835).

Also interred in the same area is John Pentland Mahaffy (1839–1919), a scholar, raconteur and wit who played a prominent part in the social and intellectual life of Dublin for over fifty years. Educated at Trinity, he held the position of tutor, Vice-provost, Provost and Professor over fifty-five years. His pupils included Oscar Wilde who spent much of his time at Mahaffy's home when the they were working on the proofs of Mahaffy's book, *Social Life in Greece from Homer to Menander*. Wilde continued his friendship with Mahaffy after university and they went on expeditions together to Italy and Greece. Another pupil of Mahaffy's was Oliver St John Gogarty, the poet, surgeon and wit.

Mahaffy, who published works on Kant and Descartes as well as on Greek and Egyptian history, was founder of the Dublin Georgian Society and President of the Royal Irish Academy. One of his memorable witticisms includes 'Ireland is a place where the inevitable never happens, and the unexpected often occurs'.

Chaloner's Corner, and the adjoining area where so many illustrious scholars from an early date are interred, is under the care of the University of Dublin.

CHRISTCHURCH CATHEDRAL CRYPT

SITUATION: CHRIST CHURCH PLACE, DUBLIN 8

PERIOD IN USE: C.1100–1900

SITUATED IN CITY CENTRE

In 1038 Sitric Silkenbeard, the first Christian king of the Dublin Norsemen, founded Christ Church or the Cathedral of the Holy Trinity for Donat or Dunan, the first Bishop of Dublin. It was built within the Danish fortifications or city walls.

The crypt, which is medieval, is assumed to be Dublin's oldest surviving building. The first burial recorded is that of Donat who is interred in the Choir, at the right-hand side of the altar. A stone coffin was discovered here in 1545 containing the body of a bishop in episcopal dress which was believed to be that of Donat.

In 1162 Gelasius, Archbishop of Armagh, consecrated Laurence O'Toole (1130–1180), Archbishop of Dublin, in Christ Church.

By 1171 the Normans, under Richard de Clare, Earl of Pembroke (Strongbow) had Dublin in their power. Their conquest was legitimised the following year through a charter granted by King Henry II. They immediately tore down the simple, wooden Christ Church and began rebuilding what is now Christ Church Cathedral. Strongbow, FitzStephen and le Gros 'set about the rebuilding of the Cathedral with commendable promptitude and generosity'. John Comyn and Henri de Loundres completed the rest of the work between 1181 and 1225.

Sir Walter Scott described Strongbow:

His stature was not of the tallest, but his person was uncommonly strong and compact. The greatest peculiarities of his frame were the breadth of his shoulders, and the great and almost disproportionate length of his arms; so remarkable, indeed, that it was said he could, without stooping, tie the garters of his Highland Hose, which are placed two inches below the knee!

He got the name Strongbow because of his amazing strength; he drew an extraordinary strong bow. In 1174 he established a priory nearby at Kilmainham for the Knights Hospitallers of St John of Jerusalem.

Strongbow died in 1176 and his obsequies were performed by Archbishop Laurence O'Toole. He was buried in the nave of Christ Church. All the ancient tombs, excepting that of Strongbow, have vanished from Christ Church. Strongbow's monument was damaged in April 1562 when the south wall of the church fell in, but it was later replaced. The small figure beside it is believed to be a piece from the original monument. Over the monument is a slab on the wall with the following inscription:

THIS :AVNCYENT : MONVMENT : OF : RYCHARD : STRA

NGBOWE : CALLED : COMES : STRANGVLENSIS : LORD : OF :

CHEPSTO :AND : OGNY :THE : FYRST :AND : PRINCYPALL : INVADER : OF :

IRLAND : 1169 : QVI : OBIIT : 1177:THE : MONVMENT :WAS: BROKEN :

BY :THE : FALL : OF :THE : ROFF :AND : BODYE :

OF : CHRYSTES : CHVRCHE : IN :AN : 1562 :AND :

SET :VP :AGAYN :AT :THE : CHARGYS : OF :THE :

RIGHT : HONORABLE : SIR : HENIRI : SYDNEY :

KNYGHT : OF :THE : NOBLE : ORDER : L : PRESIDENT :

OF :WALLES : L : DEPVTY : OF : IRLAND : 1570.

Laurence O'Toole, who died at Eu in Normandy on 14 November 1180, was canonised in 1225 by Pope Honorius III. The chapel of the Holy Ghost, in the choir in the south aisle of Christ Church was dedicated to him.

The three immediate successors to Laurence O'Toole were John Comyn, Henri de Loundres, and Luke. They were also among the principal benefactors to Christ Church and all are buried here.

In 1212 Archbishop Comyn died and was buried on the south side of the altar under a marble monument. He had repaired the church twenty-two years previously. Henri de Loundres, who died in 1228 ,was buried in a wooden tomb opposite that of Archbishop Comyn's. Archbishop Luke died in 1255 and was buried in Archbishop Comyn's tomb.

Gerald Fitzgerald, Eighth Earl of Kildare and Lord Deputy of Ireland, is buried near the high altar. Known as the Great Earl, he died from wounds received in an encounter in Offaly against O'Carroll in 1513. The King said of him 'If all Ireland cannot rule this man, let him rule all Ireland'.

The tomb of Robert Fitzgerald, nineteenth Earl of Kildare (1743), is situated against the west wall in the south transept.

There are many members of the Fitzgerald family, who contributed so much to the history of Ireland, recorded in the table of burials in the Old Register of the Cathedral. The register also contains the names of some of the members of the Irish peerage and other distinguished persons connected with Dublin who were interred in the vaults of Christ Church. These include the Rt Hon Lieut General Ingoldsby, one of the Lord Justices of Ireland.

Ingoldsby was afforded a state funeral because he died while serving in government. A description is given of the long funeral procession, which left from his house in Henry Street at 1.00 p.m. and proceeded through the principal streets of the city. It gives an idea of the form such funerals took at that time.

The procession began by forty-seven poor men in black gowns and hoods, being as many as he was years old; after whom marched two regiments of foot and two troops of horse, with five hautboys and a trumpet to sound the funeral march. They were followed by a guidon, carried by captain Haynes; a horse in black, with escutcheons; two bomb carts, kettle-drum, and five pieces of ordnance, attended by six montrosses and six gunners, together with the inferior officers of the ordnance, and the superior ones, all in mourning: after these proceeded fourteen footmen, four state trumpets and kettle-drum to sound a funeral march; the standard carried by captain Edgworth, a horse in black, two state trumpets to sound a solemn tune, five physicians, usher of the Council, three pursuivants, chirurgeon-general, six chaplains, clerk of the council, steward and comptroller, physician-general, two pennons carried by captain Jones and captain Cary, a horse in black carrying several escutcheons, the gentleman of horse holding the rein; the preacher; the gauntlets carried by captain Dallway, helmet and crest by Athlone Pursuivant of Arms, sergeant of arms in mourning, the horse in black covered with escutcheons, sword and shield carried by Colonel Morris, gentleman usher, coat of his arms carried by Ulster King of Arms, who was follow'd by a herse with the body, and then by the mourners and judges on foot; after whom went fifteen mourning coaches with six horses, and a great number of lords and gentlemens coaches.

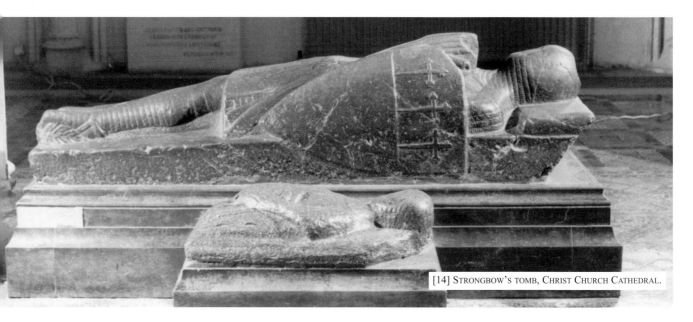

[14] STRONGBOW'S TOMB, CHRIST CHURCH CATHEDRAL.

As soon as the corpse was laid in the herse, by a signal, the ordnance fir'd a great gun every minute; and when the corpse was taken out of the herse, by a signal, the ordnance ceased firing and all the bells stopped.

It was received at the door of the cathedral of Christ Church by the whole body of the church and choir; and after the service and sermon was ended, and the corpse interred, the King of Arms made a proclamation of the titles of his posts of honour, and then by a signal, the ordnance fired three rounds, of twenty guns each round, and were answer'd by a volley of the army, who were drawn up for that purpose; one in Castle Street, one in High Street, and the horse in Christ Church yard.

Ingoldsby was buried on 9 February 1712.

A brass plate on the wall bearing the arms of Lord Grey, with the motto At vincet pauperiem virtus, has the following inscription:

SONS OF LORD GREY OF WILTON, LORD DEPUTY OF IRELAND, IN THE REIGN OF QUEEN ELIZABETH, 1580–1582 AD 1582.
HERE LIETH BURIED THE SECOND AND THIRD SONNES OF

THE RIGHT HONORABLE SIR ARTHURE GREY, KNIGHT OF
THE ORDER, LORD GREY OF WILTON, AND OF THE LADY
JANA SIBILIA, HIS WIFE, WHICH CHILDREN DIED IN THE
CASTEL OF DUBLIN, IN THE TIME OF HIS DEPUTATION
HEERE.

Lord Grey de Wilton was Lord Lieutenant of Ireland in 1580 and his main claim to fame was the putting down of the rebellion of Desmond.

The cathedral contains monuments to many distinguished religious, military, medical, musical and artistic citizens, some of whom are buried in the cathedral. These include:

Thomas Prior (1682–1751), whose memorial is in Latin, was a founder of the Dublin Society, now the Royal Dublin Society. He wrote a number of tracts such as *Absentees, The Virtues of Tar Water* and some on the linen manufacture of Ireland. He was most interested in fostering the industry in Ireland and he encouraged the wearing of linen scarves at funerals to increase the sales of the product. This custom first came into fashion at the funeral of Mr Connolly, Speaker of the Irish Commons. Prior was interred in the parish church of the village of Rathdowney.

Dr Richard Woodward, who died on 22 November 1777 aged thirty-three, was organist at Christ Church and Vicar Choral of St Patrick's Cathedral. He is interred in a vault and there is a fitting memorial to him, which bears a musical epitaph.

There is a memorial to James Hewitt, Lord Lifford, near the place of his burial. He was Lord Chancellor of Ireland and died in 1789.

Dedicated to Bishop Fletcher, DD, is a plain white tablet on the south side of the choir and of the altar. He is buried in a vault nearby. He died on 18 March 1761. For almost sixteen years he was Bishop of Kildare and Dean of Christ Church.

Some memorials to medical men include those to Dr George Renny, Director General of the Medical Department of the army in Ireland who died in 1848 at the Royal Hospital Kilmainham; Surgeon Henry Mathias, assistant surgeon of H.M.S. Enterprise, who died in 1849 at Port Leopold and Surgeon John Hamilton, Fellow and Vice-President of the Royal College of Surgeons, and Surgeon in Ordinary to the Queen in Ireland, who died in 1857.

Other important memorials include those to Francis Agard, 1577; Edward Griffith, 1632; William and Ambrose Cadagon, 1660–1693; Welbore Ellis, Bishop of Kildare, 1733; John Lord Bowes, 1767; James Viscount Lifford, 1789; Sir John A. Stevenson; Sir Samuel Auchmuty, 1822; Nathaniel Sneyd, 1833; Richard Lawrence, Archbishop of Cashel and Lismore, 1838; Lieutenant J.C. Smith, 1843; the Hon Charles Lindsay, 1846 and Lieutenant Col John W. King, 1850.

There are a number of flat slabs on the ground which are now illegible due to wear and tear. A simple slab near the doorway, facing east commemorates Richard Browne who was Sheriff of Dublin in 1605. It has the following inscription:

HERE . UNDER . LYETH . THE . BODY

OF . RICHARD . BROWNE . SOMETIME

SHERIFF . OF . DUBLIN . WHO . DEPARTED

THIS . LYFE . THE[?] DAY . OF . JULY

AN. . DOM. . 1615 . AND . HIS . WIFE,

MARGARET . STAPLES . WHO . CAUSED . THIS

MONUMENT . TO . BE . MADE . FOR . THEM

AND . THEIR . POSTERITIE.

During the years 1871–78, Christ Church was completely restored by Henry Roe. At this time, human remains were cleared from the crypt, and existing coffins were collected together and placed in an airtight vault there.

Interestingly, a small burial ground existed until the time of the restoration. It was situated to the east of the old Chapter House, the foundations of which were only discovered when the restoration was complete.

Christ Church is under the care of the Select Vestry of Christ Church Cathedral Group.

CRUAGH (OLD) GRAVEYARD

SITUATION: RATHFARNHAM, DUBLIN 16

PERIOD IN USE: 1700 AND 1800S

BUS NOS (FROM NUTGROVE SHOPPING CENTRE): 161 TO ROCKBROOK

Situated six miles from Dublin City centre and just south of Rockbrook, Cruagh (formerly named Creevagh), derives its name from Craobhach, a bushy place. The Owendoher River divides the parish of Cruagh from that of Whitechurch.

Originally there was a church in Cruagh graveyard, which was in existence at the time of the Anglo-Norman conquest. The ruin was still in existence in the last century but all traces of this have now vanished. The foundation of the church may have had connections with St Dalua of Dún Tighe Bretan or Tibradden, whose feast day is 7 January. The ancient Priory at Kilmainham owned lands in Tibradden and after the conquest, Cruagh was granted to the Bishopric of Dublin. It was subsequently assigned to the Kilmainham Priory as owners of the nearby lands at Tibradden. After the dissolution of the monasteries and religious houses by Henry VIII, the rectory fell into lay hands and at the start of the seventeenth century it was served by the Vicar at Tallaght. It was united to Ballyfermot and Palmerston some years later, but fell into disuse after troubled times.

The graveyard, which is surrounded by a high wall, looks quite dramatic on its steep slope. Old gravestones of different shapes and sizes jut out at various angles. An interesting feature of this graveyard is a low, squat stone tower which stands partly on the site of the former Church on the summit. Originally an iron-plated door led to a chamber below ground level. This door is now missing. There are a couple of narrow openings higher up and also an aperture, which gave access to a higher floor or chamber in the tower. A ladder would have been used in this case, as there was no internal stairway. This was a watchtower, which was used to protect the graveyard from bodysnatchers. Some of the early nineteenth-century gravestones contain holes, which could have been caused by bullets during a fracas with body snatchers who are known to have frequently targeted this churchyard.

A four-sided basin cut in a square granite block with a drainhole was located to the south of the site of the church, and was probably an early holy-water font.

About ninety-four memorials remain, the earliest recorded being 1728. Dr George Petrie, the antiquary who travelled through Dublin and Wicklow sketching ecclesiastical architecture, located an earlier tombstone with concentric engravings. This could lie buried like other gravestones. Many date from the 1700s and are extremely difficult to decipher.

Some of the memorials here are rather quaint, such as the one erected by Thomas Ambross, which has the face of a winged cherub carved both on the top left and right-hand sides of the gravestone. It reads:

Gloria in Excelsis Deo | IHS | This stone was erected by Thomas | Ambross of the City of Dublin Brewers | in memory of his son William who | departed this life the 14th April 1782 | aged 18 years. | Here also lieth four more of his children.

There are some local people commemorated with memorials here. Below are a few of the inscriptions:

IHS | This stone and burial | place belongeth to Thos Plunkett of Cruagh & his | posterity. Here lieth | three of his children | 1762.

IHS | This stone and burial place belongs | to Mr John Hyland and his posterity | AD1794. Here lieth the body of his | Father Mr Michael Hyland who depar | ted this life in December 1762 in the | 90th year of his age. Here lieth the | body of his Mother Mrs Judith Hyland | who departed this life in February | 1778 in the 102nd year of her age.

[15] THE GRAVESTONE ERECTED BY THOMAS AMBROSS, OF THE CITY OF DUBLIN BREWERS, IN MEMORY OF HIS SON, WILLIAM, WHO DIED ON 14 APRIL 1782.

[16] THE WATCHTOWER AT CRUAGH, RATHFARNHAM, WHICH AFFORDED PROTECTION AGAINST GRAVE ROBBERS, WHO WERE KNOWN TO FREQUENT THIS BURIAL GROUND.

Those interred here came from localities such as Killakee, Willbrook, Ballymount, Bohernabreena, Edmondstown, Rockbrook, and Templeogue. There were also people with city addresses and people from as far afield as Clontarf. Some had large families such as:

IHS | This stone was erected | by Danl. King of New | Street in the City of Dublin | in memory of his wife Mrs | Mary King who departed | this life June 24th 1778 aged 56 | Here lyeth 10 of their children.

On the eastern side of this graveyard, the new Cruagh cemetery is located which was opened in 1944 and which is still in use.

Cruagh is under the care of Dublin County Council.

CRUMLIN (ST MARY'S) CHURCHYARD

SITUATION: CRUMLIN, DUBLIN 12

PERIOD IN USE: C.1100 – 1952 [CLOSED EXCEPT FOR THOSE WITH BURIAL RIGHTS]

BUS NO (FROM CITY CENTRE): 150

Crumlin village is situated two and three quarter miles form the General Post Office. The Lansdowne Valley through which the river Camac flows is the original Cruimghlinn, meaning a crooked glen, from which the village of Crumlin derives its name.

The church and churchyard dedicated to St Mary is on the site of an early twelfth century church, which was also dedicated to St Mary. Enclosed by a high wall, it is situated at a bend on the road, which is at the junction of St Mary's Road and St Agnes' Road. It is adjacent to the new yellow-brick Church of Ireland church, which opened in 1942. The churchyard is somewhat oval in shape with a rectangular piece added on to the back of it.

A document of 1496 records that there was once a village cross. From time immemorial it was the custom in the neighbourhood for mourners attending a funeral procession to walk bareheaded around the cross, and when it was no longer there, they walked around the original site of the cross.

In 1594, insurgents from Wicklow burned the village. In doing so, they badly damaged the fabric of the church and removed portions of the lead roof for the manufacture of bullets. By 1630 the church had been rebuilt and was in good repair.

King William and his victorious army encamped in Crumlin in 1690 for two days after the Battle of the Boyne. It was here that he issued his proclamation to stop King James's brass money being coined, except at reduced rates of valuation.

The church of St Mary was rebuilt in 1818 with the help of a loan of £1,000 from the Board of First Fruits. It comprised a neat stone structure, which adjoined an ancient tower. In the tower there were some fragments found from a memorial to a lady-in-waiting to Queen Anne. Apparently, this memorial was once in the churchyard, but it was removed to the tower for safekeeping. Nothing of it remains today. Over the church door is the replica of a small skull.

In the same year, the Commons at Crumlin were enclosed by an Act of Parliament. The annual horse races that had been held here over the years had become intolerable to the inhabitants, and were brought to an end.

St Mary's is an interesting churchyard as it contains the remains of many of the original old landowning families of Crumlin, like the Deanes, the Purcells and the Shaws who lived in the old manors like Crumlin House and Kimmage Manor.

In the churchyard, there are some memorials dating back to the 1600s. There are two dedicated to members of the Deane family of Ravensthorp in Northamptonshire and of Pinnock in Gloucestershire at the close of the seventeenth century. The inscription of the first memorial reads:

JOS: FIL: SEC: JOS : ET ANN DEANE NAT: APD

RAVENSTHORP : IN COM : NORHAMP 60 DIE JAN:

1648, ET NUP : ELIZ : FIL JOH : PARKER ARCHEP.

DUBLI N ET OBIIT APD DUB : DECIMO OCTA I DIE

JAN : 1698 ET SEP : APD CRUMLIN VICISSIMO

DIE EIUS 2. MENSIS. FERENDO NON FINENDO.

A Major Joseph Deane, who was prominent in the political movements of the period, lived in Crumlin. He probably occupied the royal manor house, of which no trace now remains. In the latter half of the seventeenth century, he owned a lot of land, which included Terenure and the greater portion of the lands in Crumlin. He married twice and had a son, Joseph, by his first wife. Joseph married a daughter of Dr John Parker, Archbishop of Dublin and he predeceased his father.

Deane's second wife was a daughter of Maurice Cuffe of the Desart family from Clare and they had a son named Edward. The memorial is inscribed:

ELIZ : FILIA MAU : CUFFE .AR : NATA.

....APD : QUIN IN COM : CLARE, 10 : AUG : 1625

....NUP : JOS DEANE AR : 80 FEB : 1652.

OBIIT 30 AP : 1698.

JOS : FIL : EDW : ET ANN DEANE AR

NAT : APD PINNOCK IN COM : GLOC 2

DIE FEB : 1623

OBIIT 210 DECEMBRIS 1699

The Deane grave was situated inside the communion rail and this memorial is now in the porch of the tower.

Nearby was the grave of the Purcell family who settled in Crumlin at the end of the sixteenth century. There are a number of memorials to this family. A John Purcell was named as the principal

Catholic resident in the district according to the religious census taken in Crumlin in 1766 by order of the Irish parliament. The family lived in Crumlin House. Their memorial consisted of a slab of limestone, supported on four square legs of granite and it lay against the east wall of the church. It bore the following inscription:

IGN. PURCELL, ESQR HIS BURIALL PLACE |
His first wife MARGARET PURCELL | Alias SWEETMAN died the 13th of June | 1682. His second wife Ellenor PUR- | -CELL Alias PLUNKET died the 6th of | Jany 1691. | Not lost but gone before. IGNATIUS PURCELL, Esqr., | obt. 3rd of March, 1791. | Died 31st of Decr 1851 HENRITTA FRANCES O'NEILL, | daughter of Major BRISTOW and wife of | IGNATIUS FRANCIS PURCELL, Esqr | Also IGNATIUS FRANCIS PURCELL | of Cromlyn House, Co. Dublin, Esqr., 14th Augt 1856. | Trusting in the merits of Christ | Here also are deposited the remains of SELINA E. PURCELL, | wife of Jno.F. Purcell Esqr who departed this life on the | 7th day of October, 1823, in her 22nd year.

Sadly, two or more memorials to the Purcell family were badly vandalised quite close to the location where the original tomb stood against the east wall of the church. The burials date from the early part of the seventeenth century.

The religious census of 1766 indicated that the principal Protestant resident was George Thwaites. He was buried in the churchyard, but nothing remains of his memorial which was vandalised. It bore the inscription:

This Monument was Erected to the memory of GEORGE THWAITS Esqr of the City of Dublin Brewer who departed this Life May 25 1782 aged 66 years. Here lieth the Body of ELIZABETH his Wife who died Decr 19 1789 aged 43 years. Here also lies three of his Children MARIA, GRACE, EMILIA.

There is a particularly large granite memorial to the left of the church, which is inscribed:

Family vault of | The Rt Hon Sir Frederick Shaw | 3rd Bart of Kimmage and Bushy Park | Recorder of Dublin and M.P. for TCD. Died 1876.

Frederick Shaw built the original Kimmage Manor. Other members of the Shaw family, who were originally from county Kilkenny, are interred in Rathfarnham churchyard. When Shaw died at the age of seventy-four, the family left the manor and it was leased to Erskin Chetwode Elliott. The Holy Ghost Fathers moved to Kimmage Manor in 1911 but have sold off much of the land for housing development. Chetwode Elliott is buried in the churchyard and his memorial still remains. James Elliott, the Rector of St Mary's, erected it in 1857 to the memory of members of his family. The Reverend James Elliott is commemorated with a memorial in the porch of the tower.

[17] St Mary's Church in Crumlin showing the old tower.

Some other old tombstones commemorate the MacCreery Family, one of whom died in the Island of Ceylon and another from Shanganagh, Co. Dublin 1794–1851, Alderman Reynolds, who died in 1772 and members of the Gerrard family from 1751.

Some inscriptions refer to people from the inner city whose trades are included on their memorials. Below is a sample:

Mathew Byrne of Cole Alley, Baker, who died on 2 August 1757 aged sixty-eight years; John Johnston of Parliament Street, Silk Manufacturer, who died on 23 August 1823 aged thirty years; John Morrin of Cork Bridge, Brewer; Walter Teeling of Earl Street, Grocer, who died on 1 August 1774 aged fifty-four; John Jones of Ash Street, Cotton Manufacturer; Joseph Jones of South Earl Street, Merchant, who died on 26 August 1797 aged forty years; Mrs Corrigan of Brabazon Street, Baker, died 1793; Benjamin Matthias, Upper Coombe, Clothier, 1774–1784, Thomas Ord of Cork Street, Tanner, 1802 and Michael and Oliver Ferral, Teapweaver and Sheerman, 1751.

An unusual feature in this churchyard is a subterranean passageway, which is surmounted by a stone archway. This was supposedly used as a type of safe to contain bodies where they were kept and guarded continuously for nine days. Apparently, after nine days, they would be of little use to the grave robbers and were buried.

In 1952 the churchyard was closed by Ministerial order except for families holding burial rights. The church fell into disrepair and the graveyard became overgrown.

The church, which is the principal building of historic interest in the area and the churchyard, which is noted for its birdsong, are being restored and the memorials cleaned up. The Crumlin Historical & Preservation Society were the instigators of this major project and deserve much praise for their work. When the restoration work has been completed, the building will be used by the Historical Society as a Heritage and Community Centre and as a venue for exhibitions and lectures of a cultural nature. It will help preserve the history and heritage of the Crumlin area for future generations by making it accessible to local people and visitors.

Perhaps this venture will prompt and encourage other communities to preserve their local history in a similar fashion.

Dalkey (St Begnet's) Churchyard

SITUATION: CASTLE STREET, DALKEY, CO. DUBLIN

PERIOD IN USE: 1500 TO 1826

BUS NO (FROM CITY CENTRE): 8 OR DART

Dalkey is a coastal village situated eight miles south-east of the city. Its name is derived from Dalkey Island, which is the Norse word for *Thorn Island*.

In the Middle Ages, Dalkey was a town of considerable importance being the principal emporium for the commerce of Ireland. It was a landing place for merchandise from abroad. The harbour was considered very favourable for the business of the town, as vessels were safe in the shelter of Dalkey Island, which afforded them protection from the north-east winds. The water in the area was also of a depth which enabled a vessel to sail at any hour. Larger ships found the navigation of the Liffey impossible. Dalkey was therefore used until the close of the sixteenth century and until the adoption of Ringsend as the port of Dublin.

An enchanting description of Dalkey in the sixteenth century is given by Elrington Ball:

To a traveller coming over Killiney Hill on a fine summer's day, a pretty picture then presented itself, as the town, with its busy port, broke upon his view. Its walls, its castles, and its church stood out clearly in the sunlight and beneath them the blue water in the sound crowded with shipping.

Later, Mr Peter Wilson, the well-known bookseller, who published the Dublin *Almanac* or *Directory* of the day, recalled that in 1770 the street, owing to its rocky surface, had been impassable for carriages and difficult for a horse to traverse. It was levelled and the old road which ran on the north side of the town was then only used on the occasion of funerals.

Originally seven strongly fortified castles guarded the town, two of which still remain in Castle Street. These fortified houses date from the fifteenth and sixteenth centuries. One is known as Archbold's Castle and the other, which is named Goat Castle, is incorporated into the Town Hall.

The earliest surviving building is the medieval ruined church of St Begnet in Castle Street, which is adjacent to the Town Hall. The church is dedicated to St Begnet the Virgin, the patron saint of Dalkey,

73

who is supposed to have flourished in the seventh century, and whose feast day falls on 12 November. The Normans rebuilt it, but at the beginning of the seventeenth century it was in a ruinous condition, and apart from the curate's family, the only people at the service were some English and Scottish fishermen who attended during the fishing season.

The ruins of the church comprise a nave, chancel and a belfry. After the Restoration, the parish was united to Monkstown, and the little church of St Begnet has not been used since.

[18] The ruined medieval church of St Begnet, Castle Street, Dalkey.

There are approximately sixty-three monuments in St Begnet's graveyard. Of note is the monument which commemorates the victims from the *Prince of Wales* shipwreck. It is inscribed:

Sacred to the Memory of the soldiers belonging to His Majesty's 18th Regement of Foot and a few belonging to other corps who activated by a desire of more extensive service nobly volluntered from the South Mayo and different regements of Irish Militia of the line and who were unfortunately shipwrecked on the this coast in the Prince of Wales packet and perished on the night of the 19th November 1807. This tribute to their memory has been erected on their tomb by order of General the Earl of Harrington Commander of the Forces in Ireland.

Merrion and Carrickbrennan graveyards also contain shipwreck memorials.

Most of the people interred in this churchyard are from the areas of Dalkey, Kingstown and Glenageary.

A memorial of some local history interest is that of Hugh Dempsy who called himself the King of Dalkey:

This stone was erected by Mr Murtagh Dempsy of the City of Dublin in Memory of his affectionate son Hugh Dempsy Block Maker of said City who departed this life April 7 1790 aged 33 years.

There is a memorial erected by a husband and father, which commemorates his wife and their five young children:

Erected by John Foley of Kingstown in Memory of his beloved wife Catherine who died 26th Novr. 1844 aged 36 years, and five of his children who died as follows:

Hugh the 19th April 1840 aged 10 years.
Julia Ann 28 Nov. 1841 aged 3 years.
Marg. 3rd Decr. 1843 aged 2 years.
Dennis 23 Decr. 1843 aged 9 months.
Margt. 10th Octr. 1844 aged 3 weeks.

Access to the graveyard is through the adjoining Dalkey Castle and Heritage Centre, which is open throughout the year.

St Begnet's Church and Churchyard is under the care of the Environment Department of Dún Laoghaire Corporation.

DEAN'S GRANGE CEMETERY

SITUATION: DEAN'S GRANGE, CO. DUBLIN

PERIOD IN USE: 1865 TO DATE

BUS NOS (FROM CITY CENTRE): 45, 46A

The Burial Act of 1855 resulted in the closure by law of many of the older churchyards within the city and county of Dublin due to overcrowding. In 1861, the Board of Guardians of Rathdown bought a large tract of land in Dean's Grange for the purpose of creating a new cemetery. This was opened in 1865 and is the largest cemetery in south county Dublin. Over the years there were various changes in the authority which administered the cemetery subsequent to the Local Government Acts of 1898, 1899 and 1930. It is now administered by the Dean's Grange Burial Board.

The cemetery, which is open to all religious denominations, contains two churches, which were built in the grounds for holding both Catholic and Protestant services for the dead. The Catholic Church is on the right of the Main Avenue and the Protestant one is on the left. These are now rarely used.

The Main Avenue is wide and flanked by nicely shaped yew trees. The cemetery comprises sixty acres and slopes gently from the west side. It has the Dublin Mountains as a backdrop and a view of Killiney Head is visible from parts of it.

At the turn of the century Catholics were interred in the area of the cemetery known as the North Section and Protestants were interred in the South Section. The number of sections in the cemetery has now increased to sixteen. These later sections are named after various saints. The older sections contain a greater variety of monuments and also more shrubbery and trees.

The first burial took place on 28 January 1865. It was that of Anastasia Carey, who worked as a servant at St Joseph's Orphanage, which was run by the Daughters of the Heart of Mary in Tivoli Road, Kingstown (now Dún Laoghaire). The orphanage, which was built in 1860, was demolished some years ago. Miss Carey's grave is difficult to locate as it is completely hidden with ivy and overhanging shrubbery. To reach it, turn right at the top of the Main Avenue and follow this pathway past the little church, which is on the left-hand side. Just beside the tenth yew tree on the right-hand side, there is a memorial to James Gaffney of Booterstown. Turn a sharp right past this and continue in a direct line towards a copse like area. Anastasia Carey's grave is located here under shrubbery (31/32K north). It is enclosed in a rectangular area, which contains three graves pertaining to St Joseph's Orphanage. On her grave is inscribed:

Pray for the repose of the soul | of | Anastasia Carey | who died of typhus fever | caught in the discharge of her | duty at St Joseph's Orphanage | during the prevalence of an | epidemic 26th January 1865, | aged 40 years.

Beside it there is a cross, on top of which is inscribed the words SPES UNICA and on the base St Joseph's Orphanage Kingstown. It commemorates some of the people connected with the institution. The front of the cross is inscribed:

Pray for the soul of | Catherine Hunt | who died 8th March 1867 aged 24 | also for the soul of | Mary Byrne | who died 14th May 1878 aged 75 | also | Bridget Byrne | died Sep. 29 1890 | aged 82.

There are further names inscribed on each side of the cross.

The third memorial in this enclosed rectangle bears the following inscription:

Pray for the soul of Antoinette le Coispellier, Directress of St Joseph's Orphanage, Kingstown, who fell victim to her zeal and charity, in attending the orphans during an epidemic, 25th February 1865 aged 31 years. Greater love than this no man hath, than to lay down his life for his friends. [30 KN]

There are many eminent people buried in Dean's Grange some of whom are mentioned below.

In the south-west section in row O, John Howard Parnell [1843–1923], Charles Stewart Parnell's elder brother, was buried. He emigrated to the United States in 1866 and lived in Alabama for a time. In 1872 he returned to Ireland and farmed in Co. Armagh. He inherited Avondale after the death of his brother in 1891 and, unable to make it financially viable, sold it in 1899. He was a Member of Parliament for South Meath from 1895–1900 and in 1904 was City Marshall of Dublin. He wrote *C.S. Parnell: A Memoir*, which was published in 1916. John Howard Parnell appears in *Ulysses* as does a former well-known newspaper vendor, an uninhibited and witty Dublin character Davy Stephens who is also interred in Dean's Grange. James Joyce describes him in *Ulysses* 'minute in a large capecoat, a small felt hat crowning his ringlets'. Stephens was known as the 'prince of the news vendors' and was called 'Sir' Davy Stephens. He had a monopoly on newspaper sales to the passengers on the mailboat with his news-stand at Kingstown (now Dún Laoghaire). An amusing confrontation between Stephens and King Edward VII on the King's visit to Ireland in 1903 provides for the epithet 'a king's courier'.

Tyrone-born Dr Augustine Henry (1857–1930) was a celebrated botanist who had a most interesting life. After graduating in medicine in 1879 he worked with the Custom's Service in China. Whilst there, he sent a remarkable collection which consisted of over one thousand plants to Kew Gardens in London. He then moved to Formosa where he published the first account of the Formosan flora. At the same time, he studied law and became a member of the Middle Temple. In 1900 he returned to Europe and went to

Nantes in France where he studied forestry. With H.J. Elwes, he published *Trees of Great Britain and Ireland* which comprised seven volumes. Henry developed the School of Forestry at Cambridge University and in 1913 was appointed Professor of Forestry at the College of Science in Dublin. He died in March 1930 in Ranelagh, Dublin. To reach his grave, continue up the Main Avenue. At the top, continue straight up the narrow pathway past a rather large mausoleum on the left marked 'Glorney 1911'. Henry's grave is a few paces further on the right-hand side. [56 1 4 North]

His memorial is a plain granite upright stone, which bears the following inscription:

To the beloved memory | of | Augustine Henry | 1857–1930 | He was the first to reveal by his travels | and collections the surpassing richness | and interest of the flora of China | His work in the East has beautified the | Gardens of the West and his profound | research has established on a scientific | basis the study of all the trees that grow | In Great Britain and Ireland | And his wife Elsie (Alice Helen) Henry (1882–1956) who carried on his greatest work to its successful | conclusion in our Botanic Gardens and who enriched our era | By her gracious personality.

Writers interred in Dean's Grange include:

Constantine Curran (1880–1972) was well known in the Dublin literary, artistic and musical world. He studied at the old Catholic University where he first met James Joyce and they remained friends until Joyce's death in 1941. Curran was called to the bar but never practised. His works include *Dublin Decorative Plasterwork of the Seventeenth and Eighteenth Centuries* (1967), *James Joyce Remembered* (1968) and *Under the Receding Wave* (1970). Curran died on 1 January 1972. His friend Niall Montgomery wrote in an appreciation of Curran that he is of those of whom it can be truly said that '*dum viveret insignitus est signaculo Sanctae Trinitatis*' which translates as 'while he was alive, he was marked by the seal of the Holy Trinity'. Seamus Murphy designed his memorial. [121 K St Patrick]

Frank O'Connor (Michael O'Donovan) (1903–66), the short story writer, was born in Cork. His childhood is recounted in his biography, *An Only Child*. He died in Dublin on 10 March 1966. His memorial is a stone with Michael O'Donovan inscribed on it and also his pen name. [Section N. St Patrick. 79/80]

Donagh MacDonagh (1912–68), poet, playwright, short story writer and also son of the poet and patriot Thomas MacDonagh, was born in Dublin. He was Justice for the Dublin Metropolitan Courts at the time of his death on 1 January 1968. [Section N. AO 137]

Brian O'Nolan [Flann O'Brien, Myles na gCopaleen] (1911–66), Ireland's greatest modern satirist, always considered himself to be a Dubliner, although he was born in Strabane. Co. Tyrone. In 1940, he started writing his satirical column for *The Irish Times*, 'Cruiskeen Lawn' which appeared at least three times a week for twenty-five years. He died on 1 April 1966. To reach his grave, go to the top of the Main Avenue and continue straight up the pathway past the large mausoleum on the left. Continue to a large cross, which is on a grassy mound at the corner. Turn left and continue straight past the Republican Plot on the right-hand side. It is just beyond this on the right at a corner. [20-A-West]

Michael Farrell (1899–1962) who was born in Carlow and studied medicine at University College is remembered for his novel *Thy Tears Might Cease*. He abandoned medicine for business and broadcasting and the writing of his novel, which was the talk of the town in literary circles. Farrell never quite got around to editing the long manuscript, which was later edited by his friend, the writer Monk Gibbon. It was published posthumously (1963) and became a best seller. [15 G2 St Mary]

[19] A LARGE WHITE MARBLE MONUMENT WITH A BRONZE BUST MARKS THE GRAVE OF JOHN MCCORMACK (1884–1945), IRELAND'S GREATEST LYRIC TENOR.

Pádraig Ó Siochfhradha (1883–1964) *An Seabhac*, was born in Dingle and worked for some years in the civil service. A lifelong promoter of the language movement, he published many books on Irish, including *Jimín Mháire Thaidhg* and *An Baile Seo 'gainne*. He died on 11 November 1964. [83-Q-St Patrick]

Richard Irvine Best (1872–1959), renowned Celtic scholar and former Director of the National Library, he appears in the 'Scylla and Charybdis' episode in *Ulysses*. Best was author of a number of works including a two-volume *Bibliography of Irish Philology and Manuscript Literature, Publications 1913–1941*. Grave No: 66 H SW

John McCormack (1884–1945), acclaimed as the greatest lyric tenor of his time, is commemorated with a large white marble wall into which is incorporated a bronze bust. Born in Athlone, he entered for the tenor competition in the *Feis Ceoil* of 1903 where he was awarded the gold medal. As a result, McCormack got offers of concert engagements throughout the country and his career mushroomed from there. He went on to study in Italy and on his return met James Joyce on several occasions in the company of Richard Best of the National Library. Best was keenly interested in the *Feis Ceoil* and both he and McCormack encouraged Joyce to enter in 1904. McCormack made his operatic debut at Covent Garden in 1907 and continued with appearances with the Chicago, Boston and Metropolitan Opera Companies in the United States. After a few more opera seasons, he chose the concert stage where he proved to be the greatest concert attraction of his time. McCormack, one of the best loved of all Irish singers, died at Glena, his home in Booterstown on 16 September 1945. To get to his grave, take the first right turn inside the main gate. Continue on straight and then take first turn left. Take the second turn on the right and McCormack's memorial is a short walk up on the right-hand side. [119–120. E & F. St Patrick]

[20] AN INTERESTING MONUMENT COMMEMORATING MARY EDITH COLEMAN (MRS ALSAGER) WHO WAS DECORATED BY EMPEROR WILLIAM WITH THE ORDER OF THE IRON CROSS.

John Boyd Dunlop (1840–1921) was quite a remarkable man. He was born in Scotland and became a veterinary surgeon. He set up his own practice in Belfast. During his calls in the surrounding area, he travelled by dogcart. The roads were rough with cobblestones and he felt very sorry for people who had to travel by bicycle with their solid tyres. It made for a bumpy ride. He invented the pneumatic tyre, applied for a patent and came to Dublin where, in 1889, he founded the first Pneumatic Tyre Co. at 67 Upper Stephen Street. He was not an avid cyclist himself but he did appear occasionally on his bicycle, which he purchased in 1888 for demonstration purposes. Not anticipating the future growth and success of the business, he sold his interest in the company and thereby lost out financially. The demand became so great that the Pneumatic Tyre Company had great difficulty in meeting the orders. Dunlop, who cut a bit of a dash with his thick white hair and flowing beard, was Chairman of Todd Burns in Henry Street. He lived for thirty years in Dublin. Grave No 72 & 73 C & D-S.W.

Two former Taoisigh interred here include John Costello (1891–1976) [119, 120-M-St Patrick] and Seán Lemass (1899–1971) [38.39-R-St Patrick].

There are memorials to a number of people associated with the theatre; among them is Barry Fitzgerald (1888–1961), the actor, whose real name was Joseph Shields. He worked as a civil servant and performed in the Abbey Theatre in his spare time so he took the name of 'Barry Fitzgerald' to distinguish his acting from his day job. He eventually became a full time actor in 1929. In 1934 he toured in the United States where he was voted best character actor of the year for his part in *The Plough and the Stars* as Fluther Good. He remained in Hollywood for over twenty years appearing in numerous films. He won an Oscar for his performance as Father Fitzgibbon in the film *Going My Way*, and in 1959, he returned to Ireland where he died on 4 January 1961. He is buried with his brother, actor Arthur Shields (1896–1970) [55, 59-A.-St Nessan].

Anew McMaster (1894–1962), the tall and handsome actor/manager, is remembered for his outstanding performances as Shylock, Richard III, Oedipus and Coriolanus. He toured Australia, and in the United States, he played the part of James F. Tyrone in Eugene O'Neill's masterpiece, *Long Day's Journey into Night*. He died on 24 August 1962. Seamus Murphy designed his memorial. [St Patrick N 210].

F.J. McCormick (Peter Judge) (1889–1947), the actor who joined the Abbey Theatre in 1918 and acted in over five hundred plays at that theatre is buried with his wife Eileen Crowe the actress. Seamus Murphy designed their memorial. [121, 122 G.H-St Patrick]

Noel Purcell (1900–1985), the star of Irish stage and character actor, appeared in almost a hundred films dating from 1935. Some of his films included *Captain Boycott*, *Moby Dick* and *Mutiny on the Bounty*. [85-E – St Oliver]

There are over a hundred military graves throughout the cemetery in various locations. Some stand out as they are of uniform size, light grey in colour, bear the insignia of the regiment and are in pristine condition. A few are dispersed in the wooded area to the right, just inside the main gate. Five in this vicinity include the following and are inscribed as follows:

J. Reilly | Able Seaman, RN. 215472 | HMS 'Salmon | 24th September 1918. Aged 32. [Grave No NI 136]

90834 Private | P. Prendergast | Royal Defence Corps | 27th May 1920.
[Grave No N.R. 127]

T | 33489 Driver | M. Murray | Royal Army Medical Corps | 30th June 1818.
[Grave No XX.73]

M2 | 20 33377 Corporal | R. Lennon | Royal Army Service Corps. | 25th September 1917.
[Grave No N.E1.90]

73108 Corporal | J. V. Tierney | Royal Engineers | 5th January 1915 aged 24 | also | Cpl W.L. Tierney, MM. | Royal Engineers | Died 12th January 1923 aged 28.
[Grave No N.HI.109.]

In St Patrick's Section [Plot No H 173] is the unmarked grave of Lancashire born Joseph Edward Woodall (1896–1963), a recipient of the Victoria Cross. A member of the 1st Bn of the Rifle Brigade (Prince Consort's Own) he was awarded the Victoria Cross for 'his most conspicuous bravery and fine leadership' at La Panerie near the La Bassée Canal in France on 22 April 1918. The success of the operation on this portion of the front is attributed almost entirely to his coolness, courage and disregard for his own personal safety. He was commissioned 2nd Lieutenant in March 1919 and became an honorary Captain before his retirement in September 1921. Woodall, who lived in Sandycove, died on 2 January 1962 and the name 'King' is on the gravestone, which marks his plot.

Just behind the offices to the left off the Main Avenue in the first row, is a most interesting inscription on a memorial, which reads:

In loving memory | of | Mary Edith Coleman | Who died at Blackrock | on Sept 23 1906 | For her devoted care of the wounded soldiers | Both French and German | In the Franco-Prussian War | In the year 1870 | Under the auspices | Of the Red Cross Society | She was as Mrs Alsager | Decorated by the Emperor William | With the Order of the Iron Cross.

A large white marble memorial erected to the memory of Captain James Vaughan by his widow Margaret comprises a cross at the bottom of which is an anchor supported by a chain. Modern gravestones do not contain the same amount of information about a person's career. It is inscribed:

Sacred to the memory of | Captain James Vaughan RC, CB | Who departed this life 29th April 1873, aged 44 years. | He entered the Royal Navy in the year 1841 on board the HMS 'Scout' and was present at the operations on the River Plate. | As Lieutenant, he served in the Baltic and Black Seas during the years 1854–56 | And in the latter on board HMS 'Britannia' took Part in the attack on the batteries of Sebastopol. |

In 1857 he joined HMS 'Shannon' with Captain Sir William Peel, VC. KCB as Senior | Lieutenant, and proceeded to India. During the mutiny he served as second in | command of the Naval Brigade under that Officer and on his death from smallpox | assumed the sole command. He advanced to the relief of Lucknow and there dis | tinguished himself by his coolness and daring in taking his guns within a few yards | of the walls, and breaching them for the storming party. | For his services with the Brigade he was promoted to the rank of Commander, was | awarded the companionship of the Bath, and on his arrival in England was further | advanced to the rank of Captain. |

As well as being a thorough sailor, he was an accomplished and gallant officer | an affectionate and devoted husband, a warm and sincere friend, and died beloved | And regretted by all who knew him.

In 1916, the military authorities sent a number of bodies to be buried in the cemetery which were coffinless. There is a Republican Plot, which contains a number of memorials, one of which is inscribed:

Fionn Connolly Edwards youngest daughter of | Comdt. General James Connolly IRA, | Signatory of the Proclamation of the | Irish Republic 1916 | Died 9 April 1976 | RIP. [18 A West]

Another stone here commemorates

James Patrick Byrne | Irish Citizen Army | 1916–1923 | He served neither | King or Kaiser.

[21] THE MEMORIAL IN THE REPUBLICAN PLOT, WHICH CONTAINS THE NAMES ON THE ROLL OF HONOUR OF SEVENTEEN VOLUNTEERS KILLED IN ACTION BETWEEN 1916 AND 1922.

Similar to other maritime graveyards such as Merrion, Carrickbrennan and Dalkey, Dean's Grange contains the victims of sea disasters. One of these occurred on 14 November 1881 and involved the *Solway*, which was en route from Glasgow to Bristol in high seas with a cargo of goods such as sugar, whiskey, oils and rum. There were thirty-three people on board when a fire broke out causing damage to the ship's mast, bridge and deck. Assistance was sent from Kingstown to guide the *Solway* in, but on arrival six people had already been burned to death and five were presumed lost.

The second catastrophe happened on Christmas Eve in 1895. A Russian ship, the *Palme* got into difficulties in gale force winds, was unable to negotiate an entrance into the harbour and was blown northwards towards Seapoint. Two life boats set off, the first one overturning in the gale with the loss of all on board. Two crew members from the second boat were lost and the rescue attempt was abandoned as it was deemed too dangerous. Eventually a tug managed to reach the *Palme* and rescue its crew without any further casualties. The attempted rescue operation with the two lifeboats resulted in the death of fifteen local men. They are interred in two different sections of the cemetery depending on their religion, the Catholics in the North Section and the Protestants in the South Section. [87–88, H. North–86, 87, 88, 89–1, North and 15, 16, 17 N2, South–17 02 South]

There are some unusual monuments in the cemetery such as that of John Gardiner Nutting, first Baronet of St Helens, Co. Dublin who was born 24 July 1852 and died 18 February 1918. This is quite a remarkable monument with steps leading up to a platform and surrounded with balustrades. It is situated 76, 77 78 M7N – South West.

Another unusual monument is that of the Talbot Power family. This large corner plot is railed in and there are six crosses laid flat on the ground to commemorate different members of this family. There is also a tall monument bearing the family coat of arms. On this monument is inscribed:

> *Sir John Talbot Power Bart of Edermine Co.Wexford, died 4 December 1901 and In loving memory of Jane widow of Sir James Power of Edermine Co.Wexford daughter of John Talbot of Castle Talbot Co.Wexford who died November 29 1893.*

The Talbot Power family was connected with the locality as Leopardstown Park was once the home of James Talbot Power who bought the house in 1877. He was the grandson of the founder of Power's Distillery in Dublin. Other family members lived at Ayesha Castle in Killiney.

Also from the area was Joe McGrath (1887–1966), founder of the Irish Hospital Sweepstakes in 1930 and well-known racehorse owner and breeder who died at his home in Cabinteely. He is buried at [26-27-28/E&F St Patrick].

There are a number of plots of religious orders in Dean's Grange, such as the Christian Brothers, the Holy Ghost Congregation, Daughters of the Cross, Irish Vincentians, the Little Sisters of the Assumption and the Missionaries of the Sacred Heart.

Shanganagh Cemetery, which is situated on the left-hand side of the old Bray Road, just beyond Shankill Church, is the new extension of Dean's Grange cemetery since 1964.

The cemetery is under the care of the Dean's Grange joint Burial Board.

OPPOSITE PAGE: [22] THE MEMORIAL TO MICHAEL FARRELL (1899–1962), WHOSE POSTHUMOUSLY PUBLISHED BOOK *THY TEARS MIGHT CEASE* BECAME A BESTSELLER.

DONNYBROOK CHURCHYARD

SITUATION: MAIN STREET, DONNYBROOK, DUBLIN 4 [IN THE VILLAGE BESIDE THE GARDA STATION]

PERIOD IN USE: C.800 – 1880 [EXCEPT THOSE WITH BURIAL RIGHTS]

BUS NOS (FROM CITY CENTRE): 46, 46A, 46B

The name Donnybrook or *Domhnach Broc* is derived from the old Celtic church, which was founded by St Broc on the site occupied by the graveyard.

At the time of the Anglo-Norman conquest, there was a church in Donnybrook on the site of the existing graveyard which probably had its origins in this religious establishment of St Broc.

Archbishop Comyn, the Archbishop of Dublin, dedicated the church of St Mary on the same site sometime in the period between 1181–1212. The church was rebuilt and restored by Archbishop King in 1720. The congregation eventually became too large for it and it was replaced by a new church dedicated to St Mary, which was built in 1827. This is situated at the junction of Anglesea and Simmonscourt Road and was opened for Divine Service in 1830. The materials of the old church in the graveyard in Donnybrook were removed and sold. Just a small piece of wall remains near the centre of the ground. This is presumably the remains of the old church. There are some fine trees in this well kept graveyard.

The original entrance, now bricked up, was at the south end. The entrance to the graveyard is now beside the Garda Station on the main street in Donnybrook. It comprises a stone archway of Tullamore limestone which was erected by the Dublin Stock Exchange in 1893. It contains a plaque which is inscribed:

> *This memorial is erected by the members of the Dublin Stock Exchange to the memory of THOMAS CHAMNEY SEARIGHT, for many years Registrar to their Society who died May 27th 1890, and whose remains are buried in this Churchyard.*

Some of the people who were associated at an early date with St Mary's are interred in the churchyard. Included are members of the Fitzwilliam family who had their own chapel built onto the church in the early sixteenth century. The first recorded burial is that of Sir Richard Fitzwilliam in 1595. In 1635 Nicholas Fitzwilliam was buried 'with ancestors'.

Lodges Peerage of Ireland states that:

Oliver, the second Viscount Fitz-William, who was created Earl of Tyrconnell for his signal services to the Royalist cause 'lies buried under a handsome tomb of black marble, in the Chapel of the family's foundation in Donnybrooke-Church, with the inscription, over which are the arms of Fitz-William'. It reads:

Here lyeth the Body of the Right Honourable And most Noble | LORD OLIVER, Earl of Tyrconell, lord Viscount FITZ-WILLIAMS, or Meryonge, Baron of Thorn-Castle, who died at his House | in Meryong April 11th 1667, and was Buried the 12th day of the same month.'

[23] Donnybrook Graveyard with remaining wall of St Mary's Church of Ireland in the centre of the picture.

Richard, 6th Viscount Fitzwilliam of Merrion, who succeeded his father in 1743 and died 25 May 1776, was also interred in the family chapel. The family tomb is now missing.

The graveyard contains the remains of many distinguished ecclesiastics. These include Archbishop William King (1650–1729), who died at his Palace of St Sepulchre's. He had expressed a wish to be interred in Donnybrook on the north side of the churchyard. He was buried on the 10 May 1729. Three days later the *Dublin Intelligence* gave the following report:

Saturday night last the remains of our Archbp. was interr'd at Donebrooke, in a very decent tho' plain manner, being accompanied thither by most of our nobility and gentry, and thousands of our citizens. The corpse was put above 2 foot under water, in a grave 9 foot deep, over which a monument will be erected.

Apparently, a monument was to have been erected over the grave, but the Archbishop's executor died shortly afterwards, and the work was never carried out.

Other ecclesiastics of note include Bishop Clayton who died in his house at 80 St Stephen's Green (now part of Iveagh House) on 26 February 1758. His burial, along with the others listed below, were recorded in the *Donnybrook Parish Register*.

1758 Robert Clayton, DD Bishop of Clogher, buried in the churchyard of Donnybrook, 1st March. 'Cathren Clayton, ye Bp.'s wife' buried in same place, 8th January 1766 –

Clayton's memorial, which is a very large stone, reads:

Here lyeth ye body of Doctor Robert Clayton, Lord Bishop of Clogher, who was born in the year 1695, and was elected Fellow of Trinity College in 1714. He resigned his Fellowship in the year 1728; and the same year married Katherine, daughter of Lord Chief Baron Donnellan. He was promoted to the Bishopric of Killala in the year 1729, and died in 1758, in the 64th year of his age. To enumerate all his qualities would take up too much room for this place. His character as a Christian, and abilities as a writer, appear by his works. He lived esteemed by good men; he died regretted by many, most lamented by his afflicted widow.

Bishop Clayton's mother is buried with him as noted in the *Donnybrook Parish Register* in 1716 'Buried, Madam Cleton, in the Chancell of Donnybrook 1st February'.

The Reverend Richard Graves, who had lived in Harcourt Street, in the Parish of St Peter, is interred in the vault of the Graves family. Amongst other family names, the following inscription appears:

And of the Very Revd Richard Graves DD Dean of Ardagh who died March 31, 1829, aged 65 years.

The Reverend John Wynne, who was Precentor at St Patrick's Cathedral and a former Keeper of Archbishop Marsh's Library, was buried on 21 January 1762 in Archbishop King's grave.

A number of former curates of the parish of Donnybrook were interred in the graveyard. These included the Reverend Gore Wood, who was buried on the 25 May 1800. The Reverend Matthew West, who was buried on the 13 September 1814, had published a volume of poetry and was described as 'a gentleman whose impressive eloquence as a preacher, and cultivated talents as a scholar, were highly and deservedly appreciated by all that were acquainted him'.

The Reverend George Wogan who had been curate in the parish for twenty-six years had a tragic end to his life. He was brutally murdered in his house in Spa-field near Ballsbridge on 21 April 1826 and was buried two days later in the churchyard. He was aged seventy years. Two men from Booterstown, named Denis Hynes and George Stanley, who received sentences of death for a highway robbery committed the same night on the Blackrock Road, confessed to the murder and were subsequently hanged.

A limestone cross not far from the entrance commemorates another parish rector:

Sacred | to the memory of | Revd Arthur Gore Ryder, DD | Rector of Donny-Brook. | Sub Dean of Ct. Ch. Cl | who passed away | Feb. 21st 1889, | Aged 64. | 'Blessed are the dead which die in the Lord, for they rest from their labours'

The last two burials to take place in Donnybrook were those of the Reverend Gore Ryder's two sisters, Elizabeth in 1935 and Amy the following year.

The graveyard contains the remains of many distinguished citizens in the fields of architecture, art, literature, history and medicine.

Sir Edward Lovett Pearce (1699–1733), the noted architect who was described as the 'Inigo Jones' of Ireland, died at his house in Stillorgan on 7 December 1733. Born in County Meath, he was elected Member of Parliament for Ratoath in 1727. In 1730, he succeeded Thomas Burgh as surveyor-general. His major work was the Parliament House, College Green (now the Bank of Ireland). He also worked for Speaker Connolly for whom he designed most of Castletown House in Celbridge. His final work was the obelisk in Stillorgan, Co. Dublin. The small gardener's house, now restored, in the formal garden at the Royal Hospital Kilmainham is attributed to him. No memorial for him was found in the graveyard. His burial was noted in the *Donnybrook Parish Register*:

1733 Sir Edward Lovet Pearce, MP buried in the churchyard of Donnybrook, 10th December. There also was interred 20th January 1738, his brother, the Right Hon Lieut.-General Thomas Pearce, who 'was at once Governor, Mayor, and representative in Parliament, of the city of Limerick;' and Lady Pearce, 17th July 1749.

[24] THE PLAQUE TO THE MEMORY OF DR RICHARD MADDEN (1798–1886) ERECTED BY THE NATIONAL GRAVES ASSOCIATION.

On the right-hand side wall inside the gateway is a nice tribute in the form of a plaque, which commemorates Sir Edward Lovett Pearce. It was erected by the Royal Institute of the Architects of Ireland and was unveiled on World Architecture Day 1990.

Dr Richard Robert Madden (1798–1886), the noted physician and writer, is buried here with his father and other family members. He qualified as a doctor in London and furthered his medical studies in Paris and Naples. He practised in the Near East and worked in Jamaica in connection with the abolition of slavery. He also spent some time in Lisbon as special correspondent of the *Morning Chronicle*, after which he was appointed Colonial Secretary for West Australia, where his work involved the aborigines. On his return to Ireland, he became Secretary to the Dublin Fund Board. He became aware that Anne Devlin was living in abject poverty and organised support for her for the rest of her life. Madden wrote *The Life and Times of Robert Emmet* (1847) and a number of works about his travel experiences. He is perhaps best known for his main work, *The United Irishmen: Their Lives and Times* (4 Volumes, 1842–46). He died on 5 February 1886 at 3 Vernon Terrace, Booterstown Avenue and is commemorated with a memorial in the graveyard. The National Graves Association has a tablet on his grave with the inscription:

> *To the memory of | Richard Madden M.D. | Irish Historian, Author | And Benefactor of Anne Devlin | Erected in the Centenary year | of his Death 1986*

One of the first members of the Society of the United Irishmen, Leonard McNally (1742–1820), the playwright and lawyer, is also buried here. A notorious informer, he appeared in court on behalf of Wolfe Tone, Robert Emmet, Napper Tandy and other members of the United Irishmen and fought a duel with Sir Jonah Barrington in defence of their honour. At the same time, he accepted large fees from the government to betray them. He died on 13 February 1820 at his house at 22 Harcourt Street. His grave is unmarked but he is probably in the family grave of William Nally.

The eminent Dublin physician, Bartholomew Mosse (1712–1759), is buried here in an unmarked grave. Mosse had connections with Donnybrook as his father-in-law Archdeacon Charles Whittingham, who died in 1743, had been a rector there. Mosse had been acutely aware of the pitiful conditions of the Dublin poor at the time of their lying-in, and in 1745 opened a small hospital for them in George's Lane, which was the first of its kind in the British Isles. As the space was inadequate, he acquired a larger plot at the present site of four acres and nineteen perches from William Naper. He was a remarkable man who raised most of the finances for the building himself, through lotteries, subscriptions, grants and some of his own money.

On 8 December 1757, the Rotunda Lying-in-Hospital, designed by Richard Cassels, was opened with Mosse as its first master. Sadly he did not enjoy the fruit of all his work and effort for long. In the winter of 1758 he became ill. Alderman Peter Barre loaned him his house at Cullenswood in Ranelagh. Mosse died here aged forty-seven on 16 February 1759. On 20 February a short obituary notice appeared in Sleater's Public Gazetteer,

> *At Cullin's wood, near Miltown, of a lingering illness, Dr Bartholomew Mosse, one of the Guardians, Founder and Master of the Lying-in Hospital in Great Britain Street, the first of its kind in his Majesty's dominions, which was opened in George's lane by Dr Mosse in March 1745, where, by subscriptions and other benefactions, he fitted up 28 beds, with all necessaries for women, children, nurses etc.*

91

Mosse's hospital is certainly a magnificent monument to posterity.

Near the centre of the graveyard is the only surviving vestige of the church and, superimposed on this, is a tablet commemorating Mosse. It was carved by Tania Mosse, a descendant, and erected in 1996 by the Governors of the Rotunda hospital near the site of his unmarked grave.

Benjamin Higgins (1719–1795), Mosse's biographer, commenced work at the Rotunda when it first opened. He remained there as registrar for forty years. Close to Mosse in life, he expressed a wish to be buried near him. Higgins' gravestone is No B99. There is an unmarked spot adjacent, which is assumed to be that of Mosse.

William Ashford PRHA (1746–1824), had the reputation as the foremost landscape painter of his time in Ireland. Born in Birmingham, he came to Ireland when he was aged eighteen to work with the Ordnance Survey. Three years later, he was exhibiting his paintings. A Fellow of the Royal Society of Artists in London he contributed to its exhibitions. Between 1800 and 1821, he contributed on a regular basis to exhibitions in Dublin. Ashford was involved with the establishment of the Royal Hibernian Academy and was elected its first president. Sadly, his presidency was short lived. He died the following year on 17 April 1824 at his house at Sandymount Park which was designed by his good friend James Gandon. He was buried in Donnybrook churchyard.

In the Annals, the Reverend Beaver H. Blacker notes for the year '1843 The Right Hon John Radcliff, LL.D, buried in the churchyard of Donnybrook, 21st July'.

The following inscription is on his tombstone:

Here are interred the mortal remains of the Right Hon John Radcliff, who died on the 18th July, 1843 in the 78th year of his age. For 27 years he fulfilled the offices of Judge of the Prerogative Court and Vicar-General of Dublin; during which period he devoted himself with unexampled diligence to the publick service, combining abilities of the highest order with untiring patience and spotless integrity. In him is lost to see family and friends a sincere Christian, gifted with the sweetest temper and most affectionate heart; and to the poor a benefactor. 'Mark the perfect man, and behold the upright; for the end of that man is peace.' Psalm xxxvii 37.

Dr Radcliff was for many years Vicar General of Armagh. His son, the Reverend Richard Radcliff (1794–1818), is buried near his father.

In the *Donnybrook Parish Register*, it notes that:

in 1845 Mr and Mrs Orson and two children, buried in the churchyard of Donnybrook, 5th February; their bodies having been found in the ruins of their house [on Dodder-bank, near Donnybrook Green], which was consumed by fire under very mysterious circumstances on the morning of the 3rd instant.

Like Golden Bridge, St Mark's, Bully's Acre and some other graveyards, Donnybrook churchyard contains the remains of some victims from the cholera epidemics in the 1800s. When the main street was widened in 1931 and the entrance was moved back some fifteen feet, a mass grave was discovered. The bodies were reinterred at the southern end of the churchyard.

In 1879, 600 bodies were discovered in a mound in Ailesbury Road. These dated back to the ninth or tenth century when there was a bloody massacre by the Danes. These bodies were interred in the churchyard.

Donnybrook was long celebrated for its annual fair, which was founded in 1204 by Royal Charter. It was mainly a horse fair, which was held in August and lasted for fifteen days. During that time, shabby tents were erected and there was riotous behaviour, debauchery and noise.

When Donnybrook became a residential area, the neighbours objected and the fair was suppressed in 1855 by the buying-out of the original charter for £3,000 from the Madden family. Joseph Madden (1742–1799) and his brother Edward Madden (1739–1830) father of the physician, Richard Madden, are interred in the churchyard in nos. B59 and B60 respectively.

The manufacture of hats was formerly carried out in Donnybrook. Beaver-row was probably so named after this factory which was founded there in 1811 and owned by Joseph Wright who was originally from Co. Antrim and is buried in the churchyard.

The Reverend John Moore (1751–1840), who is buried in the churchyard, has an interesting military connection by association. His son, Major Richard Thomas Moore of the 12th Regiment was present at Napoleon's death in St Helena.

In 1847, it was recorded that many improvements were effected in the old churchyard of Donnybrook, which had been in a very neglected condition for some time. Over the years, it became overgrown again with memorials lying covered. It is great credit to the late Cecil King who organised volunteers through An Taisce and with the help of Dublin Corporation to clean up the churchyard which contains some very fine trees. The late President Cearbhaill Ó Dálaigh officially opened it on 1 May 1976.

Inside the gate and up the four steps, a most useful plan of the churchyard can be found on the left-hand side, which divides it into sections and gives some of the names of those interred and pinpoints the location of their graves.

The key is available from the adjoining Garda Station. This churchyard is under the care of Dublin Corporation.

[25] THE TABLET COMMEMORATING DR BARTHOLOMEW MOSSE (1712–1759) BUILDER AND FIRST MASTER OF THE ROTUNDA, CARVED BY TANIA MOSSE, AND ERECTED IN 1996 BY THE GOVERNORS OF THE ROTUNDA HOSPITAL.

DRUMCONDRA CHURCH AND CHURCHYARD

SITUATION: CHURCH AVENUE, DRUMCONDRA, DUBLIN 9 – OFF DRUMCONDRA ROAD UPPER

PERIOD IN USE: FROM MEDIEVAL TIMES [THE CEMETERY IS CLOSED FOR BURIALS EXCEPT FOR THOSE WITH EXISTING RIGHTS]

BUS NOS (FROM CITY CENTRE): 3, 11A, 13A, 16A

Popularly known as 'God's Little Acre', this well kept cemetery which is one of Dublin's gems dates back to medieval times. It was a popular burial ground prior to the opening of Prospect Cemetery [now Glasnevin] in 1832. On any Sunday of the year, funerals could be observed stretching in an endless line from the Rose Tavern in Dorset Street to the Cat and Cage in Drumcondra.

It is adjoins the grounds of All Hallows College, which used to be known as Drumcondra House. A Church in the cemetery has connections with the Coghill family, the former owners of the house.

Marmaduke Coghill [1673–1738], the son of Sir John Coghill, Master of the Chancery of Coghill Hall in the county of York, built Drumcondra House in 1725. He had moved from Belvidere House, now incorporated into St Patrick's Training College, just across the road.

Marmaduke died of gout, unmarried, on 9 March 1738 and was interred in the family vault at St Andrew's Church, Suffolk Street. There was not sufficient space here for the monument that his sister Mary (who had inherited Drumcondra House) planned to commemorate him with.

So, in 1743, Mary had the present parish church of St John the Baptist (Church of Ireland) built in the graveyard to house the fine monument erected to the memory of Marmaduke Coghill, Chancellor of the Exchequer of Ireland, which can be found on the north side of the church. A statue of Coghill sits in official robes – to his right there is a figure of Minerva, and on the left is Religion, both in white marble. The monument was executed by Peter Scheemakers, a noted Dutch sculptor who was responsible for many of the monuments in Westminster Abbey. Underneath is the coat of arms of the Coghill family and a long inscription outlining the main events of Marmaduke's life.

Of interest is a brass plaque commemorating James Gandon [1742–1824], which was erected by the Royal Institute of the Architects of Ireland in recognition of Gandon's outstanding contribution to the architecture of Dublin.

A stained glass window at the east end of the church executed by Early & Company of Camden Street which portrays the ascension of Christ, commemorates James Duncan Long who was incumbent of the parish and who died on 4 January 1864. The memorial was organised by his son the Reverend T. Long, rector of St Michan's Church in Church Street who presided at Charles Stewart Parnell's funeral in October 1891.

The graveyard has associations with many famous architects, actors, antiquarians, doctors, engineers, poets, brewers, bankers, patriots, musicians and military men.

Just south of the Church is the grave of Francis Grose [1731–1791] the antiquary who produced two volumes on Irish antiquities, which appeared the year he died. He was the son of Francis Grose, the Richmond jeweller who was famous for being commissioned to fit up the Crown for King George II. When he was young, Francis Grose joined the Surrey Militia, of which he became Adjutant and Paymaster. Unsuited to the life, he resigned and resorted to other pursuits. He travelled through England, Wales and Scotland and produced important work on the antiquities in the places that he visited. It was to him, while he was working in Scotland, that Robert Burns alluded in the well-known lines:

A chiel's amang you taking notes,
And faith he'll prent it.

Grose always did his own illustrations, which included one of himself actually sketching on his own grave in this churchyard!

On the large stone slab is inscribed:

To the memory | of | Captain Francis Grose, | Who while in cheerful conversation | With his friends, | Expired in their Arms | Without a sigh, | 18th of May | 1791 | Aged 60 | Also his friend | James Gandon | Architect | Born 1742 – Died 1824 | Captain Grose | Was a Friend of Robert Burns | And the Inspirer of Tam O'Shanter

James Gandon was born in London, the only son of a French father and a Welsh mother. He was educated in Hereford and later at Shipley's Academy before working for William Chambers the architect. He came to Dublin and lived in at 7 Mecklenburgh Street and later in Lucan, which is situated some miles from Drumcondra. He said that on his death he wished to be buried with his friend Francis Grose.

An article printed in the *Irish Builder* dated 13 March 1874 relates a distressing incident, which happened on the day of Gandon's funeral. It was a very wet day and the heavy slab that covered Grose's grave in which Gandon was to be laid had been removed and was lying on the damp clay. While the gravediggers were bustling about, the slab slipped on the loose clay and rolled in upon the coffin in the bottom of the grave, smashing it, and the skull of the occupant.

[26] THE GRAVE OF CAPTAIN FRANCIS GROSE, AND HIS FRIEND, JAMES GANDON.

Gandon designed some of Dublin's most famous public buildings including the Four Courts (1786), the Custom House (1791), and the Kings Inns in Henrietta Street (1785). He was also responsible for the magnificent stable yard (1790) at Carrigglas Manor in County Longford, the only surviving example of his agricultural work. This manor has another intriguing link with this churchyard.

This is where the Newcomen Tomb is of interest. In 1772 Mr William Gleadowe married Charlotte, the daughter and sole heiress of the late Charles Newcomen of Carrigglass Manor and assumed their name while retaining his own. He was knighted in 1781 and represented County Longford in the Irish Parliament. Unlike the La Touches, his banking competitors, four of whom sat in the House of Commons, he voted in favour of the Act of Union and received £20,000 for his vote, together with a peerage for his wife. He was a Director of the Royal Canal Company and Newcomen Bridge was named in his honour in 1791. In 1804 Sir William Gleadowe Newcomen bequeathed to the ministers and churchwardens of this parish, and to their successors, a Royal Canal debenture for £100. The interest of six per cent was to be used to purchase bread and provisions for the poor of the parish.

His death in August in 1807 was reported in the *Dublin Correspondent* as follows:

At Killester House, on Friday last, after a long and painful illness, Sir William Gleadowe Newcomen, Bart: Principal of the oldest Banking House in Ireland. He married Charlotte, daughter of the late Charles Newcomen of Carrigglass, in the County of Longford, Esq, since created in her own right, Viscountess Newcomen. He is succeeded as Principal in the Bank and in Honours and Estates by his son, The Honourable Sir Thomas Newcomen, Bart.

On the death of Sir William, his son Thomas Viscount Newcomen succeeded him and inherited his mother's title and the bank. After the collapse of the bank in 1825 the Viscount shot himself and died unmarried at Killester House. The tomb that bears the family coat of arms has the following inscription:

Here lies the Body of Thomas Gleadowe, Esq, | Of the City of Dublin, who departed this life the 21st day | Of June 1766, aged 72 years. Here also lieth the | Body of his wife Teresa Gleadowe, who departed this | Life the 14th day of June, 1788 aged 82 years. | Here lieth the body of Sir William Gleadowe- | Newcomen, Bart, who departed this life the 21st day | Of August 1807, aged 66 years. Here also lieth the | Body of the Right Honourable Thomas, Lord Viscount | Newcomen, who died on the 15th day of January, 1825 | Aged 48 years.

There is a rather imposing tombstone of the Lentaigne family from Caen in Normandy. Benjamin Lentaigne, the son of a lieutenant of dragoons, was born into a Royalist family in Caen in 1773. During the French Revolution, the family suffered dreadfully and two of Benjamin's brothers were beheaded at the guillotine. Benjamin had a narrow escape from prison and fled first to Flanders and then to England. Here he studied surgery from 1792 to 1795, after which he was chosen as assistant surgeon to the 5th Dragoons.

Benjamin Lentaigne accompanied the regiment to Ireland. He was the military doctor who attended Wolfe Tone when he was condemned to death for his part in the Rising of 1798. Tone learnt that he was to be hanged publicly at Newgate Prison and made a desperate effort to cut his throat with a penknife to escape execution. Dr Madden, in his *Lives of the United Irishmen*, gives an account of how Lentaigne was summoned to treat Wolfe Tone. 'They say I know everything' Tone remarked, 'but you know, doctor, there are things I do not know. I find I am a bad anatomist'. Lentaigne advised Wolfe Tone that he must stay still and silent for he was in imminent danger of death. 'I can yet find words to thank you, sir,' Wolfe Tone replied. 'It is the most welcome news you could give me. What should I wish to live for?'

Sacred to the memory of Benjamin Lentaigne MD a native of Caen in Normandy | Firm in his faith, true to his King, | preferring honour to interest | he forsook his country | To follow his exiled princes. | Ranging himself under their banner, | he adhered to their fortunes | Long after hope had fled - | and then sought asylum in Ireland, | where the amiable qualities of his heart | attached to him many affectionate friends, | whilst his distinguished talents gained | the esteem and admiration of its worthy | inhabitants. | Wept by the poor as a protector, | mourned by his friends as a brother, | Regretted by all as an ornament to | human nature. | He departed this life October X1X, MDCCCX111 aged XL1

Also in this family grave is Sir John Lentaigne KT, BA FRCSI | President of the Royal College of Surgeons in | Ireland 1908–9 | Who died 30 March 1915. Aged 59 years. | And for his dearly loved wife Phillis | Mary, | Who died 12 Dec 1893 aged 34 years. | Also for their third son John, | Who died 10 January, 1890, aged 2 [?]years.

Dr John Lentaigne, the above's father, presented a manuscript to the library of the Royal College of Surgeons of Ireland in 1851 which was written by John Ardern of Newark in the year 1349. Ardern was a distinguished surgeon of his day. It is now known as the *Lentaigne Manuscript* and comprises 110 leaves of vellum in Latin with one passage in English. These writings represent the earliest documents in these islands from a known source on the subject of surgery.

The inscription continues:

And in loving memory of their youngest son | 2nd Lieut. Victor Lentaigne | 2nd Battn. The Connaught Rangers | Killed in action at the battle of the Aisne | Sept 14, 1914 and buried near Soupir.

A small neat squat square of granite with the plough and the stars engraved on it marks the grave of

Seamus McGowan, | Irish Citizen Army, | 1874–1965.

McGowan was the model for the man who went to Knocksedan to catch butterflies in Seán O'Casey's play *The Shadow of a Gunman.*

The remains of the celebrated actor, Thomas Ryder, who died in 1791 in Sandymount, are interred here in an unmarked grave. Ryder, a man of great talent and boundless energy, became manager of Smock Alley Theatre in 1772 and was described as being a most versatile actor in tragedy, comedy, opera, and farce. He played a number of different characters over a period of twelve years and it was said that he was almost every night before the public.

One of the few remaining Mort Safes in the city of Dublin is to the west end of the church. It is a high cage-like iron structure with the four sides of the grave and the top covered in with iron railings. On the end is a small gate, which is padlocked. This afforded protection against bodysnatchers.

This ground | Was enclosed by | Mr and Mrs Thunder | New Church Street | Brewers | As well as for themselves and posterity | As a mark of respect | To the Memory of their parents | Who | With many of their | Children and grandchildren | Lie here interred | AD 1828.

Set into the north boundary wall is the grave of the Jameson family. John Jameson, who was born in Scotland in 1773, established the Bow Street Distillery in Dublin. His son John, who married Anne Haig from Fife, Scotland became High Sheriff of the City of Dublin. He and his wife are also mentioned on the headstone.

Coincidentally, an employee at the Distillery was Thomas Furlong [1794–1827] the Wexford poet. An unusual monument marks his grave. Standing on a solid ornamental quadrangular base, it is a pyramid of mountain granite on each side of which is a neatly sculptured laurel crown. On one side is a black marble slab, which reads:

To the Memory of | Thomas Furlong, Esq | In whom the purest principles of | Patriotism and Honor | Were combined with | Superior Poetical Genius, | This memorial of Friendship, | Is erected by those who valued and admired | His various Talents, Public Integrity, | And Private Worth. | He died 25th July, 1827, aged 33 years. | May he Rest in Peace.

Furlong, the translator of *Carolan's Remains*, came to Dublin at the age of fourteen and worked for a grocer before being employed with John Jameson, the eminent distiller, where he remained until his early death. Jameson is said to have wept like a child on the day of Furlong's funeral. As regards location, they were not parted too far by death.

Thomas Moore praised his poetry. Furlong's friend, the Revd Charles Maturin, sent copies of Furlong's poetry to Sir Walter Scott who agonisingly searched the Dublin bookshops for it during his visit in 1825.

[27] ONE OF THE FEW REMAINING MORT SAFES IN DUBLIN IS IN DRUMCONDRA CHURCHYARD. THIS CAGE-LIKE STRUCTURE GAVE PROTECTION AGAINST BODY SNATCHERS.

Along the back wall, there is a railed space in front of which is a tablet to the Mallet family, but there is no record in the church registers of a Mallet burial. The family had an engineering works in Ryder's Row off Capel Street.

To the south east of the church is the grave of Jimmie Mulkerns (1886–1956), who was a political prisoner in Wales. He put on a few shows whilst in prison and always dressed as a rajah. On his grave is the inscription The Rajah of Frongoch.

In an unknown and unmarked grave lie the remains of Patrick Heeney [1881–1911], the composer of the music of the Irish National Anthem, which was published by Bulmer Hobson in 1912. The words were by Peadar Kearney. Heeney unfortunately did not live to see it in print. There is a plaque on the wall near the entrance gate commemorating Heeney.

Nearby and close to the entrance is the grave of the architect George Semple, whose most noted work is Essex Bridge. He designed St Patrick's Hospital and the granite spire of St Patrick's Cathedral, which are both associated with Dean Swift. The inscription on his tombstone reads:

Here lieth the body of Mr George Semple, of the City | Of Dublin, Architect, whose skill in his profession, simplicity of manners, | unaffected piety, and rectitude of heart, | gained him the applause of all good men. He departed | this life on the 13th day of April, 1782, aged 73 years. | His daughter, Eliza Keatinge, ordered this stone and Inscription to be done as a small, but grateful mark of filial duty.

Drumcondra Church and churchyard is under the care of the Select Vestry of Drumcondra.

[28] A PLAQUE INSERTED INTO THE WALL OF THE CHURCHYARD COMMEMORATES PATRICK HEENEY (1881–1911) WHO COMPOSED THE MUSIC FOR THE NATIONAL ANTHEM.

FRIENDS' BURIAL GROUND

SITUATION: TEMPLE HILL, BLACKROCK, CO. DUBLIN

PERIOD IN USE: 1860 TO DATE

BUS NOS (FROM CITY CENTRE): 7, 7A & 8

Prior to the opening of the Friends' Burial Ground at Temple Hill, there were a couple of others in the city, which included one in Cork Street and one close to St Stephen's Green where the Royal College of Surgeons is now sited. In 1805, this Quaker cemetery in York Street was purchased as a site for the new college. Nothing now remains of either of these burial grounds. There are records in the form of a *Notice of Interment* pertaining to the burials such as:

Joshua Fayle the elder, being deceased, his friends are desired to accompany the funeral from his son's house in Meath Street; to the Burial Ground in Cork Street, tomorrow at half past twelve o'clock 2nd Month (Feb) 4th, 1773.

And a forebear of the Bewley family:

Susanna Bewley being deceased, friends are requested to attend the funeral, from her late dwelling in Earl Street to the Burial Ground in Cork Street tomorrow evening at 5 o'clock. Four Month, 21st 1779.

Deborah Walker being deceased. Friends are requested to attend her funeral, from her late dwelling house (No 74) in Capel Street, to Friends Burial Ground at Stephen's Green before 5 o'clock tomorrow evening.

One of the later Notices of Interment listed as 'Dublin 8th of 9th month 1859 to Cork Street' was a member of the famous Walpole family:

Margaret Walpole being deceased Friends are informed that it is intended to convey her remains from her late residence, Richmond Street, to Portobello, for interment in Friends' burial Ground, Cork Street on the sevenths day morning, the 10th instant, at 9 o'clock.

The first interment in Temple Hill took place on the 6 March 1860. It was that of Hannah Chapman. The notice read:

Hannah Chapman being deceased, Friends are informed that it is intended to convey her remains from her late residence, 3 Willow Terrace, Williamstown, for interment in Friends' New burial Ground, Temple Hill, at half-past twelve o'clock on the month, the sixth instant.

All the gravestones, which contain just the names and the dates of those they mark, are of uniform size. This is in accordance with the Quaker rule. Some of the Quaker families interred here include the Allens, Bewleys, Grubbs, Fairbrothers, Goodbodys, Pims, Todhunters, Sparrows, Walpoles and Warings.

The burial ground at Temple Hill comprises seven acres, which contains some really magnificent trees planted by Horace Walpole. Some varieties date to the 1860s and are tall and majestic. The avenue, which is shaded on either side by holm oaks, is particularly beautiful. This arboretum gives a lovely fresh smell of firs and pines, and encourages a variety of birds, which seem to provide delightful birdsong right throughout the year. It is a haven of both natural beauty and tranquillity and is certainly amongst the nicest and best-kept burial grounds in the country.

Among those interred here include:

Horace Walpole (1880–1964), who was very much involved with the planting at Temple Hill. Many of the plants and shrubs came from his garden at Mount Usher, Ashford, Co. Wicklow where he lived. He was a member of the well-known Walpole family who had a business at 9 Suffolk Street in Dublin which specialised in damask and linen manufacturing.

Alfred John Webb (1834–1908), the biographer and publisher, was a contributor to the *Freeman's Journal* and other papers. He is best known for his work *A Compendium of Irish Biography* (Dublin 1877). He died on the 30 July 1908.

Sir John Barrington (1824–1887), who died at his home in Killiney, was twice Lord Mayor of Dublin, in 1865 and 1879 respectively. He was a member of the firm of Barrington and Co. of Great Britain Street.

Sheila Pim (1909–95) was the daughter of Francis Henry and Margaret Townley Pim. She wrote seven novels, the first of which was entitled *Common or Garden Crime*. Among her other works is a biography of the Irish plant collector, Augustine Henry, entitled *The Wood and the Trees*, which was published in 1966.

Jonathan Pim (1806–1885) was a well-known Quaker who died at his home in Monkstown on the 6 July in 1885. He was educated at the famous Ballytore School and then worked in his father's counting house. It was during the famine of 1846–47 that he came to the fore as a notable figure in offering relief. His book, *Condition and Prospects of Ireland*, appeared during this time. Both this and another work, *Transactions*, were written as appeals for radical land reform in Ireland. After the famine, he bought an estate in the west of Ireland, for the purpose of benefiting the tenantry. A kind man, he took the first opportunity to enable his tenants to reap the benefits of the Land Act and gave them the opportunity of becoming the owners of this land.

Pim was one of the original founders of the Dublin Statistical Society and was its President for many years.

In 1862 he collaborated with Dr William Harvey, an eminent botanist, in the volume *Charles and Joshua, or Friendly Conversations between a Churchman and a Quaker*.

The Friends' Burial Ground is under the care of the Dublin Monthly Meeting of the Religious Society of Friends in Ireland.

OPPOSITE PAGE: [29] VIEW OF THE FRIENDS' BURIAL GROUND. ALL THE GRAVESTONES ARE OF UNIFORM SIZE IN ACCORDANCE WITH QUAKER RULE.

GLASNEVIN CEMETERY

SITUATION: FINGLAS ROAD, GLASNEVIN, DUBLIN 9

PERIOD IN USE: 1832 TO DATE

BUS NOS (FROM CITY CENTRE): 40, 40A, 40B, 40C

Originally called Prospect Cemetery and consisting of nine acres, Glasnevin is now the largest cemetery in Ireland and covers over one hundred and twenty acres. This land, along with an area that stretches as far as the Holy Faith Convent in Glasnevin, was once attached to the Priory of St Mary's Abbey, Dublin. At the Reformation, all church lands passed into Protestant hands. In this way, Dr Charles Lindsay, Dean of Christ Church Cathedral and later Bishop of Kildare, acquired the old monastic lands of Glasnevin.

The cemetery, which is situated two and a half miles from the city Centre, is the largest in Ireland and is non-denominational. It was the wish of Daniel O'Connell [1775–1847], who founded the cemetery, that all facilities should be given for the unrestricted exercise of religious rites by members of every creed and denomination.

Enclosed by high walls, there were a number of watchtowers set at each of the angles in the boundary wall. Cuban bloodhounds were also kept in the grounds until 1853 to guard against bodysnatchers.

Before the land was purchased as a cemetery, it comprised mainly of woodlands. Some of these mature deciduous trees, such as the oak, the sycamore and other varieties, still remain in parts of the cemetery, which lends a lovely parkland landscape. On top of this land, the cemetery was designed and a labyrinth of paths were laid out. More young trees have been planted along some of the avenues. There are rows of graves running east to west named after letters of the alphabet. Rows running south to north are numbered.

The original entrance to the cemetery was located in Prospect Square but on account of a nearby pub, the entrance was changed to Finglas Road in 1879. For over a hundred years, most of the burials have taken place before noon. A rule stipulated that only those who lived more than twelve miles from the General Post Office could be buried after that time.

James Joseph McCarthy (1817–1882), the architect responsible for the revival of the 'Irish Gothic', designed the mortuary chapel just inside the main gate. The chapel contains a number of carvings executed by James Pearse (1839–1900). Both James Joseph McCarthy [Jf 24] and James Pearse [OH 10 all] are interred in the cemetery.

The grounds were blessed on 21 February 1832 and the following day the first burial took place. This was Michael Carey, aged four, of Francis Street [043] and on his memorial in Curran's Square is inscribed:

Michael Carey, the first ever interred in this cemetery 22nd February 1832

Since the opening of Glasnevin cemetery 169 years ago, major historical events have taken place in Ireland. The vast majority of people interred in the cemetery are ordinary Dublin citizens, but many men and women who have profoundly influenced the evolution of modern Ireland are buried here.

In 1847 the cemetery committee agreed that there should be a memorial of some significance to honour Daniel O'Connell, the 'Liberator'. The tower to commemorate him dominates the entrance area of the cemetery. Designed by George Petrie, the antiquary, it is 160 feet in height. In his original plan, Petrie had included in his design a round tower, a high cross and a chapel to represent Irish architecture in the early Christian period. All these were to be placed on a raised platform. Only the tower was built, which was larger than Petrie had intended. The tomb where O'Connell was placed in 1869 contains some fine carvings. Around the wall of the crypt are inscribed his many achievements. Other members of the O'Connell family, including his wife, three of his sons and his daughter are buried in an area off the crypt. The last member of the family was a great-great-grandson of O'Connell who was interred here in 1970. O'Connell was originally buried on 8 August 1847 in the O'Connell Circle section which is located much further back in the cemetery and his remains were transferred to the crypt beneath the tower in 1869.

In the O'Connell Tower Circle there are forty-two crypts. Generally, those buried in these crypts had either money or influence. On the right-hand side of the steps leading down into the O'Connell crypt is a large cross, which commemorates The Very Revd John Spratt DD who died in 1871 in the seventy-fifth year of his age and the fifty-first of his ministry [A 1 O'Connell Tower Circle]. He was the provincial of the Carmelite Order for many years and organised the building of the church in Whitefriar Street in 1826. Father Spratt was involved in many worthy causes, such as St Peter's orphanage. He was Honorary Secretary of the Roomkeepers' Society for nearly forty years. He founded St Joseph's Night Refuge in Cork Street for the homeless poor, and the asylum for the Catholic female blind formerly at Portobello and now at Merrion. He was one of the first to join Father Mathew in the Crusade against intemperance. Of interest on the plinth of the cross are three carvings: the Carmelite Church in Whitefriar Street, St Joseph's Night Refuge which was founded in 1861 and the Temperance Pledge.

There is a huge variety of monuments and memorials at Glasnevin. These represent the work of some of the finest nineteenth-century sculptors, such as Sir Thomas Farrell who is responsible for the bust of

[30] The monument to the Reverend William Walsh DD, Archbishop of Dublin and Primate of Ireland. On the left are other clerical memorials and the O'Connell monument is to the rear.

Sir John Gray, MP, and the fine marble memorial in the form of a statue of actor Barry Sullivan (1821–91). This is to the left of the O'Connell Tower Circle. Sullivan is portrayed as Hamlet in the churchyard scene in the play. On one hand he holds the skull of Yorick. On the plinth, which supports it, is inscribed:

Barry Sullivan | After life's fitful fever | He sleeps well. [RE 32st &33].

Thomas Farrell is also interred in the cemetery [Vault B26].

Other sculptors of note buried here include John Hogan (1800–1858), who did some fine monumental work for Glasnevin and Mount Jerome Cemeteries and whose work includes the statue of Daniel O'Connell in the City Hall [E25, 26] and Christopher Moore (1790–1863), whose work mainly consisted of portrait busts. He executed the metal statue of Thomas Moore in Westmoreland Street, which was erected in 1857. [Ja 62 Garden].

The older part of the cemetery is situated near the original entrance gate off Prospect Square, in the area around Curran's Square and the Chapel Circle. Here the monuments are mainly of Edwardian and Victorian style such as inverted torches and urns. It is noticeable that few crosses appear in this section.

John Philpot Curran (1750–1817) is commemorated here with a magnificent eight-foot high, classical sarcophagus, from the design of John Thomas Papworth, and modelled on the tomb of Scipio Barbatus in Rome. It is made of Irish granite, each block weighing between four to five tons. It bears the simple inscription, CURRAN [LMN 51-57]. Curran, who was father of Sarah, was a lawyer and defender of Wolfe Tone. He died in London in October 1817 and was buried in one of the vaults in Paddington church. Curran's last thoughts were about Ireland and the cemetery committee in Dublin undertook the task of transferring his remains back home to Ireland. Twenty years later, on a gloomy November day, with a fierce storm raging and the thunder clapping overhead, his remains were brought to Glasnevin where he was buried by torchlight.

There are a number of Celtic Crosses in the cemetery and some of the finest examples may be seen in the area around the O'Connell Tower Circle. One of these crosses, executed by sculptor James Pearse, is opposite the main entrance gate and commemorates Ellen Burke. It is well worth examining it carefully. The images depict the life of St Patrick on the four panels, which support the shaft of the cross. There are various emblems such as round towers, shamrocks and wolfhounds on this and on other monuments, which signifies a patriotic symbolism and an Irish cultural identity. Beside this cross, at the edge of the circle under a silver birch tree is a flat stone slab, which marks the grave of Roger Casement (A 16 7 & 17). He was hanged in Pentonville prison on 3 August 1916. His remains were returned to Ireland, and after a State funeral, were interred on 1 March 1965. The inscription on his slab reads:

Ruairi | MacEasmainn | Roger Casement | a d'fulaing bas | ar son | na hEireann | 3 Lunasa 1916 | + | R.I.P.

Inside the main entrance, to the left are a number of clerical graves in neat rows, which are interspersed by two large monuments. The first commemorates the most Reverend William Walsh DD (1841–1921), Archbishop of Dublin and Primate of Ireland (1885–1921), who died on 9 April 1921. The second, which is directly opposite the mortuary chapel, commemorates his Eminence Edward Cardinal MacCabe, DD) Archbishop of Dublin and Primate of Ireland (1816–1885), who died at his residence in Kingstown on 11 February 1885. His last words were a request that he might be buried without any pomp in 'the poor ground' at Glasnevin. His funeral procession on 17 February 1885, from the Pro-cathedral where he had lain in state, took half a day to reach Glasnevin. Despite the snow, many thousands followed on foot. He was buried in what was then the poor ground. His elaborate canopied monument, which has a mosaic floor with symbols of the four Evangelists, was designed by the architect George Coppinger Ashlin (1837–1921), a former pupil and later a partner of Edward Pugin. Sir Thomas Farrell sculpted the figure of Cardinal McCabe. C.W. Harrison and Sons were responsible for the carved ornaments on the monument.

Many of the religious orders have their plots in the same area, which is named 'The Walk'. These include the Augustinians from Thomas Street [AH+Bh, 5-8], the Christian Brothers [MH-OH, 4-9], the Dominicans [AH-CH, 15-21 1/2], the Franciscans of Merchants Quay [AH-CH, 9ST-15 1/2], the Carmelites of Whitefriar Street [Oc & Pc, 48-51] and the Society of Jesus. Jesuits in the main Jesuit plot include the poet Gerard Manley Hopkins, whose name is inscribed in Latin on the large granite Jesuit memorial cross 'P. Gerardus Hopkins obiit Jun. 8 1889 aetat.an. 44.' Included amongst the names on this memorial is Father Conmee, Superior of Gardiner Street community, who pursues his imperturbable way through the pages of James Joyce's *Ulysses*. Other Jesuits interred here include Aubrey Gwynn (1892–1983), historian, Timothy Corcoran (1872–1943), Professor of Education at University College, Dublin, Fr E.J. Coyne (1896–1958), pioneer of Irish social studies and promoter of adult education and education for industrial workers, Lambert McKenna (1870–1956), an early sociologist and promoter and defender of Trade Unions, James Cullen (1841–1921), founder of the Pioneers, John Ryan (1894–1973), great historian of Irish monasticism and Frank Shaw (1907–1970), Professor of Irish at University College, Dublin.

A beautifully carved Celtic cross by Brendan Crowe was unveiled on 26 June 1999 for the poet and storyteller John Keegan (1809–1849) [Zg 248], who died of cholera in the South Dublin Poor Law Union on 30 June 1849 aged thirty-three. He was interred in an unmarked grave in the Old Poor Ground. He was born in Shanahoe in Co. Laois in 1809 and was educated at a hedge school. His simple but beautiful and moving poems include 'Caoch the Piper', 'Bouchalleen Bawn', Tales of the Rockites' and 'Dark Girl'.

His Legends and Poems, which were collected by Canon John O'Hanlon (mentioned later), were published in 1907.

Another poet who died the same year as Keegan was James Clarence Mangan (1803–1849) [Jb 34]. He contributed to the same magazines and papers as John Keegan, which included *The Nation*, *The Irish Penny Journal*, and *The Dublin University Magazine*. Mangan's *Anthologia Germanica* was published in 1845, but he is probably best remembered for his powerful songs and ballads such as 'Dark Rosaleen', 'The Nameless One' and 'Lament for Kincora'. Mangan, like Keegan, died as a result of the cholera epidemic which swept through Dublin in 1849. Only three persons are said to have followed his body to the grave. There were 11,357 burials in 1849 as a result of cholera, which represented the greatest number of burials in any one year at Glasnevin.

[31] THE CLASSICAL SARCOPHAGUS OF JOHN PHILPOT CURRAN BY GEORGE PAPWORTH IS MODELLED ON THE MEMORIAL OF SCIPIO BARBATUS IN ROME.

John Keegan Casey [1846–1870], known as the poet of the Fenians and author of 'The Rising of the Moon', a famous poem about the 1798 Rebellion, has a remarkably ornate grave with a high cross and a base with carvings of Irish themes (Nc 7). He was very popular and over 50,000 followed his funeral to Glasnevin.

Other writers buried in Glasnevin include Brendan Behan [1923–64], one of the most successful Dublin playwrights of the century. His memorial is an unusually shaped granite stone with a bronze inset [VA21 South]. Edward Martyn [1859–1924], playwright and co-founder of the Irish Literary Theatre, is buried in an unmarked grave in the area known as the General Poor Ground. The Palestrina Choir, which he had established in 1899, sang the Benedictus as he was lowered into the earth. The Poor Ground is located in the north-east of the cemetery near Violet Hill. Dora Sigerson [1866–1925], the poet, designed the fine 1916 memorial in the cemetery. She had strong Republican sympathies, which are reflected in some of her poems. She is buried beneath the grass verge in the O'Connell Circle [F34 all, O'Connell Circle]. Maura Laverty [1907–66], novelist and playwright, is buried quite near the memorial chapel [EF24 all Dnc]. Patricia Lynch (1898–1972), writer of children's stories and author of over fifty books which were translated into many languages, is interred in St Brigid's. Her story 'The Turf Cutter's Donkey' (1934) was serialised with illustrations by Jack B. Yeats for the *Irish Press*.

Seumas O'Kelly [1875–1918], journalist, playwright and author of the novella *The Weaver's Grave* [NB 48] and Christy Brown [1932–81], the novelist, poet and artist, are buried in St Paul's section [IF 50, St Paul], as is the legendary Luke Kelly (1940–1984), the ballad singer from the Dubliners [LE 39]. St Paul's Section is across the Finglas Road, opposite the main entrance to the cemetery.

A railing encloses the grave of Charles Stewart Parnell [1846–91] politician, agitator for Home Rule, leader of the Irish Parliamentary Party in the 1880s, and 'uncrowned king'. It is a mound and was known as the Poor Ground, as many victims of the famine and the cholera had been interred there. It is to the left of the mortuary chapel.

It is marked with a simple, unworked, naturally weathered granite boulder, which was located on a hillside near Poulaphouca in Parnell's native Wicklow. It was transported to Glasnevin cemetery in October 1939. It was simply inscribed PARNELL. Parnell's American mother, Delia Stewart, was buried beside him in 1898. It is now known as the Parnell Circle. There are a number of Giant Redwood trees and some Cedar of Lebanon in the surrounding area.

Parnell's last meeting was in Creggs, a small town on the borders of Roscommon and Galway. On 30 September 1891, some friends left him to the boat in Kingstown. He promised them he would return in ten days' time. As always, he kept his promise, but this time there were grief stricken crowds on his return and deep spontaneous emotion.

[32] THE GRANITE BOULDER WHICH MARKS THE GRAVE OF CHARLES STEWART PARNELL. HE REQUESTED THAT HIS GRAVE BE MARKED BY A SIMPLE STONE.

Parnell's funeral was the largest ever at the cemetery. Parnell's brother, John Howard, and his sister Emily, described the funeral as 'one of the most impressive sights ever witnessed'. His remains arrived back from Brighton and a service was held at St Michan's Church before being moved to the City Hall for the lying-in-state. More than 30,000 people filed past the remains. The cortège left the City Hall at 2.30 p.m., led by members of the GAA marching six deep. Six black horses drew the wreath-burdened hearse. Behind, with his master's boots and stirrups reversed, followed the twenty-five-year old Home Rule, Parnell's favourite horse. One hundred and fifty thousand people filled the streets and fifty thousand took part in the procession. Forty bands from all over the country participated.

Dusk fell and the roadside lamps were being lit as the procession approached Glasnevin cemetery at 6.30 p.m. As the Chief was being lowered, a breathless silence was broken only by the sobbing of strong men. What has been described as a fiery globe travelled swiftly, across the darkened sky. The mourners denuded the surrounding shrubs, trees and walls of ivy, and kept the sprigs as mementoes of that tragic day. The ivy leaf became the emblem of Parnell. Ivy day is now commemorated each year on the Sunday closest to 6 October when a wreathe is laid on his grave. This is organised by the Parnell Memorial Committee, which was formed in 1937 and which was responsible for the memorial, which marks his grave.

Coincidentally, nearby a white marble headstone marks the grave of John Stanislaus Joyce (1849–1931) and his wife Mary Jane née Murray (1859–1903)[XF6 ½ & 7 Dublin Sect. W]. John Stanislaus was a passionate supporter of Parnell and to the end of his life remained a Parnellite, railing against false friends and betrayers. John Stanislaus had bought this plot in November 1880 on the death of John Augustine his first child who was aged only eight days. Other of his children are also interred here and include Freddie, Georgie, Baby and Eva Joyce. After the death of John Stanislaus in 1931, it was his son James Joyce who had the gravestone inscribed.

James Joyce devotes the entire 'Hades' chapter in *Ulysses* to the funeral of the fictitious character Paddy Dignam. Mary Jane Murray's burial place is alluded to in this chapter when the mourners are passing near it,

> *Her grave is over there, Jack, Mr Dedalus said. I'll soon be stretched beside her. Let Him take me whenever He likes.*

Dignam's funeral is based on a real funeral, which was that of Matthew F. Kane, a Dubliner who drowned on 10 July 1904. John Stanislaus Joyce attended Kane's funeral in Glasnevin. Kane was buried in St Brigid's section [II 238 1 | 2]. On 16 June 1988, a new gravestone was unveiled with much ceremony for Kane by the Dublin and some overseas Joyceans. The inscription reads:

MATTHEW F. KANE | 1865–1904 | Chief Clerk | Chief Crown Solicitors Office | Dublin Castle | Beloved Friend | Of Countless Dubliners | And model in JAMES JOYCE'S | ULYSSES | For | Patrick Dignam | Martin Cunningham | William Shakespeare | Matthew F. Kane. | Accidental drowning | Dublin Bay.

Many other characters that appear in *Ulysses* are also interred in Glasnevin 'How many! All these here once walked round Dublin. Faithful departed. As you are now so once were we.'

Just some of those included are Joseph Patrick Nannetti, MP (1851–1915) member of Dublin Corporation and foreman at the *Freeman's Journal*. His cross is inscribed:

In loving memory of | J.P. Nannetti MP, J.P. | Formerly Lord Mayor of Dublin | Who departed this life | 26th April 1915.

Nannetti's grave is to the left-hand side of the mortuary chapel on the pathway and is three memorials down on the left [HF 25 South Section].

Timothy Harrington (1851–1910), barrister and former Lord Mayor of Dublin who was an active member of Parnell's Home Rule Party, is buried quite close to Parnell [Grave no: Ug 4 Dublin]. Harrington appeared for a Constable Henry Flower who was accused of murdering a woman on 23 August 1900. Henry Flower became Leopold Bloom's pen name. Then there is John Henry Menton, a solicitor and commissioner of affidavits with offices at 27 Bachelor's Walk. In fiction, he was a former employer of Dignam [Grave no: Zg 148 Garden].

Alderman John Hooper, editor of the *Evening Telegraph* and father of Paddy Hooper, an old friend of Bloom, appears both in the 'Hades' and 'Ithaca' chapters in *Ulysses*. Bloom thinks of Hooper as he walking through the cemetery after Dignam's funeral. He sees a bird perched on a poplar branch and it reminds him of the wedding present that Alderman Hooper had given to him and Molly. Hooper who lived at 22 Belvedere Place, died aged fifty-one in November 1897 [Zg 178½].

Canon John O'Hanlon (1821–1905) MRIA, who appears in the 'Nausicaa' chapter in *Ulysses* celebrating benediction, was the parish priest of Our Lady Star of the Sea Church in Sandymount. He is commemorated under a large Celtic cross at plot [Eh-19], which is off 'The Walk' on the left-hand side below the Jesuit Plot. It is difficult enough to locate his grave, but use the memorial to John Larkin on the left-hand side of the 'The Walk' as a guide. It is a few rows in behind this. The inscription on the cross reads:

Erected to the memory of | The reverend John Canon O'Hanlon MRIA | Parish Priest of Sandymount AD 1889–1905, | Author of the lives of the Irish Saints | And many other historical works | Who died on 15th May 1905, aged 83 years. This monument has been erected | By his parishioners and friends | To record their sorrow and his loss and | Their veneration for his learning and holiness | RIP.

[33] THE MONUMENT TO MICHAEL CUSACK (1847–1906), FOUNDER OF THE GAA. 'THE CITIZEN' IN THE CYCLOPS CHAPTER IN *ULYSSES* IS BASED ON CUSACK.

Canon O'Hanlon is best remembered for his monumental work, *The Lives of the Irish Saints* (9 Vols. 1875), which took thirty years to complete and includes the lives of 3,500 saints covering 8,500 pages. Born in Laois, he studied in Carlow and was ordained in St Louis in 1847. He started his writing career here, contributing to many journals. He was editor of the *St Louis Newsletter* and two of his books, *An Emigrant's Guide to the United States* and an *Abridgement of Irish History* were published here. He returned to Ireland in 1853 as a result of poor health and was appointed curate of St Michael and Johns before being appointed to Star of the Sea in Sandymount. He was secretary of the Daniel O'Connell Monument Committee in 1881. Canon O'Hanlon now lies close to the Laois born poet, John Keegan (1809–1849), whose writings he collected in *Legends and Poems*.

Michael Cusack (1847–1906), organiser of the GAA on whom 'the citizen' in the Cyclops chapter is based is buried on the left-hand side on the perimeter of the old O'Connell Circle [Dg-163.5].

A memorial plaque was erected by the National Graves Association and unveiled on 14 July 1968 in the cemetery to commemorate James FitzHarris, known as Skin-the-Goat whose name appears in the 'Eumaeus' episode of *Ulysses*. He was the Dublin jarvey, who drove the two 'Invincibles' to the Phoenix Park on 6 May 1882 when Lord Frederick Cavendish, the Chief Secretary for Ireland and Thomas H. Burke, the Under-secretary were assassinated.

FitzHarris was offered bribes from the British Government in Ireland to inform on the men. He was offered £10,000, which was a substantial sum in those days, and transport to any foreign land of his choice if he divulged information. He declined, and although found not guilty of murder, was sentenced to penal servitude for life for his part in the affair [UH 159 ALL].

Thomas H. Burke (1829–82), the Under-Secretary for Ireland, is buried in the South Section (ZB 74 South Section E).

The area to the east of the O'Connell Tower and to the right of the main entrance contains the graves of many of the most celebrated figures that shaped the history of the county.

The grave of Michael Collins (1890–1922), which is a limestone cross, is on the right-hand side of the main gate down past the offices. The large attendance at his funeral was second only to Parnell's [Gd 82 all South New Chapel]. Collins was a member of the delegation that negotiated the Anglo-Irish Treaty on 6 December 1921 and became chairman of the Provisional Government which was formed to implement it. He became Commander-in-Chief of the government forces following the outbreak of civil war in June 1922. He was shot in the head in an ambush at Béal na Bláth between Macroom and Bandon on 22 August 1922. Collins' fiancée, Kitty Kiernan, is buried close by [FD 68.5. South Section E].

In the same area are the Irish Army Plot and also the UN Plot in which are interred members of the army killed while serving with the United Nations.

Nearby is the grave of Anne Devlin (1778–1851), the faithful and devoted servant of Robert Emmet. A niece of Michael Dwyer, she was imprisoned following the failure of Emmet's rising in 1803, and despite being tortured, she never divulged any information. After her release, she spent her remaining years living in the slums of Dublin in abject poverty. Dr Richard Madden befriended her and went to America to raise funds to allow her some comfort in her remaining years. Sadly, when he returned, she was already dead and had been buried in a section reserved for paupers. Dr Madden organised to have her remains transferred 'to that part of the cemetery, which is in the most request – very near the spot there the remains of O'Connell are deposited'. He erected a monument over her grave, on the top of which is a cross and on the base an Irish wolfhound lying on a bank of shamrocks [Vc 45 all South]. The inscription reads:

115

To | the memory | of | Anne Devlin | (Campbell) | the faithful servant of | ROBERT EMMET | who possessed some rare | and many noble qualities | who lived in obscurity and poverty | and so died | on the 18th day of September 1851 | Aged 70 years | May she rest in Peace. Amen.

The Republican Plot is to the right of the O'Connell Tower. Here are interred the remains of many of those killed in both the War of Independence and the Civil War. Amongst others they include Thomas Ashe (1885–1917), John Devoy (1842–1928), Liam Mellows (1892–1922), Michael Joseph O'Rahilly (1875–1916), Cathal Brugha (1874–1922), Jeremiah O'Donovan Rossa (1831–1915), Countess Constance Markievicz (1868–1927) and Maud Gonne MacBride (1866–1953). Her son, Seán MacBride, the republican, politician, lawyer and recipient of the Nobel Peace prize who died in 1988, is buried with her [TD24 all 25 ½sth].

John O'Leary (1830–1907), the Fenian and journalist, is buried under a Celtic cross on the near side of the Republic Plot. O'Leary's main work is *Recollections of Fenians and Fenianism* (two volumes, 1896). In his poem entitled 'September 1913' W.B. Yeats wrote:

Romantic Ireland's dead and gone, It's with O'Leary in the grave.

Adjacent to O'Leary's grave is that of James Stephens (1825–1901), who was a founder member with Luby and others of the Irish Republican Brotherhood or the Fenian movement. [RD 40 South New Chapel]

The grave of Eamon de Valera (1882–1975) and his wife Sínéad (née Flanagan) (1878–1975), Irish scholar and folklorist is marked with a plain granite memorial (YD 11 & 12, Snc). De Valera served as Taoiseach seven times and twice as President. Before his retirement from office in 1973, he was the oldest serving head of state in the world.

Seán T. Ó Ceallaigh (1882–1966), who also served two terms as President, is buried in St Brigid's Section (AH64 & 65. St Brigid).

The grave of James Larkin (1876–1947), 'Big Jim', is a tall oblong granite stone on which is inscribed

James | Larkin | 1876–1947 | The Labour Leader. He was a trade unionist and founded the Irish Transport and General Workers Union in 1909. This catered for unskilled workers in Dublin, many of whom lived in really dreadful conditions in the slums. Larkin's campaign culminated in the great lock-out in Dublin in 1913 [VD 25 South New Chapel].

Not too far away is the grave of Frank Ryan (1902–1944), the republican and socialist who had a most colourful career. A graduate in Celtic studies and a founder of the Dublin branch of the National Union of Journalists, he fought in both the Irish and Spanish Civil Wars on Republican sides. He died in Germany

116

on 10 June 1944 and many years later, through the work of the National Graves Association, his remains were repatriated to Glasnevin [TD RD 22 all south].

William Dargan (1799–1867) was responsible for the construction of the first railway in Ireland from Dublin to Kingstown (Dún Laoghaire) which opened in 1834. He organised and financed the Dublin Industrial Exhibition of 1853. The National Gallery of Ireland on Merrion Square was built to commemorate the services he provided. A statue of Dargan executed by Thomas Farrell is on the lawn outside the National Gallery [TD 40 South Section E].

Frank Duff (1889–1980), the civil servant who initially worked with the Society of St Vincent de Paul was a co-founder of the Legion of Mary in 1921. In 1928, the Legion opened a hostel for destitute men in Brunswick Street named the Morning Star and later a hostel for destitute women. The Legion now has branches in Scotland, London, Paris and America [HA 23 all sth].

[34] THE GRAVE OF DUBLIN JARVEY JAMES FITZHARRIS, KNOWN AS 'SKIN-THE-GOAT'.

117

Thomas Bodkin (1887–1961), a lawyer and expert on art who was a Director of the National Gallery from 1927–1935, was responsible for acquiring the Hugh Lane Collection for Dublin. He is buried in Grave No. FD 46 South.

A simple granite stone marks the grave of Sir Alfred Chester Beatty (1875–1968), the New York-born mining engineer. He made a gift to the National Gallery of paintings to the value of over one million pounds. He also donated his private collection of Oriental manuscripts and printed books to the Irish nation. It is now housed in the Chester Beatty Library in Dublin Castle. A Freeman of Dublin and the first honorary citizen of Ireland, he was given a state funeral as a mark of respect and appreciation [SD 53 South Section E].

Hanna Sheehy-Skeffington (1877–1946), the suffragette, feminist and nationalist, was co-founder in 1908 with Margaret Cousins of the Irish Women's Franchise League. Their aim was to fight for votes for women in any future Home Rule bill. Hanna was married to Francis-Sheehy Skeffington (1878–1916), the journalist and pacifist who was shot dead without trial on 26 April 1916 in Portobello Barracks. Bear right at the main entrance and pass the administration office. Take the last turn to the left and continue straight on. On the left-hand side, two graves in, is the headstone of the Skeffingtons. They are buried together almost opposite the grave of Brendan Behan. [LA 18 South]

Margaret Burke Sheridan (1889–1958), Ireland's first international *Prima Donna*, who sang with John McCormack and made her debut in Puccini's opera 'La Bohème' on 3 September 1916, is buried in the shadow of the O'Connell Tower [XD 16 & 17 1/2 Sth].

Peadar Kearney (1883–1942), songwriter and revolutionary, worked as a house painter and was also associated with the Abbey Theatre as property man and small-part actor. He wrote a number of well-known songs including 'Down by the Glenside' and 'The Tri-coloured Ribbon'. In 1907 he wrote the words for 'The Soldiers' Song' which later became the National Anthem. He is buried in the Republican Plot. Patrick Heeney, who wrote the music, is interred in Drumcondra churchyard.

There are several veterans who survived the horrors of the *Charge of the Light Brigade* who are buried in Glasnevin. James Devlin, late of the Adjutant-General's Office at the Royal Hospital Kilmainham was one, and is buried in the South Section [AC 74 South Section E]. Another was Major John Dyke who died on the 7 September 1864 aged thirty-seven years of tubercular consumption at Portobello Barracks in Dublin with only two shillings to his 'credits'. Dyke, who was born in Dublin, enlisted in Liverpool in May 1846. He served in the 11th Hussars and rode the twenty-three year old 'Crimean Bob' as a farrier in the *Charge* that both of them remarkably escaped unscathed. Dyke was entitled to the Crimean medal with clasps for Alma, Balaclava, Inkerman and Sebastopol. He is buried in Plot No. [B60 – 194], which is unmarked.

Interestingly, Crimean Bob, a chestnut coloured horse of fifteen hands, returned to the barracks in Cahir where the Duke of Cambridge directed that he was not to be sold when he became unfit as was the practice at that time. On 9 November 1862, old Bob died, to the sincere regret of the whole regiment, and he was buried with military honours within Cahir Barracks. A commemorative tablet bore the inscription:

Alma / Balaclava / 11th (P.A.O.) Hussars | Underneath | Lies Crimean Bob | A veteran Troop Horse | Who after passing unharmed | through the memorable | Crimean Campaign | Died at Cahir Barracks | On the 9th November 1862 aged 34 years.

His memorial was known to be still in Cahir in 1973, but by 1991 it had been purchased and brought to England, where it is now in the Museum of the Royal Hussars.

A Boer Memorial was unveiled in October 1901. It commemorates two of the 59,000 people who died in the Boer War. The inscription reads:

To the memory of Patrick J. Lawlor and Peter J. Murphy, Orderlies of the Irish Hospital who died in South Africa in the year 1900, of disease contracted in the discharge of duty. This monument has been erected by their comrades of the Irish Hospital. R.I.P.

Similar to Mount Jerome, there are two memorials erected in Glasnevin dedicated to members of the Royal Irish Constabulary and the Dublin Metropolitan Police. These are situated on either side of a pathway, facing each other, directly behind the old O'Connell Circle.

Zozimus (1794–1846), whose real name was Michael Moran, was born in Faddle Alley, off Black Pitts in the Liberties. Blinded since infancy, he became famous as a storyteller and ballad writer. W.B. Yeats fondly wrote of him as The Last Gleeman:

Free from the interruption of sight, his mind turned every movement of the day and every change of public passion into rhyme or quaint saying. He was the admitted rector of all the ballad mongers of the Liberties.

He dressed in a scalloped cape and battered high hat and carried a blackthorn stick and became a well-known Dublin character. He died in a top back room at 14½ Patrick Street and is commemorated with a limestone memorial, which was erected during the Dublin Millennium in 1988 [AG 30 Dublin Section W].

There are free guided tours of the cemetery covering the main monuments. These are courtesy of the Dublin Cemeteries Committee and are available to the public. They are held every Wednesday and Friday throughout the year. For information on these tours telephone (01) 830 11 33.

Glasnevin Cemetery is under the care of Dublin Cemeteries Committee.

GLENCULLEN (OLD) CHURCHYARD

SITUATION: GLENCULLEN, CO. DUBLIN

PERIOD IN USE: 1824–1908. CEMETERY CLOSED EXCEPT FOR THOSE WITH BURIAL RIGHTS

BUS NO: 44B FROM THE CITY CENTRE [HAWKINS STREET]

Gleann Cuilin, which means the Glen of the Holly, is about a thousand feet above sea level overlooking a beautiful glen. A stone wall surrounds the old churchyard in Glencullen on the site of the former church dedicated to St Patrick. This was erected in the year 1824 and is now a ruin. It was built with donations from the public and with the financial assistance of Christopher Fitz-Simon who also donated the site from his estate. He lived nearby at the Gandon designed Glencullen House.

Interestingly, it was at a dinner party in Glencullen House in 1823 that the idea for Daniel O'Connell's Catholic Association originated. O'Connell, who later founded Glasnevin Cemetery, had connections with the Fitz-Simon family through his daughter Ellen, who was married to Christopher Fitz-Simon. The marriage took place at Westland Row on 16 July 1825. Nearby at Glendoo is the rock where Daniel O'Connell addressed a crowd of nearly 2,000 people concerning his plan for the formation of The Catholic Emancipation Committee.

At the gable end of the ruin is a now almost illegible tablet, which reads:

St Patrick's Chapel | Erected AD 1824 | To the Honour and Glory of God

The external stone steps leading to its west end gallery may still be seen. The church was an old style east-west building and had a mud floor. It was in use until the present church was completed in August 1909. Glencullen is in the parish of Sandyford.

Father Patrick Smyth, who was ordained in Maynooth, and sent as an assistant to Father William Flood in Sandyford in 1823, was instrumental in providing the church at Glencullen. This hard-working and able priest administered to the prisoners on board the ships destined for the British penal settlements overseas and celebrated Mass in the hulks in which these prisoners were cramped. These unwieldy vessels were moored off shore in Dún Laoghaire before setting off for their long sea voyages to the penal colonies.

The burial ground at Glencullen was opened the same year as the church in 1824 and there are approximately forty-six memorials remaining. Among those buried here are Father Smyth. His grave is one of the few which is railed and is located at the very back of the churchyard almost behind the church he had built in the early days of his ministry. The stone is inscribed:

Erected to the memory of Patrick Smyth, Parish Priest of Sandyford and Glencullen, who was ordained in 1815, came to this parish in 1823 and died, to the regret of his devoted flock, on 28th May, 1860. Requiescat in pace.

There are members of families who had lived in the area for many years interred here. These include the Fitz-Simon family who took over the Fitzwilliam interest in Glencullen in 1671. The Fitz-Simon plot, which contains three headstones enclosed by large granite kerbstones adjoins one side of the church.

Sacred to the memory of | Christopher O'Connell Fitz-Simon, D.L., J.P. | 1830–1884 | his wife | Agnes (nee Leyne) | their children | Christopher 1867–1910 | Richard 1868–1894 | Daniel 1872–1948 | Edward died in S. Africa 1873–1939 | May 1871–1953

Sacred | to the memory of | Lieut. Col. | Henry FitzSimon | late 29th B.N.I. | died 7th Sept. 1865 | and of his wife Marianne Fitz-Simon | died 5th April 1899 | also their daughter | Ellen Fitzsimon | died 7th Feb 1937.

In loving memory of | Henry O'Connell Fitz-Simon | born 13th April 1837 died 11th April, 1902 | and of | Eliza his wife | born 18th Sept 1832 died 14th Feb 1901 | Requiescant in Pace | In te Domine speravi | Non Confundor in aeternum.

Others include the Roe and Lenehan families who have long been associated in the area with farming and the stone quarries. There are quite a number of headstones to the Roes, which include three family headstones alongside each other:

Sacred | to the memory of | Hugh Roe who depd this life | April 7th 1865 aged 84 years | also his son Cornelius who depd | May 21st 1867 aged 31 years | and two other sons who died young.

Erected | by | Hugh Roe | in memory of his beloved father | Thomas Roe | who died 29th July | 1890 aged 81 years | also of his sister | Elizabeth Leary | who died 26th April 1864 aged 21 years | and of his brother | John Roe | who died 28th May 1891 aged 43 years.

Two headstones to the Lenehan family are within a railed enclosure, one of which reads:

Erected by | James Lenehan | in memory of his beloved father | Patrick Lenehan | who died Aug 27th 1870 aged 72 years | Also his mother Margaret Lenehan | died March 1st 1862 aged 54 years | and of James Lenehan | Grange Rathfarnham, (formerly of Ballybrack) | died 30th April 1944 aged 77 years | his daughter Mary | died 5th Aug 1919 | and John Lenehan | Woodside House Sandyford | beloved husband and father | who died 14th March 1977 aged 73 years.

John O'Rorke, owner of the old Jamestown House in Kilternan [now derelict], erected a memorial to:

121

[35] ᴇɴᴛʀᴀɴᴄᴇ ᴛᴏ ᴛʜᴇ ɴᴏᴡ-ʀᴜɪɴᴇᴅ ᴄʜᴜʀᴄʜ ᴏꜰ Sᴛ Pᴀᴛʀɪᴄᴋ ᴀɴᴅ ᴏʟᴅ ᴄʜᴜʀᴄʜʏᴀʀᴅ, Gʟᴇɴᴄᴜʟʟᴇɴ, Cᴏᴜɴᴛʏ Dᴜʙʟɪɴ.

John and Mary his parents | Edmond and Bridget | his brother and sister | also | of James Archbold | his only son | who died 16th February 1860 | aged 9 years | and his dear wife | Cecilia Emily | who died 20th February 1868 | RIP | They shall not return to us | But we shall go to them.

According to local lore, the old cemetery at Glencullen did not escape the bodysnatchers or sack-'em-up men, as they were known. Glencullen would seem to be a bit far out to travel, but come they did! However in this case they were unsuccessful. A story is recounted whereby an actual battle took place between grave robbers and some local men. The locals had been forewarned of the impending raid and laid in waiting. The grave robbers had come for a recently interred body but were confronted – shots were exchanged before the robbers retreated and fled. Evidence of the fight was to be observed on some of the older tombstones until the recent past. So stealthy were these grave-robbers that they were known to have shod their horses with rubber shoes to make their travel silent!

The new St Patrick's church is somewhat similar in size to the former one and is down a few hundred yards from it. The new graveyard, which was opened in 1908, contains the grave of Canon Maurice O'Shea, which is located immediately to the rear of the church. A native of Limerick, he presided over the parish at a time of great development. He was instrumental in providing new schools in the Sandyford area and also one in Kilternan in 1963. He also set up the beautiful oratory at Leopardstown Hospital.

Old Glencullen cemetery is under the care of the Roman Catholic Parish of Sandyford.

122

GOLDEN BRIDGE CEMETERY

SITUATION: ST VINCENT STREET WEST, INCHICORE, DUBLIN 8

PERIOD IN USE: 1829 TO 1869 (EXCEPT THOSE WITH BURIAL RIGHTS)

BUS NOS (FROM CITY CENTRE): 51, 51B, 68 & 69

Inchicore is two miles west of Dublin city centre. Nearby is Golden Bridge, which was known for centuries as Glydon Bridge. It was here that a site was chosen for the first Catholic Cemetery in Dublin (until Glasnevin was opened in 1832). Though nominally a Catholic burial place, it was also open to other sects. It was located between the former Richmond Barracks (now redeveloped), which was built in 1807 to house the 91st Foot Regiment and the 92nd Highland Regiment, and the Grand Canal.

Daniel O'Connell and the Catholic Association bought the land, which comprises three statute acres, for £600 from a Protestant named Mathias O'Kelly. Archbishop Murray delegated the Reverend Father George Canavan to bless the new site at Golden Bridge and it was officially opened on 15 October 1829, six months after the Act of Catholic Emancipation had been passed.

A high limestone wall encompasses the almost rectangular cemetery. There is a pathway around the inside perimeter and two pathways, one from the eastern end and one from the north-west end, lead to the centre of the cemetery. Here there is a mortuary chapel, which was once a rather lovely feature resembling a classic Roman temple, but is now in a disgraceful condition due to vandalism. Beneath it is a room, which was originally provided for the watchmen and their guard dogs, which were generally Cuban bloodhounds. These men with their dogs kept a vigil against the many bodysnatchers or sack-'em-up men. They were so called on account of the method they used to acquire the bodies. They dug at the end of the grave, placed a noose around the feet of the body, and pulled it up and placed it in a sack. It is recorded that firearms were provided for some of the watchmen at Golden Bridge.

Among the first burials in Golden Bridge was that of the Reverend Father Lawrence Whelan, who in penal days had been a pastor at Dolphin's Barn. His remains, when removed from underneath the earthen floor of that chapel, evoked memories of the past. The Reverend Father James Callan, who was curate of St James's church, died on 8 February 1825 and is also interred here.

With the opening of Glasnevin Cemetery [formerly named Prospect Cemetery] in February 1832, the number of burials at Golden Bridge decreased.

The famine took its toll in Dublin as well as in country areas and the south-east corner of the cemetery was used as mass graves for the victims. Later on, as with Bully's Acre nearby in Kilmainham, there were a number of people who died as a result of the Asiatic cholera epidemic which invaded Ireland for the first time in 1832 and claimed a horrific amount of victims. Many of the victims were buried here.

In the autumn of 1866, the Committee of Golden Bridge Cemetery received numerous letters from the quarters of the 92nd Highlanders in Richmond Barracks. It requested that steps be taken to render the cemetery less obnoxious to the troops quartered in the barracks and suggested that it be closed, or if not, that interment be made as far away from the barracks as the nature of the ground would admit. The many reports undertaken indicated that the cemetery was in good condition and contained absolutely no threat to the military.

[36] VIEW OF PORTION OF GOLDENBRIDGE CEMETERY, INCHICORE.

A further cholera epidemic occurred in 1867. This resulted in an increased amount of funeral traffic which caused a commotion when passing Richmond Barracks and annoyed the military personnel. Fuel was added to an already smouldering fire.

On 9 June 1868, *The Dublin Gazette* contained an announcement which read:

All parties having any objections to the proposed order for closing the said burial-ground are hereby informed that they are at liberty to appear before the Privy Council in support of these objections, either personally, or by counsel, on the fifteenth day of July next.

On 15 July 1869, the Privy Council held a hearing at which The Right Hon Abraham Brewster, then Lord Chancellor, presided. The result was the virtual closing of the cemetery. It also limited interments to those already holding burial rights.

Among those buried in Golden Bridge are William T. Cosgrave (1880–1965), the first President of the Executive Council of the Irish Free State (1922–32). Professor Brian Farrell, the historian and broadcaster, wrote

We buried William T. Cosgrave on a wet day in Dublin. There was not even a tricolour on the plain, wooden coffin. The unpretentious ceremony might have marked the passing of any simple, gentle old man, laid to rest after a dutiful life of service to his family community.

The cross on his grave bears the simple inscription:

W.T. Cosgrave | died 16 November 1965 | Louisa Cosgrave | died 16th June 1959 | Requiescant in Pace.

A mound in a circle with a cross marks the burial place of the orphans from the Orphan House in Harold's Cross Convent. It bears the date of 1831.

The river Camac, which flows from Brittas through Inchicore and Kilmainham, joins the Liffey just below Heuston Station. In bygone days, like the Dodder, it had a number of watermills on it. In the cemetery, there is an inscription, which is reminiscent of these days. It reads:

This stone was | erected by | the Millwright Society of | Dublin | in memory of a deceased | brother Thomas Purcell | who depd this life 27th Jany 1839 | aged 32 years | May he rest in peace.

A number of clergy are also interred here. These include priests from the neighbouring parishes of St James's and St Audoen's:

Crux Mihi Salus | Sacred to the memory of | the Revd John Doyle | who for a period of twenty years | discharged the duties of the R.C. curate of St James's Parish in this city | He lived enthroned | in the hearts of the

parishioners | and in the 54th year of his age | and the 23rd of his ministry entered into the repose of the | just on Good Friday the 14th day of April | 1843 | Requiescat in Pace.

The grave of a young priest from St Audoen's parish is inscribed:

The heart felt tribute of sorrowing friends | to the memory of the | Revd James Dempsey | of St Audoen's Parish | Dublin. | Invested with the greatest dignity | to which mortal can be raised | the ambassador of God to man | and discharging his high trust with | fidelity and zeal | It seemed good to his heavenly master | to take to himself | almost in the onset of his glorious course | Respected by the rich beloved by the poor | he was called to a better life | on the 20th of Decr 1830 | in the 32nd year of his age | And it seems his thread of life to sever | Yet dry your tears arrest the rising sigh | His soul indeed has winged her flight forever | But lives with angels in her kindred sky.

Also interred here is Father James Harold (1744–1831), who was parish priest of Rathcoole in 1798. Following the destruction of his house by fire, Father Harold was arrested by the military, and although not charged, was deported to the penal colonies in Australia where he arrived in Sydney after a lengthy sea journey on board the *Minerva*. After spending some time on Norfolk Island he was given permission to leave Australia and returned to Ireland in 1810 via Rio de Janeiro and Philadelphia. The inscription on his grave gives no details of his historical connections:

Beneath this stone lie entombed the mortal remains of the Revd. James Harold and the Revd. William D. Harold. The former was during many years Parish Priest in this Archdiocese. He died on the 15 August 1830 in the 87th year of his age, a faithful Christian and a firm friend. The latter was of the Order of Preachers, and a member of their house in Denmark Street. The few years of his public ministry were spent in zealous discharge of all his sacred duties. Pious, upright, and benevolent, he expired on the 15 December 1830 in his 29th year, leaving many who revere his memory and deplore his death.

Golden Bridge Cemetery, which contains a total of 1,100 headstones, with reference to 4,402 people, holds the remains of a population mostly from the Dublin area. Dr Michael Egan and Mr Richard Flatman have recorded all the inscriptions over a period of eighteen months of what must have been painstaking work.

The cemetery is kept locked. The key is available from the caretaker's house, which adjoins the burial ground.

Golden Bridge is under the care of the Dublin Cemeteries Committee, The Office, Glasnevin Cemetery, Finglas Road, Glasnevin.

126

GRANGEGORMAN MILITARY CEMETERY

SITUATION: BLACKHORSE AVENUE, DUBLIN 7

PERIOD IN USE: FROM 1878 [NOW CLOSED EXCEPT TO THOSE WITH RIGHTS]

BUS NOS (FROM CITY CENTRE): 10 AND 37

OPENING HOURS: 10 A.M.–4 P.M.

This cemetery, comprising five-and-a-half acres of nicely wooded land adjacent to the eastern boundary of the Phoenix Park on Blackhorse Avenue, dates from 1878.

It was opened as a burial ground for members of the British Army and their families. Many who served in the British Forces during the First World War were buried here including over one hundred soldiers killed in Dublin during the 1916 Rising.

Of note in this graveyard is the standard size of most of the headstones compared to those in places like Mount Jerome or Glasnevin cemeteries which contain monuments of every shape and size.

It can be approached either by Blackhorse Avenue or through a pedestrian gate from the Phoenix Park. Beside the pedestrian way is a larger gate known as the Funeral Gate which has three small crosses on top of it indicating that it is the cemetery gate. This gate has not been opened for years, with the exception of Pope John Paul II's visit in 1979, when it was used to give added access to visitors entering the Park to attend the ceremonies.

This gate was formerly used for funeral processions coming out from the Park to cross what was then Blackhorse Lane, which up to the early 1940s was just a muddy laneway. When the road was built it became Blackhorse Avenue. It derived its name from the old Blackhorse Tavern.

The graveyard has an imposing entrance with large stone pillars. Inside on the left-hand side is a recently discovered well. Formerly, there were rings on the wall for the purpose of tying the horses. It was customary to have a well in any army installation and here it would have been used to water the plants and of course the horses. For an officer's funeral, six horses would have pulled the gun carriage and there would have been three outriders.

Beside the well is a building now used for housing garden machinery. This building was once a morgue where bodies were left overnight. The insets for the former four sentry boxes, two at each end, can still be seen.

The grounds are formally laid out and it is certainly one of the nicer cemeteries in the Dublin area.

In Victorian times many scented plants such as *cyrynga* lilac and *philadelphus* were used here. Two magnificent American Giant Redwood trees, which are quite unusual to find in a burial ground, overshadow the avenue. Most of the trees are planted in pairs and include English weeping yew, Irish yew, Cedar of Lebanon, and an unusual Spanish evergreen.

Close to the boundary walls on both the left and right-hand side, are rows of children's graves of different denominations which include Church of England, Church of Ireland, Roman Catholic and Wesleyans and children who came from the nearby Royal Hibernian Military School in the Phoenix Park.

On the left side on entering the gate, situated down at the boundary wall in plot 222, is the grave of Company Sgt Major Martin Doyle, who was awarded both the Victoria Cross and the Military Medal. Doyle was awarded five medals from the British Government for his service in the First World War. The stone on his grave was erected by his 'old comrades in the Regiment' and reads:

Coy Sgt Major | Martin Doyle V.C. M.M. | Royal Munster Fusiliers | Died 20th Nov 1940

Born in New Ross in 1894, he joined the 18th Royal Regiment at Kilkenny Barracks when he was fifteen and served in India. He returned to Ireland in 1914 at the outbreak of the war and was posted to France with the Royal Dublin Fusiliers, where he fought at the Battle of Mons. He became a Company Sergeant Major and transferred to the 1st Battalion of the Royal Munster Fusiliers. He won the Military Medal in March 1918 when serving at Hattenfield in France.

Again in France, near Riencourt, Doyle displayed outstanding courage and won the Victoria Cross which was presented to him by King George V at Buckingham Palace on 8 May, 1919. He retired from the British Army two months later, having served for nine years and five months. He then served for over fifteen years in 'regular' Irish Army service followed by one and a half years in the Reserve. This courageous man died at the age of forty in Dublin at Sir Patrick Dun's Hospital.

The last official Government hangman, Alfred Pierpoint, is also interred here:

In loving Memory of | Alfred Wallace Pierpoint | Rifleman Royal Irish Rifles | Died 21st March 1946 | And his loving wife Maud | Died 8th November 1969

An intriguing grave is to that of Capt. M. Clarke who was one of the six hundred at Balaclava who rode into the Valley of Death in the Charge of the Light Brigade so poignantly, recounted in Tennyson's poem.

Cannon to right of them
Cannon to left of them,
Cannon to front of them
Volley'd and thunder'd.

Clarke was fortunate to have survived. Confusion over orders during the Battle of Balaclava when Raglan's message had been misunderstood, resulted in an action that cost the lives of 247 men. Out of some 630 men who charged, 110 were killed in action, 196 were wounded (some later dying as a result) and 57 were taken prisoner. The number of horses killed was 362.

To the Memory | of | Capt. M. Clarke | Paymaster | 2nd Bn. 18th the Royal Irish Regt Late Adjt. 8th [Royal Irish] Hussars | Died 27 December 1878 | Aged 61 years | He was one of the six hundred | At Balaclava | Erected by the Officers of the 2nd bn 18th Royal Irish Regt | Here also is interred | Grace his wife | Who died 24 January 1884 | At Ash Surrey | Aged 67 years | Be thou faithful unto Death.

On 10 November 1918, a month before Armistice Day and the end of the First World War, three torpedoes fired by the German submarine UB-123 sank the mail boat, HMS Leinster. The Leinster, which was operated by the City of Dublin Steam Packet Company, maintained the mail service throughout the First World War. Of the 757 people on aboard, 501 were lost in the worst disaster in the Irish Sea. Since over 500 soldiers were passengers, a large number of the victims were buried in this cemetery. Of the 150 military graves resulting from the ill-fated ship, 145 are located in this cemetery. They include Irishmen who were returning to the front and other soldiers who were going on leave to Britain from units of the Irish garrison.

Among them were twenty-four-year-old M. Flaherty of the Irish Guards and Lieut Comdt George Richard Campbell, whose entire family were victims. Other casualties included Colonel William Mosse and his wife Ellen who were returning to Italy where Mosse commanded a garrison battalion of the Munster Fusiliers.

[37] THE GRAVESTONE OF CAPT. M. CLARKE, WHO RODE IN THE CHARGE OF THE LIGHT BRIGADE.

129

[38] THE GRAVESTONES OF SOME OF THE 600 SOLDIERS WHO WERE ENGAGED IN THE FIRST WORLD WAR. INCLUDED AMONG THEM IS THE GRAVE OF THE UNKNOWN SOLDIER.

Others were thirty-three year old Lance-Corporal William O'Mahony of the 1st Royal Dublin Fusiliers, Henry Thomas Doyle, aged twenty-eight, a 2nd lieutenant in the Wellington Regiment of the NZEF and William Dillingham a twenty-four-year-old private from the Scottish Horse, from Bedfordshire.

The graves of six hundred soldiers, including the Unknown Soldier, who were engaged in the First World War, are in neat rows of military precision. Of interest is the fact that each soldier buried has the insignia or emblem of his regiment engraved on his headstone. Some of the many regiments included are:

Argyll & Sutherland Artillery, Army Cyclists Corps, Black Watch, Cameron Highlanders, Cameronians [Scottish Rifle], Canadian Field Artillery, Canadian Infantry 4th Battalion, Connaught Rangers, Cheshire Regiment, Dorset Yeomanry, 5th Dragoon Guards, East Kent Regiment [Buffs], East Lancashire Regiment, East Riding Yeomanry, Grenadier Guards [3rd Bt], Highland Light Infantry, Hussars 4th [Q.O], Irish Guards, Royal Inniskilling Fusiliers, 2nd King Edward's Horse, King's Liverpool Regiment, King's Own Scottish Borderers, 8th King's Royal Irish Hussars, King's Shropshire [Light Infantry], Labour Corps, 5th Lancers, Lancers [Empress of India], Leinster Regiment, 2nd Batt London Rgt. Royal Fusiliers, Machine Gun Corps, Middlesex Yeomanry, Military Police Corps, Munsters, New Zealand Army Service Corps, New Zealand Wellington Regiment, Prince of Wales Volunteers – South Lancashire Regt. Queen Mary's Army Auxiliary Corps, Rifle Brigade, Royal Air Force, Royal Army Medical Corps, Royal Army Ordnance Corps, Royal Army Services Corps, Royal Artillery, Royal Berkshire Regiment, Royal Canadian Dragoons, Royal Corps of Engineers, Royal Defence Corps, Royal Dublin Fusiliers, Royal Engineers, Royal Field Artillery, Royal Garrison Artillery, Royal Irish Rifles, Royal Marine Labour Corps, Royal Scots Fusiliers, Royal Warwickshire, Royal Welsh Fusiliers, Seaforth Highlanders, South Lancashire, Scottish Horse, South Irish Horse, South Lancashire Regiment, Welch Regiment, Westmoreland & Cumberland Yeomanry, West Yorkshire Regiment, Wiltshire Regiment, and the Worcestershire Regiment Yorkshire Hussars.

On entering the main gate, on the right-hand side just behind the lodge, is a fine memorial wall, which consists of a main plaque in the centre with four plaques on either side containing names.

The centre plaque is inscribed:

1914–1918   1939–1945

THOSE HONOURED | ON THESE PANELS | GAVE THEIR LIVES | IN TWO WORLD WARS | AND ARE BURIED | ELSEWHERE IN IRELAND.
THE FACING MEMORIALS | COMMEMORATE THOSE OF | THEIR COMRADE IN ARMS | WHOSE GRAVESTONES ARE IN | CORK MILITARY CEMETERY.

HOWTH (ST MARY'S) CHURCH (NATIONAL MONUMENT)

SITUATION: CHURCH STREET, HOWTH, CO. DUBLIN

PERIOD IN USE: 1470–1973

BUS NOS (FROM CITY CENTRE): 31, 31B. DART TO HOWTH STATION

Howth forms a peninsular promontory, occupying the north side of Dublin Bay and joining the mainland by a low sandy isthmus half a mile wide. The harbour, built in 1807, was originally the chief packet station. The village is nine and a half miles from Dublin city centre. The name of Howth is derived from the old Norse word Hofuth, meaning a promontory or head. Binn Eadair, the Hill of Eadar is the Irish name.

The old abbey and burial ground are situated on a height at the end of Church Street, which runs parallel to the sea front. The entrance is through a gate and down some steps. There is a fine view overlooking the harbour, which takes in Ireland's Eye, and further beyond, Lambay Island. Two sides of the burial ground have high battlement type walls.

Sigtrygg (Sitric) King of Dublin, founded the first church on this site about 1042. In 1235 this church was amalgamated with the one on Ireland's Eye, and Luke, Archbishop of Dublin, founded a new church on land granted by Sir Almeric St Lawrence. Howth Castle has been the seat of the St Lawrence family since the sixteenth century, but the first St Lawrence, Almeric I, had settled in Howth in the twelfth century, when he was granted a manor by Henry II. His motte-castle was near to where the abbey is today, on the site of the Martello tower, on a height at the head of the east pier.

Much of the present abbey dates from the late fourteenth or early fifteenth century. Various alterations and additions were carried out on it in the fifteenth and sixteenth centuries, such as the raising of the gables, the building of the bell cote and the addition of a new porch and south door. The present church has two aisles, whereas the original one of 1235 had probably just the one.

In the south-east corner of the south aisle of the abbey is the chantry. This is the portion that the St Lawrence family of Howth Castle modified to use as a private chapel.

This contains the tomb of Christopher St Lawrence, thirteenth Baron of Howth, who died in 1462 and his wife, Anna Plunkett of Ratoath. The tomb was carved around 1470. On the top is the effigy of the

Knight and his wife. The sides and the ends of the tomb, which are elaborately carved, include a scene of the Crucifixion, St Michael and the dragon, an abbess, St Thomas of Canterbury, St Katherine of Alexandria holding her wheel, and St Peter holding a key.

On the south wall an inscription reads:

The Honourable William Almericus St Lawrence | died the 15th day of April 1820 aged 13 years.

Another stone on the right of this reads:

Almerica Isabella Maria fourth Daughter of the Rt Honble the Earl of Howth departed this life May 5th 1855. Aged 4 months.

There are several memorials and plaques within the precincts of the church.

On the south wall of the nave is one inscribed:

[39] Interior of St Mary's Church, Howth.

William Wylde of Worcestershire a Plantagenet was interred here AD 1843 and Mary his wife AD 1837. Leaving issue one son.

On a marble tablet on the south aisle wall is one inscribed to Captain Mudge as follows:

Sacred to the memory of Captain William Mudge R.N | F.R.A.S. who departed this life on the | 20th July 1837 aged 40. Under his command was | conducted the Important Nautical Survey of Ireland. | He was one of the Commissioners for the Improvement | of the River Shannon and other extensive | improvements in this country. Science has lost one | of its brightest ornaments, society one of its most valued members.

Underneath this memorial is a slab which reads,

Capt. W. Mudge, R.N. died 20th July 1837.

A marble tablet on the south wall commemorates his wife and son. It reads:

Also to the Memory of Mary Marinda, widow of Captain Mudge R.N. who died 31st May 1864 and their son William Tertius Fitzwilliam Mudge, First Lieutenant of HMS Orpheus wrecked off Manukau Bar New Zealand 7th February 1863 aged 65 years. RIP

The church was collegiate and was served by a college or community of clerics. To the south of the abbey are the ruins of the fifteenth/sixteenth-century college where the community once lived.

The windows and entrances to the abbey are blocked up with ironwork to protect the interior, and the key is available from a local person whose name is on the notice at the entrance. A gravelled path kerbed on both sides surrounds the abbey on three sides.

The burial ground was closed from 31 May 1973 by ministerial order and is under the care of Dublin Corporation.

[40] ELABORATE CARVINGS ON THE ST LAWRENCE TOMB AT ST MARY'S ABBEY IN HOWTH.

KILBARRACK CHURCHYARD

SITUATION: DUBLIN ROAD, SUTTON, DUBLIN 13

PERIOD IN USE: C. 1654 TO DATE

BUS NOS (FROM CITY CENTRE): 31A, 31B AND 32A. DART TO BAYSIDE STATION

Kilbarrack Churchyard is situated five and a half miles north-east from Dublin city centre between Clontarf and Sutton on the coast road. Kilbarrack is reputed to be the site of an early church, which was founded by St Berach in the sixth century. The name Kilbarrack is derived from the church of Berach. St Berach's well, which was noted for its curative powers for eye ailments, was situated to the north of the church.

Originally belonging to the monastery of the Blessed Virgin, the scant ruins of the chapel of Mone, commonly known as the Abbey of Kilbarrack, remain. The Capelle de Mone or Killmona indicates the church on the bog or marshy land. The earliest part of the ruin dates from the late twelfth or early thirteenth century. Interestingly, this was the votive chapel of the mariners who frequented Dublin bay. On their arrival, they had prayers offered up for the repose of the souls of the sailors who had perished at sea. Up until the time of the Reformation in 1538, ships entering into the port of Dublin paid an annual fee to this church. At this time, like so many other churches, Kilbarrack fell into disrepair and there is little mention of it after this. The ruins comprise a nave, chancel and part of a side aisle. The ruin is protected by an iron railing, so it is not possible to enter and view the memorials inside it.

The churchyard, built on the strand near the great sandbank, which was named the North Bull, was once unfettered by a fence or boundary walls. The present wall, which encompasses three acres, is a recent structure. The area contains about a thousand memorials the majority of which are made of limestone. There were others recorded previously which have since disappeared. Some may possibly have sunk in the soft sandy soil. The earliest memorial dates from 1654 and records the name of Howard.

Kilbarrack churchyard, which is on a slope, is noted for some famous and infamous people who were interred there. Among them is the notorious Francis Higgins (1746–1802) known as the 'Sham Squire'. He converted to Protestantism, and by posing as one of the landed gentry, he enticed a lady of means, Mary Anne Archer, into marriage. A sentence in Newgate Prison ensued for this offence. He also made financial gain from the operation of shady gaming houses. When he owned the *Freeman's Journal*, he used its pages to attack any opponents of the government, especially the United Irishmen. As a government informer, he is in all probability the 'F.H.' who was recorded as receiving £1,000 'for the discovery of Lord Edward Fitzgerald'. He was implicated in the murder of Oliver Bond who died suddenly in prison in September 1798. Higgins died on 19 January 1802 at his house, 82 St Stephen's Green, Dublin. Two years later, a magnificent memorial was erected to him in Kilbarrack churchyard. However, it did not survive too long, as after his death there was an utter abhorrence towards him:

> an alderman of the old corporation, who resided in Howth declared in 1820 that in riding into Dublin he would never pass Kilbarrack without ridiculing and insulting the Sham Squire's grave.

The burial grounds on the north side of the city did not escape the ravages of the sack-'em-up men! In 1833, the *Irish Penny Journal* contained a feature with the title of 'Deadwatcher'. In it it referred to the grave robbing in this churchyard. The accompanying woodcut illustrates the grave robbers in action accosting a relative by placing a bag over his head and tying it! Kilbarrack church serves as the backdrop.

The two Antrim born brothers, James (1869–1938) and Eoin Mac Neill (1867–1945) are buried here. Their memorial is just outside the west end of the church. James Mac Neill, after a successful career with the Indian civil service, succeeded T.M. Healy as second governor-general of the Irish Free State. Eoin Mac Neill was an eminent historian, and with Douglas Hyde and others, founded the Gaelic League in 1893. In 1908 he was appointed professor of Early Irish History at University College Dublin. He was founder and commander of the Irish Volunteers and the Minister of Education in the first Free State government. His publications include *Phases of Irish History* (1919) and *Celtic Ireland* (1921).

Some notable local people interred include members of the Sweetman family of Kilbarrack and Raheny who were a well-known brewing family in the eighteenth and nineteenth centuries. Their brewery was situated somewhere between South King Street and the

[41] KILBARRACK CHURCH AND GRAVEYARD IN SUTTON, COUNTY DUBLIN.

Royal College of Surgeons on St Stephen's Green. John Sweetman was the first of the family to be buried here in 1720. South of the church, is a memorial to Patrick Sweetman, his wife Mary (Thunder née Dodd) and daughter Catherine Browne. Around the time of their marriage, they lived at Fox Hall in Raheny. Patrick died in 1777 aged sixty-eight and Mary died aged ninety-two in 1784. She was some years older than her husband.

Perhaps the most notable member of this family was John Sweetman (1752–1826), the United Irishman. There is a memorial plaque on the wall of the ruined church, which reads:

John Sweetman | United Irishman | 1798 | is interred close by | RIP | Erected by the National | Graves Association. In his memory.

John Sweetman, who was a member of the Catholic Committee and secretary of the Dublin branch, was a close friend of Wolfe Tone. On account of his politics, he was jailed, and on his release, remained in exile for a number of years in Holland and Paris. From Paris, he submitted a design for the new Catholic Cathedral in Dublin. The *Irish Ecclesiastical Record* for December 1917 had an interesting report written by the Reverend Daniel Downey

On Easter Tuesday, March 28th 1815, the foundation stone of the 'Metropolitan Chapel' was laid. A beautiful design submitted by John Sweetman of Raheny had been approved and accepted. Mr Sweetman was not a professional artist or architect, but he was a man of rare architectural knowledge and keen artistic sense – from 1798 he had been in political exile.

Of military interest in the churchyard is the memorial to the four soldiers who were killed in the First World War. Privates F. and E. Brady from the same family were killed in November 1915 within 16 days of each other. Lieutenant Richard Gardiner Brewster was killed in action in France on 21 March 1918 and W. J. Powell was killed at the Dardanelles on 14 July 1915.

There are several young men from areas in the city who died during the War of Independence and are commemorated in Kilbarrack. They are buried elsewhere. Among them is Frank Flood of Summerhill Parade whose parents erected a memorial to him in Kilbarrack. A lieutenant in the IRA, he was aged nineteen when he was executed in Mountjoy Prison on 14 March 1921. He was buried in the prison yard. Among others commemorated are Seán Doyle from Amiens Street who died from wounds he received from an attack on the Custom House and Dan Head from Seville Place, who was killed by British forces during an attack on the same building.

Kilbarrack Churchyard is under the care of Fingal County Council.

KILGOBBIN (OLD) CHURCHYARD

SITUATION: KILGOBBIN, ENNISKERRY ROAD

PERIOD IN USE: UNKNOWN–1905

BUS NO (FROM CITY CENTRE): 44. ALIGHT AT KILGOBBIN LANE

The remains of an eighteenth-century church built by Archbishop King to serve the parishes of Taney and Cruagh are on the site formerly occupied by a church dating back to the time of the Anglo-Norman invasion. The founder is said to be St Gobban who had an early monastery, Cell Gobban, here and whose feast day is the first of April. It has even been attributed to An Gobán Saor, the well-known architect and builder in stone who was born in the sixth century. The earliest mention of this church was in 1179 as Technabretnach, translated in 1530 by Archbishop Alen in a note as 'the house of the Welshmen'.

The church, which occupies a scenic position in the centre of an elevated site, remained in use until 1826 when the new church in Kilternan was built on another site. The Board of Works carried out basic repair work on the structure such as pointing. Some of the older slabs within the church are unfortunately daubed with paint.

One of the former rectors was a colourful personality. He was the Reverend Patrick Crawley who succeeded in 1772 and had the distinction of being the tutor of Sir Jonah Barrington the historian, judge and writer. Like his pupil, Crawley was quite a remarkable character and is described by Barrington in his *Personal Recollections* as a man in knowledge excelled by few, but singular in his movements from his immense size and peculiarity of dress. In his time, the collection of tithes was unattended with danger, and although content to accept less than his due, Crawley nearly lost his life on one occasion while out with his collector.

Close to the entrance of the old churchyard is a fine twelfth-century ringed granite cross [Nat Mon] about ten feet high on a square base which has a bullaun on the south west side. The cross was found buried in the graveyard in the middle of the last century. Nearly half of the upper part has been broken off. On the east face is the Crucifixion in low relief, while on the west face a figure of Christ may be seen clad in a loose garment reaching down to the ankles.

On the outside wall outside on the right-hand side of the entrance gate of the churchyard is a metal plaque to the Richardson family. Their vault is cut deep into the side of the slope. The inscription reads:

138

The | family vault of | John Richardson | Kilgobbin

John Richardson, a mason and builder, was a churchwarden of Kilgobbin Church in the 1820s. He was also contractor for the new Church in Kilternan. Later on, his family were landowners and farmers in the district.

Of interest to military historians is the tall cross on the western edge of the churchyard which commemorates the brave men from the locality who were killed in the First World War. To read the inscription on the plaque, it is necessary to descend three small granite steps. These are adjacent to the cross but are hidden by briars. They lead on to a little railed-in balcony, which overlooks a large field:

Hoc Sig | In Vin | In memory of | the officers and men of this district who fell in the Great War, 1914, 1918 | Royal Field Artillery. | Lieut. Eric Manly, John Casey, | Royal Garrison Artillery. | Lieut. Richard Talbot Scallan. | Royal Engineers. | Edward Grady | Irish Guards. | John Quinn, Denis Doyle, John Doyle, Edward Byrne, | Edward Farrell, William Murphy | Queen's Royal West Surrey Regt. | John Brennan | Royal Irish Regt. | Andrew Belton, George Mason. | Royal Inniskilling Fusiliers. | Lieut. E. Arthur Trouton, W.S. Collen | Duke of Cornwall's Light Infantry | Hugh Dwyer | Royal Irish Rifles. | Christopher Mulligan. | Royal Irish Fusiliers. | John Redmond, Michael Carey | Connaught Rangers. | William Murphy. | Argyll and Sutherland Highlanders. | John Carey. | Royal Dublin Fusiliers. | Lieut. William Symes Drury, Laurence Mooney, George Mahon | Philip O'Connor, William Gatercole, Joseph Doyle | Machine Gun Corps. | David Nolan | 50th Batt Canadians | James Dwyer.

Within the confines of the ruined church, is a slab resting on the ground, which is enclosed by railings. In it are the remains of the Reverend Henry Kearney who was rector of Kilternan parish for thirty-six years.

Sacred to the memory of | the Reverend Henry Kearney, A.M. | for 36 years rector of Kilternan parish | who died the 6th day of June 1855 in the 72nd year of his age | a devoted soldier of Jesus Christ | when few were on the Lord's side | he contended boldly against error | a faithful shepherd of his Master's fold | he led his flock in heavenly pastures | and while thus walking in the fear of God | he won the respect and love of men. | Underneath also rest the remains of his wife | Mrs Elizabeth Kearney who departed this life the 15th day of May 1834 | Blessed are the dead which die in the Lord from henceforth | Yea saith the spirit and one may rest from their labours and their works do follow them.

There are a number of families from the immediate locality interred within the confines of the ruin. They include the Cuthbert sisters who lived in Kilgobbin. Their grave, which is located at the north side, reads:

139

[42] THE TWELFTH-CENTURY RINGED GRANITE CROSS NEAR THE ENTRANCE TO THE OLD KILGOBBIN CHURCHYARD.

In memory | of | Jessy Barbara Cuthbert | who died 15th February 1875 | aged 61 years | Also of | Cecilia Margretta Cuthbert | who died 15th August 1881 | Aged 72 years.

A railed in horizontal slab commemorates the Bayly family, substantial landowners, also from Kilgobbin:

Here rest | the mortal remains of | Ellen Letitia | Second daughter of Emmanuel James Bayly | of this parish esquire and | Margaret Eleanor his wife | born January 18th 1837 | died June 9th 1853 | Here also is interred | William Bernard Bayly | an infant child of the above parents | born March 5th 1842 | died August 6th 1842 | Also Alice Isabel Smith | who died August 12th 1877 | aged 8 months | Emanuel Bayly | born March 16th 1810 | died March 25th 1877.

In the south-east corner is a vertical memorial to the Strong family of Glenamuck. It reads:

Here rests | with her husband | Joseph Strong | and her mother Elizabeth Houston | Elizabeth Strong | born October 15th 1785. Died September 2nd 1873 | Then are they glad because they are at rest and so | he bringeth them into the heaven where they would be | Psalm cviii. 30.

Inside the west wall is a memorial to Thomas Callaghan, a farmer who died on 19 October 1780 aged seventy-two years. He was actually buried outside the church, but his memorial was moved inside when the church fell into disuse. Some time before his demise, he had passed his large farm on to his son Robert. Tragically, Robert died before his father aged forty-two and is buried close to the outside wall of the west side of the church.

This stone was erected in memory | of Mr Robert Callaghan late of | Kilgobbin, farmer who | lieth here | interred and departed this life | the 5th day of May 1779 | aged 42 years.

In the churchyard itself there are monuments to the Trumbles of Woodside dating from 1801, the Deakins from 1721 to 1821, the Millikens from 1799 to 1883, members of the Davis family from 1740 to 1927, the Taylors of Harold's Grange from 1727 to 1892 and the Harknesses from 1794 to 1901.

Towards the western side is a large railed-in horizontal slab [one of three] to members of the Prior family. The long inscription commences in Latin and continues:

Robert Young Prior, T.P. S.T.C.D | Here also are buried | Revd Hugh Edward Prior, rector of Clonmel | who died 1st Sep 1856 aged 50 years | Second son of above named Thomas Prior D.D. Vice Provost T.C.D. Meriel Neville wife of H.E. Prior | who died 5th March 1890 aged 86 years. | Meriel Anna third daughter of H.E. Prior | who died 13th Oct. 1856 aged 18 years. | Here also is | Mary S. Phillips | died 16th Feb. 1894 aged 85 years. | Widow of Richard E Phillips of Mount Rivers, Newport Co. Tip. | only daughter of Revd Thos Prior D.D. Vice Provost T.C.D. | Blessed are the dead which die in the Lord.

There are a number of memorials, which are hidden beneath the ground in this churchyard. Some of the remaining slabs are damaged and are difficult to read.

Kilgobbin Churchyard was closed by Ministerial Order in 1905. It is under the care of Dublin County Council.

Kilgobbin (New)

Situation: Kilgobbin on the Enniskerry Road

Period in use: From the 1920s. [now closed except to those with burial rights]

Bus No (from city centre): 44. Alight at Kilgobbin Lane

Enclosed by a granite wall, this cemetery is located on the eastern side of the slope of the Old Kilgobbin churchyard.

Like most cemeteries, Kilgobbin has its share of military men and casualties of war. A small limestone cross marks the resting place of:

Charles Henry Freeman, | Late Royal Irish Regiment, | Died 4 March 1950

There are six small limestone crosses in a row to the Manly family, some of whom were military men. The family had casualties in both world wars:

In Memory of Eric Manly, | Lieut. R.F.A. | Aged 21 | Killed in action near Ypres | 18 July 1917 | Ubique Quo Fas et Gloria dicunt Also

Lt. Col. L.A. Manly M.C. | Lancashire Fusiliers | Killed in Action in | North Africa 28 November, 1942

A marble stone marks the resting-place of Private Mcdermott:

In fond memory | of | Pte. Michael Jos Macdermott | South Saskatchewan Regt [Canada] | died 5th Aug. 1945 of wounds | received in action in | East Holland | aged 24 years | RIP.

An inscription carved in granite commemorates:

The Peace of God | which passeth | understanding | Herbert Maxwell | Lenox-Conyngham | Bt Lt

Colonel D.S.C. A.V.C. | died March 15, 1918, aged 47. | 'Nothing is here for tears, | Nothing but well and fair | And what may quiet us in a death so noble.'

A simple limestone memorial marks the grave of Hilary Heron:

Hilary | Heron | 1925–1977 | Sculptor

Much of her early work was carved in wood. In 1956 she represented Ireland with Louis Le Brocquy at the Venice Biennale.

Some of the residents from neighbouring houses are interred here, such as Edmund Darley from nearby Fernhill and Boss Croker of Glencairn.

[43] THE SIMPLE MEMORIAL TO HILARY HERON, SCULPTOR.

In loving memory of | Edmund Sanders Darley | of Fern Hill | born on 26 October 1846 | died 27 September 1912. | Rest in the Lord | looking for that Blessed hope and the | glorious appearing of the great God | and our Saviour Jesus Christ

Fernhill is situated on the north-east slope of the Three Rock mountain on the Enniskerry road. The Darleys were builders and some members of the family were architects. There was also Judge William Darley who created a magnificent garden and collected plants from all over the world.

Many of the trees in the estate date back two hundred years and some other plants were introduced from the Himalayas by the William Hooker expedition. The giant Wellingtonian redwoods are particularly spectacular. In the 1930s, the Darley property passed to the Walker family, who continued the tradition of plant collecting. The garden at Fernhill is open to the public.

A tall, carved limestone cross marks the burial place of the well-known local character, 'Boss' Croker:

In loving memory of | Stella Bowman | of Glencairn | born March 24 1868 | died June 1914. | R.I.P. On slab: Richard Welsted Croker | born Nov. 23rd 1841 | at Clonakilty, County Cork, Ireland | died at Glencairn, April 29th – 1922 | R.I.P.

Croker's family emigrated from Cork to the United States when he was a small boy. He made a lot of money in dubious circumstances and had an unsuccessful marriage which produced two sons and two daughters. Both sons died tragically, one in a car accident and the other from a drug overdose. Eventually Croker fled to Berkshire in England. He imported a string of American-bred racehorses and employed Charles Morton, one of the most successful trainers of the day. However, the English racing fraternity did not accept Croker. He returned to Tammanay Hall for a period before coming back to Ireland. In 1904 he bought Glencairn, a fine house designed by Benjamin Woodward [subsequently the residence of the

British Ambassador]. He acquired a lot of land around the house, where he set up a racing stables, a stud and quite magnificent gallops where he had his horses trained.

In 1907 Croker had great success with his horse, Orby, which won the Epsom Derby, the Baldoyle Plate and the Irish Derby. Since then, only twelve horses have managed the Derby double. Croker was a Catholic and belonged to the faith of the majority of the country. On winning the Epsom Derby one old lady quipped, 'Thank God…we have lived to see a Catholic horse win the Derby'. Boss Croker was conferred with the Freedom of the City of Dublin after Orby's English Derby win.

Mrs Croker, who had refused to grant her husband a divorce, died in America in September 1914. Boss, then aged seventy-two, travelled to her funeral and returned a few weeks later to Ireland with his new bride Beulah Edmonson, a twenty-three-year-old Cherokee Indian princess!

[44] View of Kilgobbin Churchyard showing the Boss Croker memorial in the centre.

Croker died aged eighty-one in the winter of 1922. Mass was said in his private chapel in Glencairn. The pall-bearers included his wife, Arthur Griffith, Oliver St John Gogarty and Alfie Byrne. He was interred in an unusual casket, which contained a window on one side. He was wearing his full morning attire. A tomb made of Barnacuilla granite was constructed at Glencairn into which this casket was placed. Croker had requested that the bones of his beloved horse Orby, who died in 1918, should be exhumed and reburied beside him. Orby is buried in the grounds of Glencairn alongside Rhoda B, its dam.

The next occupants of the house decided to remove the Croker casket from Glencairn, but the key was missing and the granite could not be dismantled. So a local man opened the tomb and Croker was removed to Kilgobbin, where he is buried with his former housekeeper, Stella Bowman, who it is rumoured was somewhat more than a housekeeper.

Boss Croker once remarked that Sundays in Dublin were very cheerful.

On Sunday mornings the funerals enliven the streets leading to Prospect Cemetery. Forty, fifty, or sixty cabs and outside cars with four to six passengers in each often follow a single hearse. And as time goes on, so great is the anxiety to arrive before the gates are shut, that three funerals will race up Sackville Street three abreast, each trying to be the first to make the narrow Cavendish Row. I've often stood at Nelson's Pillar and enjoyed it better than Baldoyle or the Curragh. Sure, where do you think I first saw Orby's Mother!

In an unmarked grave near Croker's is the burial place of the unfortunate Lizzie O'Neill, a lady of the night who had lodgings in a house at Newmarket in the Liberties. Known as Honour Bright, her body was found lying on the road to Ticknock on 9 June 1925. This is a very tragic story of the unclaimed body of a murdered victim.

This graveyard is under the care of Dublin County Council.

KILLESTER CHURCHYARD

SITUATION: KILLESTER AVENUE, DUBLIN 5

PERIOD IN USE: UNKNOWN. THE GRAVEYARD WAS CLOSED IN 1876

BUS NOS (FROM CITY CENTRE): 27 AND 27B. DART TO KILLESTER STATION

The churchyard of Killester is situated on Killester Avenue, which once formed part of the famous 'green lanes'. Formerly known as Killester Lane, this area was the last portion of the ancient route to the sea. It is off the Howth Road and three miles from Dublin city centre.

The name Killester derives from the ancient name *Quillesra*, or in Irish *Cill Esra*, which means the church of Esra.

Until 1934, it contained the remains of a chapel dedicated to St Brigid, the virgin abbess, who was born in the sixth century at Foghart near Dundalk. This medieval little chapel, like its sister church in Raheny, probably fell into a ruinous state with the suppression of the monasteries around 1536. Some years ago, Lewis gave a description of 'some remains of the church, which, from its circular arches, appears to be very ancient'. He also described the parish 'commanding fine views of the Dublin and Wicklow Mountains, and of the Bay of Dublin'. There were several large houses in the area such as Killester House, Maryville, Woodville, Hollybrook House and Hollybrook Park.

A new church, which was built in 1924 on another site nearby on the Howth Road, Killester, contains a relic of St Brigid.

Before reaching the churchyard, there is a high old wall which formerly encompassed part of Lord Howth's estate. A partially ivy covered wall encompasses the old churchyard. Leaning against the outside wall by the footpath is a small stone, which commemorates Michael Neville, a native of Clare who was executed in the churchyard during the civil war in 1922.

Nothing remains of the old church, not even the ruin described by Lewis. The churchyard looks slightly unkempt. This is due to the fact that roughly half of it has sunk to a lower level which creates a large hollow. This is filled with rocks and stones. The remainder contains a number of memorials dating back to the 1700s. A few are still upright, the rest are lying on the ground and some dating to the 1700s are buried in the rubble. A number of those interred here were involved in various trades:

There is one for instance to a Mr James Gernon from the City of Dublin who was what was termed as a 'Linnen Draper'. As his memorial was partly sunk his dates are unknown.

146

James Byrne a 'Glover' from Fishamble Street in the City, erected a memorial to his wife, Rebecca Byrne. She died on 18 December 1737.

Another memorial containing no dates is that of a Cooper. It reads:

This stone and Burial Place Belongeth to Mr Edward Banon of the City of Dublin Cooper and his posterity. Here lieth 4 of his children and 3 of his grandchildren.

Then there is a memorial to a mason:

Here Lyeth the Body of Pouck Quinn, Mason Who departed this life June the 14. 1773

William Dowling, a vintner from Little Strand Street in the City of Dublin, erected a memorial to Margaret, his eighteen-year-old daughter, who died on 6 May 1792.

Samuel Edwards, a merchant from Drogheda Street, erected a memorial to his wife Mary, who died on 25 March 1784, and to fourteen of her children.

There is also a memorial to Patrick Meade of George's Hill in the City of Dublin, who died aged fifty-five on 19 December 1821. It also mentions his son, Master Thomas Meade, who was a student for six years in the Jesuit College of Kildare. It states 'his talents could not be surpassed by any of his age, his conduct was exemplary ...'

The churchyard is locked and is under the care of Dublin Corporation, Environmental Section.

[45] THE MEMORIAL STONE ON THE OUTSIDE WALL OF KILLESTER GRAVEYARD, TO MICHAEL NEVILLE WHO WAS EXECUTED IN 1922.

Killiney Church and Churchyard (old) (national monument)

Situation: Marine Avenue West, off Killiney Hill Road, Killiney, Co. Dublin

Period in use: unknown

DART (from city centre): to Killiney Station

Killiney derives its name from Cill Inghean Leinin, meaning the church of the daughters of Leinin. This indicates that these five holy women who are said to have flourished in about the sixth century founded the church.

This sixth century monastic site is on the descent of a hill overlooking the sea. It is best reached by walking up to the top of the laneway, which is almost opposite the DART station. The church, which was in use until the seventeenth century, is now a ruin. It possibly dates from the eleventh or twelfth century and consists of a nave and chancel with the later addition many centuries later of an aisle on the northern side.

An unusual feature is the small Greek cross carved in relief on the soffit or underside of the lintel over the square doorway at the western end. Even though there are a few houses in the area, the small narrow lancet shaped east window in the chancel has a beautiful and uninterrupted sea view. The north aisle contains a baptismal font and an early Christian granite cross which is affixed to the wall. After the dissolution of the monasteries, the church was given to the Dean of Christ Church, and was served in the sixteenth century, by the chaplains of Dalkey.

A fine granite wall encompasses the churchyard. There is a gravel path around the perimeter with a few seats placed at intervals. Interspersed with an old yew and some holly trees, is a number of young trees, which have now been planted and certainly enhance the place.

Over the years, many of the memorials in this churchyard were covered up. Others, on account of their antiquity and decoration, unfortunately went missing. One of the oldest decipherable memorials bears the following inscription:

This stone was erected by Patrick Burk of Castle Town Delvin, Co. Westmeath, in memory of his brother John Who departed this life July 30 1791 aged 39 years.

[46] KILLINEY CHURCH AND CHURCHYARD.

There are several people from the surrounding areas, such as Monkstown, Kingstown, and Dalkey. The first is a clergyman:

Here lieth the remains of the Revd Dudley Ryves late
Minister of the parish of Monckstown and its Unions.
Dept. this life March ye second 1801.

Erected by Thomas Masterson of Ballybrack in memory of
His father and Mother and Brothers Christopher and William AD 1861

This stone was erected by Jms. Maher of Kingstown in
mem. of his beloved brother John Maher who dept. this
life 28 April 1828 aged 26 years.

Erected by Elizabeth Bryan of Dalkey in memory of her
Beloved husband Bartholomew Kavanagh died
22 May 1857 aged 57 years. Also 5 of his
Beloved children who died young.

A little plaque, once on the wall near the entrance gate, summed up the antiquity of this monastic site in the following words,

Petrie dates this gem of early Irish churches from the sixth century. Here for 1000 years God was worshipped by Gael, Dane and Norman, united by their one Faith. Many of them rest beneath the shade of its venerable and hallowed walls.

The churchyard, which is locked, is kept neat and tidy and is under the care of the Select Vestry of Killiney. The Corporation of Dún Laoghaire maintains it.

[47] AN EARLY-CHRISTIAN CROSS IN KILLINEY CHURCH.

Kill o' the Grange Church and Churchyard (St Fintan's — National Monument)

Situation: Clonkeen, Co. Dublin

Period in use: Unknown. Closed by Ministerial Order in 1864

Bus Nos (from city centre): 45 (Eden Quay) or 46a (Fleet Street)

The name of Kill o' the Grange or Dean's Grange derives its name from the fact that in the Middle Ages the land was owned by the Augustinian Canons of the Priory of the Holy Trinity which had one of its farms or granges here. With the Reformation, when the Priory became secularised, the last Prior became the first Dean of the reorganised Cathedral now named Christ Church. The farm came to be known as the Dean's Grange.

The entrance gate to the ruined St Fintan's Church and churchyard, which is encircled by a high stone wall, is kept locked. Although a National Monument, it is not signposted. It is situated adjacent to the Kill Abbey housing estate, which is just off Kill Lane. Nearby is the original old house named 'Kill Abbey' which has lost its original characteristics but bears the date 1595. Between this house, which is west of the churchyard, and outside the boundary wall of the churchyard, is a bullaun stone half-sunken into the grass. There was also a well in the same area, which was covered over.

St Fintan founded the original church in the sixth century. The chancel was added possibly as late as the sixteenth century. The doorway and belfry were later additions. The church was among the churches allotted to the Priory of the Holy Trinity and was first mentioned in 1179. The Priory had extensive tracts of land ranging from the foot of the Three Rock Mountain right down to the sea at Killiney.

The graveyard contained a number of items of great historical interest, such as a circular flat stone with a Greek cross; a cross-inscribed slab wrecked by vandals, and also what was described as a 'small triangular fragment with an incised equal-armed cross 13 cm wide with splayed extremities'. Sadly, these are now gone. A number of the remaining gravestones have been daubed with paint. Most of the people interred here were from the immediate neighbourhood of Kill o' the Grange, Kingstown, Newtown Park, Monkstown, Blackrock, Cabinteely, Williamstown and Bray.

Some of the older stones include memorials to members of the Finigan and Runnell families. The stones bear the inscriptions:

Here lieth the body of Jane Finigan who departed this life 12th day of September 1692. And also here lieth ye body of Peter Finigan who departed this life the 12th day of June 1694. This stone was caused to be made by Brian Finigan for him and his posteritie. Also the body of Mrs Judith Butler alias Finigan who departed this life 14th Oct. 1790 aged 75 years.

Here lieth the body of Mathias Runnell deceased November 20th 1760 aged 76.

[48] St Fintan's Church and Graveyard, Kill o' the Grange, County Dublin.

Two stones bear coats of arms. These include memorials to members of the Byrne and Hinchy families:

Sacred to the memory of Robert Byrne Esq of Cabinteely who was born in Dublin on the 20 May 1768 and died in Buonos Ayries in Lisbon on Monday 7th January 1799 after a long and tedious illness. He was married on Sunday the 7th January 1790 to Mary only daughter of Robert Devereux Esq of Carigmessan Co.Wexford by whom he had issue Mary Clare, Clarinda Margaret and Georgina Mary Byrne.

This Stone and Burial Place Belongeth to David Hinchy Esq of Rockville in the County of Dublin. Here Lieth the Body of the above David Hinchy who dept. this life May 8th 1820 aged 80y.

One memorial of military interest refers to Edward Timmons who died in the Crimea:

Erected by Thomas Timmons in memory of his beloved Father and Mother, John and Mary Timmons and also his brother Edward Timmons died in the Crimea. Above Thomas Timmons his beloved wife Rosanna. Also their children Mary, Peter, Margaret and Rosanna who died young.

A rather sad inscription of a young man, Robert King, who died a few years after the opening of the railway line from Dublin to Kingstown follows:

Erected by William King in memory of his beloved son Robert C. King who was killed at the Blackrock Railway Station Dec. 11th 1858 aged 17 years.

This churchyard is under the care of Dublin County Council, Environment Department, Sandyford Depot, Sandyford Industrial Estate.

KILTERNAN CHURCHYARD (OLD)

SITUATION: BISHOP'S LANE, OFF GLENCULLEN ROAD, KILTERNAN, CO. DUBLIN

PERIOD IN USE: UNKNOWN. CLOSED BY MINISTERIAL ORDER IN 1948

BUS NO (FROM CITY CENTRE): 44. ALIGHT AT THE WOODEN CHURCH OF OUR LADY OF THE WAYSIDE. PROCEED UP GLENCULLEN ROAD FOR ABOUT 500 METRES TO BISHOP'S LANE, A CUL-DE-SAC THAT IS SITUATED OFF A SHARP BEND

This small, pleasant and scenic churchyard, which has a backdrop of mountains, is surrounded by a granite wall on three sides. The fourth side at the end of a slope is encircled by a row of deciduous trees, beyond which there is a bridge and small stream. There is both a gateway and a stile on the northern wall that fronts Bishop's Lane. The ground level was raised considerably due to the many interments in the cemetery.

The ruins of an early Christian church remain. Little is known of the history of St Tighernach, or Tighernan, who has been attributed to the foundation of the church and whose feast day is celebrated on 8 April. He was born in Errew in the parish of Crossmolina in Co. Mayo and flourished towards the close of the fifth century.

The MacGillamocholmogs family, a clan who had long ruled South County Dublin, was the owner of Kilternan at the time of the Anglo-Norman invasion, and by befriending the invaders, was allowed to retain the land. Some time later, the ruling chief of the clan granted Kilternan to William de Carrew, an Anglo-Irish Norman who in turn gave it to the monks of St Mary's Abbey. It is likely that this church was served by one of its members. During the thirteenth and fourteenth centuries, the parish would have been subjected to raids by the Irish who lived in the mountains close to the border of the Pale. In the fourteenth century, a disagreement with their neighbour, the Harolds of Kilgobben, over the precise boundaries of the Abbey's lands, led to an enquiry. Kilternan remained in the ownership of the monks until the dissolution of the monasteries by Henry VIII.

The church, which does not have a chancel, is a simple oblong structure. There is little mortar in evidence, a common feature of early Irish churches. The square-headed doorway at the west end is now blocked up. On the south window of the church is a round, hollowed stone which is perforated. W.F. Wakeman has described it as 'a very remarkable relic of ecclesiastical furniture'. It was found near the church and was probably used as a baptismal font.

154

Within the confines of the church, there are six headstones. In the churchyard itself, thirty-three memorials remain. Of the memorials with discernible dates, fifteen date back to the 1700s. Many of these are extremely difficult to read. The earliest would seem to be to Darby Byrn, which is in the confines of the church. Follow the pathway to the church and turn right on entering. There is a group of four erect stones in a row and it is the third one out from the wall. It is in poor condition.

IHS | Here lieth ye body | of Darby Byrn | who dyed Jan 2(7?) | 1727 aged 6(0?)years | Also his wife Ann | Byrn who dyed | Decm ye 10 1729 | aged 5(6?)years.

Another Byrne whose stone is also in poor condition is in the confines of the church almost directly in front of the entrance:

IHS | This stone and bur(ial) | place belongeth to Murr | agh. John Byrne, brothers. | Here lieth the body (of) | John Byrne who dep | arted this | life June | the 7 aged 65 years | Also Murragh Byrne | who departed this | life August the 29 | 1779 aged 74 yers | God be mercyfull | to their souls and | their posterirty.

Tucked in the north west corner of the church is a granite stone :

IHS | This stone and | burial place be | longeth to Joh | n Lynch and his | posterity. Hea | re lieth the b | ody of Owne | Caffary whoe | departed thi | s life the 29 of | September 17 | 62 aged 18 year | s

In this churchyard the older memorials are mainly made of granite. There were a number of stonecutters working in the vicinity especially around Glencullen, where there were a few small granite quarries. Samuel Beckett who walked frequently in this area with his father mentions them in his works. In 'First Love' 'I saw the mountain, impassable, cavernous, secret, where from morning to night I'd hear nothing but the wind, the curlews, the clink like distant silver of the stone-cutters' hammers' and again in *Malone Dies* 'The hammers on the stone-cutters ring all day like bells.'

A local stonecutter erected a stone to the memory of his father. It is rare for the place of origin of the person to be commemorated inscribed on the memorial.

Gloria in Excelsis Deo | IHS | Memento Mori | This stone was erected by | Mathew Plunket of Kilgobbin in the | County of Dublin Stonecutter to | the Memory of his father Michl Plunket | who departed this life March the 20th 1806 | aged 42 years | Also two of his sisters who died young

A man with the unusual name of Daniall Grumbly, who was born in 1698, is commemorated on an erect stone outside the south wall of the church that tilts slightly forward:

Here lieth the Body | of Daniall Grumbly | who departed This | Life November the 1 | 1758 Aged 60 years | Also his son Simon Grum | bly who departed this | life April the 16th 1797 | aged 66 years.

A small narrow stone commemorates a person with yet another unusual name:

Heare | lieth | the body | of Mary | Naile a | nd her | poster | ety | 1759

The names of Byrne and Doyle seem the most popular with four memorials to each of these names.
One fine yew tree remains in the churchyard.
This churchyard is under the care of Dublin County Council.

KILTERNAN CHURCHYARD (NEW)

SITUATION: ENNISKERRY ROAD, KILTERNAN, CO. DUBLIN

PERIOD IN USE: C.1841 TO DATE

BUS NO (FROM CITY CENTRE): 44. ALIGHT AT BUS STOP FOR JAMESTOWN HOUSE

Situated against a backdrop of mountains and a view of the sea to the fore this churchyard is neat and well kept.

The parishes of Kilgobbin and Kilternan were united by an Act of Parliament in 1824. John Semple, who was the architect for this church [Church of Ireland] designed about fifteen churches for the dioceses of Dublin, Kildare, Ossory, Ferns and Leighlin.

Kilternan church was erected in 1826. It displays the typical Semple features, which are narrow lancet windows between buttresses and a slender tower supporting a narrow spire. It cost £1,900, of which £900 was a gift from the Board of First Fruits, £500 from Lord Powerscourt, and £500 raised by assessment. It served Kilgobbin parish when the church there fell into disuse.

There are some interesting memorials inside the church, which include a small stained-glass panel attributed to Austin Molloy which was presented to Kilternan church by Major R.H.C. and Mrs Green of Sandyford.

Three former rectors of the parish are also commemorated. These include Edward Hughes, DD rector from 1879 to 1894; Thomas Arthur MacMurrough the O'Morchoe who was rector of the parish for twenty-eight years until 1921 and who is commemorated with a window erected by his parishioners and friends. Canon Francis Ernest Byrn who was rector from 1922 to 1951 (wooden plaque) and a marble plaque in the church porch commemorates the Reverend William Newcombe Vickers, incumbent of the parish of Kilternan, who died on the 25 November 1857 aged forty-two years.

Some families from the locality who are interred in the churchyard also have memorials within the church. These include the Jellett family who lived in the neighbourhood of Sandyford. They have three memorials which consist of a staircase and brass plate under a window which commemorate Hewitt Poole Jellett, 'KC Serjeant-at-law' who died 10 March 1911. There is also a gallery in the church which is in loving memory of Phyllis (bluebell) Jellett who died on 10 August 1907, aged four and a half years.

Edmund Sanders Darley, late of Fernhill, whose grave is in Kilgobbin Cemetery (new) is also commemorated here. There is also a window and a bell in the tower in memory of the Rt Hon Mr Justice Murphy of Glencairn who died on 5 September 1901.

Of military interest is the memorial window by the artist, Sir Ninian Comper, to Lieut Edmund Arthur Trouton of the Inniskilling Fusiliers who was killed in action at Thiepual, France on 1 July 1916 aged twenty-four years.

There are approximately two hundred and twenty memorials in the churchyard. Most comprise families from the area such as Walker and Rutherford. There are four Jellett memorials in a row.

[50] KILTERNAN CHURCH AND CHURCHYARD.

Nearby are graves with the following inscriptions:

In dearest memory of | Mary Moore Hughes | daughter of | Rev E Hughes DD | Later rector of this parish | At rest Sept 11th 1915 | When the even was come, Jesus saith | Let us pass over unto the other side.

In | Loving memory | of | Lt. Col. Vernon Beadon MC | I.A. Burma Commission | Died 14th August 1985 | Aged 82 years | And of his wife | Beryl Edith Beadon | Died Dec. 1947

Just inside the entrance gate there is a memorial to The O'Morchoe which reads:

In Christ | Arthur MacMurrough Murphy | The O'Morchoe | Died March 7th 1918 aged 83 years | And his wife | Susan Elizabeth | Died April 23rd 1924 aged 83? Thomas Arthur MacMurrough / The O'Morchoe | Rector of this Parish for 28 years | Died Nov 18th 1921 aged 56 | And of his wife | Anne | Died Feb 26th 1958, aged 86 | And of their 2nd son | Lt. Col. Kenneth Gibbon O'Morchoe | Died Dec 22nd, 1962 aged 68.

Filling the corner inside the exit gate of the churchyard is a raised flower bed with granite stones which contains a variety of lovely plants:

Planted | In memory of | Jessie O'Morchoe | 1898–1987

This is imaginative and adds a nice touch to the churchyard.

This churchyard is under the care of the Select Vestry of Kilternan.

159

MERRION CEMETERY (BELLEVUE)

SITUATION: MERRION ROAD, DUBLIN 4

THIS CEMETERY IS SITUATED ON THE LEFT-HAND SIDE OF BELLEVUE AVENUE, WHICH ADJOINS THE TARA TOWERS HOTEL ON THE MERRION ROAD. IT IS HIDDEN DIRECTLY BEHIND THE PETROL FILLING STATION

PERIOD IN USE: FROM CIRCA 1300–1866

BUS NOS (FROM CITY CENTRE): 5, 7, 7A, 8, 45

The cemetery, which is bounded on three sides by a wall, is almost square in shape. A fence is on the remaining side. It is not known when it was consecrated or by whom. In 1978 it was turned into a public park which is under the care of Dublin Corporation. A pathway runs around the perimeter. It contains a few trees one of which is a yew.

Originally there was a church here which is supposed to have been erected by Sir John Cruise of Merrion Castle in the fourteenth century. Dalton in 1837 states that 'the old church presents some few but insignificant remains, in the middle of a graveyard most scandalously open to every species of insult and desecration'. Nothing of the church remains today.

Later in 1894 when the Revd R.S. Maffett copied the grave inscriptions, he wrote that there had been no burials in the graveyard since it was closed thirty years before. At that time it contained a good many trees and was in fair condition. At some places there was a quantity of minute bones appearing on the surface. According to the Revd Beaver H. Blacker 'three letters descriptive of the wretched state of this burial place appeared in *Saunders News-Letter* on the 19th, 25th and 31st May, 1865'.

This cemetery is best known for the fact that it contains the remains of the soldiers who perished in the transport packet the *Prince of Wales* which departed Kingstown harbour along with two large transports on Wednesday morning the 18 November 1807. There were one hundred and twenty passengers on board. The following day, amidst one of the worst snowstorms ever remembered, the *Prince of Wales* was observed heaving about the bay and trying to return towards the harbour. As darkness fell, the gale increased in its ferocity with the boat firing several distress signals for help to no avail. The gale was too bad and no assistance was forthcoming from the shore. One hour before midnight, the *Prince of Wales* struck rocks off Seapoint and sank. Of the one hundred and twenty passengers on board, most were recruits of the eighteenth regiment under the care of Lieutenant McClean who drowned with his fellow soldiers. At dawn on 20 November, the scene along the shore must have been quite horrific.

From this shipwreck only Captain Jones, some of the crew and two officers escaped. The captain launched the long boat and rowed off as quickly as possible! Before doing so, he is alleged to have removed the ladder leading from the hold to the deck, thus depriving the passengers below of an escape route. After the inquest, Captain Jones, along with the mate and steward, were arrested on a charge of murder for the removal of the ladders as the crew made good their escape. Eventually, the Crown found the evidence to be insufficient and abandoned the proceedings.

[51] A VIEW OF MERRION CEMETERY.

[52] THE MEMORIAL TO THE SOLDIERS WHO PERISHED ON 19 NOVEMBER 1807 WHEN THE *PRINCE OF WALES* WAS SHIP-WRECKED OFF SEAPOINT.

The memorial, which is now barely legible, is on the gravel pathway close to the north boundary wall, on the right-hand side of the entrance gate:

Sacred | to the memory of the Soldiers | belonging to his Majestys 18th Regiment[sic] of Foot and a few belonging to other | Corps who actuated by a desire of mor[e]Extensive Service NoblyVolunteered[sic] | from the South Mayo and different | regiments[sic]of Irish Militia into the line | and who were unfortunately Shipwrecked[sic]on this Coast in the Prince of Wales Packet | and Perished[sic]on the Night of the 19th of | November 1807 this Tribute to their | Memory has been placed on their Tomb | by order of General the | Earl of Harrington | Commander of the Forces in Ireland.

162

Although this burial ground dates back to the 1300s, as usual many of the memorials are now missing. Only sixty-six remain and many of these are upright memorials. There are six slabs on the ground, some of which are partly broken, and one slab, which is on four supports.

One of the earliest inscriptions on a memorial is dated 1692. Charles J. Wallace and F. Elrington Ball transcribed it in the late 1800s. It reads:

Riley IHS | This buriall place | belongs to Thomas | Riley Patrick Riley | Richard Rialey and | theyer posterit y | March the 25 1711- | Here lieth the | body of Fargvs | Riley who depart | ed this life the 18 | day of March 1692.

A limestone cross commemorates:

IHS | This burial Place | belongeth to | Charlis Reilly & | his posterity 171[Broken] | His daughter Ca | thrine died Sep | the 2nd 1721.

Another older memorial of granite is:

+IHS. Here lies the | body of Willm Daily who | died May 20th 1774 aged 53 years.

+IHS This stone & burial | place belongeth to Morgan Ryan | for him and his pos | terity. | Here lyeth ye body of Charles Ryan son to | Morgan Ryan who depart | ed this life ye 28th June 1726.

The following entry is of interest as it refers to Butterstown. In various old documents the parish of Booterstown is termed Ballybotter, Ballyboother, Butterstown and Boterstone.

Glory in Excelis Deo | This stone was erected by Ann Tully [of?] Butterstown Lane in memory of her | [belove?]d husband Stephen Tully who | [departed this?]life the 22nd Jany 1815 \ [aged?]46 years. (Gravestone now missing).

IHS. | This stone and burial place be | longeth to Mr Andrew Purcell of | Georges Quay rope maker & his | posterity erected 1780. Here lieth ye | body of his father and mother Thos & | Mary Purcell & too [two] of the above Andrews | children Thos & Martha.

The precise date of the closure of this graveyard was 1 May 1866. It is now under the care of Dublin Corporation.

MERRION ROW BURIAL GROUND (HUGUENOT)

SITUATION: 10 MERRION ROW, DUBLIN 2

PERIOD IN USE: 1693–1901

SITUATED IN CITY CENTRE

Covered in a mass of bluebells in the spring, this little cemetery situated in Merrion Row is the oldest Huguenot non-conformist cemetery in Europe. The two Huguenot non-conformist churches in Dublin were the Chapel of St Brigide's which was in a private rented house in Wood Street off Bride Street and the Chapel of Lucy Lane (now Chancery Place). Some ground near Newmarket was obtained as a cemetery attached to St Brigide's church, but no trace of it now remains. This congregation moved to Peter Street in 1711.

Towards the end of the seventeenth century, the Huguenot congregation at Bride Street acquired their own cemetery at Merrion Row adjoining St Stephen's Green. Definite boundaries of St Stephen's Green were still unmarked on *Sir William Petty's Map* of 1655. Nine years later, the Corporation needed funds and eighty-six lots on the perimeter of the Green were leased out to tenants for building. The area of St Stephen gave way to St Stephen's Green when the leases for the plots were perfected in the autumn of 1664.

In 1693, Lot 10 which fronted onto Baggot Rath and St Stephen's Green, was allocated as the French Burial Ground or Huguenot cemetery. Originally it was leased to Peter Ward, a brewer, who sold his interest for the sum of £16.

The burial ground is clearly shown on *Rocque's Map* of 1765 with Stable Lane to the rear and 'the road to Ball's Bridge' to the fore. Baggot Rath became Merrion Row in 1776. A map from 1840 illustrates the layout of the cemetery as it is today. Over the entrance to the gateway, 'Huguenot Cemetery 1693' is etched in granite. In 1936, Dublin Corporation moved the gateway, wall and railings back four feet.

The earliest gravestone, dated 1710, is the only one with an inscription in French and it reads:

.... LE CORPS DE | ....(JO)VGLAS DECEDE LE | ....JUILLET 1710 | NATIF DE | CLERAC EN GUINE AGE DE | 53 ANS MARCHAND DUBLIN | ET DE SON FILS DECEDE LE | 14 FEVRIER 1710 | 1L

The cemetery has one path which divides the area into two parts. On either side, the ground is divided up into burial plots for various Huguenot families. At the end of the pathway in the back wall is a memorial porch, which was erected by the Huguenot Society in 1880. It bears the inscription

164

Erected in loving memory of those whose mortal remains have been laid within this cemetery.

In the available records, there are more than three hundred burials recorded, but it is estimated that over double this number are interred in the burial ground. They include many from the army and from various professions and trades, for example, Paul de Blosset, a Colonel Infantry; Phillippe Girard, who was an officer and a native of Arles; Tracen Dambon, ex William III Huguenot Regiment; Henri Dabzac, who was a former professor at Trinity College Dublin; M. La Coste, a teacher; John Law, a medical doctor and Peter Du Bedat, who had banking connections.

Some of those with big family plots include the names of Badier, Dabzac, Boileau, Tardy, Marland, D'Olier, Maziere, Law, Lunell, Mallet, and Du bedat.

James Joyce mentions the name Du Bedat in the 'Lestrygonian' chapter of *Ulysses*:

'May I tempt you to a little more filleted lemon sole, miss Dubedat? Yes, do bedad. And she did bedad. Huguenot name I expect that. A miss Dubedat lived in Killiney, I remember. Du de la French.'

The Du Bedat family originally came from the province of Guienne. Members of the family married into other Huguenot families and were prominent in stockbroking, banking and merchandising in the city of Dublin. The Du Bedat plot is on the right-hand side near the back wall. One of the family memorials reads:

IN MEMORY OF | WILLIAM DUBEDAT ESQr. | OF THE BANK OF IRELAND WHO DEPARTED THIS LIFE | ON THE 12 OF NOVEMBER 1859 AGED 74 YEARS | THE REMAINS OF WHOSE ANCESTORS ARE | ALSO INTERRED IN THIS GROUND | THIS STONE IS ERECTED BY HIS SONS AS A MARK OF THEIR AFFECTION. | MARY, WIDOW OF THE ABOVE Wm DUBEDAT | DIED MAR 23 AGED 72 | FRANCIS DUBEDAT DIED 21 NOV 1857 AGED 36 YEARS.

Members of the D'Olier family are interred here and their names are listed on their memorial. This name would be familiar to many, as D'Olier Street is named after a descendent of Isaac D'Olier who fled from the Toulouse area in France after the revocation of the edict of Nantes and joined the army of William of Orange.

There is a burial plot for the Boileau family, some of whom left Toulouse in France in 1685. The foundation of the well-known Dublin firm Boileau and Boyd wholesale chemists' dates back to 1700. A member of this family, John Theophilus Boileau worked in St Bride's Church as a churchwarden along with James Napper Tandy, the United Irishman who died in Bordeaux in 1803. Both Boileau and Tandy had their names inscribed on the church bell. On the demolition of St Bride's in 1898, the bell was moved to nearby St Werburgh's.

The Boileau memorial is inscribed:

HERE LIETH THE REMAINS OF Mr SIMEON BOILEAU | WHO DIED 1st JULY 1767 AGED 50YEARS. | ALSO THE REMAINS OF THE LATE Mr JOHN BOILEAU HIS | BROTHER AND THOSE OF THE LATE THEOPHILUS DESBRISAY ESQ | THIS STONE WAS ERECTED TO THE MEMORY OF THE ABOVE | SIMEON, BY HIS SON THOMAS BOILEAU.

The graveyard which belongs to the French Huguenot Fund was restored in 1988. This was funded through a grant from the French Ministry of Foreign Affairs in conjunction with FÁS and was reopened in November 1990 by the Ambassador of France. The burial ground was planted after a design based on seventeenth and eighteenth century Huguenot sources, using traditional plants.

Although there are only thirty-six stone memorials in this cemetery, there are two hundred and forty families known to be buried here. Traditionally, Calvinist Huguenots were not inclined to use headstones.

In May 1999, the Huguenot Family Names Triptych of Irish limestone tablets was unveiled. It is on the wall on the left-hand side inside the entrance. It was commissioned by the French Huguenot Fund and executed by the sculptor Seamus Dunbar. The names of the two hundred and forty surnames of the families are inscribed on this limestone triptych. It is a truly lovely memorial in this little oasis in the city centre.

Just beside this memorial, is another smaller one which was unveiled the same day. The inscription reads:

FONTAINE | In memory of Jaques Fontaine | 1658–1728 | And his courageous wife | Anne Elizabeth Boursiquot | Fontaine fled France in 1685 | Served as minister in Cork | and on the Bere peninsula | Established a classical school | in St Stephen's Green in 1709 | His memoirs stand as a | remarkable testimony of the | Huguenot experience. | This stone given by descendants in America | 15th May 1999.

The burial ground is under the care of the Huguenot Trust

[See also: Cabbage Garden, Peter Street, and St Luke & St Nicholas Without]

[53] INSRCIPTION OVER GATEWAY OF HUGUENOT CEMETERY, MERRION ROW.

Moravian Cemetery

Situation: Whitechurch Road, Dublin 16
Period in use: From circa 1750 to date
Bus No (from city centre): 15C

The entrance to the Moravian cemetery is a through a large archway with an iron gateway. Two steps lead to the main pathway, which divides the burial ground in two grassy halves. The males are buried on one side and the females on the other. A high wall surrounds the perimeter.

The Moravian church was introduced to Ireland in the mid 1700s. In the 1740s Benjamin Latrobe, a young graduate of Trinity College, headed a mission in Skinners' Alley. While in London he heard John Cennick, the Moravian evangelist, preach and invited him to Dublin. As a result of Cennick's visit a Moravian congregation was set up in 1750, and within a few years, eighteen churches and forty locations for preaching were established throughout the country.

The Moravian Church of the United Brethren in Dublin was built about 1760 in Bishop Street. It fronted on to Kevin Street where it may still be seen. It is no longer used as a church. There was also an almshouse nearby in Whitefriar Street.

The land for the burial ground in Whitechurch was purchased in the early 1760s from a mill owner and was a bequest of Andrew Moller. In 1764 the first person was interred. He was John Tellschig, a native of Moravia and the Provincial in Ireland. He was a popular man and an estimated five hundred people followed his funeral cortege from the Church in Bishop Street to the burial ground.

All the memorials are flat on the ground, which is unusual. The following are some early inscriptions from the Moravian burial ground:

Mary McLouglin Born Sept. 1698, d. 22 Augt 1722

Mannah Binns; b April 1st 1723, d. Sept 9th 1787

Benigna Salome Lodge; b. Nov 24th 1760, d. March 1786

Elizabeth Carmichael; b. Augt 24th 1766, d. Nov.29th 1788.

The Revd Javobus Amandis Eberle; born at the Moravian Mission Station,

Herrnhut Greenland; died in Dublin, 13th Sepr aged 38 years.

John Connolly; born 25 April 1729; died Augt 14th 1798.

Daniel Walsh, b. Dec. 1723; d. Sept 12th 1777.

In July 1980, the Synod of the British Province removed its name from the official role in accordance with the wishes of the Dublin congregation. As a result the Dublin congregation ceased to exist on 31 December 1980.

The burial ground is under the care of the Irish District, British Province of the Moravian Church.

[54] THE FORMER MORAVIAN CHURCH ON KEVIN STREET.

Mount Argus Churchyard

Situation: St Paul's Retreat, Mount Argus, Harold's Cross, Dublin 6

Period in use: 1894 to date

Bus Nos (from city centre): 54a

Situated off Kimmage Road Lower, the site for the retreat house of the Passionist Fathers at Mount Argus was purchased in 1856. There was a red brick house there at the time known as 'Mount Argus', which was used before the new retreat house, was completed. Building commenced four years later and it was dedicated in 1863. The church was completed in 1878 and extended in 1936.

The church has many interesting associations. For many years it has been the associated with the Garda Síochána. James Pearse, father of Patrick and Willie Pearse, carved a statue of Our Lady and a pulpit in the church. It was at Mount Argus that James Pearse was received into the church. Patrick Pearse came to confession at the monastery on Good Friday 1916, three days before the Easter Rising. Father Ignatius Spencer, a great-great-great-grand uncle of the late Princess of Wales, was one of the first Passionist preachers in Dublin.

The community graveyard is situated behind the railing to the right-hand side of the church. There are circa 172 graves here marked with small neat memorial stones. In the centre is a high Celtic cross, which commemorates Father Sebastian Keens.

A Memorial marks the grave of Father Fernando Saavedra who died on 1 May 1922 aged seventy-four years. He was vicar at Mount Argus for a time and is known for the Saavedra move in the game of chess.

Father Paul Mary Packenham, who was the first rector and superior of Mount Argus, died less than eight months after his arrival in Ireland in 1856. His grave is marked with a memorial which is inscribed:

The Honble and Very Reverend | Fr. Paul Packenham | Died March 1st 1857 | Aged 36 years.

Father Packenham was a son of the Earl of Longford and a nephew of the Duke of Wellington. He had converted to Catholicism in 1850 and had been a captain in the Grenadier Guards before joining the Passionist order.

Father Charles of Mount Argus, was born Andrew Houben on 11 December 1821 in Munstergeleen in Holland. He served as a conscript in the army, and when he was twenty-four, he joined the noviciate of the Passionists in Belgium where he was ordained on 21 December 1850. Known as Charles of St Andrew, he was sent to England two years later. Here he met Paul Packenham who helped him with his English lessons.

Father Charles first came to Ireland in July 1857 and spent nine years at Mount Argus when he returned to England. He was recalled to Mount Argus in January 1874 and remained there for the rest of his life. During his years at Mount Argus, there was a steady stream of people each day that came to receive his blessing. They came from all parts of Ireland, England, Scotland and America. When Father Charles' health deteriorated, he continued to work tirelessly and went out to sick calls in atrocious weather at all hours of the night. Many cures were attributed to him and his fame spread rapidly.

[55] St Paul's Retreat, Mount Argus, Harold's Cross. Behind the railing is the community graveyard.

James Joyce mentions him in *Ulysses*, 'Then perform a miracle like father Charles'. The character of Cranly in *Ulysses* was a friend of Joyce's named J.F. Byrne. Byrne recounts in his book entitled *Silent Years* how he suffered with eye problems and was treated unsuccessfully at St Vincent's Hospital by two specialists.

Then someone suggested that Byrne be brought to Father Charles.

I had heard, of course, about Father Charles, for you couldn't have lived in the Dublin of these years without hearing of his sanctity and his miraculous good works. Indeed, he was the uncanonized saint of the city of Dublin when he came to me and stood before me and I looked up into his rapt face, I beheld a vision of unutterable holiness, and as I felt the soft caress of his emaciated fingers all over my closed eyes I was in a state of near ecstasy.

The following days Byrne's eyes were normal and he never suffered with them again.

Father Charles of St Andrew died on 5 January 1893, and was buried on 9 January, in the community cemetery. His funeral was said to have attracted more mourners than that of Parnell. On 3 November 1937 he was exhumed when his coffin was replaced with a lead coffin. On 30 November 1949, by order of the Holy See, his body was transferred from the cemetery to the church at Mount Argus where it is now entombed in a white marble sarcophagus at the top right-hand side of the church. On top of the tomb is a bust of Father Charles.

Engraved on the front of his white marble tomb with gold lettering is the following:

Blessed Charles of Mount Argus
Passionist
1821 – 1893
Beatified by Pope John Paul II
16th October 1988

St Paul's Retreat, Mount Argus, is under the care of the Passionist Congregation.

Mount Jerome Cemetery

Situation: Harold's Cross, Dublin 6

Period in use: 1836 to date

Bus Nos (from city centre): 16, 16a, 19a, 54a

Mount Jerome derives its name from the Reverend Stephen Jerome who was a Vicar at St Kevin's Parish in 1639. At the time this parish encompassed part of the lands in the Harold's Cross area. By the seventeenth century, the Earl of Meath owned the lands and leased various sections of it out to prominent Dublin families.

The original house on the estate of Mount Jerome, which was built in the early eighteenth century, is used today as the administrative offices for the cemetery. It had a tree-lined avenue and was enclosed by high walls. In the mid-eighteenth century, the Wilkinson family lived here. By the end of that century, John Keogh (1740–1817), the Catholic leader who was born in poor circumstances and became a successful businessman, leased the lands from the Earl of Meath. The estate of Mount Jerome was described as a beautifully picturesque demesne adjoining the village with 'a venerable mansion embowered in trees'.

At the time of the establishment of Mount Jerome Cemetery, Harold's Cross was a rural area, with some handsome villas and the Grand Canal passing close to the village. There were cotton, paper and flourmills in the vicinity and a green, which was taken over by the Rathmines Commissioners in 1894 and converted into a public park.

The land was purchased by the General Cemetery Company of Dublin, formed under the provisions of an Act of the fourth and fifth years of William IV in 1834 'for establishing a general cemetery in the neighbourhood of the city of Dublin. Samuel Lewis described the cemetery as being on gently elevated ground 'embellished with lawns and shrubberies, and wholly surrounded with lofty trees of venerable growth, giving it an air of seclusion and a solemnity of aspect peculiarly appropriate'.

The cemetery, then comprising of twenty-six acres and enclosed by a wall, was for the interment of people of all religious denominations, though in the nineteenth and early twentieth centuries it was the main burial place for members of the Protestant religion. Catholic burials took place mainly at Goldenbridge and Glasnevin cemeteries, which had been established in 1828 and 1832 respectively. The first Catholic burials did not occur in Mount Jerome until an industrial dispute took place in Glasnevin cemetery in the 1920s.

Plans were made with the Grand Canal Company for the improvement of the canal road leading from Portobello, and for exemption from toll of all carriages passing to or from the cemetery. There are various stories about funerals and the shiny black-plumed horses, being put through their paces along this stretch of road, and then on the approach to Mount Jerome cemetery, the rein would tighten and the pace would slacken to a more respectable speed.

Père-Lachaise in Paris was opened in 1804. Mount Jerome opened its gates in 1836 just three years before Highgate Cemetery (1839) in London. Bishop Whately consecrated it on the 19 September 1836.

John Howard Louch, who designed the gate lodge and the nearby Church of Ireland, also surveyed and designed the layout for the cemetery. His son, Fitzgibbon Louch, later redesigned the church in the gothic style. At the end of the main avenue and facing directly on to it, is a gothic style chapel (1847) created by William Atkins, whose design was influenced by Augustus Pugin. The chapel contains a number of interesting mural tablets.

In 1984 Mount Jerome Cemetery was purchased by Massey the undertakers.

The cemetery, now forty-seven acres, is symmetrically laid out with radiating walks, which were once gravelled. The walks, pathways and avenues, which total almost twenty miles, all have names such as the Avenue, the Long Walk, the Low Walk, the North, South, East and West Walks or the Catacombs. Some have been named after people, such as Purser's Walk and Guinness' Walk. These were two brewing families whose vaults may be seen on their respective walks. Both families were original shareholders in the General Cemetery Company. Other names include Drummond's Walk, Parker's Walk, and Neville's Walk. Some have interesting stories attached to them, such as the Nuns' Walk and the Orphans' Walk. The former name commemorates the Sisters of Charity, who had a convent adjacent in Greenmount Estate, founded by Mother Mary Aikenhead in 1845. Orphans' Walk was named for the orphan children from the Masonic Orphans' Schools and the Protestant Orphans' School on the South Circular Road. Other names reflect the tree types which once grew on the original estate such as Hawthorn Walk, Yew Walk, Laurel Walk, Laburnum Walk and Cypress Walk. This lends a certain environmental charm and is most useful when locating graves.

A crematorium has been built in the middle of the North Walk, the positioning of which interferes with the symmetry of the original design by Louch. Once tree-lined, the North Walk linked up with seven other walks, which had as its centrepiece a large fountain. This has been replaced by a circular flower bed, which lends some colour to the area. A memorial at this junction has the following thought provoking inscription

Life how short | Eternity how long.

173

[56] The Gothic-style chapel designed by William Atkins at the end of the Main Avenue in Mount Jerome Cemetery.

The cemetery, which contains one of the finest collections of funerary monuments in the country, has a treasure of Victorian memorials, varying in height, which give the landscape an interesting perspective. These were designed by eminent sculptors and noted architects of the day, including Thomas Harrison, Thomas Kirk, John Louch, Sandham Symes and George Papworth. The stone used in these memorials varied. In some cases Carrara marble was used for the sculptured angels on monuments. Michelangelo chose the marble for his works at Carrara, a small place located between Pisa and Florence. Other stones used at Mount Jerome included Kilkenny limestone, granite from the Dublin and Wicklow hills, and in some cases, purple slate. Imported stone was also used, such as red granite from Aberdeen and Portland and yellow sandstone from England.

Mount Jerome has a list of the most distinguished names on its rolls dating from the Victorian era and contains a widely diverse collection of famous people in every field. There are patriots, writers, playwrights, poets, churchmen, military men, architects, scientists, engineers, surveyors, surgeons, mathematicians, sculptors, artists, legislators, musicians, merchants and members of the Royal Irish Constabulary and the Dublin Metropolitan Police. Due to space limitations, just some of these are listed below. A walk around this cemetery, or along any of its paths, is a voyage of discovery and many names inscribed on memorials are familiar.

Among the many churchmen interred in Mount Jerome is the Reverend William Conygham Plunkett (1828–1897), Archbishop of Dublin. In 1871, he became fourth Lord Plunkett on the death of his father. His grave is located to the right, off Hawthorn Walk, before it joins the Long Walk [C91-145 vault].

Writers include William Carleton (1794–1869), the great novelist, storyteller and interpreter of the Irish people. Some of the most notable men and women of the time attended his funeral.

Carleton's widow and children erected a miniature obelisk of limestone, which showed his bearded profile, and his name was ringed with the poet's wreath of honour. The inscription said that this was 'to mark the place wherein rest the remains of one whose memory needs neither grave stone nor sculptured marble to preserve it from oblivion'. In time, his memorial fell into disrepair, and was restored by the William Carleton Memorial Committee. At the unveiling on the 15 August 1989, Dr Benedict Kiely said in his oration that Carleton, as a novelist, had taken up the issue of tenants' rights, emigration and famine and had put down on record the Irish people as he remembered them before the famine, before they were practically wiped out. Irish people have not much changed, he said.

For Carleton's memorial, from the main entrance, take the first set of little steps on the right-hand side off the Avenue. The memorial is second on the left [C3754.130].

John Kells Ingram (1823–1907), the poet and scholar, was born in County Donegal. He spent fifty-five years associated with Trinity College where he studied and later held the positions of Professor of

Oratory, Professor of Greek, Librarian, Senior Lecturer and Vice-Provost As a literary man, Ingram is remembered best for his famous lyric 'The Memory of the Dead', a martial poem which was known as the 'Irish Marseillaise'. Aged twenty, he published it anonymously in *The Nation*, though he did not formally acknowledge it until he was aged seventy-seven as he was reluctant to be associated with the sentiments he had expressed in it. Ingram died on 1 May 1907 aged eighty-three.

Who fears to speak of Ninety-Eight?
Who blushes at the name?
When cowards mock the patriot's fate,
Who hangs his head for shame?

To reach Ingram's grave, take the first left turn inside the main entrance on to the Laurel Walk. Continue to the first bend and turn right at the headstone for James Samuel Wauchope Craig on the right-hand side. Take the second turn right after this. Ingram's grave is fourth on the left-hand side [C3367.127].

Sir William Wilde (1815–76), the writer and archaeologist and father of Oscar Wilde, was one of the foremost eye and ear specialists of his day. Known for his generosity, he set up a dispensary for poor people, which was the precursor of St Mark's Ophthalmic and Aural Hospital in Lincoln Place. His books include *The Beauties of the Boyne and The Blackwater* (1849), *Lough Corrib and Lough Mask* (1867), and in 1858 he published a descriptive *Catalogue of the contents of the Museum of the RIA*. Dr Wilde died on 19 April 1876.

A marble plaque to his wife, Lady Wilde, was mounted on the Wilde family tomb. This headstone was unveiled 3 February 1996 to mark the occasion of the one hundredth anniversary of her death. The *Freeman's Journal* described her as 'a woman of the most versatile attainments, genuine intellectual power and commanding character'. She was buried in an unmarked grave in London. Merlin Holland, the great-grandson of Lady Wilde, introduced the ceremony at Mount Jerome. The writer Ulick O'Connor recited Oscar Wilde's sonnet 'Helas'. As he did so, a lone swan flew over and disappeared into the distance towards the west.

Tread lightly, she is near
Under the snow,
Speak gently, she can hear
The lilies grow.

William Wilde's grave is at the top of the Avenue and left just in front of the chapel. The headstone is the third on the left-hand side [C678.108].

Thomas Caulfield Irwin (1823–92), poet, writer of fiction and classical scholar, was born at Warrenpoint, Co. Down. A vegetarian, he had a great love and concern for all animals and had a special affection for cats. He was strongly influenced by the English poets, Keats, Shelley and Tennyson and was a great observer of men and nature. Irwin's works include *Versicles* (1856), *Irish Poems and Legends* (1869), *Songs and Romances* (1878), *Pictures and Songs* (1880), *Sonnets on the Poetry and Problem of Life* (1881) and *Poems, Sketches and Songs* (1889). He died at his home, 36 Upper Mountpleasant Avenue, Rathmines on 20 February 1892.

To reach Thomas Caulfield Irwin's tomb, turn right at the chapel for the Hawthorn Walk and turn right into the Long Walk. Approximately seventy yards away, the thirty-sixth grave down on the left-hand side is the memorial to Irwin, which is a limestone cover on a granite plinth [C946.93].

Thomas Davis (1814–45), poet, nationalist and journalist, was born in Mallow, County Cork, in October 1914. A man of vast charm, Davis portrayed great enthusiasm in the national cause, and through his essays and patriotic verse, published in *The Nation*, won popular support for its principles. An influential member of Young Ireland, he was a supporter of the Repeal Association. Among his best-known poems are 'A Nation Once Again', 'The West's Asleep', and 'Lament for the Death of Owen Roe O'Neill'. Davis died aged thirty of scarlet fever on 16 September 1845 at his mother's home at 67 Lower Baggot Street.

[57] THE MONUMENT TO SIR WILLIAM WILDE (1815–76), THE NOTED SURGEON AND ANTIQUARIAN AND FATHER OF OSCAR WILDE. ON THE SAME MONUMENT IS A MARBLE PLAQUE COMMEMORATING LADY WILDE.

To reach Davis's grave, turn right to the Low Walk inside the main entrance. Turn left then for the Long Walk. Take the first pathway on the left-hand side, passing the headstone for Sir Rowan Hamilton on the right-hand side. Take a right turn between the headstones for Bradley and Sherrard. The tall Celtic cross, recently restored, which marks Davis's grave, is the first on the left-hand side [C5474.115].

Joseph Sheridan Le Fanu (1814–73), novelist and short story writer, was born in Dublin and educated at Trinity College. His works included *The Cock and the Anchor* (1845), which gives a colourful picture of eighteenth century Dublin with its duels and alehouses. After his wife's death in 1851, he was devastated with grief and was rarely ever seen. He became a recluse and was known as 'the invisible prince'. He then wrote twelve novels, which included *The House by the Churchyard* (1863), a macabre story about a haunted house. Le Fanu died on 7 February 1873, in his fifty-ninth year, at his home, 18 Merrion Square. His obituary in the *Dublin University Magazine*, of which he had been Editor from 1861 to 1869, read,

> *he was a man who thought deeply, especially on religious subjects. To those who knew him he was very dear. They admired him for his learning, his sparkling wit and [his] pleasant conversation, and loved him for his manly virtues, his noble and generous qualities, his gentleness, and his loving, affectionate nature.*

To reach Le Fanu's grave turn right at the main entrance to the Low Walk and continue to the Nuns' Walk. On reaching a bend, there is a white limestone headstone to Kathleen Keane. Le Fanu's grave, a flat vault with limestone top, is to the left of this [C399.122].

John Millington Synge (1871–1909), the playwright, was born in Dublin and educated at Trinity College. Synge was the first playwright in Ireland to write for an Irish audience about Irish matters. He spent five successive summers in Aran. His plays include *In the Shadow of the Glen*, *Riders to the Sea*, *The Well of the Saints*, *The Playboy of the Western World* and *The Tinker's Wedding*. He was engaged to Molly Allgood, the actress, but sadly became ill and was admitted to the Elphis Nursing Home. He took with him the manuscript of his final play *Deirdre* (which he decided to call *Deirdre of the Sorrows*) in case he felt well enough to work on it. Whilst there, he asked to be moved to a room from which he would be able to see his beloved hills once again — the hills where he had loved to wander since his childhood, and about which he wrote with so much feeling. He died on the 24 March 1909. Synge's epitaph reads:

> *A Silent sinner, nights and days,*
> *No human heart to him drew nigh,*
> *Alone he wound his wonted ways*
> *Alone and little loved did die*

[58] THE RECENTLY RESTORED CELTIC CROSS MARKS THE BURIAL PLACE OF THOMAS OSBORNE DAVIS (1814–45), POET AND NATIONALIST. 'HE SERVED HIS COUNTRY AND HE LOVED HIS KIND.'

To reach Synge's grave, turn right at the chapel for the Hawthorn Walk. Beyond the junction with the Long Walk, turn left up the narrow concrete pathway. On the right-hand side is a headstone for Dawson. Follow the narrow concrete pathway, passing at intervals on the left-hand side the headstones for Norton, Smyth and Dallas. A headstone for Bloster is directly ahead. Synge's headstone is second to the left of this. [C9468.38].

George FitzMaurice (1877–1963), the playwright and author of *The Country Dressmaker* (1907), *The Pie Dish* (1908), *The Dandy Dolls* (1913) and other plays, is buried nearby on the second turn left off Neville's Walk. A native of Listowel, Co. Kerry, FitzMaurice's monument was erected by Duagh Historical Society in association with the North Kerry Literary Trust [C19-29414].

George William Russell (1867–1935) or AE as he was known, poet, painter, mystic, organiser for the co-operative movement, economist and editor, was born in Lurgan, County Armagh. A prominent figure in the Irish Literary Revival, he died in Bournemouth on 17 July 1935. The inscription on his memorial reads:

> *I moved among men and places*
> *And in Living I learned the*
> *Truth at last I know I*
> *am a spirit, and that I went*
> *forth in old time from the*
> *Self-ancestral to labours yet*
> *Unaccomplished.*

To reach AE's grave, turn right at the chapel for the Hawthorn Walk. Fork left up Neville's Walk and continue up Archbishop's Walk. Turn right at the junction with Consecration Walk. As a guide, the headstone on the left corner is for McGrail. Twenty-five graves down on the right, there is a narrow pathway between the headstones for O'Rourke and Cooling. AE's grave, a flat stone on the ground, is the fifth row in on the right [A76.401.11217].

Máirtín Ó Cadhain (1906–1970), born in the *Cois Fharraige Gaeltacht* of County Galway, was a novelist, short story writer and an authority on Irish literature and culture. UNESCO chose his novel *Cré na Cille* (1949) for translation into several European languages. Included in his other works are *Idir Shúgradh agus Dáiríre* (1953), *An Aisling* (1961), *An tSraith ar Lár* (1967), and *An tSraith Dá Tógáil* (1970). Ó Cadhain died on 18 October 1970 [CRB+4-465-37967].

Lord Longford (1902–61), Edward Packenham, 6th Earl of Longford, playwright and producer, became a Director of the Gate Theatre in 1931. Many of his own plays and translations were produced in

179

the theatre. The burial place of Lord Longford and his wife Christine (nee Trew), also a playwright, is marked by a memorial which is the work of the sculptor Seamus Murphy RHA. On either side of the memorial, a theatrical mask is carved. Turn left at the chapel for the Guinness Walk and the grave is the fifth one on the right-hand side [C53-35538]. It reads:

Edward Arthur Henry | Sixth Earl of Longford | Poet and Patriot | Born 29th Dec 1902 | Died 4th Feb 1961 | and | His wife | Christine | Writer and Dramatist | 1900–1980

Further up, near the top of the Guinness Walk on the right-hand side and just behind the family vault of Arthur Guinness of Beaumont, Co. Dublin, is the grave of Edward Dowden (1843–1913), the Shakespearean scholar, critic and writer who was appointed Professor of English Literature at Trinity College in 1867. Amongst his works are *Shakespeare, His Mind and Art* (1875), *A Shakespeare Primer* (1877) and his *Life of Shelley* (1866) [C5-14017].

Dublin-born Paul Smith (1920–1997), the novelist and playwright, is interred at the corner of the entrance to the garden section on the South Walk. Among his works are *Esther's Altar* (1959) and *The Countrywoman* (1962), *The Stubborn Season* (1962), *Stravaganza* (1963) and *Annie* (1972) [C8-48145].

A few paces up on the same side of the South Walk is the memorial to Colonel Fritz Brase (1875–1940), who was brought over by the Irish Government in 1923 to found the Army School of Music. Brase, who studied in Leipzig was a master pupil of Max Bruch and was the youngest ever court conductor in Berlin [C25462-62-67].

Facing the top of the Guinness Walk, where it meets with the South Walk, there is the grave of the L'Estrange family. Three graves up from this is the family sepulchre of H.E. Flavelle. On top of it is the Masonic symbol, the Compass. These Masonic symbols may be seen on other gravestones throughout the cemetery.

Among the distinguished sculptors and architects buried here are Newry-born Thomas Kirk (1772–1845) RHA, who was responsible for a number of church memorials, busts and statues, including the statue of Admiral Horatio Nelson which surmounted the former Pillar in Sackville Street (now O'Connell Street). His works may be seen in the Royal Dublin Society, the Royal College of Surgeons in Ireland and Trinity College Dublin. Kirk's son Joseph designed the family grave, which has a Freemason symbol engraved on it. It is on The Avenue. It is the fifth memorial up after the first set of little steps on the right-hand side [C130-843].

The architectural works of George Papworth (1781–1855) include many of the country's municipal and ecclesiastical buildings such as King's Bridge, the courthouse in Castlebar and the church in Whitefriar Street. He was responsible for some monuments both in Mount Jerome and Glasnevin cemeteries. He died on 14 March 1855 aged seventy-five. His grave is situated to the east of the Cypress Walk [B68-179-7673].

John Skipton Mulvany (1813–1870) designed the beautiful building of Broadstone Station which lies at the junction of the Western Way with Phibsborough Road and Constitution Hill (Midland & Great Western Line). He was involved with work concerning the first railway in Ireland, the Dublin and Kingstown Railway, which was constructed by William Dargan. At the time, the terminus for this line was at the former Salthill Hotel which Mulvaney designed. He was also responsible for other buildings in the area such as the clubhouse of the Royal Irish Yacht Club, which is considered to be his masterpiece, and the Royal St George Yacht Club. The magnificent terraces of houses such as Longford Terrace and the houses in Belgrave Square in Monkstown are just part of his legacy.

Dargan chose Mulvany to design his house, Mount Anville, which is noted for its large campanile tower. On 29 August in 1853 Queen Victoria and Prince Albert called to see Dargan at the house near Goatstown. In August 1865, the house was sold to the Sisters of the Sacred Heart. Mulvany died on 12 May 1870. His grave is halfway down the Laburnam Walk [C134-511].

Cork-born Sir Richard Morrison (1767–1849) and his son William Vitruvius Morrison (1794–1838) belonged to a family of noted architects. William became a partner in his father's business early in his career. They left a great legacy in their work on a number of large stately homes around Ireland. This included enlargements and neo-classical interior design for the houses at Fota Island in Carrigtwohill, Co. Cork, and Barons Court, in Co. Tyrone. Killruddery House, the 1820 Elizabethan Revival mansion in Bray, Co. Wicklow which incorporates a seventeenth century house, was built for the tenth Earl of Meath by Richard and William Morrison. Ballyfin House near Portlaoise, which was built for Sir Henry Charles Coote, is considered to be the Morrison masterpiece. It is now a school run by the Patrician Brothers.

[59] THE GRAVESTONE OF PLAYWRIGHT JOHN MILLINGTON SYNGE (1871–1909).

William, who predeceased his father, died on the 16 October 1838. The Morrison memorial, which consists of a raised casket on a plinth, contains the remains of Sir Richard Morrison, William Morrison and other members of the Morrison family. The relevant inscriptions on the plinth read:

To the memory of | William Vitrivius Morrison, Architect RIAI | This monument is erected | By his parents whose only solace in their bereavement | is that God and Saviour with whom | They trust he liveth | He died October 16th 1838 aged 44 years.

Sacred to the memory of | Sir Richard Morrison Knight | Founder and Vice President of the Royal Institute | of Irish Architects | Died October 31st 1849 | Aged 82 years.

To reach the Morrison memorial, take the Hawthorn Walk from the chapel and turn left at the Long Walk. Take first left, and the memorial with its raised casket is just in on the right [63 – 199 vault].

Jacob Owen (1778–1870) was born in Wales and was assigned in 1832 as engineer and architect to the Board of Public Works, which had been established the previous year. The state buildings in the city came under his care and he carried out work on Dublin Castle, the Four Courts, the Viceregal Lodge (now Áras an Uachtaráin) and the Royal Hibernian Military School (now St Mary's Hospital).

Owen died in England aged ninety-two and was buried in Mount Jerome on 2 November 1870. His vault is at the end of the South Walk almost facing the top of the Guinness Walk [B210].

The grave of the Kerry-born sculptor Jerome Connor (1876–1943), who spent much of his life in the United States, is marked with a simple upright slab. In 1968 Connor's statue of Robert Emmet was unveiled outside St Stephen's Green West, which was then opposite Emmet's birthplace (now demolished). In 1978, his bronze Eire, was sited in Merrion Square [A98 – 497 – 25947].

[60] THE GRAVE OF JACK BUTLER YEATS (1871–1957), THE PLAYWRIGHT, NOVELIST AND PREMIER PAINTER OF THE TWENTIETH CENTURY, AND HIS WIFE, MARY COTTENHAM YEATS, WHO DIED IN 1947.

Sarah Henrietta Purser (1848–1943), the portrait painter and stained-glass artist founded *An Túr Gloine* (the Tower of Glass) in 1903. Her painting of Countess Markievicz gained her many commissions in London. In 1924 she founded the Friends of the National Collections and was instrumental in acquiring Charlemont House as the Municipal Gallery of Modern Art. Her grave bears the simple inscription:

Sacred to | the memory | of | Sarah Henrietta Purser RHA | Born 22nd March 1848 | Died 7th August 1943 | Fortis et Strenua.

To reach the memorial, take the first turn right inside the main entrance, which is the Low Walk, and continue to the Nuns' Walk. At the bend, there is a white limestone headstone to Kathleen Keane on the right-hand side. Purser's grave is directly opposite this [C121-19521].

Jack B. Yeats (1871–1957), playwright, novelist and premier painter of the twentieth century, was born in London. From the age of eight to sixteen he lived in Sligo with his Pollexfen grandparents and later said 'From the beginning of my painting life, every painting which I have made has somewhere in it a thought of Sligo'. During the 1930s, he wrote a number of prose works and plays, which include *Sligo* (1930), *Sailing Swiftly* (1933), *The Amaranthers* (1936) and *The Careless Flower* (1947). Three of his plays were produced at the Abbey Theatre: *Apparitions* (1933), *La Noo* (1942) and *In Sand* (1949). Jack B. Yeats died on 28 March 1957. His funeral service was held at St Stephen's Church, Mount Street Crescent. The Yeats Museum in the National Gallery of Ireland, which was opened in March 1999, is a tribute to the artistic achievements of the Yeats family. It is dedicated primarily to the work of Jack B. Yeats.

To reach Yeats' grave, turn right at the chapel for Hawthorn Walk. Continue straight to the fork, taking the left for Neville's Walk. At the first tree, take a sharp left. The grave is the sixteenth in on the right-hand side [C41.27646].

The Dublin painter Walter Osborne, (1859–1903), who studied in Antwerp under Verlat for two years, spent a decade travelling in Spain, Brittany, England and Holland, where he painted landscapes in oil and watercolour. He is represented in the National Gallery with a number of his paintings, including *Apple Garden at Quimperle* and *St Patrick's Close, Dublin*. He died on 24 April 1903 [C24 11 11 3].

Just to the right off the Hawthorn Walk, the Thomas Drummond (1797–1840) memorial may be seen. The work of George Papworth, it consists of a very imposing sarcophagus which is surmounted on a pedestal which forms the walls of the vault where the remains of Drummond are interred. The highest monument in this area, it bears the following inscription:

LAST WORDS | 'Bury me in Ireland | The land of my adoption. | I have loved her well, | And served her faithfully.'

183

Drummond, who was born in Scotland, served as Under Secretary from 1835–40. In 1815 he joined the Royal Engineers and it was while serving with the army that he developed the 'Drummond' limelight which is used in the theatre. As well as his involvement with the Royal Irish Constabulary, he was involved with the Poor Law in Ireland. He died in office aged forty-three.

Nearby on the Hawthorn Walk, is the Cusack Memorial designed by Sandham Symes. This is in the form of a sarcophagus, which is contained within a temple, raised on a pedestal. The sarcophagus bears the inscription

James William Cusack M.D. | Born 26 May 1788. Died 25 September 1861 [C89 2956 vault on left of path].

Other unusual Victorian memorials on the Hawthorn Walk include the Harvie Memorial. Surmounting this large monument is a dog (now headless) which sits alertly on his owner's cloak. According to the story, the dog failed to rescue his master who was drowning. It stood on his master's cloak barking furiously for assistance, which unfortunately arrived too late. When the dog died, he was buried with his master. A nice ending to this touching story of a man and his dog [C88 vault on left of path].

Almost opposite the Harvie Memorial is the Gresham Tomb, which also has an unusual story in its design. It originally had a bell, which could be sounded if necessary by the lady who was interred here. She had a fear of being buried alive and her casket had special spring locks fitted, which could be opened from within in case of emergency. [C90 vault on right of path].

Just at the start of the Hawthorn Walk, on the right-hand side, is the memorial to John Bernard Logier [C88-287]. Logier, a Huguenot, whose parents had fled from France, was an author of textbooks on music. He was for a time the organist at Westport, Co. Mayo. He invented a method of piano teaching that spread worldwide, and bears his name, the Logier Method. He died on 14 July 1846. The inscription reads:

He was by birth a German | But by choice | A citizen of Great Britain | He attained to professional eminence | As inventor of the | Logerian system of music | As a Christian | He was enabled by the grace of God | In life and in death | To rejoice in | The hope of the gospel.

To the left of the Long Walk, as it is approached from the Hawthorn Walk, there are three large rectangular areas. Each of these contains a memorial. The first one reads:

Interred in this plot are the remains of persons originally buried in the graveyard attached to St Bridget's Church in the City of Dublin and removed to this cemetery pursuant to the provisions of the Dublin Improvement to Bull Alley 1899 Act.

184

The second reads:

This plot contains the remains transferred from St Thomas's Graveyard, Marlborough Street Dublin 1925–26.

The third area contains the remains of Huguenots who were transferred from the Peter Street Burial Ground, which ceased to be a cemetery when the site was redeveloped. The remains of all the deceased were removed and reinterred in accordance with the rites of the French Reformed Church in Mount Jerome in 1966. A large memorial stone marks the plot, bearing the name and date of death of each person, ranging from Barthelemey D'Arabin, 31 January 1713, to Thomas Daniel, November 1829. Flanking two sides of this large plot are some of the original memorial slabs from Peter Street Burial Ground which are laid flat on the ground.

[61] A CLOSE-UP VIEW OF THE TOP OF THE DRAMATIC HARVIE MEMORIAL ON THE HAWTHORN WALK. IT DEPICTS A PINING DOG STANDING ON HIS OWNER'S CLOAK; HE WAS UNSUCCESSFUL IN RESCUING HIM. WHEN THE DOG DIED, HE WAS BURIED WITH HIS MASTER. THE HEAD ON THE MEMORIAL WAS REMOVED FOR SAFEKEEPING AFTER IT HAD BEEN DAMAGED.

[62] THE UNUSUALLY DESIGNED
GRESHAM TOMB. IT CONTAINS A BELL
ON TOP WHICH IS LINKED BY A CHAIN
TO THE COFFIN WHICH HAS SPRING-
LOADED LOCKS AFFIXED IN CASE THE
LADY INTERRED WAS BURIED ALIVE.
THE TOMB IS SITUATED ON THE
HAWTHORN WALK.

Adjoining St Bridget's plot is a striking red obelisk, which commemorates the members of the Royal Irish Constabulary who were interred in the cemetery. It includes General Sir Duncan McGregor, Commander of the 93rd Highlanders and Inspector General of the Irish Constabulary (1838–1858) who died in 1881 and Frederick James Bail, Assistant Inspector General of the Royal Irish Constabulary who died on 27 March 1918. The Royal Irish Constabulary was formed by Thomas Drummond in 1836 as an armed police force and disbanded in the autumn of 1922 with the establishment of the Civic Guards, an unarmed police force.

There is also a memorial to mark the burial place of members of the Dublin Metropolitan Police. A number of these died at a young age, the victims of typhoid, for example,

John Quinn, B. Divn died 20 Jan 1896 aged 23 years; Robert Turner B. Divn Died 1 May 1901 aged 19 years; Thomas Cross A. Divn died 22 Sept 1911 aged 24.

The DMP, founded in 1786 was an unarmed police force covering Dublin city and county and Co. Wicklow. In April 1925, the DMP became part of the Garda Síochána under the Police Forces Amalgamation Act 1925. To reach the DMP memorial, turn right off the Avenue and take the Laburnum Walk. Half way along this walk on the right-hand side is the family vault of The Hone Family. Directly opposite this and one row in, is the DMP memorial on which ten names are inscribed.

The cemetery also contains the remains of a number of Irishmen who served with the British army in various regiments. They fought in the Napoleonic Wars, the Afghan Wars, the Indian Mutiny, the Boer War and the World Wars. Many fell in far foreign battlefields. Some survived and their graves provide their names, regiment, and date of death. Others who fell are commemorated with memorials in the mortuary chapel such as Lt Col Darcy Kyle, who was the youngest son of Samuel, Lord Bishop of Cork. He died aged forty-two on 11 October 1857, whilst commanding the Royal Inniskilling Fusiliers at Peshawar during the Indian Mutiny.

There are two survivors from the Charge of the Light Brigade and three recipients of the Victoria Cross buried in Mount Jerome.

The two 'Chargers' include Trumpeter John Brown of the 17th Lancers, who died on 26 February 1905 aged seventy-one [c25-12120]. The other is Captain James William Kelly of the 4th Light Dragoons, who later transferred to a foot regiment as Paymaster. He died on 8 January 1887 at 7 St George's Place in Dublin. His grave is marked by a marble headstone [c7072 / 38].

Lt Col John Augustus Connolly won the Victoria Cross in the Crimea and died on 23 December 1888 aged fifty-nine [88-163-6931]; Major General Arthur Thomas Moore won his VC in Persia. He died on the 25 April 1913 aged eighty-two [156-c-14036.]; Colonel Hans Garret Moore won his VC in South Africa in 1877. He died on 7 November 1889 aged fifty-four years. [c 25 and 26 – 7903]. His memorial reads:

To the beloved memory of | Colonel Hans Garrett Moore VC C.B | Late Commanding Officer Argyle and Sutherland Highlanders | and formerly Connaught Rangers | who was accidentally drowned in Loch Derg | during a gale October 7th 1889 | Age 54 years | He served with distinction in the Indian Mutiny, the Ashantee War 1874 | The Kaffir War 1877–1878 | and the Egyptian War 1882. | He received the Victoria Cross | for endeavouring to save the life of a | soldier left alone surrounded by Kaffirs. | This monument is erected by his sorrowing sister | HM Bird.

This memorial is difficult enough to locate. The easiest way to approach it is to turn left at the chapel for the Guinness Walk. Some metres up on the left-hand side is an oblong memorial to a John McCormack. Turn left here (there is no pathway) and cross to the tree. The memorial to Moore is just before this tree.

Among the eminent doctors interred in Mount Jerome are Sir William Wilde (1815–1876) (mentioned above); Robert Graves (1796–1853) who was attached to the Meath Hospital for a number of years, and known for 'Graves disease' (exophthalmic goitre) [C19-1698], Robert Adams (1791–1875), who was the first doctor to describe the 'synovial' cyst [C27-1509 vault] and Abraham Colles (1773–1843), surgeon to Dr Steeven's Hospital, known for the 'Colles fracture' [92 – 744]. To reach the family vault of Abm Colles Esqre take the Hawthorn Walk from the chapel, turn right down the Long Walk, and the vault is sixth down on the right-hand side.

Notable historians interred in the cemetery include William Hartpole Lecky (1838–1903), whose grave is located off the Laburnam Walk [C136-1183]. The grave of George Petrie (1789–1866), the antiquary, is easy enough to locate. From the main entrance, go up the Avenue and take the second set of little steps on the right-hand side. Walk straight ahead and at the facing marble cross, turn left. Ten paces up is the raised, flat, grey memorial stone bearing a Celtic motif with Petrie inscribed at the head of the stone and his dates at the bottom [C110-2603].

187

Sir William Rowan Hamilton (1805–1865), the mathematician and astronomer, was born in Dublin and educated by his clergyman uncle in Trim, Co. Meath. His interest in mathematics started at an early age. He entered Trinity College in 1823 and in 1827, while still an undergraduate, was appointed Professor of Astronomy and Superintendent at Dunsink Observatory. His greatest work, *The Elements of Quaternions* was published posthumously in 1866. A great lover of poetry, included among his friends were William Wordsworth, Maria Edgeworth, Samuel Taylor Coleridge and Robert Southey. His grave is inscribed:

Here lie | The mortal remains | of | Sir Rowan Hamilton Ll.D. | Royal Astronomer of Ireland | He was born August 4th 1805 | He died September 2nd 1866.

To reach Hamilton's grave, turn right onto the Low Walk inside the main entrance. Turn left then for the Long Walk. Take the first pathway on the left-hand side and Hamilton's grave is the second on the right-hand side [C116-3489].

George Francis Fitzgerald (1851–1901), the renowned physicist, is buried in a grave with other family members. There is no mention on his gravestone of his remarkable achievements. Fitzgerald's contraction theory of 1889 led the way to Einstein's special relativity theory of 1905. He died on 21 February 1901 [20/21-7953].

John Joly (1857–1933), was another distinguished physicist, engineer and geologist. Born in Offaly, he studied at Trinity College, and on graduation in 1883, taught in the School of Engineering. From 1897 to 1933 he was Professor of Geology [C17-20221].

Alexander Thom (1801–1879), the son of Walter Thom and Margaret Turner, was born in Moray in Scotland. In 1813 his father moved to Dublin for a position as editor of the *Dublin Journal*. Alex followed him to assist him with the *Journal*. Later he had his own business, Alex. Thom & Co., with an address at 87–89, Middle Abbey Street and printed *Thom's Official Directory of the United Kingdom of Great Britain and Ireland*, the first issue of which appeared in 1844. When he was writing *Ulysses*, James Joyce had frequent recourse to the information provided by *Thom's*. In his obituary, printed in *The Irish Times* on the 14 January 1941, his friend C.P. Curran wrote

He contained Dublin.... If Dublin were destroyed, his words could rebuild the houses; if its population were wiped out, his books could repeople it. Joyce was many things, but he was certainly the last forty volumes of Thom's Directory thinking aloud.

Alexander Thom would surely have been pleased at this comment! [C115-5372]

If Alexander Thom left us his *Dublin & County Street Directory* that listed the occupants of both business and residential premises, Sir Richard Griffith (1784–1878) left a valuable source for the researcher and genealogist in his *General Valuation of Rateable Property in Ireland* (c.1850–64), which lists every dwelling and land holding in the country at the time of valuation. It lists the names of the occupiers, their immediate lessers and the places and valuations of their holdings. Griffith, a geologist and civil engineer, was born in Dublin. In 1808 he surveyed the coalfields of Leinster for the Royal Dublin Society. He was involved with the improvement of the Shannon navigation and was Chairman of the Board of Works from 1850 to 1864. He died on 22 September 1878.

To locate the Griffith memorial, take the East Walk at the chapel [C87 2276 vault]. His memorial is located eight graves up [from the corner with Hawthorn Walk] on the right-hand side of the East Walk. At the base of the memorial is a book with a cross on the page. The inscription on the grave reads:

In memory of | Sir Richard John Griffith Bart | Born 20th September 1784. Died 22nd September 1878 | Aged 94 years.

Up further on the East Walk on the left-hand side before the convergence with all the other avenues, is the grave of Henry Hutchin Stewart [C11-5395] which is inscribed:

In memory of Henry Hutchin Stewart, M.D. | Founder of the | Stewart Lunatic and Idiotic Asylum | at Palmerstown County Dublin | Died 3rd Dec 1879 aged 82 years.

[63] The Huguenot memorial stone in Mount Jerome Cemetery.

In an obituary in the *Gardeners' Chronicle* Ninian Niven (1799–1879) was described as 'a landscape gardener with very few equals'. Born near Glasgow, he came to Dublin to work as Head Gardener to the Chief Secretary at the Phoenix Park. He designed the parterre and Yew Walk at the Viceregal Lodge (now Áras an Uachtaráin) and the garden of the Chief Secretary's Lodge (now the residence of the US Ambassador).

In 1834, Niven was appointed as curator of the Royal Dublin Society's Botanical Garden and was responsible for the layout of some of the paths which were laid in the 1830s which remain today. He encouraged people to donate unusual and rare plants to the garden, and in this way, built up a good collection at minimum cost. He published a circular containing details and advice of the collection of plants and seeds when abroad. In 1838, Niven set up his own business as a landscape gardener and nurseryman in Drumcondra and designed a number of demesne gardens. These included the gardens of two distilling magnates, that of Alderman Roe at Nutley, and Edermine, the estate of Sir James Power Bt, which overlooked the river Slaney in Wexford. He also designed gardens at St Helen's in Booterstown, Santry Court, Killakee, Athgarvan in Co. Kildare and Baronscourt in Tyrone. Niven died on 18 February 1879 [C106-177].

Mount Jerome with its rich heritage is gradually being restored. Details concerning the location of graves are available from the Administration Office during the hours 9.30 a.m.–12.30 p.m., Monday to Friday.

Mount Jerome, privately owned, is under the care of Masseys.

PETER STREET BURIAL GROUND (HUGUENOT)

SITUATION: DUBLIN 8

PERIOD IN USE: 1711 TO 1879

SITUATED IN CITY CENTRE

There was a Huguenot Chapel of St Peter, also known as 'French Peters' on the south side of Peter Street, opposite where the Adelaide Hospital used to be. This was built in 1711 after a problem arose in St Brigide's congregation in Wood Street concerning the lease of the house. The first pastor was Monsieur Joseph Lagacherie. This chapel continued in use to the year 1814 until the death of the chaplain, Monsieur Subremont. Attempts were made to reopen it in 1815 and 1828. It was finally demolished in 1840.

There was a cemetery attached to it, which opened at the same time as the chapel in 1711. The famous Huguenot artist, Gabriel Beranger, was interred here. Beranger painted in Dublin from 1750–1817. With the Italian architect, Signor Bigari, he travelled around Ireland on behalf of the Antiquarian Society of Dublin, and sketched places of historical interest. Throughout his journey, he kept a diary, which was regarded by Sir William Wilde as an important account of the time. Beranger's wife, Elizabeth Mesteyer, a Huguenot, was also buried in Peter Street.

Some inscriptions from the memorials were fortunately copied before they became too weather-beaten to decipher. They included an array of the most beautiful musical French names of professional, military, artistic, religious and trades-people who contributed so much to the city of Dublin. To delve into the pedigree and the family history of some of these families uncovers some of the most fascinating and amazing stories. Some of the memorials include:

This stone and burial place | Belong to | John Villebois of City of Dublin, Merchant | And John Villebois, eldest son of above | Died 26th April 1775, aged 20 years | Also of his sisters and | Brothers who died very young.

Mr Le Docteur Benjamin Barrington Domville | Died 19th October 1774

Underneath lie the remains of | Major John Corneille | Who died the 10th July AD 1792 aged 67 years | This stone was laid here | To mark the place of his burial | For the satisfaction of those who | Knew his virtues and revere his | Memory.

191

Corneille was descended from Rodolph Corneille of Amsterdam, the renowned shipbuilder who built a fleet of ships for Louis XIV, including one reputed to have been the largest in the world.

There was a memorial to Paul Magin of his Majesty's 46th Regiment of Foot who was born at Cologne Sur La Sprée in 1700, and died on the 17 April 1797. His wife, Henrietta D'Aulnis De la Lande, who was born in London in 1714 and died in Dublin on 13 January 1779, was buried with him.

The Reverend Gaspard Caillard, who was pastor in Peter Street from 1720 to 1739 was interred here. He also worked as pastor in Portarlington, which some claim was founded by the Huguenots. This town flourished due to the Huguenots' industrious and hard-working nature. Caillard's best-selling book, entitled *Sermons Sur Divers Textes de L'Ecriture Sainte*, was published in 1728.

The last interment took place in 1879. In 1967 the remains of all the deceased were removed and reinterred in accordance with rites of the French Reformed Church in a plot of ground in Mount Jerome Cemetery. The Reverend François Dubois officiated at the ceremony. The memorials from Peter Street were laid to the left and right sides on top of this plot but are not visible. A large memorial stone in Mount Jerome marks the plot bearing the name and date of death of each person.

A plaque inserted in a wall in Peter Street marks the site. It reads:

From the 19th December 1711 | This was the site of 'French Peters' | The church of the | non-conforming French Huguenots | Until the remains were removed | and reinterred in | Mount Jerome Cemetery in 1967.

The cemetery in Peter Street became part of the former site of W.R. Jacob and Co. Ltd, the biscuit manufacturer.

[See also: Cabbage Garden, Merrion Row and St Luke & St Nicholas Without]

Raheny (St Assam's) Church and Churchyard

Situation: Raheny Village, Dublin 5

Period in use: Unknown. Closed in 1925 except those with burial rights

Bus Nos (from city centre): 29A, 31A, 32A, 32B. DART to Raheny Station

Raheny, formerly named Rathenny, is situated on the Howth Road four and quarter miles north-east from Dublin city centre. It derived its name from *Rath Éanna* or the Fort of Éanna. The outline of this fort was still to be seen up to 1869 around the area of the old church. This is situated on a high mound at the end of the main street. Raheny is supposed to have formed part of the district called Rechen, which together with Baelduleek (Baldoyle) and Portrahern (Portrane), was granted by Anlave, King of Dublin, to the Church of the Holy Trinity, in 1040.

Archdall also notices it under the name of Rathena, as the birthplace or residence of a saint about the year 570, at which time there may have been a religious establishment here. Early saints in Ireland tended to locate their cells in isolated places. As the saint's fame spread, disciples would join him, and in time, the original cell would develop into a monastery. St Assam is associated with Raheny. One account describes him as a disciple of St Patrick and a talented metal-worker. He later became the first bishop of Elphin in County Mayo. His feast day is the 17 February. A holy well was also dedicated to him.

The church, which was originally dedicated to St Assam, was a small plain building said to have been reconstructed about the year 1609. It was rebuilt in 1712, as a stone inserted in the wall indicates. Not of great architectural merit, it was on a site of great historical interest dating back to at least the twelfth century.

Interestingly, Patrick Grattan, D.D., the grand father of Henry Grattan, was rector here from 1680 to 1703.

In 1888, All Saints' Church, which is on a different site, replaced the old church of St Assam's. Most of the old church was removed in 1920, the walls being reduced to three feet from the ground and leaving just the east gable, which looks quite imposing where it stands on a mound high above the street. On either side of the frame of what was formerly the east window, are placed three white marble mural tablets, all of which have been damaged and broken so badly that they are now quite illegible. The first

193

one on the left-hand side commemorates members of the Finn family. John Temple James Finn lived at the Larkhill estate in Drumcondra.

> *Sacred to the memory of James and Elizabeth Finn, late of King's Inns, Dublin,*
> *whose remains are interred at the East end of this church; the former departed*
> *this life May 10th, 1829 aged 52 years; the latter October 20th 1833, aged 60 years.*
> *Their sons John Temple James Finn and William Finn, have erected this monument*
> *as a mutual token of Gratitude and Affection in remembrance of their unceasing*
> *Parental love and attention; always shewn them by their Beloved and Regretted*
> *Parents.*

[64] ST ASSAM'S CHURCH AND GRAVEYARD, RAHENY.

The second mural tablet on the right side of the window commemorates the two sons of the Reverend Robert William Burton who was one time rector of the parish. The mural reads:

Sacred to the memory of Robert Edward and of John, the beloved sons of the Revd Robert Wm. Burton, Rector of this parish. The former died at Sidmouth, Devon, on 19th February, 1850, aged 16 years; the latter died at Meeanmeer, near Lahore, serving with his regiment, H.M. 51st Light Infantry, on 4th January, 1852, aged 19 years. 'I am the Resurrection and the Life' – John X1.25.'

The third memorial, which was placed just below the Revd Burton's memorial, had the following inscription;

This stone is erected to the memory of Robert Harrison, of the City of Dublin,
Esqr., who departed this life the 25th March, 1769, aged 70 years. Here also lie
interred three of his children, Robert, Harry and Matilda.

The churchyard is somewhat oval in shape and contains about thirty-nine memorials mostly made of limestone. These include memorials to Edmund Archbold, who died in 1711, and a memorial for the relatives of Mr Law, who was formerly a banker in the city. Another memorial commemorates the Grogan family. John D'Arcy, the brewer erected a headstone in memory of his mother and father-in-law, Peter and Jane Segrave, in 1845. There are some old trees, including yews, in the churchyard.

The churchyard, which is kept locked, is under the care of the Select Vestry of Raheny and is maintained by Dublin Corporation.

RATHFARNHAM CHURCHYARD

SITUATION: RATHFARNHAM VILLAGE, DUBLIN 14

PERIOD IN USE: UNKNOWN. NOW CLOSED FOR BURIALS

BUS NOS (FROM CITY CENTRE): 15C, 16, 16A

Rathfarnham village is situated four miles south-west from Dublin city centre. Rathfarnham Castle, the main historical building in the area, was originally the seat of the Loftus family, with Archbishop Loftus taking up residence there in the year 1585. It was during the troubled times of 1641 that the Castle was first used for the purpose for which it was built, which was for interposing a strong military station between Dublin and the mountains on the principal road leading to the south.

The Castle passed through various hands, the last owners being the Jesuits. It is now state-owned and open to the public.

During the 1600s, it was reported that the village was the scene of so many skirmishes and encounters between the Dublin settlers and the mountaineers, that it became a very undesirable place of residence and fell into a decayed condition.

A description was given at the turn of the century about the lovely rural access to Rathfarnham. It said:

> The bridge of Rathfarnham, over the Dodder, is several hundred yards from the village, the approach to which is rising ground, thickly shaded in summer by the trees of the demesnes on each side. The neighbourhood abounds in pretty seats and villas, commanding rich views of the Dublin Mountains and bay.

The village itself consists of one long irregular street with the spired and towered Church of Ireland on the right-hand side which was built in 1784. There are a number of memorials in the church commemorating many of the older families from the area. Included are two stained glass windows to members of the Yelverton family, one to the Jones family and three plaques commemorating members of the Shaw family.

There is a tenuous connection with Percy French and the church. Dr Houston Collisson, who was a very talented musician, was appointed organist here in 1885. He became friendly with French and they collaborated to produce the first Irish musical comedy, which was staged on 27 April 1891 at the Queen's Theatre in Pearse Street (then Great Brunswick Street) to a full house. It was called *The Knight of the Road* and was later renamed *The Irish Girl*. Later they produced another musical entitled Strongbow, which was staged, at the Queen's Theatre in 1892. Percy French died on 24 January 1920, and amazingly, Collisson died within the same week in London after holding a memorial service for Percy French.

There is no through traffic permitted through the main street now, which has been bypassed with a new road. In this way, the street certainly retains some of its former peacefulness.

Off the street, at the northern end of the village is the short lane, which leads through a large iron gate to an area of high ground. Here lies the ancient church and cemetery, which overlooks Shaw's Wood and the Dodder Valley to the west

A ruin in the centre marks the site of a church dedicated to SS Peter and Paul which according to Ball stood there at the time of the Anglo-Norman conquest. About the year 1780, it was described as a plain building with a small chancel and a modern porch. It became too small for the congregation and was seemingly in a very decayed state. In 1783, a grant of £400 was voted by Parliament for the building of a new church, the foundation stone of which was laid in 1784 by the Revd Philip Homan. It was on a different site, which has already been mentioned. On 7 June 1795, in response to a petition signed by Sir George Ribton of Landscape, Barry Yelverton of Fortfield and the Marquis of Ely, it was consecrated for divine worship.

In the cemetery and within the confines of the ruined church, there are approximately 166 memorials still remaining. All except about thirty-two have legible engravings. As in most cemeteries, there are of course a large number of unmarked graves of the many poor people who were interred here over the centuries. The letters IHS are inscribed on some stones, indicating the burial of Catholics.

There is one particular decorated slab indicating that the graveyard is of great antiquity. This is situated slightly to the north-east of the church. However, the earliest legible headstone inscription is dated 1689:

Here lyeth the body of William Phillips, who deceased ye 27th of Novemr 1689

Another old memorial is to Clark:

Here lyeth the body of Jane Clark the wife of John Clark, who deceased May ye 23 1698. Also the body of the above named John Clark who died Septbr the 20th 1720 aged 54 years.

One inscriptions reads:

This stone belongeth to John Creathon of Patrick Street and his posterity
Here lieth many of his children.

197

And tho here they lie in putrid state,

Reader think surely will be your fate,

And whilst you have that power that's given to man,

Pray merit a seat in heaven.

An interesting memorial is that of Ellen Crone which reads:

Sacred to the memory of Ellen Crone, for many years the devoted nurse and friend in the family of Abraham and Charlotte STOKER, and in whose services she died on 29th March 1869 aged 68 years

A plaque in the Rathfarnham Church of Ireland states that Abraham Stoker was for fifty years in the Irish Civil Service, Dublin Castle, and died at La Cava in Italy on 12 October 1876, aged seventy-eight. Abraham and Charlotte Stoker were the parents of Bram Stoker, the novelist and theatrical manager, best remembered for his book *Dracula*.

[65] THE ARCHWAY OF THE RUINED CHURCH IN RATHFARNHAM CEMETERY WHICH IS ON THE SITE OF AN OLDER CHURCH DEDICATED TO SS PETER AND PAUL.

Within the confines of the ruined church lie the remains of Archbishop Magee with several of his family. Magee was involved in a dispute in 1823 because of his refusal to permit Catholic burial ceremonies in Protestant-controlled graveyards. The tomb is somewhat raised and enclosed by railings.

In memory of William Magee DD, archbishop of Dublin, who died 18th of August 1831 in the 67th year of his age. And his second son Thomas Perceival, archdeacon of Kilmacduagh, died 16th of December 1854 in the 58th year of his age. Here are also interred the remains of Elizabeth Smith, third daughter of the above named Archbishop Magee and widow of the Revd Charles Smith, formerly rector of Arklow, born Novr 15th 1800, died Decr 27th 1873 aged 73 years. Here is also interred the remains of Margaret, eldest daughter of the above named Archbishop Magee & widow of the late William Hunter Esqre, the Lodge, Coleraine, Born 7th May 1795, died 21st October 1880 aged 85 years.

Also within the confines of the church, are three graves of the Shaw family which was prominent in the area. Of Scottish descent, William Shaw came to Ireland in 1689 from Hampshire. He was a Captain in King William's army and fought in the Battle of the Boyne. His mother whose maiden name was Markham, was a sister of the Archbishop of York and a direct descendant of Oliver Cromwell. Shaw was granted lands in Counties Kilkenny and Cork.

In the middle of the eighteenth century, Captain Shaw's great grandson, Robert Shaw, came to Dublin from Kilkenny and became a successful merchant in Capel Street. He later became Accountant General of the Post Office in Dublin. In 1785, he leased Terenure House, and in 1787 rebuilt part of it i.e., the front portion of what is now Terenure College. In 1796 Robert Shaw junior, aged twenty-two, married Maria Wilkinson, the daughter of his neighbour Abraham Wilkinson. For her dowry she received £10,000, Bushy Park House and over a hundred adjoining acres. The same year as his marriage, he inherited Terenure House on his father's demise. In 1799 he became a partner, contributing capital of £20,000 in a bank in Fleet Street, which was subsequently transferred to Foster Place. It was known as Shaw's Bank, and in 1837, was amalgamated with the Royal Bank of Ireland. In 1798, Shaw became, MP in the Irish Parliament for New Ross, and after the Act of Union, for which he voted, he was the MP for Dublin in the English House of Commons from 1804 to 1826. He held many civic offices in the city, including Lord Mayor in 1815–16. He was made a freeman of Dublin and in 1821 King George IV created him a Baronet. He died in 1849.

Sacred to the memory of Abraham Shaw, second son of Robert & Maria Shaw, who departed this life at Bushy Park on Monday the 21st August 1815 in the 17th year of his age. Beloved and lamented by all who knew him, he calmly resigned his gentle soul into the hands of his father & his God. Seed sown on earth to ripen for eternity;

199

Maria Lady Shaw died 28th March 1831 in the 54th year of her age. Lydia Cecilia died Novr 1st 1835 aged 33 yrs. Elizabeth Maria June 18th 1836 aged 13. Revd George Augustus, curate of Rathfarnham, Sept 1st 1839 aged 24. Major Beresford William, late 5th Fusiliers, Octr 20t 1847 aged 40. Sir Robert Shaw Bart March 10th 1849 aged 75 yrs. Also Sir Robert Shaw of Bushy Park, 2nd baronet, born 28th Sept. 1796, died 19th Feby 1869. Also Charles Shaw QC, born 27th July 1817, died 9th Dec 1870.

[Through Sir Robert Shaw (1796–1869), George Bernard Shaw, one of the greatest playwrights and wits of the English stage had a slight connection with Terenure. His grandfather, Bernard, was one of the Kilkenny Shaws]

In ever loving memory of Lt. colonel Sir Frederick W Shaw DSO, 5th Bart, of Bushy Park, Terenure, died 15th July 1927. And of his wife Eleanor Hester De Vere, died 13th Feb 1946. And of their youngest daughter Eile de Vere Shaw, died 27th April 1949.

Sir Frederick Shaw, who was educated at Harrow and Oriel College, Oxford, was a Deputy Lieutenant for the county and High Sheriff in Dublin in 1907. He was Colonel of the Royal Dublin Fusiliers from 1907 to 1913. He saw service in the First World War. He raised and commanded the 8th Service Battalion of the Royal Dublin Fusiliers 1914–1916 and the 2nd Garrison Battalion RI Regiment, 1916–18. He was awarded the DSO.

The churchyard contains the remains of many of the leading families in the Rathfarnham area over the last three hundred years such as the Griersons and Yelvertons:

Sacred to the memory of George Grierson of Rathfarnham House in this parish, king's printer for Ireland, only son of Hugh Boulter Primrose Grierson and Mary WILKINSON of Dublin. He was a man worthy to be held in remembrance for his services to his country in originating the reformation of farming in Ireland. Died 28th August 1821 aged 58. And of Charlotte his wife, only child of Thomas, eldest son of James THORNTON of Greenville, Co. Cavan, died 21st August 1812 aged 45. Also of their children Constantia Letitia & Charles Loftus Burgh who both died young. Maria Hester who died unmarried 22nd July 1860 aged 64. Constantia who died unmarried 10th August 1863 aged 62.

Rathfarnham House was later sold to the Loreto Order. While owned by Mr Grierson, it was a model farm noted for the production of prize crops and cattle.

The Yelverton graves read:

Sacred to the memory of Mary the Dowager Viscountess Avonmore, whose mortal remains are deposited here. This stone is erected by her afflicted daughter Mary Yelverton as a tribute of affection & duty to her beloved & revered parent. Dowager Mary Viscountess Avonmore, who departed this life Friday the 30th May 1834 in the 65th

year of her age, was the widow of William Charles, second Viscount Avonmore, who lies buried in the church of the

parish of Llanarth, Co Monmouth. Beneath lie (sic) the body of the Honble George Frederick William Yelverton,

2nd son of the 3rd Viscount Avonmore, died 26th of Feby 1860 aged 41.

To the memory of Barry John, Viscount Avonmore and Baron Yelverton, died 24th October 1870 aged 80 years. Also

Cecilia Viscountess Avonmore, his dearly loved wife, who died 1st Feby 1876, most deeply regretted, aged 69 years.

On the top of the stone is a crest.

There is a tablet on the wall of Rathfarnham church erected by Sir William Cusack Smith to the memory of an earlier Barry Yelverton who built Fortfield House in 1785. He is said to have been one of the greatest orators that ever adorned the Bar of Ireland. It reads:

In the adjoining cemetery are deposited the mortal remains of
Barry Viscount Avonmore, late Lord Chief Baron of the Court
of Exchequer in Ireland, who departed this life on the 19th day of
August, in the year of our Lord 1805. In consideration of having
long been honoured with his lordship's friendship Sir William
Cusack Smith, Baronet has obtained a kind permission of which
he avails himself with gratitude and pride by consecrating to his
respected memory this tablet. It is a plain one but it bears the
name of Yelverton, and therefore is not unadorned. The abilities
and worth which it might with truth record it, however, cannot be
necessary to commemorate here, of merits so recent and so eminent
as his, on the minds of the present generation the impression must
be strong; while considering the eventful periods which his life
embraced, and the elevated and active sphere in which it was his
lot to move, to transmit those merits to posterity seems the task of
the historian to whom, accordingly and fearlessly, it is surrendered
by the friend.

[66] THE GRAVESTONE OF ELLEN CRONE, THE NURSE AND FAITHFUL FRIEND OF ABRAHAM AND CHARLOTTE STOKER, THE PARENTS OF BRAM STOKER.

A poignant memorial is that to two former young friends:

YOUNG

Beneath this stone are deposited the mortal remains of two young friends, Master Walter Young of Monaghan &
Alexander CROSSLE of Anahoe House, County Tyrone. They were playmates in infancy who, having being separated
(sic) by the contingencies of life, are now met at a distance from their native homes, to part no more. The former
departed this life on the 22nd September 1824 aged 13 years, the later on the 14th of February 1825 in the 12th
year of his age. [Memorial broken in two parts]

There are also many parishioners, merchants and tradesmen from the city of Dublin interred in this
churchyard such as:

Here lieth the body of Mr Thos Ahmuty late of the city of Dublin, merchant, who departed this life the (5th?) day
of June 1775 aged 41 years. And here also lieth two of his children.

IHS memento mori. here lieth the body of Mrs Mary Carr and her posterity. She departed this life the 2nd march
18[0]0 aged 46 years. This stone was erected by her beloved brother Thomas BROWN of the city of Dublin, sadler.
Here lyeth the body of the above Mr Thomas Brown who departed this life July the 10th 1811 aged (6?) years.

The churchyard is under the care of Dublin Corporation.

RATHMICHAEL CHURCHYARD

SITUATION: RATHMICHAEL, CO. DUBLIN

PERIOD IN USE: FROM 1600. IT IS NOW CLOSED EXCEPT FOR THOSE WITH BURIAL RIGHTS

NOT ON BUS ROUTE

The easiest way to reach this lovely rural churchyard is to pass the present Church of Ireland in Rathmichael and continue on the Rathmichael Road, which leads to Ballycorus. Some metres up this road there is a lane to the left, and 300 metres up this lane is Rathmichael Church, the remains of a Round Tower and the cemetery. Remains of the old stone cashel or fort surround the cemetery. In his ecclesiastical account, Ball writes that Rathmichael is the most attractive site of a Celtic religious foundation to be found in the southern portion of the County Dublin.

St Comgall of Bangor is reputed to have founded the first church on this site, which was a monastery. It was built on a mound circa three hundred and fifty feet in diameter. The present ruined nave and chancel church dates from medieval times but incorporates part of the earlier church. It is a most interesting site.

Attached to the southern exterior wall of the building are a number of unusual early Christian grave-slabs with concentric markings and a cross, which were unearthed during the last century.

Nearby, at the south-west end of the nave, is the stump of a round tower, which is built of large rough blocks set in courses with smaller stones inserted in the spaces. It is one of four such towers in County Dublin, although there was one known to have stood beside the church of St Michael-le-Pole in Dublin city.

There are quite a number of memorials dating back to the 1700s. Many of these are buried or partly buried in the ground. The Reverend R.S. Maffat transcribed some of them.

An upright granite slab bears the inscription:

This stone and bu | rial place belongeth | to Thomas Traynor | Hamilton (of)Rassellen (?) and His posterity Here Lyeth the remains | of him who died | March the 2nd 1769 | aged 76 years.

To the south-east of the round tower are some of the earliest legible headstones, a few of which have similar ornamentation, which comprises clearly defined curved ornamental branches meeting at the top of the stone. Part of the bottom of these headstones lies buried in the earth.

Here Lieth the Body | Of Hvgh Denisson | Deceasd Febry ye 1st | 1724 aged 60 yr | Hvgh Denisson the | youngr Died 1751 | Ioan | Denisson Died April ye | 13 1754 Aged 82 yr.

A similar patterned upright stone is near the remains of the round tower and is inscribed:

Here lieth the | Body of Mary Mc | Cormack deceasd Mar | ch ye 1. 1753 aged 65yr | Lord have Mercy on Her Soul | Amen.

Here lieth the body | of Edward McNally | Deceasd Janry the 6 1758 | Aged 48 yrs

At the northern side of the churchyard is a headstone commemorating one of the local people from Loughlinstown. It is inscribed:

Ellen, wife of Richard Thompson, 1881

Richard Thompson had been Master of Loughlinstown Union.

Close to the east end of the northern boundary is a flat stone to Charles Edward and John Trench West, 1871. These were the two young sons of Mr West, a barrister from Loughlinstown House, which was located in the vicinity of the churchyard.

Two children from the city are commemorated with an upright slab with a clearly cut inscription, which reads:

Here lieth the Body of Garret | Kelly son of Michael and Martha Kelly of Montague | Street who departed this | Life 21st July 1808 | Aged 16 years | Also of their Daughter Mary | Aged 8 years.

In the vicinity of this churchyard, in a lane leading down to the Old Connaught road is a most interesting small twelfth century cross, which is supported on a base. There is a crucifixion on either side, one, which is in high and the other in low relief.

Rathmichael churchyard is under the care of Dublin County Council, Environment Department.

[67] THE STUMP OF THE ROUND TOWER NEAR THE SOUTH-WEST END OF RATHMICHAEL CHURCH. IN THE FOREGROUND IS
THE GRAVESTONE OF HUGH DENNISSON, DATING TO 1724.

St Andrew's Church and Churchyard

Situation: 26 Suffolk Street, Dublin 2

Period in use: 1171–1916

Situated in city centre

St Andrew's Church is situated on the corner of Andrew Street and Suffolk Street. This is no longer a place of worship and was sold recently by the Church of Ireland and converted for use as the city's main Tourist Information Centre.

St Andrew's parish was founded in the eleventh century, with the original church at the corner of Dame Street and Church Lane. A cemetery adjoined it, no trace of which now remains. In 1631 an unpublished Remembrance Roll stated that this church

> in the tyme of the late warrs when the enymy did without controule approch to the cittie walls became desolate and soe hath contynued ever since, whereby it hath in a manner lost the name of a church.

As a result a portion of it was converted into stables for the horses of the Viceroys.

A new church was erected between 1670 and 1674 near the present site, which was then called 'the old bowling green'. It was dedicated to St Andrew the Apostle and was after an oval model by William Dodson by which it acquired the name 'the round church'. This church and adjoining burial ground is clearly marked on *Brooking's Map* (1728) and *Rocque's Map* (1756).

In 1763 the parish petitioned the Parliament, pointing out that the church was in a ruinous and dangerous condition and that the churchyard was much too small for the interment of the dead. It informed the House

> that there is, contiguous to the churchyard, ground in lease from the city, which may for a small sum be purchased; that part of this would sufficiently enlarge the burying-ground, and open a communication with Chequer-lane, a passage there being very much wanted....

The House of Commons referred it to the Parliamentary Committee, which reported that £2,000 would be required for the church repairs, and said that it would be necessary to enlarge the burial ground of the parish. The church was duly repaired and James Lever, the father of Charles Lever, the novelist and doctor, carried out all the interior work.

The church was destroyed by fire on the 8 January 1860 and replaced by the present church, which opened in 1866. It is to the design of Lanyon, Lynn and Lanyon of Belfast. The entrance, which is in Andrew Street, is through a granite porch. Centred over the main entrance, there was a statue of St Andrew by the sculptor Edward Smyth (1749–1812). This was unusual, as apparently it was the only one erected over any Protestant church in the city. This statue, which looks sad and eroded and was once used for target practice, is now sited unobtrusively to the rear of the building. As a work of art and with its historic association, it certainly deserves a more prominent position.

[68] ST ANDREW'S CHURCH, ST ANDREW STREET.

A diagram dating back from the early 1800s shows the old Round Church and the burial ground, which was situated to the rear and on either side of it. It contained quite an amount of graves. It was recorded by G.N. Wright in 1825 that there was a burial ground attached which was preserved with much decency, but contained no remarkable tombs. In 1859, Thomas Drew surveyed this burial ground and he copied about two hundred and fifty inscriptions.

In 1916, only one of the graves which was connected with Lord Carbury's family was preserved. The inscription on it is difficult to decipher.

Situated close by is the monument erected to the memory of the troops from the 74th (Dublin) Company of the 16th Battalion of Imperial Yeomanry who fell in the Boer War 1899–1902. This is in its original position and consists of a polished marble column on a pedestal of Portland stone surmounted by a crown.

The following names of those who lost their lives are inscribed on the panel:

William G. Dawson, Robert Owen, Thomas Dowling, Walter D. Jeffares, Francis Knight, B.R. McElveen, Charles Mercier, Sutherland Pike, Alfred B. Smyly, Hugh Talbot-Crosbie, Edward Deane-Freeman, Carl J. Greene, Samuel Spence, Ernest R. McLean, Charles A.V. Bonynce, John Olliffe, R.C. Brady, Charles Gallis and James Carlisle.

On the back panel is inscribed:

This memorial was unveiled on the 5th May 1904 by HRH The Duke of Connaught, KP, Rt Hon The Earl of Meath, HML Patron, C.B. White, M.D. Vice President, A.M. Milligan, Hon Treas, R. Eager & J. Thompson, Hon Secs.

Many of the parishioners of St Andrew's were from well-known and respectable families who were engaged in trading or connected with the business world. St Andrew's was close to the stock exchange and was once known as the Church of the Irish Parliament. Some of the memorials within the church were dedicated to them, but were all removed when the interior of the church was altered to accommodate the Dublin Tourism Centre. The beautifully tiled altar floor was removed and incorporated into Drimnagh Castle, and the organ was moved to St Werburgh's church.

The Revd John Travers, nephew of the poet, Edmund Spencer, was rector here in 1693. He erected, at his own expense,

a commodious building, wherein were several apartments for the convenient lodging of poor widows, formerly housekeepers of this parish, and two rooms particularly set apart for a school for the charity girls, and lodging for their mistress.

Among the notable people buried here is Esther Van Homrigh, known as Vanessa. When she died on 2 June 1723 aged thirty-six, she was buried near her father Bartholomew Van Homrigh and her sister 'Molkins' in St Andrew's Church.

Jonathan Swift first met Vanessa, whose liaison with him is related in *Cadenus and Vanessa*, in Dunstable in 1707. Her father had been Lord mayor of Dublin in 1697, and in 1714, Vanessa came to live in the Abbey, in Celbridge, Co. Kildare. She also spent time in Dublin at the Van Homrigh's house at Turnstile Abbey (now Foster Place), College Green which is close to St Andrew's Church. Vanessa was described as follows by Orrerry:

Vanessa was excessively vain … she was fond of dress; impatient to be admired, very romantic in her turn of mind; superior, in her own opinion, to all her sex; not without some agreeable accomplishments, but far from being either beautiful or genteel … happy in the thoughts of being reputed Swift's concubine; but still aiming and intending to be his wife.

She never did become Swift's wife.

Interestingly, provoked by Swift's rejection of her, Vanessa left George Berkeley half of her property, having previously, it is said, accorded it in her will to Swift. She had only met Berkeley briefly on one occasion.

Andrew Cumpsty, a man of many talents who styled himself, 'master gunner of Ireland' died on 24 November 1713 and was buried in St Andrew's churchyard.

Cumpsty also ran a school at the 'Earl of Galway's Arms in Castle-Lane', where he taught 'arithmetick, geometry, trygonometry, astronomy, algebra, guaging, surveying, navigation, dyaling, gunnery, fortification, and the use of globes and instruments'. As well as teaching, he compiled astrological observations and almanacs. The final almanac compiled by him was issued for the year 1714.

[69] THE STATUE OF ST ANDREW, BY SCULPTOR EDWARD SMYTH (1749–1812).

Francesco Geminiani (1687–1762), the Italian violinist and composer who died in Dublin on 17 September 1762, was buried in St Andrew's. Born in Lucca, he studied under Corelli and Scarlatti. During his career, he lived at various periods between Italy, England, and Paris. He also spent long spells in Dublin, and from 1733 to 1740, he lived in Spring Gardens, a house in the lower end of Dame Street. A concert hall was attached to his home and here he received his pupils and gave recitals. Geminiani encouraged Carolan, the Irish harper, to compose a concerto in the Italian style. Mrs Delany, the eighteenth century diarist, mentions him a number of times in her correspondence. She refers to one of his performances which she attended, and was annoyed it only lasted under an hour, when 'I could have sat three more hours with pleasure to have heard it'. Geminiani was described as one of the greatest violin virtuosos of his time.

The earlier burials are under the church building, and their associated gravestones are placed against the walls. These stones, some of which are quite large and weathered are placed against each other on the far back wall of the site and are arranged in such a haphazard fashion that they are difficult to decipher.

Similar to St Anne's churchyard in Dawson Street, the burial ground at St Andrew's has been turned into a car park.

St Andrew's Church (vaults)

Situation: Westland Row, Dublin 2

Period in use: 1834. Now closed except to those holding burial rights

Situated in city centre

St Andrew's parish dates back to 1150, when the first church was situated outside the city wall. It is reputed to be the site on which the Danish temple of Thor and Fregjia once stood.

The present St Andrew's Church, also known as 'All Hallows' was designed by James Bolger and built in 1832/7. It replaced a smaller parish church in Townsend Street. Daniel O'Connell, who lived nearby in Merrion Square, took a great interest in its construction and presented some paintings, which include *The Martyrdom of St Thomas à Beckett*, which is situated in the south transept. Alfred Elmore (1815–1881) painted it, and a copy of it hangs in Canterbury Cathedral. O'Connell also donated the Baptismal Font of red marble, which is supported on a stone pedestal. It was nick named 'The O'Connell Font' by the locals.

Sculptural work includes a *Madonna*, *Our Lady of Sorrows*, a Carrara marble statue by William Pearse (1881–1916), which is on the altar in the mortuary chapel of the church, and *The Ascension* by John Hogan (1800–58).

There are several memorials within the church to commemorate families who are interred in the vaults. Amongst these is the Farrell Memorial [Vault No. 6], which is on the top right-hand side of the nave. It is a large white marble piece; one of the finest executed by the sculptor John Hogan. In 1843, it was erected in the church by the parents of the little girl who is portrayed in the work. It reads:

Sacred to the memory of Miss Jeannette Mary Farrell, | Who departed this life the 10th November 1838. | They who instruct many unto Justice shall shine as stars for all Eternity. Daniel X11.V.3 | Being made perfect in a short space she fulfilled a long time. Wisdom 10.V.13

This monument was erected by her sorrowing parents | Thomas and Margaret Elizabeth Farrell | As a record of her great devotion to God's love and service and of the zeal | For the religious instruction of the poor children of this parish.

In the vaults of this church are also interred | John son of the above named Thomas and Margaret Farrell | Who died on the 31st march 18?2 | The said Thomas Farrell who died on the 18th November 1852 | And Margaret Elizabeth

Farrell who died on the 9th October 1867 | Also James Farrell who died 8th October 1881. | Thomas Arthur Farrell, died 29th December 1898. R.I.P.

Close by is the large Netterville memorial in white marble. It bears the family coat of arms, underneath which is inscribed *Crucidum Spiro Fido*.

This monument has been erected by | Arthur James 8th Viscount Netterville | To the memory of his very dear beloved wife | Constantia Frances Viscountess Netterville | Who died at Paris, deeply lamented | On the 21st day of January 1870 | Aged 48 years. | May she rest in Peace | Also of the above named | Arthur James 8th Viscount Netterville | of Dowth Co Meath | Who died April 7th 1882, aged 76 | And his sister | The Honble Maria Netterville | Who died at Paris, March 4th 1890.

The church contains forty-nine vaults, some representing the families of eminent people.

On the main passage, vault No. 3 on the left side is that of the Hon Viscount Netterville. The title was created in 1622. James Lord Viscount Netterville, who was the first of the family interred here, died on 13 February 1854. The title became extinct with the death of the Rt Hon Arthur James Viscount Netterville of Dowth, Co. Meath, on 7 April 1882. Nearby to Dowth Hall is the ancient burial mound of Dowth. Apparently, the sixth Viscount Netterville, who was known to be slightly eccentric, used to sit on top of it and 'attend' Mass by focusing his telescope on a distant church.

Vault [No. 4] of Sir Dominic Corrigan (1802–1880), who had his medical practice nearby at 4 Merrion Square West, is a little further along on the same side of the main passage. He is interred here with other members of his family. Born in Thomas Street, Dublin, he studied medicine in Edinburgh. When he returned to Dublin, he set up a medical practice and became Dublin's leading physician. A lecturer in medicine at the Carmichael School, he first described 'Corrigan's pulse'. He was five times President of the Irish College of Physicians. As well as publishing many important medical papers, Corrigan wrote a travel book entitled *Ten Days in Athens*. He praised the climate of a health resort in Arcachon near Bordeaux, which helped to promote it, and as a result, the citizens named a street, *Allée Corrigan*, in his honour.

Corrigan died on 1 February at his home, Inniscorrig, Coliemore Road in Dalkey, and four days later was interred in the crypt of St Andrew's Church.

The Priests' Vault [No. 8] contains the remains of seventeen clergy, six of whom are commemorated with memorials in the church. The first priest interred was the Revd Thomas Carr, who died on 8 June 1834 aged sixty. The next three priests The Revs. Thomas Carroll, William O'Grady and Edward Morris, who died in 1839, 1846 and 1848 respectively were all in their early thirties.

A couple of the clerical memorials include one to the Revd Walter Meyler PP of St Andrew's and Dean of the Diocese of Dublin. He is commemorated with a marble bust. A native of Ferns, Co. Wexford, he was parish priest of St Andrew's for thirty years and died in 1864. The Meyler Memorial bears the following inscription:

Venite : Ad : Me : Omnes | In memory of | The Very Reverend Walter Meyler | Dean of Dublin | This monument was erected | By his friends and parishioners | As a lasting tribute to his exemplary piety | And zeal during a period of thirty years | Which he devoted to the discharge of the duties of | Parish priest of St Andrew's | He died on the V. January MDCCCLXIV in his eightieth year.

Just inside the mortuary chapel on the wall there is a memorial to the Revd John Brennan CC who died on 11 December 1907. It reads:

Pray for the soul of | the Revd John Brennan | Late curate of this parish | He was distinguished for his untiring zeal | In the discharge of all his duties | especially for | His advocacy of temperance | and for | His charity to the poor | His remains are interred | In the vaults of this church. | The altar in this chapel | is erected to his memory | By some of his many friends.

Some family vaults include those of John Walsh [No. 13] of Castlehill, Co. Mayo, Robert Hoey [No. 15], Kilmacud House, Stillorgan, Vault [No. 23] of the family of the late John Farrell Esq of Merrion Square and Moynalty, Co. Meath and of the late Thomas Farrell of Merrion Sq and Robertstown, Co. Meath, Vault [No. 24] James Harrison, Montpellier, Monkstown, Vault [No. 26] Lt Col C.R. Chichester, Runnamoat, Roscommon, Vault [No. 28] Nicholas Francis Coppinger and Vault [No. 29] the family of Sir Bernard Burke, CB Ulster and Mr Richard Gradwell of Dowth Hall. Vault [No. 27] contains the remains members of the Barnwall family including Sir Aylmer Barnwall Bt who was engaged at the Battle of Waterloo.

Terence Farrell RHA (1798–1876), the sculptor, is interred in Vault No. 44. He was born in Creve in County Longford and came to Dublin in 1810 where both Edward and John Smyth taught him. He was later a pupil of and assistant to Thomas Kirk in his Jervis Street studio. Farrell was well known for his portrait busts, a number of which were of notable people.

This church is of literary interest as it was here that Leopold Bloom, in the Lotus-Eaters episode in *Ulysses*, watched the priest celebrate Mass.

The vaults are under the care of the Roman Catholic Parish of St Andrew.

[70] St Andrew's Church, Westland Row, which contains forty-nine vaults.

St Anne's Church and Churchyard

SITUATION: DAWSON STREET, DUBLIN 2

PERIOD IN USE: 1720 – C.1870

SITUATED IN CITY CENTRE

The parish of St Anne's was established in the year 1710. The site for the church was a gift from Joshua Dawson and vested by him in trustees,

to the intent and purpose that a parish church, vestry, and other rooms and conveniences necessary for a church, might be built thereon, for the use of the vicar, ministers, and parishioners of the parish.

Included were a vicar's house, a garden and a churchyard. Some years later, at the request of the parishioners, the original site was exchanged for the one on which the church now stands. G.N. Wright recorded that

the parishioners [of St Anne's] are rather of the higher classes of society, as it is in a most respectable and fashionable neighbourhood.

The architect Isaac Wills designed the church, which is situated on Dawson Street opposite South Anne Street. Work commenced on it in 1720. It is portrayed on *Brooking's Map* (1728) as having an impressive front, but this was altered to a less elaborate form and in 1868, it was refronted by Deane and Woodward with its present Romanesque façade.

The interior of the church has a shallow rounded apse, a single span vault and a gallery supported by pillars of carved oak. It has particularly nice reredos panels, which were inserted in 1905. A theme is the bread of life and there is a sheaf of wheat in one of the panels.

On either side of the chancel there were originally two recesses in the wall, which were fitted with shelves. One of these remains. Every Sunday, some loaves of bread are left here, which are available for deserving cases after Sunday and early Monday services. There is an interesting explanatory inscription beneath the shelves, which reads:

The Right Hon Theophilus Lord Newtown of Newtown
Butler bequeathd to the Poor of St Anne's Parish for

ever Thirteen Pounds per annum to be distributed in
Bread at five shillings each week, 1723

Some of the earlier rectors of this church included Daniel Hearn, born in 1693, and a graduate of Trinity College. He was great-great-grandfather of the noted writer, Lafcadio Hearn.

Others included John Madden, Thomas Smyth (1752), Richard Chaloner Cobbe (1764), Hugh Hamilton (1767), Benjamin Domville (1768), Thomas Leland (1773), H.L. Walsh (1785), Robert Fowler (1789) and John Pomeroy (1794).

There is an amusing story concerning the Revd John Madden who was Vicar of St Anne's and Dean of Kilmore. One of his parishioners who lived close by in Molesworth Street, was Richard Parsons, described as a man of humour and frolic, who was created first Earl of Rosse in 1718.

He was fond of all the vices which the beau monde call pleasures, and by those means first impaired his fortune as much as he possibly could do; and finally, his health, beyond repair.

When the Revd John Madden heard that his neighbour the Lord Rosse was approaching death, he thought it his duty to send him a letter outlining the various points of his dissolute past life. He urged the Lord in the short time remaining to repent. When Lord Rosse read it, he resealed it, and using the messenger who had delivered it from his Reverend neighbour the Dean, he redirected it to Lord Kildare. Kildare was in every respect a contrast in character to Rosse and was so indignant at receiving such a letter from the Dean that he went straight to the Archbishop of Dublin to complain about him.

Upon reading the letter, the Archbishop summoned the Revd Madden who came immediately. He asked him if he had written the letter and the Revd confirmed that he had. The Archbishop informed him that unless he rescinded what he had said, he would have to resign his position in the church. Lord Kildare decided to sue the Dean. The archbishop, who was aware that the Dean would be ruined if he decided to defend the suit against the Lord, recommended to him that he ask Lord Kildare's pardon. 'Ask his pardon,' said the Dean, 'Why the man is dead!' 'What! Lord Kildare is dead!' 'No, Lord Rosse.' 'Good God,' said the Archbishop, 'did you not send a letter yesterday to Lord Kildare?' The Dean replied he did not but had sent one to the unhappy Earl of Rosse as he thought it his duty to write to him in the manner he did. On questioning the messenger, the mistake was rectified, and the Dean saw, with real regret, that Rosse died as he had lived, a jester to the end. The only person who suffered from the Lord Rosse's last joke was the poor messenger who lost his job!

Lord Rosse died in his home in Molesworth Street on 21 June, 1741, and was interred in St Patrick's Cathedral where he is commemorated with a marble plaque surmounted by a bust.

Felicia Hemans, the lovely and celebrated poet who died aged forty-one on 16 May 1835 in her home at 21 Dawson Street, is buried in a vault under the south-western side of the chancel. The stained glass windows in this church were put in between 1859 and 1860, and one to Felicia Hemans was constructed in the chancel after an appeal made two hundred and fifty pounds. Charles Dickens did not give a donation towards the appeal because, 'I would rather read Mrs Hemans by her own light than through the colours of any painted window that ever was or will be contracted for'. Wordsworth paid special poetic tribute to the memory of this remarkable woman and gentle poetess by commemorating her in his Epitaphs (number xii, stanza 10). A small white marble tablet with some lines of her own poetry marks the place where she was buried:

> Calm on the bosom of thy God,
>
> Fair spirit, rest thee now!
>
> E'en while with us thy footsteps trod,
>
> His seal was on thy brow.
>
> Dust, to its narrow house beneath!
>
> Soul, to its place on high,
>
> They may have seen they look in death
>
> No more may fear to die.

Laetitia Pilkington, whose memoirs were published in three volumes between 1748 and 1754, is interred here with her father who was a distinguished Dutch doctor in Dublin. Her memoirs, which are anecdotal and spiced with scandal, include her memories of Dean Swift. Her memorial, which is the newest in the church bears the inscription:

> In the Crypt | of this Church, near | the Body of her honoured Father | John Van Lewen M.D. | lies the Mortal Part of | Mrs LAETITIA PILKINGTON | Whose Spirit hopes for | that Peace, thro' the infinite Merit of | Christ, which a cruel & merciless | World never afforded her. | Died July 29th 1750

There are many famous people interred in the vaults of the church. In 1908, the Reverends Hon B.J. Plunkett and H.L. Denny carried out a search of the area underneath the church. Beneath the centre of the church, a passage runs north and south, at the south end of which there was a trap door leading to the churchyard. At the north end is an opening through which coffins were lowered into the passage. From this passage run four galleries, two to the east and two to the west, off which are the vaults.

The family vault of C.G. Otway is here. The following inscription is on the coffin plate:

Revd Caesar Otway | Died | 10th March 1842 | Aged 62 years.

In 1827, William Carleton met the Reverend Otway, who was co-founder of the *Christian Examiner*, a magazine associated with the established church. Under the influence of Otway, Carleton contributed sketches of Irish country life to the magazine, including a description of his pilgrimage to Lough Derg.

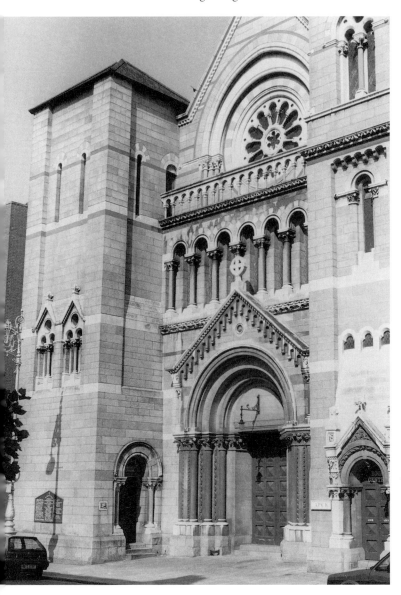

The churchyard, which lies east of the Church, is now converted into a car park with all the memorials removed. It was reported to be exceedingly crowded and contained the remains of many notable people. General Anthony St Leger (1732–1786), founder of the St Leger Sweepstakes at Doncaster in 1776, was buried there. Also included are Dr Brocas, Dean of Killaloe, Dr Stopford, Bishop of Cloyne, and the surgeon John Creighton, who introduced the Jennerian vaccination to Ireland in 1800 and who was twice President of the Royal College of Surgeons in Ireland in 1812 and 1824. The Revd Beaver H. Blacker recorded the inscriptions on a number of the memorials, including that of The Right Hon Lieut. General Pomeroy which read:

Here lieth the body of the Right Honble. Lieut.Genl. JOHN | Pomeroy, who departed this life the 10th day of June, | 1790, aged 66 years. He was Lieut. Genl. of His Majesty's | Forces, Colonel of the 64th Regiment of Foot, one of His | Majesty's most Honble. Privy Counsel, and Representative | in Parliament for the Borough of Trim, in the County of Meath. This tomb is erected to his memory by his nephew and heir, the Honble. and Revd. JOHN POMEROY.

Nearby and raised on a granite sarcophagus which was railed in was the burial placeof

Copeland Grattan, M.D., Surgeon 56th Regiment, who died on 27th May, 1850, loved and esteemed by all who knew him.

It is a pity that the churchyard of St Anne's was not retained, as it contained so much information inscribed on the memorials about the people interred there from all walks of life.

The church is noted for its number of interesting memorials, which include ones to Lord Downs, Hon Tankerville Chamberlain, and Miss Elizabeth Phibbs. The latter, executed by Smyth, is a rather beautiful white marble female figure leaning over a funeral urn. Sir Hugh Lane, nephew of Lady Augusta Gregory and founder of the Municipal Gallery, is also commemorated. A stained glass window commemorates Christopher Digges La Touche who was born in 1856 and died 27 November 1914.

Two members of the Witherington family are buried in St Anne's. Marriages in the church included that of Wolfe Tone to Martha Witherington on 21 July 1785 and also Bram Stoker, author of *Dracula* married the tall and graceful Florence Balcombe on 4 December 1878. Oscar Wilde, who considered her to be 'exquisitely pretty' had formerly courted her.

The church and crypt is under the care of the Select Vestry of St Anne.

OPPOSITE PAGE: [71] ST ANNE'S CHURCH, DAWSON STREET.

St Audoen's Church and Churchyard

Situation: Cornmarket, Dublin 8

Period in use: 1190–1885

Situated near city centre

St Audoen's is the only medieval church which remains in the city and has the distinction of serving its parishioners on a continuous basis for over eight hundred years. Dedicated to St Audoen or Ouen, Bishop of Rouen and patron St of Normandy, it was founded at the end of the twelfth century and was once a group of guild chapels, being as it was in the neighbourhood of many guildhalls. The only one remaining today is the Tailor's Hall, which was built in 1710 in High Street. It is possible that St Audoen's was built on the site of a former church, as a ninth century decorated grave slab was found. Known as 'the Lucky Stone' this is now mounted in the church porch.

St Audoen's Church is situated just inside the inner city wall of medieval Dublin. A passageway alongside it leads down to what remains of the city wall in Cook Street and St Audoen's Arch, the only remaining gate of Norman Dublin dating to 1240 AD. The restoration and preservation of this section of the Old City wall and Gate was part of Dublin Corporation's contribution to European Architectural Year.

St Audoen's, which is somewhat rectangular in shape, is divided into four sections. One quarter of it is occupied by the Norman church and nave and is the Church of Ireland parish church. On Sunday mornings before the service, the delightful peal of the six bells, three of which were cast in 1423, may be heard ringing out over this part of old Dublin.

St Audoen's was the burial place for many well-known families in the sixteenth, seventeenth and eighteenth centuries. These included those of Ball, Bath, Blakeney, Browne, Cusack, Desminier, Fagan of Feltrim, Foster of Bally-Dowd, Fyan, Gifford, Gilbert, Malone, Mapas, Molesworth, Penteny, Perceval, Quinn, Talbot, Ussher and Wemys.

The north wall of the church contains some seventeenth century wall-tombs on which there are no visible inscriptions. Recently restored, they are said to be those of the Sparke and Duff families. Both show figures of a man with his wife and children circa 1620. There are two small bronze tablets bearing the dates 1719 and 1730, which mark the site of the burial places.

Part of the church floor is paved with medieval grave slabs, but due to age, the lettering on them is now almost illegible. Some other graves in the floor mark the resting place of Lord Mayors and Aldermen of the Corporation. Nearby, at the corner of Skinners' Row and Nicholas Street, was a building known as the Tholsel where the Corporation held their meetings.

Dr Edward Parry, Bishop of Killaloe, and two of his sons, John and Benjamin, successively Bishops of Ossory, are buried in the vestibule of the church. Dr Parry died of the plague in Dublin in 1650. John Parry bequeathed an annual rent-charge of forty shillings for the preservation of his family tomb which, having been enclosed by him in 1681 with 'a rail and banister', got the name of the 'Bishop of Ossory's Chapel'. Many generations of the Parry family are interred here.

The burial place of Sir Matthew Terrell, a knight who died in 1649, is marked, and under the east window, is the vault of Robert Maple who died on 8 January 1618.

St Anne's Chapel, which was built about the year 1430 for the Guild of St Anne, is to the south of the nave. Due to a fall in the number of the congregation, the roof was removed from the whole of the eastern end of the church, and in 1823 it was also removed from St Anne's. It is now under the aegis of Dúchas, which has re-roofed and restored St Anne's and created a Visitor Centre with a most interesting display, incorporating the history of St Audoen's church.

St Anne's formerly contained a number of memorials, some of which date to the fourteenth century and may be seen as paving on the floor. There is a wall memorial dedicated to the memory of John Malone Esq, Alderman of Dublin, who died on 20 October 1592. It is recorded that

John Malone of the Sept of O'Malone in ye County of Westmeath was shireve of Dublin in Ano 1581, and afterward Alderman, and deceased a little before his tyme of beinge Mayor. He had to wife Mary daughter of Michaell Penteney Mayor of Dublin by whome he had issue Edmund, and three daughters ...

The memorial, only a part of which remains, was placed over the sarcophagus on the south wall of the aisle. The sarcophagus bears the names of John Malone and Mary Pentony. On the west end, it has the inscription

JOHN MALONE, MARY PENTONY, virit post funera virtus

and on the east

Ecce Rei domo clauditur omnis homo.

Many interesting features remain in St Anne's Chapel. Excavations revealed a cobbled lane, which went from High Street towards St Audoen's Arch. On the south wall there is a piscina which was used for washing the sacred church vessels.

221

Sir Roland Fitzeustace, Baron of Portlester, built the Portlester Chapel as a private chapel in 1455. Dedicated to the Virgin Mary, it is on the southern side of St Audoen's church. Fitzeustace, who was Chancellor and Treasurer in Ireland for a time, died in 1496 and was buried in Kilcullen, Co. Kildare at the Franciscan Abbey, which he built. His effigy and that of his wife Margaret was once in the Portlester Chapel and was moved inside the Norman church under the bell tower. The inscription reads:

Pray for the soul of Roland Fitzeustace of Portlester who gave this Chapel in | honour of the Blessed Virgin Mary: also for the soul of Margaret his wife and | for the souls of all the faithful departed: The year of our Lord 1455.

The Portlester Chapel also contained a slab commemorating members of the Terrell family:

Here under lyeth the bodies of Richard Terrell, Alderman, Mayor | of the city of Dublin, merchant and also of Walter Terrell, | Alderman,..and of their posterity. John Terrell, Alderman, son of the said Walter Terrell who hath caused this | monument to be made the 16th day of December Anno .. | Super est quod super est[What still abides above]. Here also lyeth the body of Matthew Terrell, the eldest son of Sir | John Terrell, knight, late Mayor of this city who caused this | monument to be finished in anno 1619. Obiit..

In the same section, a Dublin tailor was interred whose memorial bore the inscription:

Here under lyeth the corpses of George Dowde of Dublin taylor | who deceased 22 February in Anno Domini 1636 and his loving | wife Ismay Bagott departed this life the of in Anno | Domini upon whose souls the Lord have mercy Amen.

The Portlester Chapel, and the Chancel or northern aisle (built circa 1300) which is beside it, were unroofed in 1773 as the building was too large for the requirements of the parish. In 1887, the floor was concreted and the tombstones were laid horizontally on the ground. Many are missing and it is difficult to decipher the inscriptions on any of the remaining stones.

Some older memorials with incised lettering include:

HERE THOMAS HARVYE AND ELINOR HIS WIFE DOE | LYE SHE DYED AT YE AGE OF 17 JVNE 22 1673 HE AT | THE AGE OF 32 YEARES AT LAZIE HILL MARCH 19 | 1677

HEREVNDER LYETH THE BODY OF Mr SAMVELL | DISMYNERS SON TO ALMA [i.e. alderman] JOHN | DISMYNERES WHO DEPARTED THIS LIFE THE 13 | OF NOVEMBER 1690

An old slab with the inscription in relief was copied but only the following was legible:

...ERETON OF DVBLIN | MARCHANT WHO DE | CEASED THE IX DAY OF MAY ANNO | 1610. | HIER LYETH.

222

A memorial to William Molyneux (1656–1698) is intact. Molyneux, the philosopher and patriot, was interred in the family vault in the chancel northern aisle of the church in 1698. Born nearby in New Row on 17 April 1656, he was educated at Trinity College and the Inner Temple, London. He was known for his various works on philosophy, natural history and astronomy. He was joint Surveyor of the King's buildings and Works in Ireland and was first secretary of the Dublin Philosophical Society, precursor of the Royal Irish Academy. He went to live in Chester, during the war of 1689–91 and became friends with Locke. It was here that he wrote *Dioptrica Nova*, which was the standard work on optics for some time. He returned to Dublin and was elected MP for Dublin University.

In 1698, Molyneux's last and most celebrated work was published. This was entitled *The Case of Ireland's being Bound by Acts of Parliament in England, Stated*. This work caused uproar as it proposed the arrest of the English Parliament for the destruction of Irish woollen manufacture. Molyneux died on 11 October 1698.

[72] ST AUDOEN'S MEDIEVAL CHURCH IN CORNMARKET AS SEEN FROM ST AUDOEN'S PARK, THE FORMER CHURCHYARD.

223

Another old memorial in this area bore the following inscription:

Nicholas Skarly of Dublin Marchant caused this stone to be sett | heere for himself and his Wife Elizabeth Fleming and for their | posterity. The year of our redemption 1637. +IHS Blessed are | the dead which die.

The graveyard was situated to the west of the arch of the church. It was used as the burial place for the prisoners who died at the Newgate gaol which, at that time, was situated at the corner of the Cornmarket and had been one of the gates of the city wall.

The graveyard is now St Audoen's Park and there is a stone here commemorating James Napper Tandy (1738–1803), the United Irishman whose house was in Cornmarket. He was baptised in St Audoen's on 16 February 1738, where he was later churchwarden in 1765. He entered politics as a representative of the guild of merchants of the Common Council of the city.

No gravestones remain in this churchyard. Being as it was in the heart and commercial centre of a bustling medieval Dublin, many of the people who were buried here were wealthy merchants and also tradespeople. The names of the local streets indicate the trades, which were in operation from an early date. These include Cook Street (1270), from the Guild of Cooks once resident here, Weavers' Square from the weavering trade which was once brisk in the Earl of Meath's Liberty, Corn market, Fishamble Street (1467) being the place where fish was sold, Winetavern Street, Skinners' Row (1367), Skippers' Lane and Merchants' Quay.

There are merchants, craftsmen and mariners from near and far interred in the graveyard. Below are extracts from the inscriptions of some of the gravestones, which are now, missing, and which were copied by the late Edward Evans and published in the *Irish Builder* in 1886.

This stone was erected to the memory of William | Doolittle, of Bridge Street, in the city of Dublin, | Merchant, and his sister, Elizabeth Doolittle, otherwise Slator, who departed this life the 14th August 1796, | both aged 48 years. Who, whilst they lived, loved and | feared God, and was affectionate and kind to each other, | well loved and respected by all their acquaintance, | (and) happy are they who are in such a state (pre)pared | at all times to meet their God. (here also) lieth 4 of | their children.

Here lieth the body of Mr Thomas Mason, of Chester, | late of the City of Dublin, Merchant, who departed this | life the 25th day of May, 1759. For him and his | Posterity.

Here also lyeth the remains of Mrs Catherine Townson, | wife of Thos. Townson, of Dolphin's Barn-lane, tanner, niece of the above Thos. Mason, who departed this life | the 19th day of November, 1773, aged 42 years.

Also the remains of Mrs Margaret Johnson, wife of | John Johnson, of Marlborough Street, and Clark of St Thomas's, Dublin, niece of the aforesaid Thomas Mason, | and sister of the above Catherine Townson, who departed this life the 5th day of August, 1779, aged — years.

Erected in memory of John Birkett, of Whitehaven, | Mariner, who departed this life the 18th August 1788, | Aged 64.

This stone was erected by Mr James King, Manufacturer | in Glasgow, in memory of his brother, Mr John | King, formerly of the Parish of Kilmadock, in the Co. | of Perth, Scotland, but late of King's Inns Quay, City | of Dublin. He departed this life the 1(?)Of May 1804 | aged 5(0) years.

This stone is sacred to the memory of Sir Anthony King, | Knt., Alderman of the City of Dublin, who departed this | life 1st Sept. Anno 1787. | His spirited and unwearied exertion as a Magistrate for | the Peace and Welfare of the City will ever be remembered | with gratitude. The tears of the poor whose necessities he was to relieve, bespeak his private virtues. | This stone is also designed to perpetuate the memory | of Sarah Atkinson, otherwise King, wife of the above | Sir Anthy King. | Here lyes also the body of Anthony King, Esq, Son of | the above-named Sir Anthony King, who dyed the 19th | day of September Anno 1797. Aged 55 years.

St Audoen's Church is under the care of the Select Vestry of St Patrick's Cathedral Group.

St Audoen's Churchyard, now a Park, is under the care of Dublin Corporation.

The Visitor Centre, which contains an exhibition on the history of St Audoen's Church, is now located in St Anne's Aisle. It includes part of one of the oldest pavements in the city. This section is under the care of Dúchas/The Heritage Service. There is an Information desk and guided tours are available.

OPENING HOURS: MAY — WEEKENDS ONLY: 9.30 A.M.–5.30 P.M.

1 JUNE–30 SEPTEMBER: 9.30 A.M.–5.30 P.M. DAILY

St Bride's Church and Burial Ground (demolished)

Situation: Bride Street, Dublin 8

Period in use: unknown–1890s

Situated close to city centre

ormerly situated on the corner of Bride Street and Bride's Alley (now named Bride's Road), St Bride's or St Brigid's is of interest as it was one of Dublin's oldest and most important parishes in the city. Significant in medieval times, and one of the six parishes outside the city walls, it later included the parishes of St Michael le Pole and the old St Stephen's. On 12 March 1672, Richard Steele (1672–1729), the playwright and essayist, was baptised in St Bride's church.

In 1684, St Bride's church was rebuilt, and in 1886, it was united to St Werburgh's. It had a gallery on either side and at its west end. It contained a number of monuments, which included one to Sir William Cooper, Bart. Mrs Pleasants was commemorated with a sarcophagus made of white marble surmounted by the family arms. Her husband, Thomas Pleasants (1728–1818), was a generous man, and during his lifetime, he gave over £100,000 towards various causes. These included a donation for the building of the Meath Hospital, a contribution towards the entrance gate of the Botanic Gardens and a stove-house in the Liberties. He established an asylum for female orphans in Camden Street, which was opened in 1818. Pleasants Street, off Camden Street was named after him.

There was a small burial ground adjoining the church, which contained about seventy memorials. There were possibly other unmarked graves. The grounds were enlarged by The Reverend W.H. Irvine (1825–1828). Thomas Pleasants is interred here. Affixed to a wall, was a tablet, beneath which was a limestone slab on supports. The inscription on the tablet read:

> *Mr Thomas Pleasants by his last Will and Testament | directed that he should be buried in the same Grave | with his Wife Mildred, otherwise Daunt, and that his | Executors should have a Monument erected to her | Memory, as well as to that of her father George Daunt; | and thereby also desired that the Grave should never | more be opened; which Monument has been erected | in the Church AD: 1819.*

Mr O'Hanlon, the keeper of the Record Tower, was also buried here. He was killed by an insurgent named Howley in 1803. At the time, O'Hanlon was attempting to arrest him.

This burial ground contained a tomb of the Domville family, which read:

Here lie interred the Bodies of | Benjamin Barrington Esq who died | Decr. 1748 age 61. Margaret his wife, daughter of William Domville, Esq | who died Feby. 11th 1768 aged 81. The Revd Benn Domville D.D. son of the | above mentd Benn & Margt Heir at Law | and Inheritor of the estates of the Late Will: DOMVILLE, Esq of Loughlinstown in the | County of Dublin, who died on the 19th day | of Octr. 1774, in the 64th year of his age.

The popular clergyman, the Revd Richard Drury who held the curacy of St Bride's for forty-four years, was married in the church in 1807 and buried there 1827 aged sixty-nine. It was said of him that, despite his labours, he died an unrewarded curate. He lived in Exchequer Street, later in St Peter's Row and then in Bride Street. The Revd Philip Skelton, who was a close friend, often stayed with him when he visited Dublin. There is an amusing account of the visit of Dr Peckwell, the Huntingdonian, to St Bride's in 1783. The Revd Skelton was sitting next to the Revd Drury at the reading desk in St Bride's during the sermon, whilst Dr Peckwell preached over their heads and flung his arms about 'like the arms of a windmill'.

St Bride's church was demolished in 1898 for Lord Iveagh's improvement and redevelopment of the Bull Alley area incorporating the Guinness Trust Buildings. The bell from St Bride's, along with some of the wall memorials and memorial stones from the burial ground, were transferred to nearby St Werburgh's, and its organ was moved to the National Museum. The remains of those buried at St Bride's were transferred to a plot in Mount Jerome Cemetery.

St Catherine's Churchyard

SITUATION: St Catherine's Park, Thomas Street, Dublin 8

PERIOD IN USE: 1552–1894. Now Closed

BUS NOS (FROM CITY CENTRE): 51B, 78A

The first church on this site dates from 1185. It was close to the Abbey of St Thomas (of Canterbury). Consequently, the street on which it fronted was known as Thomas Street. Some of the oldest names of the streets are derived from the ancient churches of our city. St Catherine's and St James's were under the auspices of the Abbey of St Thomas. Between 1760 to 1790, the present church of St Catherine, with its splendid classical façade designed by John Smyth, was built to replace an earlier one, which was by that time in ruins. The planned spire for the new church was never erected.

In September 1966, the church was closed, deconsecrated and given to Dublin Corporation with the proviso that it would be put to community use. It was transferred then to the Bell Tower Trust, a voluntary group which carried out a lot of restoration on the building. St Catherine's is now used as administrative headquarters for CORE (City Outreach through Renewal and Evangelism). Funds were raised and restoration work commenced in January 1998. On 6 November the same year, the church was re-dedicated by the Archbishop of Dublin, Dr Walton Empey.

It was outside St Catherine's that Robert Emmet was executed on 20 September 1803 after the rebellion. A plaque commemorates the event.

The churchyard, which measures one hundred and eighty feet in length by eighty feet in width, is situated directly behind the church and is bordered by Thomas Court, Hanbury Lane and St Catherine's Lane. It was taken over by Dublin Corporation in 1986 and turned into a public park. At the time, there were 124 gravestones surviving, some of which were very old and of great historical interest.

By the time the churchyard had been transformed into a park, nearly half of these memorials had been removed. A vast amount of time, craft and workmanship went into the hewing of the stones, the wording and engraving, and with their removal, some of the history and heritage of the locality was lost.

Many of the gravestones date from the 1700s. Some of the older and more interesting ones are no longer in the churchyard, but the inscriptions were fortunately recorded. The bulk of the memorials still remaining are sited around the perimeter. Many of the inscriptions are now illegible due to age and weathering.

One of the earliest recorded memorials (now missing) was an oblong and decorated tombstone with the names of Bagot and Bathe, which was unusual, in that it had the inscription engraved around the perimeter of the stone. The IHS was underneath the top margin, and underneath this, there was a lover's knot with the initials WBE intertwined. The memorial read:

Hearunder lieth the corpse of Robart Bagot of Drogheda, marchant, survyvine ffeaffi of Sainte Katherins [C]hurch, wo deceased the 14 of Februarie 1613, and his wife Ellenor BATHE deceased the 5 of November 1616, whose souls the lord have mercy upon. Amen IHS. 'WBE'.

The churchyard contains the remains of the Reverend James Whitelaw (1750–1813) and his brother the Reverend William Whitelaw (1762–1827). Both were vicars at St Catherine's.

The Reverend James Whitelaw, author, statistician, historian and philanthropist, was born in County Leitrim and was educated at Trinity College Dublin, graduating in 1771 with a BA Degree. He laboured among the poor and established schools, industrial institutions and loan funds. He undertook a census of Dublin City in 1798 the main points of which are outlined in his *Essay on the Population of Dublin* (Dublin 1805). He worked relentlessly to relieve the distress caused in Dublin by the fall of the weaving industry after the Act of Union. He assisted in *The History of the City of Dublin* with Warbuton, the Deputy Keeper of the Records in Dublin Castle. On their demise, the Reverend Robert Walsh concluded it. Whitelaw caught a fever while administering the sacraments to patients in Cork Street Hospital. He died on 4 February 1813. His grateful parishioners commemorated him with a tablet in the church, which was subsequently moved to a new location in the Church of St Catherine and St James in Donore Avenue.

The eminent architect and engineer, William Mylne (1734–1790), is interred in the churchyard. A tablet in the church, which was erected by his brother, commemorates him. It informs posterity of the 'uncommon zeal, integrity and skill with which he formed, enlarged and established on a perfect system the waterworks of Dublin'.

In a vault in the church are deposited the remains of Sir William Brabazon Knt. He was commemorated with a monument, which was destroyed when the present church was being constructed. Brabazon was descended from the family of Roger le Brabazon, who in turn was descended from an ancient family in Normandy. Sir William Brabazon was the son of John Brabazon of Eastwell, Leicestershire. After succeeding his father, he was knighted on 20 August 1534 and appointed vice-treasurer and general receiver of Ireland, a position he held for eighteen years. In a letter from Chief Justice Aylmer to Cromwell in August 1535, he is described as 'the man that prevented the total ruin and desolation of the kingdom'.

In 1543, he acted as commissioner for receiving the surrender of the abbeys closed by Henry VIII, and as receiver of the official seals when Henry altered his title from 'Lord' to 'King' of Ireland.

229

[73] St Catherine's Churchyard, now St Catherine's Park, Thomas Street.

Included on the inscription on the tablet is that 'he was the first Englishman that planted in Conoght and wan the castle of Athlone'.

Brabazon died on 9 July 1552, at Carrickfergus. His heart is buried with his forebears at Eastwell and his body in a vault in the chancel of St Catherine's. The Earls of Meath are descended from him. There are a few street names in the area associated with this family such as Brabazon, Meath and Ardee.

An interesting inscription on a memorial, no longer in the churchyard, displays an association with far foreign fields:

Sacred to the memory of Mr Fredr Barker, stone cutter, late of this parish, who died 21st of March aged 58 years. His son Thomas died the 28th of August 1783 aged 9 months. His eldest son Fredr was killed by the French at Rugheda in Spain Dec 13th 1808 aged 27 years. Here also lie the remains of Mrs Elizabeth Barker, widow of the above Fredr Barker, who departed this life Feby 20th 1811 aged 64 years.

In respect of Frederick Barker junior, his death occurred during the Peninsular War in Spain just before Sir John Moore's retreat to Corunna. On 12 December 1808, Brigadier General Charles Stewart was in Rueda with cavalry having the night before surprised and overrun a French Post composed of fifty

230

infantry and thirty Dragoons. It would be acceptable in the circumstances to say that it was in that event that Barker was mortally wounded and died the following day as it is the only action reported in *Napier's History* of the war in the peninsula for the period 1807–1810.

In a corner of the churchyard, there was a tombstone commemorating the Protestant Orphan Society, which was founded in 1828. It contained the names of eighteen Dublin orphans aged between three-and-a-half and twenty-one, all of whom died in the 1800s. 'Suffer little children to come unto me'.

As well as two memorials to Emmet, one outside the church and the other across the street there is a plaque commemorating other men who took part in the Rising of 1803. This was unveiled on 28 September 1980. The inscription reads:

These men took part in the 1803 Rising:

Edward KEARNEY, carpenter, hanged Thomas St Sep 1

Owen KIRWAN, tailor, hanged Thomas St Sep 1

Maxwell ROACH, slater, hanged Thomas Street Sep 2

Denis Lambert REDMOND, coal factor, hanged Coal Qy, Wood Qy, Sep 8

John KILLEEN, carpenter, hanged Thomas St Sep 10

John MCCANN, shoemaker, hanged Thomas Street Sep 10

Felix ROURKE, farm labourer, hanged Rathcoole Sep 10, at his own door

Thomas KEENAN, carpenter, hanged Thomas Street Sep 11

John HAYES, carpenter, hanged Thomas St Sep 17

Michael KELLY, carpenter, hanged Thomas St Sep 17

James BYRNE, baker, hanged in Townsend St Sep 17

John BEGG, tailor, hanged in Townsend St Sep 17

Thomas DONNELLY, factory worker, hanged Palmerstown Sep 17

Nicholas TYRELL, factory worker, hanged Palmerstown Sep 17

Henry HOWLEY, carpenter hanged Kilmainham Jail Sep 28

John MCINTOSH, carpenter, hanged Patrick St Oct 3

Unveiled by Michael Mullen, Gen Sec IT&GWU, on behalf of the Dublin History Workshop Sept 28 1980.

The last burial in St Catherine's churchyard was in 1898. It is now under the care of Dublin Corporation Parks Department.

St Fintan's Churchyard

Situation: Carrickbrack Road, Sutton, Co. Dublin

Period in Use: 1850 to date

Bus No (from city centre): 31B

St Fintan's graveyard is situated on the southern side of the peninsula of Howth and is located to the right of Carrickbrack Road coming from the direction of Sutton Cross. Comprising of about twenty acres, it is in quite a spectacular location as before it stretches the whole of Dublin Bay and the city of Dublin. Behind it rises Shelmartin Hill, located in Howth demesne, where one of the biggest cromlech's in the country is sited. It is the great cromlech to Aideen, wife of Oscar, son of Oisín, grandson of Finn. Sir Samuel Ferguson wrote about it in his poem 'The Cromlech of Howth' and Gabriel Beranger made a sketch of it in 1775.

The graveyard is unusual in layout as it is on a gradual slope and comprises four different sections. These are divided by hedges, and in one case, by a wall. From the top, the first section is referred to as the 1907 Section. This is an extension of the original old graveyard, which is known as the 1889 Section. It is here that the small ruined church of St Fintan may be seen. The church is an oblong building and has a belfry rising over the gable of its western wall.

The third section is known as the 1954 Section, so called after the date it was opened, and the final section is known as the Lawn. Here there are no upright memorials. All the monuments are laid flat into the ground, giving it a spacious and uninterrupted garden appearance when viewed from the uphill older part of the cemetery. The Lawn Section was opened in 1972.

Amongst those included in this cemetery are poets, writers, actors and artists.

Padraic Colum (1881–1972) and his wife Mary Maguire (1884–1957) are buried in Section 1954. Their grave no. is B20. Enter over the stile at the entrance, and follow the path straight across the width of the section. When it winds down a little slope, turn left at the yew tree and the Colum memorial is the third grave in on the left-hand side. Their grave is marked with a large Celtic cross. Covering the grave is granite stone. Both the cross and the stone are inscribed in beautiful lettering with the following:

Mary Maguire | Colum 13 June | 1884 Collooney | Co. Sligo 22 Oct | 1957 New York City | RIP |

Padraic Colum | Poet Dramatist Novelist | Longford | 8 December 1881 + Enfield Connecticut | 11 January 1972.

Dream of me there in stirless air

Beyond the seagulls range

Above enshadowed beings we name

Time and loss and change

Mary, who was born in Sligo, was a writer and lecturer. Her books include *Life and the Dream*, *From These Roots* and *Our Friend James Joyce*, which she wrote in conjunction with her husband.

Padraic Colum was an outstanding character of the Irish Literary Renaissance. His life spanned almost a century, a period which he described as long enough to be historical. During his distinguished career, he was poet, playwright, biographer, novelist, folklorist and writer of children's books, but it is primarily as a poet that he is remembered. Apart from his plays, he published sixty-one books and various poetic broadsheets which were illustrated by Jack B. Yeats and published by the Cuala Press.

Colum died in Enfield, Connecticut, in his ninety-first year and was interred in St Fintan's on 18 January 1972. During the Requiem Mass in Beechwood Church, Ranelagh, John Montague read extracts from Colum's *Blackbird*, *Sojourner* and *The Fourteenth Station* in his beautiful poet's voice. Colum's cortège then passed through many parts of Dublin City associated with his friend, James Joyce, and out along the seacoast to St Fintan's where Dr Benedict Kiely delivered a fine oration. Due to illness, Micheál MacLiammóir was unable to attend. Edmund Krochalis from Connecticut read a fine tribute by MacLiammóir to his lifelong friend at the graveside. Below is an extract from it:

His own world, his innermost secret, lay in the bare and stony tracks, not of the desert but of the boglands of Connaught…. But Padraic Colum always found gold hidden under the sod, as well as at the foot of the rainbow. His image is before me as I speak these words: a short, sturdy figure with a face that, for all its smiling and eloquent friendliness, recalls the face of Dante. He was among the earliest poets of the Renaissance that grew out of Yeats's dreams: his lovely Thomas Muskerry was among the earliest and the finest of the older Abbey Theatre plays…. His soul will journey on forever young and joyous. May the wild earth that covers his body lie lightly over him [B Section 24 in 1954 extension].

Micheál MacLiammóir (1899–1978) is buried not too far away in St Fintan's in the new section with his companion Hilton Edwards (1903 – 1982). MacLiammóir was born Alfred Wilmore in Kensal Green, London, and came to work in Ireland with Andrew McMaster, the actor-producer who toured the country. It was through McMaster that he met Hilton Edwards, the actor-producer-director, and in 1928 they formed a partnership which became the most celebrated in the history of the Irish theatre. Together they founded the Taibhdhearc na Gaillimhe in Galway city, and in the same year they also founded the Gate Theatre in Dublin.

233

With Hilton Edwards, MacLiammóir was made a Freeman of the City of Dublin and from France he received the Chevalier of the *Légion d'honneur*. He died on 6 March 1978 at 4 Harcourt Terrace, the home he had shared with Edwards for thirty-four years. On its way from University Church, his cortège passed his beloved Gate Theatre where a wreath was placed on it. At his graveside, Hilton Edwards recited the dirge from Cymbeline:

Fear no more the heat o' the sun,
Nor the furious winter's rages;
For thy worldly task has done,
Home art gone, and ta'en thy wages;
Golden lads and girls all must
As chimney-sweepers, come to dust.

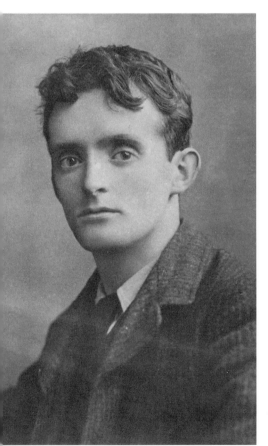

Hilton Edwards, who survived MacLiammóir by over four and half years, joined him at noon on 22 November 1982. They lie side by side in St Assam's in the Lawn Section in St Fintan's [Grave No. 6-8K].

Mainie Jellett (1897–1944) the abstract and figure painter is buried in the older section [Section F – 50]. She studied art from an early age. Aged eleven, she took lessons in watercolour painting in a class which was given by Elizabeth Yeats. In 1914, she entered the Dublin Metropolitan School of Art where William Orpen was teaching at the time. She then went to London to study at the Westminster Art School under Walter Sickert. It was here in 1917 that she first met Evie Hone (1894–1955), who became her lifelong friend. With Hone she became a student of André Lhote, and later with Albert Gleizes at his studio near Paris. Jellett held exhibitions in London, Paris and Amsterdam and her works are in many galleries including the Irish Museum of Modern Art, the Hugh Lane Municipal Gallery of Modern Art and the National Gallery of Ireland. She died on 16 February 1944.

St Fintan's Cemetery is under the care of Fingal County Council.

[74] PADRAIC COLUM AS A YOUNG MAN. (COURTESY OF MÁIRE O'SULLIVAN)

St George's (Little) Churchyard

SITUATION: HILL STREET, DUBLIN 1

PERIOD IN USE: UNKNOWN

SITUATED IN CITY CENTRE

A medieval parish of St George formerly existed with its church sited in George's Lane, near the junction of Exchequer Street and South Great George's Street, but this parish became extinct at an early date.

Sir John Eccles built the Chapel of Little St George in 1714 in Temple Street [now Hill Street] for his Protestant tenantry. This church, which measured sixty-five feet long by thirty feet wide, was closed and demolished in 1894, but the black calp tower of it still stands. A cemetery was attached to this, which was described as 'crowded in a most shameful manner'. The surface of the churchyard was several feet above the level of the street. Sir John Eccles is buried here and his gravestone is on the east wall on the right-hand side. The churchyard is now open space, and since 1930, it has been a children's playground. Many of the remaining gravestones are in an upright position around the perimeter.

A tablet on the outer wall of Church Tower reads:

This is the Burial Place of | Mr John Hindman of the | City of Dublin Carpenter | and his posterity | Here lyeth the Body of Mr | Josiah Hindman his Father | who departed this life the | 27th day of November 1738 in | the 86th year of his age.

Two upright stones in the churchyard are inscribed:

Here lies the Body of | Francies Kell Marchant of Drogheda who departed | this life December the 2nd | 1765 aged 29 years.

This stone was erected here by | Andw Spence Esq in memory | of his Love and beloved Wife | Mrs Bridget Spence who departd | this life the 29th of November 1798 | aged 45 years and in memory of | his Mother Mrs | Spence. [the inscription is partly buried]

It formerly contained the family tomb of the local Dix family. The inscription read:

Sacred to the memory of | Ebenezer Dix late of this City Obit 5th June 1824 aged 74 years | buried in the City of Edinburgh | And in this churchyard lie the remains of | Mary Dix otherwise Davies his wife obit 7th July 1820, aged 74 years | And their son | Thomas Dix a Captain in his Majesty's 57th Regt. | obit 15th Sep. 1820, aged 35 years |

235

The inscription is quite long and contains other members of the Dix family. The side tablet was inscribed:

This tablet | is erected by | William Dix | of Gardiner's Place | in this City Esqre | to the Memory of | his dearly beloved wife | Julia Dix | otherwise Hudson | obit 21st January 1840 | aged 54 years. And the end tablet was inscribed:

Erected by | William Dix and Julia his wife | To the memory of | their beloved daughter | Julia Eliza Dix | born the 5th July 1814 | Died Augt 1st 1837 aged 23 years.

The churchyard is under the care of Dublin Corporation.

[75] THE TOWER OF LITTLE ST GEORGE'S CHURCH ON HILL STREET.

St George's Cemetery (Whitworth Road)

Period in use: 1820s–1962

Situation: Whitworth Road, Drumcondra

Bus Nos (from city centre): 3, 11a, 13a, 16a, 33 and 33b to Drumcondra Station or 13, 40, 40a, 40b or 40c, and alight at stop No. 33. This is just across the road from the cemetery

This cemetery served the Parish of St George, when the parish church was located at Hardwicke Place. Designed by Francis Johnston, the church was built between 1802 and 1813. It ceased to be a place of worship in 1990.

The present St George's Cemetery is located on Whitworth Road by the banks of the Royal Canal. It was opened for interments in 1817, was consecrated on 20 May 1824 and was closed for burials by order of Dublin Corporation in 1962.

The entrance is through an archway in the old stone wall, which surrounds the graveyard, which is almost square in shape. The old Whitworth Hospital (now the National Council for the Blind of Ireland) overlooks it at one end, and houses overlook the other sides. It contains a variety of stone squares, headstones and tombstones. The place looks quite grey, as there are just a few straggly trees, which have seen better days.

The noted architect Francis Johnston (1761–1829), who played an important role in the classical renaissance at the end of the eighteenth century in Dublin, is interred here. His grave, over which a sarcophagus monument is erected, is the most prominent edifice in this area, and is reached by following the pathway straight from the entrance gate on the south to the opposite north side. Almost halfway along this path, the memorial may be seen. It bears the inscription:

Underneath is interred | the remains of Mr Francis Johnston | Who departed this life on the 14th day of May, 1829, | in the 69th year of his age. | Also | Mrs Anne Johnston, | Relict of the above named Francis Johnston, | Who departed this life on the 18th August, 1841, | In the 72nd year of her age.

Johnston's best-known work in Dublin is the General Post Office in O'Connell Street and of course his masterpiece, St George's Church in Hardwicke Place. He worked and studied under Thomas Cooley and was chief architect to the Board of Works by 1811. Johnston carried out a lot of work at the Royal

Hospital Kilmainham, having remodelled the original dining room in the Masters Quarters by extending it into the arcade. He also designed the Richmond Gate Tower at the West entrance to the hospital, and numerous churches and country houses.

Johnston lived at 64 Eccles Street, where he kept a number of bells in the stable to the rear of his house. These were rung on special occasions. Understandably it did not make him too popular with his neighbours. He presented these to St George's Church in 1828. He endowed the bells with an annual sum, which was given to the ringers to hold a dinner, the condition being that the bells were to be rung on certain occasions, one of which was his birthday! Sadly too, they tolled on his death. The bells of St George's are immortalised in *Ulysses*:

> *A creak and a dark whirr in the air high up. The bells of St George's church. They tolled the hour: loud dark iron.*

With the closure of St George's Church, and its conversion into a theatre, the bells were transferred to Christ Church in Taney and rang in the new millennium.

However, a number of interesting memorials remain in the building commemorating some of the people buried in St George's cemetery. There is a mural tablet dedicated to an academic named Charles Metzler Giesecke who was born in Augsburg in 1761. Mr Giesecke must surely hold the record for having the most letters after his name, thirty in all, engraved on any memorial in the entire country. He devoted thirty-six years to the sciences of mineralogy and geology and travelled widely in the course of his works, having spent seven years in Greenland despite its inhospitable climate. He was known to many of the crowned heads of Europe and was professor of Mineralogy in the Royal Dublin Society for nineteen years. He died on 5 March 1833. A portrait of him by Sir Henry Raeburn hangs in the Council Chamber of the Royal Dublin Society.

One of the most obvious memorials in the graveyard which towers above the rest is the tomb of Richard Carmichael (1776–1849), the eminent Dublin surgeon. This is situated to the left of the entrance.

Carmichael died as the result of an accidental fall from his horse when he took a short cut, from Dublin City to his home, over the sands at low tide. Carmichael was an immense loss to the world of medicine. He had an interesting and varied career, having served as surgeon to a regiment with the Wexford Militia. He was President of the Royal College of Surgeons in Ireland on three different occasions. The Richmond Medical School, which was founded in 1826, was later renamed the Carmichael School of Medicine.

A young medical doctor who is interred here is Ephraim McDowell, who with Carmichael and Robert Adams, founded the Richmond Medical School. He was Censor to the Royal College of Surgeons in Ireland and Surgeon to the Richmond Hospital.

[76] THE GRAVE OF FRANCIS JOHNSTON (1761–1829), THE NOTED ARCHITECT.

In his XXXVIIIth year he was removed from his sphere of usefulness | Honoured and beloved by all who knew him, | But especially by his numerous apprentices, | Who, mourning for their loss, have raised this marble | To commemorate the virtues of an excellent and amiable man.

The graveyard contains the remains of Ann Hutton, the fiancée of Thomas Davis (1814–45), the poet, nationalist and journalist. Ann first met Davis in 1843 at a dinner at her father's country home near where Beaumont Hospital is now sited. She was aged eighteen and he was twenty-nine. Her parents sent her abroad a number of times so that she might forget him, but she did not, and by late July in 1845 they were engaged to be married. Sadly, Davis died of scarlet fever on the 16 September the same year. Ann never recovered from his death and died eight years later. She was one of the Hutton family of John Hutton and Son, the well-known coachbuilders from Summerhill. The company was responsible for building the Irish State coach for Queen Victoria, which is still in use today.

Some of the military graves include:

510 Corporal R. Hurst, South Irish Horse, 4th April 1917 aged 25

The standard military gravestone bearing the emblem of the regiment may be seen near the pathway due north of the Carmichael memorial.

Nearby is:

John Thomas Lowry | lieut. 8th Kings Rgt. of Foot | Born 4th July, 1789 | Died 29th April 1888 | A good soldier of Jesus Christ 2 Timothy 11.

358528 Gunner, R.A. Deegan, Royal Garrison Artillery, 6th November 1918.

This is situated on the top of the east pathway.

Henry Christian Murphy | Died 5 Feb. 1914 aged 84 | Served at | Balaclava, Inkerman and Sebastopol | and also his wife | Georgina Emily Murphy | wounded during Rebellion | Died 29 April 1916, aged 59.

This is twenty-three paces up from the entrance gate on the left-hand side. Twenty paces further on is:

553815 Sergeant | N.F. Boxwell | wireless operator | Air Gunner | Royal Air Force | 21 August 1942 aged 19.

The cemetery is under the care of the Select Vestry of St George.

---

[77] THE TOMB OF RICHARD CARMICHAEL (1776–1849), THE EMINENT DUBLIN SURGEON.

St James's Churchyard

Situation: James's Street, Dublin 8

Period in use: 1627–1954 [Closed except to those with burial rights]

Bus Nos (from city centre): 51B, 78A

The fairly large churchyard of St James's is hidden away behind St James's church, now numbered 121 James's Street. Closed in 1963, the church is no longer a place of worship and is used for commercial purposes.

Nearby is the recently restored fountain, which is an obelisk, ornamented by four sundials. It was designed by the architect Francis Sandys and erected in 1790. Interestingly, the old custom of carrying the coffin three times around this sundial before a burial is still remembered. This was in order to recite the burial prayers prior to interment in St James's churchyard, as Catholic priests were not permitted to officiate at burials within Protestant churchyards. It was recorded that the Pope offered up a Pontifical Mass in Rome on St James's Day for the repose of the Catholics buried in St James's Graveyard.

The church of St James, which was founded in medieval times, was located on this site. It was dedicated to the Apostle, James the Greater, the patron saint of Spain and also the patron of lepers. The remains of St James are buried in Santiago de Compostela, which was one of the great pilgrimage centres and the third most important city of pilgrimage after Jerusalem and Rome.

Ireland had close connections with Compostela from medieval times. In 1220, two hospitals were founded for lepers in Dublin. St Stephen's was on a site in Mercer Street and Lazaretto was located on Lazar's Hill, which was near Townsend Street. Intending pilgrims for the shrine of Compostela stayed here. The journey, which took about four days, usually commenced from St James Gate, through which the old road from the west, the Slíghe Mór, passed to what is now High Street to become the main street of the medieval city. St James's Gate is marked on *Speed's Map of Dublin* (1610) and on *Brooking's Map of Dublin* (1728).

The earliest documented reference to St James's church is dated 1268. Following the Reformation, it was united with the parishes of St John in Kilmainham and St Catherine's. The old church of St James fell into disuse and quickly became a ruin.

By an Act of parliament in 1707, the parish of St James was separated from St Catherine's, and shortly afterwards, the Protestant church of St James was built on the site. The new church was described as a long, low and narrow building. It collapsed in 1761, but was repaired soon after.

The present church, the third to be built on the same site, was designed by Joseph Welland, architect of the Church Commissioners. It was erected in the period between 1859 to 1860. In the 1940s, the spire of the church was deemed to be in a dangerous condition, and in the late 1940s thirty feet of it was removed, leaving the spire somewhat stunted. In 1956, it was recommended by the City and Town Parish Commission that the parish of St James should be united with that of St Catherine's. The last service held in the church was on 14 April 1963 and the Archbishop of Dublin Dr George Simms was the preacher.

In 1987 to 1988 FÁS and the St James's Development Association sponsored a programme to restore St James's churchyard and record the headstone inscriptions. During the work, 705 memorials were uncovered, 537 of which had inscriptions which were legible. The burial records indicated that, between the period 1742 to 1836, the number of people who were interred in this burial ground amounted to 30,000. Well over that number must have been interred there over the centuries, the vast majority of whom would not have been commemorated with a memorial. During this work, two medieval stones dating from the fifteenth and sixteenth centuries were located which could have been remnants of an earlier church

The churchyard, which comprises one and a half acres and slopes down towards the river, is one of the oldest burial grounds in what is now the inner city. Along with Bully's Acre in Kilmainham and St Kevin's in Camden Row, it was the burial ground most used by Catholics during penal times. It is shown on *Bernard de Gomme's map of The citty and suburbs of Dublin* (1673) and it is seen quite clearly on *Charles Brooking's Map* of 1728 and *Rocque's Map of Dublin* of 1756. On all of these maps, the site is still surrounded by fields.

Just as the feast day of St John was celebrated at nearby Kilmainham, the feast of St James, which falls on 25 July, was celebrated by St James's Fair which was held in James's Street, opposite the churchyard. The graves were decked with ornaments and garlands of white paper which had been fashioned into fanciful forms. There was a holy well known as St James's Well in close proximity to St James's Gate. The fair is mentioned in Holinshed's *Chronicles*, 1577 and also described by Barnaby Rych in his *New Description of Ireland* 1610.

The will of Walter Segyne or Soggyn, proved in 1495, in which he asked to be buried 'in the church of St James without the city' is the earliest reference to a burial in St James's.

The earliest legible headstone recorded dates from 1627. There are a number of memorials, which are placed over vaults, which were erected and paid for by the relatives of the deceased.

A large monument in the centre of the churchyard commemorates Tipperary born Sir Theobold Butler, who framed the *Articles of Limerick*, in 1691. A distinguished lawyer, he was knighted in 1689. He became Solicitor General for Ireland and pleaded the Irish cause in the Commons in 1704. He was made a Knight in the Order of St James of Compostela for his loyalty to King James II during his short sojourn in Ireland. He died in his residence in nearby Nicholas Street in 1721.

The Butler monument comprises a high wall of plastered brickwork surmounted by a circular overhead on front of which are the heads of three cherubs surrounding a medallion. Beneath is a tablet bearing a Latin inscription, which was translated in the *Irish Builder* as follows:

> *This bust is a likeness of Sir Theobold Butler, an Irish lawyer, | an honour to the laws, his name and his country, Invested, not exalted, with the equestrian dignity. An advocate, Judicious, | upright, polished, eloquent, excelling in the native and his | legal dialect, not in partial Justice, not in search of favours, | not in flattering language, but in weight of arguments, innate | force of genius and a consummate knowledge of the laws. A man | whom eloquence, an unsullied faith, gravity tempered with much | humour and affability, whom a sincere and virtuous course of | life, and a mind the guardian of virtue, sagacious to unfold | the intricacies of the law, have raised to the summit of fame, | and might also, were it not for his religion, have raised him | no doubt to that of fortune. He died aged 70 the 11th of March | MDCCXX[1771], inferior only to death. James his | eldest son erects this monument to his most worthy father.*

[78] ST JAMES'S CHURCH, ST JAMES'S STREET. THE GRAVEYARD LIES TO THE REAR.

Brewing was always popular in this area of Dublin. Towards the end of the twelfth century, a large amount of ale was brewed along the course of the river Poddle, as its water was deemed suitable for the purpose. The Poddle, along with its tributary the river Coombe, was once the main supplier of Dublin's domestic watermains.

The exact date when James's Gate Brewery was established is not recorded. It was so named as it was close to St James's Gate, the ancient entrance to the city. Various names were connected with the brewery such as Giles Mee in 1670. In 1693, Alderman Sir Mark Rainsford had a brewhouse at St James's Gate where 'beer and fine ales' were made [Rainsford Street behind the brewery is named after him]. From 1715, the Espinasse family carried on the brewing business here for forty-five years, and in 1759 Arthur Guinness took over. He was a courageous man as there were ten other brewers already in this street alone.

A number of brewers, and others connected with the brewing industry, are buried in the churchyard and include William Espinasse and James Farrell.

This vault and Tomb were Purchased | and Erected for him and his Posterity. Here Lieth the body of | Miss Cordelia Espinasse Daughter of the | Above named WILLIAM ESPINASSE. Here also lieth the (body of)Above named | Mr WILLIAM ESPINASSE who departed this | life November 15th 1740 in the 48th | Year of his age | ...m Eonfants? ESPINASSE | who d. Enniskillen | May the 31st 1782 in her thirty first Year | This.....|

Gloria in Excelsis Deo | IHS | Memento Mori | This stone and Burial Place Belongs to | Mr JAMES FARRELL Brewer of Black Pitts in the County of Dublin. (details of other family members follow on)

Members of the Guinness brewery staff are also interred:

In Loving memory | of | PATRICK MCEVOY | (Late of Messrs Guinness) | Who died 6th April 1912 | Aged 51 years | 'In The Midst of Life We Are In Death' | Erected by His Sorrowing Wife | R.I.P.

And a Cooper who carried out one of the most intricate of wood crafts:

This Stone and Burial Place Belong | to Mr JAMES HARFORD of (Br)idge | Street in the City of Dublin Cooper | (and his)Posterity | Here Lyeth (the body) of Mrs HARFORD late wife of the above | Who Departed this life the 20th of (April?)1736 in the 36th year of her age | also five of their Children

A person of note is John Bonham who gave his name to Bonham Street off Bridgefoot Street. The Revd C.T. McCready cites Alderman Bonham as a hide merchant.

Here lies the Body of JOHN BONHAM of the City of Dublin | Esquire who died 29th January 1781 aged 77 years. | Also the bodies of his father and mother, and grandfather | and grandmother, and was rebuilt and embellished by his | affectionate wife and tender children. | Also the body of Mrs SUSAN BONHAM the beloved wife | of said JOHN BONHAM Esqr who departed this life the 21st | Janry 1809 aged 89 years (details of other family members follow).

The inscriptions in this churchyard give a great insight into the local history and the great variety of tradespeople who lived and worked in the area. They included skinners, coach makers, ironmongers, weavers, coopers, brewers, builders, merchants, bakers, gardeners, drapers, grocers, hatters, needle-makers, and saddlers. Local areas had names associated with some of these trades such as Saddlers' Street, Skinners' Row, Weavers' Square, Shoemakers' Street etc.

Two local skinners interred here include:

IHS | This stone Belongeth to JAMES | WADICK of Ye City of Dublin Skinner | Here lieth the Body of his Son | Thos Wadick who Departed this | Life the 8th Octr 1764 aged 25 Years | And ye Lord have mercy on his soul Also three of his children ANN TOBIES and CHARLIS | Also the Body of the Revd MR PHILIP | ROSSETER who Departed ye July 1767 | MARGT aged 38 yrs Also the body of Mrs | WADICK who Departed Ye 25th Feby 1770 | Aged 68 yrs.

and:

Requiestcant in Pace | This Stone was Erected | by Mr PATRICK GING Skinner of New | Row on the Poddle of the City of Dublin | for him and his Posterity. | Here lieth the Body of his Daughter MARY ANN GING who departed this life | the 9th of March 1787 aged 18 years. | Likewise the Remains of his Daughter ANN GING who died 11th October | 1792 in the 24th year of her age. | Also three of his Children who | died young.

There are also two coachmakers, one from Vicar Street and the other from Jervis Street:

Gloria in Excelsis Deo | IHS | Memento Mori | This stone is Erected by JOHN | SHERIDAN of Vicar Street. Coach | Maker in Memory of his Wife | SARAH SHERIDAN who Departed | this life the 3rd day of May 1795 | Aged 33 Years. Here also lieth | the Body of her Father EDWARD | MALONE who departed the 27th Feb | 1793 Aged 65 Years.

and

IHS | This stone and burial place | Belongeth to Mr PHILLIP COSTELLO | of Jervis Street Coach Maker and | his Posterity here Lyeth his Mother | ALICE COSTELLO who Departed this | Life Novr 7 1775 Aged 60 years.

and a needle-maker, a craft long gone:

IHS | this Stone and Burial Place?belongeth to EDWARD REYNOLDS | of Cook Street Needle-maker | who departed this life January | the 31st 1781 in the 50th year of his age | Here also lieth the body of | his son JOHN

REYNOLDS | Also here Lieth the body of CRISTIAN | REYNOLDS Wife to the deceased | EDw REYNOLDS who departed | this life March 21st 1785 aged 50.

Other traders included Thomas Finn, a hatter from Thomas Street who died 8 December 1772, John Elliott, an Ironmonger of Thomas Street who died 23 June 1832 and John Kearney of Patrick Street, a stone manufacturer who died in 1766.

Of the medical men interred here, James Henthorn was a well-known surgeon in the city and had close associations with the Royal College of Surgeons in Ireland, having been President there in 1822. His memorial reads:

Sacred to the memory of JAMES HENTHORN | For many years an eminent surgeon | in the City | and Secretary to the Royal College | of Surgeons in Ireland | who died in December 1832 | Aged 89 years | Also | To the memory of | Elizabeth Stanley alias HENTHORN | His Wife | who died August 29 1833 | aged 79 years.

Nearby in Bow Lane, off James's Street, is St Patrick's Hospital which was established for the treatment of mental illness. It was founded in 1745 with funds bequeathed by Jonathan Swift (the bulk of his estate). This Hospital has long associations with the history of medicine in Ireland. Edmund Lawless, who was Staff Surgeon at St Patrick's, was interred in St James's churchyard. During the Crimean War he became a prisoner of the Russians. His memorial reads:

[79] THE SLOPING GRAVEYARD BEHIND ST JAMES'S CHURCH. THE IVY-CLAD MONUMENT IN THE BACKGROUND MARKS THE GRAVE OF SIR THEOBALD BUTLER, WHO FRAMED THE *ARTICLES OF LIMERICK*, IN 1691.

In Loving Memory | of | EDMUND LAWLESS, M.R.C.S.E. | Staff Surgeon R.N. | For 13 years Medical Superintendent of St Patrick's Hospital | Born 20th March 1820 | Died 11th March 1879 | Also HARRIET His Wife | Daughter of | BENNJN NEWPORT WHITE, ESQ. | OF Cashel | Born 5th Nov. 1822 | | Died 12th May 1898. | Also of EDMUND JAMES | Surgeon S.S. Mexican | Their Eldest Son | Born 14th May 1856, | Lost at Sea Sept 1877 | 'With Christ in Perfect Peace'

Close to St Patrick's Hospital was Dr Steevens' Hospital in Steevens' Lane. It was Dublin's second oldest hospital. Swift was one of the original trustees. It was built with money left by Dr Richard Steevens to provide for his twin sister Grizel during her life. After her death, the money was to be used 'to provide one proper place or building within the City of Dublin for an hospital for maintaining and curing from time to time such sick and wounded persons whose distempers and wounds are curable'. The first patients were admitted in July 1733 and it remained a hospital until 1987, when it was taken over by the Eastern Health Board.

There is a touching memorial to one of the young nurses from this hospital in St James's churchyard which reads:

In Memory | Of | Edith Caroline Vaughan | Late of the Nursing Staff of Dr Steevens Hospital | Who Died of Fever | Contracted While On Duty | 1st February 1893, | Aged 22 years | .... | This Stone Was Erected | By Some Of The Medical Staff | Sister Nurses And Friends | Who Esteemed and Valued Her. | .... | Thy Will Be Done.

There are several religious, both Protestant and Catholic, buried here. Among them, one of the Vicars of St James's and later of St Catherine's parish.

This memorial | belongeth to | John Ellis DD | 35 Years Vicar of this | Parish | (6 of) his Children | 1755 | .... | Also the said Rev JOHN ELLIS DD | 12 Years Vicar of St Catherines who died Oct 7 1764 Aged 77.

There is a wall memorial in the church also dedicated to the Reverend Ellis. It mentions his youngest son William, Governor of Patna in Bengall who lost his life in 'ye Bloody Massacre on October 5th 1763' This was when a force of European and Indian troops took to the field under Major Adams and beat Mir Kasim in a number of engagements. Two months later, Kasim celebrated his fourth defeat by butchering in cold blood one hundred and fifty English officers and soldiers at Patna.

A later Vicar was Thomas Kingston:

In r(emberance) of | The Revd Th(omas) Kingston, M.A. | who laboured zealously and faithfully for upwards of | 40 years, as Vicar of this parish. | Sound in judgement, clear in intellect, and | uncompromising in his testimony to the truth, | he consecrated the Talents with which he was gifted | to the glory of God... | (ste)eadfast faith on his

247

Redeemer, and rejoicing \....(en)tered into rest March 14th 1867, and was | ...y Trowbridge, Wilts. (more follows, but is difficult to decipher).

There is a memorial to the Reverend Richard Connolly, Curate of St James's, who died after contracting a fever while administering to victims of the famine. It reads:

Erected | by the congregation | of | St James's Church. | To the memory | of their late Curate | The REVd RICHARD CONNOLLY A.B. | who was cut off | by Fever caught in the discharge | of | his Ministerial duties | Jany 18th 1848 | aged 31 Years. | 'Blessed are the dead which die in | the Lord from henceforth; yea saith | the Spirit, that they may rest from | their labours, and their works do | follow them'. Revs. 14th. Chap 13th.v.

Mother Mary Bellew was a notable Irish nun. Along with five others, she was one of the founders in 1717 of the first Dominican convent in Dublin at Channel Row [Now Brunswick Street North]. She resigned as prioress in May 1726 and died the following August at a young age. She was buried in St James's churchyard.

The convent account books recorded that £0.10.0 was paid for the opening of her grave: £1.10.0 for her coffin; £2.10.0 for Masses, and that a sum was also paid for the hire of coaches and sedan chairs. This was the burial place of all the nuns from Channel Row until around 1776 when a site was acquired at Mulhuddart.

St James's churchyard contains its share of military men including a victim from the *Leinster*.

In | memory of | WILLIAM SWANSON | who died 9th April 1894 | Aged 42 | and of | GEORGE WILLIAM SWANSON | his only son | Captain Royal Flying Corps | and 4th Hants Regiment | who went down in the Leinster | 13th October 1918 aged 28 | 'Thy will be done'.

There is a memorial to the Worthington family which includes the name of Albert Worthington who was killed in action at the Battle of the Somme in the Great War on 3 July 1916.

Two members of the Royal Dublin Fusiliers also rest here:

12760 Private | T. Murphy | of the Royal Dublin Fusiliers | 31st May 1915 age 35 | Gone But Never Forgotten. and *24760 Private | P. Glynn | Royal Dublin Fusiliers | 22nd January, 1920.*

Another victim of war was the Reverend Francis Cavendish Roche C.F., who died on active service at Alexandria, 14 November 1915 aged thirty-three years.

Like Bully's Acre nearby, which supplied the greatest quantity of bodies to the Dublin medical schools, St James's churchyard did not escape from these grave robbers either. In fact, in some instances, caretakers and sextons colluded with them for a price! Such was the case with a certain Mr Thomas

Owen, described as above average height with red hair, and who wore a black coat and breeches. The following notice appeared in Faulkner's *Dublin Journal* in December 1732 offering a reward of ten guineas for the capture of the said Thomas Owen, Sexton of St James's Church 'who most wickedly and feloniously removed the corpse of the late Mrs Murphy which it is supposed he sold'.

St James's churchyard was officially closed for burials in 1954 except to those holding burial rights. The last entry in the burial register is dated 11 November 1989 and relates to a funeral conducted by the late Father James Carroll, then curate of St James parish.

It is under the care of the Select Vestry of St Patrick's Cathedral Group.

St John's Church and Churchyard (demolished)

Situation: Fishamble Street, Dublin 8

Period in use: 1619–1850

Situated in city centre

The parish of St John's dates from the twelfth century and covers an area of about fourteen acres. Before the close of the twelfth century, it was attached to the church of the Holy Trinity, then under the rule of the Canons of St Augustine. The original church was rebuilt a number of times. The last, designed by George Ensor, was built between 1766–1769 and was situated on the west side of Fishamble Street, at the corner of John's Lane. In 1877 the parish of St John's was united with St Werburgh's and the church was closed the following year. It was subsequently demolished in 1884 to facilitate roadworks to link Christ Church Place with Dame Street. The site is now occupied by a public park and is under the care of the Parks Department in Dublin Corporation. The Dublin Civic Offices overlook it.

The parish was made up of people in the middle ranks of trade, although it was recorded that some of the inhabitants of Fishamble Street had accumulated fortunes. This street appears on *Speed's Map of Dublin*, which was published in 1611. As the name, an elision of Fish Shambles, implies, it was originally a place where fish was sold. Over the years, many notable people resided there, as the church records reveal. Across the street from the Church, where Kennan's premises once stood, was the Musick Hall where Handel's Messiah was first performed on 13 April 1742.

Henry Grattan (1746–1820), the patriot and orator, was baptised in this church, as was the Reverend Henry Echlin, son of Sir Henry Echlin, after whom Echlin's Lane (later Echlin Street) was named.

A graveyard adjoined the church in which over 12,500 burials took place. Here are interred the remains of a great variety of citizens which include many titled people, aldermen, sheriffs, Members of Parliament, lawyers, clergy, lord mayors, scholars, curates, goldsmiths, musicians, printers, papermakers and even some soldiers.

Those interred mainly came from the parish, with addresses at Wood Quay, Blind Quay, Copper Alley, Smock Alley, Merchant's Quay, Winetavern Street, John's Lane, Fleece Alley and Fishamble Street. Some were MPs representing various parts of the country who lived in the fashionable Fishamble Street.

A sample of the early interments recorded include the following:

25 June 1597, Christopher Ussher, Ulster-King-at-Arms, Fishamble Street; 6 September 1597, Elinor Ussher, wife of Richard, of Santry; 21 April 1599, Alderman John Ussher, uncle of Primate James; 4 June 1614, Edward Cherry, MP for Ballyshannon, husband of Lettice Aungier; 10 June 1610, Edward son of Sir Edward Pitte; 29 September 1622 William Dongan, Recorder of Dublin, husband of Lady Slaney O'Brien, daughter of the fourth baron of Inchiquin, from 15 Fishamble Street; 4 May 1624, Lady Annesley, wife of Sir Francis, MP for Armagh, afterwards Baron Mountnorris, and Viscount Valentia, from Copper Alley; 11 November 1624, Lady Ryves, wife of the Attorney-General, Lower Blind Quay; 6 September 1630, Hon Dorothy Annesley, daughter of Viscount Valentia; and 4 November 1630 Nicholas Cormick, Clerk of the Chancery, Fishamble Street.

An interesting burial is recorded for 29 June 1732.

Counsellor James Uniacke, of Mount Uniacke, Co. Cork, an old veteran of the Boyne, also on December 4, Mrs Constantia Grierson, second wife of George Grierson, King's Printer, and most accomplished scholar and friend of Dean Swift, Lower Blind Quay.

On 1 December 1706, Elinor, wife of Dean Harrison and widow of Godwin Swift was interred.

There is a particular list of burials for St John's churchyard, which comprises 164 names and which covers the period from 30 December 1641 to 13 April 1642. It contains

The names of ye poore English who having fled to this citte for refuge, and dyed in ye Parish of St John's, were buried since 30 December 1641.

There is a further list of 39 names of

Ye poore souldiers who were buried at St John's between the 24 April and 11 October 1642.

Among the clergy interred were the Revd John Read, MA, Curate of the parish with, an address in Fishamble Street, who was buried on 6 February 1787 and the Revd John Murphy, PP, who was buried on 30 November 1798.

Six stone slabs are all that remain of the memorials in St John's and these may be seen lying flat in a group on the ground in the park. The other gravestones were removed but fortunately some of the inscriptions on them were recorded.

The earliest gravestone that is mentioned is that of William Scriven, who died on 8 October 1683. A wealthy joiner, Scriven lived close by in Racket Court in John's Lane. He was granted special permission to stack his timber against the wall of the graveyard. Also in the neighbourhood in the early seventeenth century was Dr Angel Goulding, who paid a rent of fourpence halfpenny for a window overlooking the graveyard.

[80] The Church of St John the Evangelist, Fishamble Street, which was demolished in 1884. (Courtesy Irish Architectural Archive)

Among the graves recorded is one to Robert Echlin, who was born in 1635. His gravestone bore his coat of arms. There are many members of this family recorded in the burial records.

Here lyeth the bodie of | Robert | Echlin who departed this | life the 20th day of December | 1706 aged 71 years as also | the Bodie of Anne Frances | Agnes Eustace & Penelope | His children.

There were a number of families who had plots here such as the Blackleys, Davenports, Perrins, Anyons, Allens, Davises, Walshes and Higginbothams. Below are some inscriptions:

IHS | Sacred to the memory | of Travers Blackley Esqr | Late Representative in Parliament of | the City of Dublin who departed this | Life the 27th March 1796 aged 73 years. | Here also is interred his son-in-law | John Blackley Esqre who died the | 13th of October 1801 aged 34 years | and of Temperance his wife who | departed this life 10th of February 1809 | aged 49 years.

There are some generations of the Davenports mentioned on the memorial inscription:

The Burial Place of Simon and Dorcas (?) Davenport, Dorcas Shepherd alias Davenport | their Daughter; | and Simon Davenport Esqre and Dorcas Davenport | Her son and Daughter-in-law | of Cullentra in Co. Cavan and many of their children, grandchildren | and great grandchildren | are buried here. | Restored by Simon Davenport | Grandson of | Simon Davenport Esq, | June 1881.

A rhyming couplet such as the following does not often appear on a gravestone,

Here lies ye body of Thomas Oakes of Francis Street | Who departed in Full Assurance of Faith, May 1763

Sovereign Grace Redeeming Love
His theme below His song above.

John Davis from New York erected a memorial to his parents and some of his young brothers and sister in the churchyard.

Beneath this tomb lie interred | the remains of | Edward Davis who died Feby 9.1831 | aged 56 years | Maria Davis his wife who died Dec, 23rd 1849 | aged 60 years and their children | Timothy Davis | who died Feb 25 1821 aged 7 years | Amelia Davis | who died Aug 31 1832 aged 3 years | Thomas Davis who died July 21st 1840 | aged 14 years | James Timothy Davis who died Aug 21st 1824 | aged 12 months | This stone is erected here by Mr John Davis of New York U.S. | son of the above Edward and Maria Davis.

Being sited on Fishamble Street, it is not surprising that a few fishmongers were buried in St John's churchyard. There is a Molly Malone who was baptised in the church on 24 July 1663 who died at the relatively young age of thirty-three and was buried here on 13 June 1699. It has not been ascertained whether it is the same Molly Malone who inspired the ballad. The figure of Molly Malone, carved in bronze by sculptor Jeanne Rynhart, may be seen opposite the Provost's House at the end of Grafton Street, where she is portrayed selling her cockles and mussels.

The last burial at St John's churchyard took place on the 22 November 1850. It was that of Elizabeth Frances McCausland with an address at 7 Waterloo Road. A notice was then posted up on the gate, a copy of which was dispatched to all the newspapers, stating that there would be no more burials permitted at St John's churchyard. This was because of the potential danger to the public due to the already enormous amount interred in this very small space.

The parish records pertaining to St John's are among some of the most important held in the custody of the Representative Church Body Library. It contains the oldest extant parish vestry minute book, which covers the period 1595–1658 and the oldest extant register of baptisms, marriages and burials for the period 1619–1719.

St Kevin's Churchyard

Situation: Camden Row, Dublin 8

Period in use: 1226–circa 1753. Now a Public Park

Situated near city centre

A chapel was built on this site some time during the fifteenth century, which was dedicated to St Coemgen or St Kevin. The church was long in use as a place of pilgrimage, as Archbishop Dermot O'Hurley who was executed in the reign of Queen Elizabeth in 1584, was interred here. Born about 1519 and educated at Paris and Rheims, he was appointed to the see of Cashel. He was captured bearing treasonable papers in Carrick-on-Suir and tortured. Condemned under martial law, he was hanged in St Stephen's Green.

The present church, built about 1780, was described as a church, built in the shape of the letter T, like a village church, without an interior gallery. It was unroofed around 1920 and is now a ruin. It was still in use after the opening of the new St Kevin's church in the South Circular Road in 1889.

In 1903, the Reverend R.S. Maffet recorded a number of memorial stones in the churchyard, some of which are now missing. Many memorials date from the 1700s and include the names of locals from Kevin Street, Bishop Street, Castle Street, Cuffe Street, Aungier Street and Skinners' Row, representing merchants, drapers, harness-makers, goldsmiths and Inn-keepers. For example:

This Stone and Burial Place | Belongeth to Mr James Roony of | Kavin [sic] Street Inn Keeper and his | Posterity who | Died July 21st 1788 Aged 63 yrs

The Leeson altar tomb, which bears the family coat of arms, is the oldest in the churchyard. In 1680, Hugh Leeson came to Ireland as an officer in his Majesty's army. On retiring from the army, he became an eminent brewer. He married Rebecca who was the daughter of Richard Tighe, alderman of Dublin. They had four sons, three of whom died without issue. They were Thomas, William, Hugh and Joseph. Joseph, who died in 1741, succeeded his father in the business. His only son, also named Joseph, entered Parliament and was ultimately advanced to the Earldom of Milltown. The inscription reads:

This tomb was Erected by Mr Hugh Leeson | of the City of Dublin Brewer for himself | his posterity the 29th day of January 1685 | and now Beautified by his Son Joseph | Leeson the 14th day of May, 1741. | Beneath are interred the following members of the family | GRACE 1st Wife of the Honble Robt Leeson, Died 11th Nov 1833 | WILLIAM, eldest son of Sir W.E. Leeson, Died 2nd 1837 | ELIZABETH COUNTESS OF MILLTOWN, Died 22nd Jany 1842 | aged 100 | She was the third wife of the above named JOSEPH LEESON | who was created EARL OF MILLTOWN, 1760 | The HONBLE ROBERT LEESON, youngest son of the | 1st EARL OF MILLTOWN, by his 3rd wife, died 10th April 1852 | At which period this tomb was renewed by his son | SIR WILLIAM EDWD LEESON

The parents and sister of Thomas Moore are buried here. They lived at 12 Aungier Street, which occupies the site of the house where Thomas Moore was born on 28 May 1779. It was here that Moore's father carried on his business as a wine merchant and grocer. He is described as being 'tall, handsome, and full of face'. His mother, labelled with the unpoetic name of Anastasia Codd, came from Cornmarket in Wexford. Moore described her as 'one of the noblest minded as well as the most warm-hearted of all God's creatures'. Their memorial reads:

Sacred to the memory of John Moore Esqr | formerly Barrack Master of Islandbridge in the County of Dublin | Who departed this life December 17th 1825 | Aged 84 years. | Here is also interred Anastasia [sic] Moore | Alias Codd his beloved Wife | who departed this life May 8th 1832 | Aged 68 years | Also six of their Children who died young. | And their beloved Daughter Ellen | who died February 14th 1846 | Deeply mourned by her brother Thomas Moore | the Bard of his much beloved Country IRELAND.

A small stone to the left of the main entrance into the churchyard from the lane is dedicated

To the memory of Henry Oliver, aged 136 years!

A tall four-sided pillar, which tapers at the top, marks the burial place of an extraordinary Dublin-born priest, the Reverend John Austin. It is said that, as a boy, he so impressed Jonathan Swift that the Dean advised his parents to 'send him to the Jesuits, who would make a man of him'. He was admitted to the Jesuit Order at Champagne in 1735 and returned to Dublin in 1750 to the parish of St Michael and St John's where he worked as assistant priest. A renowned preacher, he established a classical school in Saul's Court near Cook Street where the majority of the Catholic youth of the city received their education, including John O'Keeffe, the dramatist. It was used as the diocesan school of Meath as well as Dublin for the training of priests. This was before the foundation of seminaries in other parts of the country. With the assistance of two other Jesuits, Father Philip Mulcaile and Father Thomas Betagh, he opened a boarding school for boys.

Father Austin was a man of extraordinary piety and learning. Together with running his school and seminary, he visited the poor of the city daily in their garrets and cellars and dedicated all he had to them in the way of food and time. The wealthier people helped him and 'while the means lasted [he] was constantly on foot administering relief to innumerable poor wretches, never resting while he had a single guinea'. He cared for his elderly mother and when she died he was so overcome with grief, that it is said he never afterwards raised his head – but drooped into a second state of childhood. He remained like this for three years, and though ignored by some, he would not have survived without the care he was given by his brother Jesuits, Fathers Betagh, Fullam and Mulcaile.

The west-facing side of the memorial bears the following inscription:

Viro Reverendo | JOHANNI AUSTIN, | Dubliniensi | Societatis Jesu, Dum Fuit Sacerdoti | In vinea Domini per annos 36, | Pio, Docto, Indefesso Operario, | Qui | Ill Calendas Octobris, AD 1784, | Aetatis anno sexto et Sexagesimo | Vitam | Apostolicis, Confectam Laboribus | cum Morte | In conspectu Domini Pretiosa | Commutavit.

[81] View of St Kevin's Church and Churchyard, Camden Row, Dublin.

On the south side is the following:

Cippum hunc | Ministri fidelis Religio Non Immemor | Vi idus Decembris, AD 1786 | Plens possuit[sic]. | Divites Admonuit | Pauperes sublevavit | Juventutem erudivit | Orphanis loco Parentis fuit | De omni hominum genere | Praeclare meruit | Omnibus omnia factus | Ut | Omnes Christo Lucrifaceret;

on the east side

A.M.D.G. | This monument is erected | To the memory of | THE REVD JOHN AUSTIN, S.J. | Who departed this life | 30th Sept. 1784, | In the 66th year of his age. | R.I.P.;

and on the north side:

This monument | Was | Restored & renovated | January 1900.

John Keogh, a prosperous merchant and a champion of Catholic Emancipation is interred here. He was the leader of the radical section of the Catholic Committee in the 1790s and headed a deputation to George III. He petitioned parliament and it was through his efforts that a Relief act was passed. In 1796 he was arrested as a United Irishman but was released after a short period. He was greatly distressed by the 1798 Rebellion and withdrew from public life. He died in 1817.

Thomas Ball of Norfolk, Captain in Fleetwood's Regiment of Horse, who came to Ireland with Oliver Cromwell, has a descendant buried in St Kevin's. He is Thomas Ball of Creggan, Co. Armagh. The inscription on his memorial is as follows:

Here lyeth the Body of Thomas | Ball Esqr who departed.... | the 9th Augst 1742 Aged 44[Y]ears. | as also the Body of Mildred Ball | otherwise Johnson his Wife, who | departed this Life on 31st July 1763 aged 55 years. Also the Body of | the Revd Joh[n]son, Brother of | the said Mildred Ball who departed | this Life 26th of Octr 1771, Aged | Seventy one Years.

In 1823 the funeral of Arthur D'Arcy, a well-known citizen of Dublin, took place at St Kevin's. He was a charitable and popular man who died as a result of a fall from his horse. His sudden death evoked great sympathy and there was a large following at his funeral. (He was the brother of John D'Arcy, later Lord mayor). A number of priests wearing scarves and hatbands were in the funeral procession, which came up Liberty Lane from Kevin Street to the churchyard. The procession entered the churchyard, and as they approached the grave, they gradually encircled it to recite the *De Profundis* and other prayers. As the Reverend Michael Blake, Vicar-General, was about to speak he was rudely interrupted by an order of Dr Magee, the Protestant Archbishop, that he must not offer any prayer over that grave! This incident

257

demonstrated the series of insults which Catholics were subjected to concerning the burial of their dead in penal times.

Another grave of note is that of Jasper Joly (1739–1823), who was a member of the Irish Volunteers in 1779. He was responsible for building the houses on Harcourt Terrace. A friend of Lord Edward Fitzgerald, he kept him in his house when he was on the run in March 1798. When Joly's house was raided, Lord Edward found refuge in a well in the garden before he escaped to Thomas Street. Joly died on 9 November 1823 aged eighty-four. Most of the burials had been carried out in this churchyard prior to 1753, though twelve burials are recorded for a period of thirteen years until 1903.

The churchyard, which is beautifully landscaped with a wide variety of flowers, shrubs and trees, makes a delightful park and is under the care of the Parks Department of Dublin Corporation.

[82] THE GRAVESTONE OF JOHN MOORE AND ANASTASIA CODD, THE PARENTS OF THOMAS MOORE, IN ST KEVIN'S CHURCHYARD, CAMDEN ROW.

St Luke and St Nicholas Without Church and Churchyard

Situation: 106A The Coombe, Dublin 8

Period in use: 1713–1922

Situated near city centre

The remains of this church and churchyard are situated in the Coombe. Up to a few years ago, this resembled a lovely little country church in close proximity to the city centre. A long narrow avenue, formerly lined with elm trees, approached the church entrance door. It had the remains of a nicely-planted garden, which included cherry trees and forsythia.

The church was built In 1708 when the Parish of St Luke was created by an Act of Parliament. Over the years, various repairs were carried out such as re-roofing in 1835 and extensive repairs in 1884.

The parish of St Nicholas Without, which comprised a long narrow strip between New Street and the river Poddle, formerly used the North Transept of St Patrick's Cathedral as its parish church. In 1861, it was re-united to St Luke's (which had been formed from part of it) and both parishes occupied the same church, which became St Luke and St Nicholas Without.

Just inside the entrance gate from the Coombe, there are the remains of tall almshouses (listed buildings) which were used for widows. There was also a poor school established here. The parish, which had a total of 480 houses, was noted for its poverty. The advertisement of the annual charity sermon was headed by the words, 'The poorest Parish in Dublin'.

The church was closed in 1975 and is no longer used as a place of worship. It was occupied for other purposes until 1981 and then lay empty. The church and churchyard were both subjected to extreme vandalism and in 1986 the church roof was destroyed by fire.

The churchyard was associated with Huguenots, although no Huguenot names are discernible on any of the headstones. There was, however, a memorial to the Huguenots within the church on a brass plate on the pulpit which read:

To the | glory of GOD | and in memory of the noble Huguenots | who came to the Parish | from their native France | for liberty of conscience | this pulpit was erected by | Mrs C.E. Smylie St Luke's Rectory | Sth Circ Road Christmas 1899.

259

[83] The old entrance from Newmarket to St Luke and St Nicholas Without.

Justice Hellen, second Judge of the Court of Common Pleas in Ireland, who died on 22 July 1793 aged sixty-five years, was buried near the entrance, in the north side of the church. His son, Robert, who died in 1796 aged thirty-nine, and wife Mrs Dorothea Hellen, who died in June 1806 aged seventy-eight, are also buried here.

Walter Thom was commemorated with a memorial in the church, which read:

In memory of | Walter Thom Esq | Author of the 'History of Aberdeen &c &c' | died 16th June 1824 aged 54 years. | and | Margaret Turner his wife | died 4th May 1842 aged 73 years | both interred in the adjoining churchyard. | This tablet had been erected by his son | Alexr Thom Abbey St Dublin.

[84] THE FORMER AVENUE LEADING TO THE CHURCH OF ST LUKE AND ST NICHOLAS WITHOUT. THE ALMSHOUSES ARE ON THE LEFT.

Alex. Thom & Co. had an address at 87–89 Middle Abby Street and printed *Thom's Official Directory of the United Kingdom of Great Britain and Ireland*, the first issue of which appeared in 1844.

Some of the headstones contained a large number of the family's deceased children, such as the following:

This stone & burial | place belongeth to Mr William | Dally Cloathier and his posterity. | Here lieth the body of the above | William Dally | who departed this life the 12th | day of June 1735 | Aged 48 years. | Here also lyeth 6 of his children.

Here lieth the body of Joseph McNab, of the City of Dublin | who departed this life | the 8th of April 1778 aged 36. | Also the body of Marebell his wife | who departed this life | 19th May 1772 | aged 48 | and the body of Theophilus their | son who died 16th May, 1773, aged 26, and 8 of their children | Here lieth the body of Ann | McNab who died 20th June 1781.

This stone and burial ground | belongeth to | Mr Wm Richey of Hanover Street, silk manufacturer | Underneath are deposited the remains of | his beloved wife Anne | aged 29 years. | Also his son Samuel aged 4 years. | and John, 23 years | his daughter Esther aged 4 years | and other children who died young.

This stone was erected by Mr Charles Haskins | of....Street for him and his posterity. | Here lieth the bodies of 5 of his children. | Arthur Haskins died Nov. 29th 1791. | aged 14 months. | Richard who died July 1792 aged 4 months | Elizabeth who died June 29th 1796 | aged ? months | Charles who died April 1799 aged 3 years | William who died Jan 12 1801, aged 7 years.

At present, it is not possible to gain entry to what remains of this derelict churchyard. The long avenue is now gone, the almshouses are roofless and the windows have been bricked up. A section of the new Cork Street / Coombe Relief Route will cut through this area, stretching from the Coombe to Ardee Street. In the Liberties / Coombe Integrated Area Plan (1998), the proposed development contained objectives which included the retention and refurbishment of the church and graveyard for community and institutional use.

St Mark's Church and Churchyard

SITUATION: 42 PEARSE STREET, DUBLIN 2 (FORMERLY GREAT BRUNSWICK STREET)

PERIOD IN USE: 1730–1950s

SITUATED IN CITY CENTRE

An Act was passed in 1707 and the following year St Mark's parish was created from part of St Andrew's. More parishes were needed for the expanding population created by the amount of new streets around Trinity College. The area covered by this new parish was bounded by the Liffey, Westmoreland Street, Nassau Street, Leinster Street, the Grand Canal and South Lotts Road. It was a parish of contrasts, as it bordered some of the wealthiest households like the Molesworth and Dawson estates, as well as some of the most deprived of households in the labyrinth of streets off the quays.

Lord Carteret, the viceroy, laid the foundation stone of the church on St Mark's Day 1729, but little progress was made on the building until the 1750s. It was aided by parliamentary grants until 1757. Archbishop Cobbe consecrated the church on St Mark's Day in 1757. With its gloomy interior and its unfinished tower, the structure is considered to be plain and even slightly dismal in appearance. The church was closed in 1971 and its bell was given to the Methodist Centenary church, because John Wesley had preached at St Mark's in the year 1747.

Trinity College acquired the church in 1971 to house part of its library overflow. It was sold to a group named the Assemblies of God in 1987 and renovated by a FÁS youth training scheme. It is now used as a Family Worship Centre. The main part of the church has been portioned off to suit its present requirements. All the wall memorials have been removed, which is a pity, as part of the heritage of the parish has been removed forever from future generations.

Oscar Wilde, one of the great dramatists to emerge from Dublin in the late nineteenth century, was born nearby at 21 Westland Row and had associations with St Mark's. His uncle, the Reverend Ralph Wilde, rector of Kilsallaghan, christened him here on 26 April 1855.

The churchyard was in use before the church was completed. It comprises over an acre, which has now been cleared of all but a couple of headstones. Some that remained have been removed to one side and are lying on the ground. Others have disappeared without trace. With their dispersal a lot of local history is lost to visitors to the churchyard. Part of it is now used as a car park and the remainder is laid out in grass.

Like St Paul's, poor relief figured largely in the parochial accounts. In the vestry minutes and churchwarden's accounts, coffins for the poor are mentioned regularly. An outbreak of cholera occurred in the parish in 1834 and the Great Famine even took its toll in the little streets and alleyways behind the Church. The records contain details of receipts and expenditure of the 'Fleet Market soup kitchen' which was established to feed the hungry during the famine period in the years 1846–47.

The entries in the burial records in the 1820s portray some of the prevailing social conditions. It makes sad reading as a number of children, and indeed some adults, are entered with no details of their name, address, age or sex, such as:

[85] St Mark's Church and Churchyard on Pearse Street (formerly Great Brunswick Street).

264

A child found dead in Lime Street. Buried 5 January 1825

A child from Cumberland Street. Buried 20 March 1825

A child from Singleton's House. Buried 31 March 1825

A Foundling. Buried 4 June 1825

An infant boy. Buried 5 October 1825.

A drowned infant was buried 8 June 1826

Other entries from this brief period include:

A man found drowned. Buried 20 March 1825

A poor woman. Name and age unknown. Buried 19 January 1825.

An inmate from Lock Hospital who was buried on 2 March 1863.

The Lock Hospital, which started in 1792 and was latterly known as the Hospital of St Margaret of Cortona, stood at the corner of Luke Street. It was demolished in the early 1950s.

On occasion, the cause of death is included and these include childbirth, rupture, smallpox, scarletina, cholera, dropsy, convulsions, croup, consumption, insanity, decay. A number of infant deaths are put down to 'teething'.

Some of those interred in the churchyard had memorials within the church, such as

To the memory of | Revd. Alexander Franklin A.M. | For 36 years Curate of this parish | Who died 28th November 1857 | Aged 80 years. | This tablet has been erected | By a friend as a tribute of esteem | For his moral and intellectual worth.

Another clergyman who contributed enormously to the parish was the Reverend A.S. Fuller, who was vicar of St Mark's in 1872.

AD | 1879 | Erected | By the parishioners | Of St Mark's | As a record of the | Munificence of the | Revd. A.S. Fuller, D.D. | Vicar: In having repewed and | beautified this church | at his own cost. | Hall Bredin M.D. | George Porte, M.R.I.A. | Church Wardens.

The architectural sculptor, Charles Harrison (1858–1913), who died at his residence in Great Brunswick Street on 14 June 1913 is buried here. One of three brothers, he was the eldest son of

265

Charles L. Harrison, a monumental sculptor from Yorkshire. There was a lot of work for sculptors with the boom in church building following Catholic Emancipation. Interestingly, James Pearse, father of Patrick Pearse, joined the firm of Harrison as a journeyman before setting up the firm of Neill and Pearse early in the 1870s.

A fine Celtic cross carved by Harrison in Ballinasloe limestone marks the burial place of Thomas Moore in Bromham in Wiltshire. In Dublin, Harrison was responsible for the stone carvings on the National Science Museum building in Merrion Street (formerly the old Royal College of Science). He did stone work on St Colman's Cathedral in Cobh and St Finian's College in Co. Westmeath. A member of the Architectural Association of Ireland, he was involved with the parish of St Mark's for up to forty years.

His memorial reads:

To | the beloved memory of | Charles Wm. Harrison | Sculptor, | Born at Cottingham, Yorkshire | 4th Oct. 1834 | died at Dublin 16th May 1903. | As a member of this | congregation for upwards of 40 years, he always took an | active interest in its welfare. | He filled the office of | Churchwarden | from 1892 until his death, | and for many years that of | Parochial Nominator & Synodsman, | during which time he heartily | co-operated in effecting many | needed improvements in the | Church and Schools of the Parish.

Also interred in the churchyard are William Wilson late of South Gloucester Street, who died 13 January 1897 aged seventy-nine years and his wife Harriet, who died 30 August 1872 aged forty-six years.

The crypt beneath the church contains ten vaults on each side of the passageway. The vaults generally contained the remains of wealthy people. These include one to the builder of Great Brunswick Street on which the church stands. It reads:

To the memory of | DANIEL CROWE builder of Great Brunswick Street | Who departed this life March the 31st 1859, aged 77 years | Also of | Catherine Crowe his wife, | who died March 14th 1858 aged 73 years. | This tablet has been erected | By their sons as a tribute of filial affection for their parents | Who always sustained an Honourable position in life | And ended their days in Peace. | 'These are they which came out of great tribulation | And have washed their robes and made them white in the Blood of the Lamb | Therefore are they before the throne of God.' Rev: vii.14.5.

Other vaults include one to

John Smith | Family | Sepulchre | 1796

and the Family vaults of

James W.L. Lendrick | 32 Leeson Street | February 1837

and

John Wilkin who died 5 February 1859.

Like many churches, St Mark's had a memorial on its west wall containing the names of the twenty-four men from the parish who died in the First World War. It read:

To the Glory of God | and in proud Remembrance | of men from the Parish of St Mark, | Dublin, who died for their country | in the Great War, 1914–1918. | Joseph Bayle, Samuel Biddy, Thomas Bould, Henry Brogan, Frederick W. Davey, George Evans, William Eyre, Walter Harpur, Frederick Harrison, Richard Harte, Charles Irwin, Edward Jones, George Lalley, John McCarthy, Leo D. Matthews, William H. Matthews, Alfred Maybury, Samuel F. Moran, Joseph Paul, William Payne, Thomas Sloane, David Walker, John Walker, Richard Walker. | 'Greater Love Hath No Man Than This.'

St Mark's Church and churchyard is under the care of the Irish Assemblies of God.

St Mary's Church and Churchyard

Situation: Mary Street, Dublin 1

Period in use: 1700–1855

Situated in city centre

St Mary's Church, no longer a place of worship, is situated between Wolfe Tone Street (formerly Stafford Street) and Jervis Street. The former churchyard is now a park.

The parish of St Mary's was created in the year 1697 when the ancient parish of St Michan's (1095) was divided into three parts which comprised St Michan's, St Paul's and St Mary's. Its name is derived from the medieval Abbey of St Mary which was founded in 1139 by the Cistercian Order. St Mary's Abbey is nearby in Meetinghouse Lane off Capel Street and is open to visitors at specified times.

St Mary's church is credited to Thomas Burgh who succeeded William Robinson as Surveyor General in 1700. It is an early classical church and probably the first galleried one in the city. The intended tower for the church never progressed beyond the first storey.

The interior was adorned with magnificent carved wooden cornices and pilasters and an organ case by Renatus Harris, which was regarded as one of the finest in Dublin. It retained many of its original features, such as the gallery and pew boxes, though now most of the interior fittings have been removed. However, some features are being retained as part of the new development. These include the churchwarden's pew and the organ.

St Mary's ceased to function as a parish church in the 1970s and was used for a short period by the Greek Orthodox Community. In 1988 it was sold and used for other purposes. Three of its six crypts have been removed, as the church is now being converted and developed into a bar and restaurant.

A number of famous people are associated with St Mary's church. When Joseph Le Fanu, the novelist and short story writer was born in 1814, his father Philip Le Fanu was the curate of St Mary's Church.

Among those who were baptised here are the Earl of Charlemont, in 1728, Theobold Wolfe Tone, in 1763, and the playwrights, Richard Brinsley Sheridan in 1751 and Seán O'Casey in 1880. The church is also noted for the fact that John Wesley first preached in Ireland here in 1747. Amongst the marriages celebrated here was that of Arthur Guinness to Ann Lee.

The funeral service of the poet F.R. Higgins, who died in the former Jervis Street Hospital on 8 January 1941, was held here before his burial in the graveyard of Laracor Church in Co. Meath.

Dr Patrick Sheridan, the schoolmaster and friend of Swift, Stella and Mrs Dingley had gallery seats for his pupils in St Mary's church.

The Ormonde family vault is contained beneath the church and a tablet commemorates the family. It reads:

In a vault underneath this church | are deposited the remains | of James Butler, Marquis of Ormonde, K.P. | Born 15th July 1774 | and who departed this life | 22nd May 1838 | and of his two sons | Richard Molesworth Wandesforde Butler | born January 30th 1818 | died February 3rd 1838 | and Charles Wandesforde Butler | Lieut. R.N. | born February 7th 1820 | died October 30th 1857 | So teach us to number our days that we apply our hearts unto wisdom. In the vault beneath the church | where lie the mortal remains of | her husband and her two sons | are also deposited those of Grace Louisa | Dowager Marchioness of Ormonde | who died May 3rd 1860 | aged 61 years.

Another memorial, which bears the coat of arms of the Newcome family, reads:

Near this place lies the remains of | Susanna Newcome | of the ancient family of the D'Oylys | Baronets in Oxfordshire | She married William Bishop of Dromore | and after the sharpest pain in childbirth | patiently breathed out her pure and pious soul to GOD | Dec, XXX, MDCCLXIX in the XXX year of her age.

There are a number of clergy connected with St Mary's Parish who were buried in the vaults and in the churchyard. Included among them was the Reverend William Fletcher DD, Dean of Kildare and Rector of St Mary's, and his wife Horora who followed him to a better life on the 23 June 1770 aged seventy-one.

A warm tribute is paid to the Revd John Magill. His memorial, which bears the Magill coat of arms, reads:

Beneath in the vault | the remains of ye Revd John Magill, A.M. | are deposited. | A Divine of polite learning & sound judgement | of exemplary conduct and an excellent preacher | The poor have lost in him a Benefactor | Widows & orphans a faithful friend & guardian | and, if anything can add to his character | many pupils of his entered Trinity college | Four of whom were elected Fellows | of our University. | He departed this life All Sts Eve | 1777 | Sacred to whose memory | This monument was erected by his affectionate | brother the Revd Moses Magill A.M.

The Revd Hugh White, a curate of St Mary's was remembered by his friends:

269

[86] PORTRAIT OF F.R. HIGGINS BY SEAN O'SULLIVAN. (COURTESY OF THE ABBEY THEATRE)

Erected by the Parishioners & his private friends | to the memory of | the Revd, Hugh White A.M. | For 17 years curate of this parish | who died May 15th 1844. | aged 49 years. | christianity found in him a no less bright example than eloquent advocate. | The tendency and power of Gospel truth | to render the believer in Jesus | holy and happy | were eminently displayed in his character and life | Constrained by the love of Christ | he laboured both in the pulpit and in private to win souls to Him. | and when lingering illness, endured without a murmur, no longer suffered him to speak in public | his pen was still employed in his beloved Masters service. 'Thanks be to GOD for His unspeakable gift.' 2 Cor. 9.15.

The Revd John Black was also curate at St Mary's and his memorial reads:

Sacred to the memory | of the Revd John Black, M.A., | for 24 years Curate of this parish | he entered into rest on the 7th of May 1883 | in the 54th year of his age | and the 31st of his ministry. | For what is our hope or joy, or crown of rejoicing? Are not even ye in the presence of our LORD JESUS CHRIST at His coming. I Thess 2 c 19 v. | Erected in loving remembrance by the | Parishioners and other friends.

The adjoining churchyard, which extends south of the church, contains the remains of Thomas Brinsley Sheridan, father of Richard Brinsley Sheridan. Thomas was a godson of Swift. He was an actor as well as being manager of the famous Smock Alley (now West Essex Street). Under his management, the 1745–6 season Smock Alley Theatre is described as unequalled in Dublin until the twentieth century. During this time he engaged brilliant actors such as Spranger Barry, Mrs Bellamy and David Garrick. Later, in England, he became a friend of Dr Samuel Johnson. When Sheridan compiled a dictionary, Johnson became irritated and said to Boswell, 'Why sir, Sherry is dull, naturally dull; but it must have taken him a great deal of pains to become what we now see him. Such an excess of stupidity is not in nature'.

Archibald Rowan Hamilton, the United Irishman, who died in Dublin on 1 November 1834 aged eighty-one, is also interred in the churchyard. He was a strong supporter of Catholic emancipation and subscribed to the Catholic Association.

Mary Mercer, a remarkable woman whose inspiration, helped provide Dublin with a hospital service, was laid to rest in this churchyard in 1735. She was the only child of George Mercer who came to Dublin from Lancashire in the 1660s. He studied medicine at Trinity College and had a most successful career as a doctor. On his death, he left a vast fortune to Mary. She devoted her time to assisting the many poor girls in the city and contributing to their welfare and education. For this purpose, she leased for a period of 999 years a site in Stephen Street. Here she built an almshouse on the former site of the Chapel of the Leper Hospital of St Stephen. Before her death, she transferred the lease to the trustees of what was to become Mercer's Hospital. It opened with ten beds on 17 August 1734. It was aided by some legacies and was among the beneficiaries of a performance of Handel's Messiah in Fishamble Street in April 1742. Mercer's Hospital lasted until 1983. The Royal College of Surgeons in Ireland acquired the building, which still retains some of the original stonework. The site now houses a hostel and the Mercer Library, which stand as a fitting memorial to Mary Mercer.

The remains of George Simpson, the founder of Simpson's Hospital, who died in 1778 are also interred here. Simpson lived nearby at 24 Jervis Street. He suffered from both blindness and gout. On his death he left his estate to found a hospital for men in reduced circumstances who suffered from similar ailments. This was opened in 1781 in Putland Street. The patients wore frock coats and top hats. By all accounts the hospital was a happy and a cheerful place, 'in the spring and summer the gay sound of the flute and violin is often heard from the benches of their little garden…' In 1925, the hospital was moved to Wyckham in Dundrum.

Dr Marlay, who was Bishop of Waterford and an uncle of Henry Grattan, is also buried here, as is John Toler (1745–1831), the first Earl of Norbury. He was the infamous hanging judge, who sentenced Robert Emmet to death. Toler was descended from Cromwellian planters and was Chief Justice of the court of

271

common pleas. A small man with grey eyes, he had the habit when speaking of inflating his cheeks at the end of each sentence, and as a result, was named Puffendorf.

A staunch supporter of Protestant ascendancy, Norbury had a weird sense of humour and even joked in court when the life of someone was hanging in the balance. He presided at Robert Emmet's trial, and more than once interrupted him in the course of his speech before his sentence. As Attorney General, he conducted the prosecution of those who were concerned with the 1798 Rebellion. He was completely insensitive to human suffering, as in the case of the Sheares brothers. He was finally, through the efforts of Daniel O'Connell, forced to resign at the age of eighty-two in 1827. The blow was greatly softened for him as he was granted a very large pension and made Viscount Glandine and Earl of Norbury. O'Connell remarked that 'he was bought off the bench by a most shameful traffic'.

Before his death in Dublin on 27 July 1831, Norbury had his last joke. He heard that Lord Erne his neighbour was near death, and feeling his own end was near, he summoned his valet: 'James', said he, 'run round to Lord Erne and tell him, with my compliments, that it will be a *dead*-heat between us.' At Norbury's burial, when his coffin was being lowered, one of the local Dublin wags quipped, 'Give him plenty of rope lads, he never spared it himself'.

St Mary's churchyard was transferred to Dublin Corporation in 1966 and converted into a public park. At that time, some gravestones were missing and those remaining were arranged around the edge of the park. At present, the park is being landscaped, and the remaining gravestones will be incorporated into any new development.

St Mary's Pro-Cathedral (Vaults)

Situation: Marlborough Street, Dublin 1

Period is use: 1827–1932. [From 1932 burials are those of Archbishops of Dublin]

Situated in city centre

Marlborough Street runs from North Earl Street to Cathal Brugha Street and dates from 1728. Formerly called Great Marlborough Street, it was name after the Great Duke of Marlborough (1650–1722).

The plans for the new Cathedral resulted from a competition which was held in 1814. John Sweetman, an exiled United Irishman who was living in Paris, submitted the most suitable plans, which were classical in design. It is quite possible that a French architect named Louis Hippolyte le Bas was responsible for them, as there are certain similarities to two churches in Paris, St Philippe-le-Roule and Notre Dame de Lorette.

The Cathedral was built on the site of Lord Annesley's former town house, which stood on the corner of Marlborough Street. George Papworth and John Taylor are associated with the completion of the work. Peter Turnerelli (1774–1839), the Belfast born sculptor of Italian parentage, executed the high altar and the relief of the *Ascension* was by John Smyth.

Archbishop John Thomas Troy laid the foundation stone of St Mary's Pro-Cathedral (formerly known as St Mary's Metropolitan Catholic Chapel) on 8 March 1815, the feast day of St Laurence O'Toole, patron of the archdiocese of Dublin. Daniel O'Connell and John Philpot Curran were present on the occasion.

Archbishop Troy died in May 1823 and his requiem was the first Mass to be celebrated in the yet unfinished Cathedral. A monument within the cathedral commemorates him, which reads:

Here lies in peace John Thomas Troy Archbishop of Dublin, who, having governed the Diocese of Ossory for ten years and subsequently the Archdiocese of Dublin for thirty-six years in a most holy manner, died in Dublin on 5th May 1823 at the age of eighty-three.

At the height of national upheaval he was a man of firm principle and most humble nature who won the love and respect of all. He disapproved equally of the vices and errors of rulers and of the insurgent movements.

This monument was erected to a most loving father-in-God by the clergy of Dublin, to whom, at his death, he had left a special example of virtue through the religious observance of the vow of poverty, a vow he had made to God in the Order of Preachers (the Dominican Order).

AD 1838

Archbishop Troy's remains are contained in the vaults. Dr Daniel Murray succeeded him and he in turn was succeeded by Dr Paul Cullen.

The Most Revd Dr Daniel Murray performed the opening ceremony of St Mary's Pro-Cathedral, which took place ten years later on 14 November 1925. O'Connell gave a speech which concluded with the following words:

If all classes of Irish men were united, if the demon of discord was cast out from among them, what a happy country, how blessed beyond example Ireland should be.

When O'Connell died in Genoa in 1847, his remains were brought back to Ireland and his coffin was placed in the Pro-Cathedral for four days before his funeral to Glasnevin. Michael Collins' funeral was also from this cathedral.

---

[87] VIEW OF THE FRONT OF ST MARY'S PRO-CATHEDRAL, MARLBOROUGH STREET.

There are two large marble memorials facing each other across the nave of the Cathedral. Both were executed by the famous Dublin sculptor, Thomas Farrell (1827–1900). One commemorates Archbishop Daniel Murray (1768–1852), who is depicted kneeling in prayer. On either side of his statue are the allegorical figures of *Meekness* and *Prudence*. This monument represented the first major commission of the Catholic Church in the nineteenth century. The other memorial commemorates Cardinal Paul Cullen (1852–1872), who played an important role in nineteenth century church history and was the first Irish prelate to be made a Cardinal. In the sculpture, he stands on a platform which is surmounted on a drum. Around this, relief figures depict different scenes of his life as Archbishop, such as tending the sick and the poor and the training of priests.

The vaulted cemetery beneath the Cathedral is quite extensive and contains the remains of 961 people some of whom were benefactors, such as the Sweetman, O'Rourke and Corballis families. It contains the vaults for the Religious Sisters of Charity and a special area for the clergy.

The vaults contain the remains of the following archbishops of Dublin:

Most Revd John Troy (1786–1823)

Most Revd Daniel Murray (1823–1852)

Most Revd Edward J. Byrne (921–1940),

Most Revd John Charles McQuaid (1940–1972)

Most Revd Dermot Ryan (1972–1984)

Most Revd Kevin McNamara (1984–1987)

The remains of Alberto Levame, former Papal Nuncio to Ireland, were transferred from Glasnevin and re-interred in the vaults in 1987. The remains of the Most Revd Ettore Felici, the Apostolic Nuncio who died on 16 May 1951, are also interred here.

There are thirty-eight family vaults. The O'Conor Don, an MP who died on 28 July 1847, has his own vault. Also interred here are Sir Thomas Esmonde, who died on 5 January 1869, Honble Charles Southwell, died 10th August 1875, Rt Hon Thomas Southwell, 3 May 1878, Sir John Ennis, Bart, Aug 1878 and Lady MacDonnell, who died on 15 February 1878.

Edward Martyn (1859–1924), the playwright, established the Palestrina Choir at the Pro-Cathedral in 1899 where John McCormack sang for some years.

The vaults in St Mary's Pro-Cathedral are not open to the public, but a visit to the Cathedral and a look at the memorials there indicate the importance it played in the church history of the time.

St Mary's Pro-Cathedral is under the care of the Roman Catholic parish of Saint Mary.

St Matthew's Churchyard

Situation: Ringsend, Dublin 4. St Matthew's Church is situated just two miles east from the city centre at the junction of Irishtown Road with Londonbridge Road

Period in use: 1723 to 1866

Bus Nos (from city centre): 1 and 3

The name Ringsend is derived from the Irish word *rinn*, meaning end or point. This refers to the point or spur of land, formerly between the river Dodder and the sea. This can be seen clearly on *Bernard de Gomme's Map* of 1673. It is a long and narrow strip of land that extends into the sea. The water is on the western side and it covers the low ground between Irishtown and the slightly rising ground of Beggars Bush.

In the seventeenth century, there was much seafaring activity in Ringsend and it was the chief landing place at the time of de Gomme's map. It became the principal packet station and Port of Dublin (later it was transferred to Howth and Kingstown). It provided a convenient landing place for Dublin-bound passengers and avoided the trouble of navigating the tidal river.

At the time, the Liffey had not yet been quayed and was winding in devious courses through a labyrinth of sands as can be seen on *de Gomme's map*. Before a bridge was built across the Dodder, Ringsend could only be approached from Dublin by a ford across this river. Generally a vehicle known as a 'Ringsend Car' was used. This was a one-horse vehicle comprising of a seat suspended on a leather strap between two shafts without springs. The noise created by the creaking of the strap distinguished this way of travel. An even shorter way to the city was to race in one of the cars over the sands at low tide.

It was here that Oliver Cromwell landed in 1649 with his 12,000 troops and caused months of havoc in the country.

The population of Ringsend increased with seafaring men and merchants. It was originally in the parish of Donnybrook, but the journey along the highway to the church in Donnybrook proved hazardous, mainly due to the frequent flooding from the Dodder. An Act of Parliament was passed in 1703 authorising the building of a church at Ringsend for the revenue officers and other inhabitants of the area. The Act authorised Viscount Merrion to convey any quantity of land, not exceeding two acres, for a church and churchyard, and the Archbishop of Dublin was empowered to apply £100 out of the forfeited tithes towards building same, an endowment which afterwards took effect in the adjacent village of Irishtown.

276

A year later, St Matthew's Royal Chapel opened. St Matthew's was in the patronage of the Crown until the disestablishment. Shortly afterwards, it became the church of a separate parish. It was rebuilt in 1878 but the original tower still stands.

Ringsend became a vibrant little village and was described in the middle of the eighteenth century in contrasting ways. It was seen as being 'very clean, healthy and beautiful....' but the *Parliamentary Gazetteer of Ireland* (1846) described it as a 'dingy, dirty, and disagreeable place; and jointly with Irishtown, forms one of the most befilthified skirts of the city'. An interesting reference in 1728 says:

> *Brooking's curious* Map of the City and Suburbs of Dublin, *published this year, will show that very great changes have taken place in Irishtown and the neighbouring districts during the last century.*

Interestingly, Irishtown and its church are shown in this map as almost surrounded by the sea, from which no small extent of ground has since been reclaimed, and the desolate appearance of the country along the south-east side of Dublin Bay is particularly striking.

There are several burials in the vaults of St Matthew's, some of which are quite early, such as that of Henry Lord Power, who on 6 May 1742, was 'Buried in ye vault of St Matthew's Chappel'. According to Mr D'Alton,

> *but for the effect of attainders, was the Lord Power of Curraghmore, and should be commemorated by the Waterford family, who enjoy what were once left to the estates of the Poers. He had claimed the estate of Curraghmore as heir male [James Earl of Tyrone] the father of Lady Catherine Poer, who on her marriage had brought over the property to Sir Marcus Beresford [afterwards created Earl of Tyrone]; but of course he failed his suit.*

The vaults also include Sir Aylmer Bourke, only son of John, Eight Viscount Mayo, and Catherine, daughter of Major Whitgift Aylmer. Catherine was born on 17 November 1743 and died on 21 July 1748 and two days later, 'was buried in the church of Irishtown, near Dublin'.

St Matthew's Church contains a number of plaques, some of which are now stored in the vaults which can be accessed from the south side of the church. A similar vault on the north side has been bricked-up for a number of years.

One of these tablets, formerly on the west wall of the south door, bore the inscription:

> *Elected by the members | of the congregation | To the memory of the | Revd. Michael Henry Wall D.D. | Chaplain for more than half a | Century of the Royal Chapel of | St Matthew Ringsend | Who died Sept. 15th 1869 | Aged 74 years. | Gifted by his Creator with many and | Rare endowments he devoted them all | To his service and the setting | Forth of his glory | 'O God, thou hast taught | me from my | Youth: and hitherto have I declared thy | wondrous works'. Psalm LXXXI.17th*

High up in the centre is a large stone plaque [by Harrison] which reads:

Pro Patrica | In proud and Loving Remembrance of the men, | brothers-in-arms, who, from this parish or connected | therewith | died in the Great War, 1914-1918, | Fighting for God, and right, and liberty. [Left-hand side]Duncan Black | Harold Cox | Frederick A. Harrison | Wm Robt Alfred Leland | Arthur Luger | Robt Daniel Mc Carthy | Michael Henry Mc Clean | George Mc Kinley | David McComb | Frank Milligan | Denis O'Brien | Richard Patterson | William Rawlins | Frank Moore Scott | Charles Victor Scott | Frederick Sessions | William Wood Vernon | John Willoughby | Charles Robert Young | Hector Albert Young. [Right-hand side] The following were | formerly members of | the St Matthew's (17th)Co. | of the Boys' Brigade:- | James Charles Bannan | James Blackmore | Walter Blackwell | Edward Davey | Walter Harper | William Louth | John Mc Gurdy | James Mannix | Frederick Morrow | William Murphy | Ernest Peel | Edward Pullen | Henry Rose | Edward Tutty | George Twamley.
Faithful unto Death.

A brass plaque also with a military connection reads:

In proud memory of | Thomas Hankey. | Rifleman 1st Batt. Royal Ulster Rifles. | 6th Airborne Division. | Killed in action on 7th June. | 1944 | Also | Bruce Samuel Hudson | Lieut. Royal Artillery. | Killed in action in Korea on 23rd April 1951 | 'We will remember them'.

The adjoining churchyard is well kept and consists of two portions, a smaller one on the north side and a larger one on the south side. The smaller section contains eighteen memorials and the larger sixty-one. Previously, they contained many more, as shown by the Reverend Beaver H. Blacker, who, in his *Brief Sketches of Booterstown and Donnybrook,* listed the headstones in the 1850s. Since then, however, a large number of the memorials have vanished.

One of the earliest interments was that of the first minister, whose memorial is missing. It was inscribed:

Here lyeth the body of the Revd Mr John | Borough, first | minister of the Royall Chappell. He died on the 10th May, | 1726, in the 41st year of his age. He was third son on the Revd Dr Elias Borough, chanter of the Cathedrall of St | Patrick and first Library-keeper of the publick library | at St Sepulcher's.

Interestingly, the Revd John Borough's father, Sir E. Borough, was a descendant of the Revd Elias Bohereau, the first Librarian of Marsh's Library, a Huguenot who fled from France in 1685.

The following suggests that the air in Ringsend was extremely good:

Mary Myers, of Ringsend, buried in the churchyard of St Matthews, 21st March, 1829 aged 103 years.

She had never (as she had informed Dr Wall) slept a night out of Ringsend, which in her youthful days 'was very clean, healthy, and beautiful, with vines trained up against the walls of the houses'.

A memorial may be seen close to the south boundary wall in the south section which marks the resting place of the young Roman Catholic Pastor of the Parish, who was interred here. Prior to 1829, Roman Catholics living in Dublin city had no cemeteries in which to bury their dead.

To the memory | of the Revd Peter Richard Clinch | Roman Catholic pastor of this Parish | who died on the 29th December 1792 | in the 29th year of his age | and the 5th of his mission | In humble hope with Christ again to rise | beneath this stone the friend, the pastor lies. | His manners open, elegant and sage; | his youth rever'd like venerable age; | his charity, which oft her all bestow'd, | and oft in sorrows for the helpless flow'd, | Alas! could not reverse the mournful doom; | And torture sunk him to an early tomb. | Here laid in peace, his honour'd ashes rest; | Here all with tenderness his virtues own, | And grateful rear this monumental stone.'

Some early interments include:

This burial-place belongs to Alexr Stephens, of Temple | Barr {Dublin}. Here lyeth his grandson, Alexr Stephens dyed ye | 11th of Feby, 1763, aged 10 months (Grave missing).

Here lieth the body of Mr Joseph Watson, late | Deputy Surveyor at Ringsend, who died the | 17th day of August, 1746, aged 66 years.

[88] THE GRAVESTONE OF THE REVEREND PETER CLINCH, THE CATHOLIC PASTOR OF THE PARISH WHO DIED IN DECEMBER 1792, AGED 29 YEARS.

This is a horizontal slab which is difficult to decipher and it is contained in the larger section of the churchyard.

A number of mariners were buried here including:

Richard Piper, mariner, died May | 24th 1750 aged 37 years (memorial missing).

Also:

James Pile | mariner | native of Brixham who departed this life | the 29th May 1855 aged 46 years.

279

Another mariner is:

Sacred to the memory of Henry Totty, late Commander of | the Brigg Hawk of Chester, who was upwards of 40 years trading from that city and Liverpool to this Port. For honesty and | integrity he might be equalle'd , but not exceeded. He | departed this life the 3rd day of July, 1799, aged 60 years. | Reader, remember an honest man is the noblest work of God [Gravestone missing].

John McNamara, a well-known collector of Irish manuscripts who is mentioned on almost every page of O'Reilly's *Chronological Account of Irish Writers* (Dublin, 1820), is interred here. A horizontal flat slab on four granite legs marks his resting-place in the larger section of the churchyard.

Here lie the mortal remains of | John McNamara, Esq late of Sandymount | formerly of Coolnahella, Barony of Tulla, Co. Clare. | who died 3rd Sept 1822, aged 58 years. | The Lord have mercy on his soul. Amen. | He was a thorough honest Irishman | and a lover of his country.

The churchyard contains the tombs of families such as the Foxes of Tully, from 1768; the Chapmans, from 1786; the Harts, from 1813 and the Vavasour family from 1762. Regarding local names of places, the name Vavasour is of interest:

Here lieth the body of John Vavasour, merchant, who | departed this life April the 2nd, 1762, aged fifty-four [Gravestone missing].

Here lieth the body of Mr Peter Vavasour | who departed this life 9th December 1782 | aged 60 years. Here lies the body of | Mrs Frances McAuliffe | otherwise in the 75th year of her age. | Also the remains of Thomas McAuliffe | her husband who died on the 10th of December 1818 | aged 64 years [Grave is located in the larger section].

Beneath this stone lie the remains of William Vavasour | Esqr of [Kildare Street] Dublin [and Williamstown Castle], LL.D., who died on the 25th day of May, | 1819, aged 75 years. Also of Anne, his wife, who died on 19th October, 1823, aged 76 years [Gravestone missing].

[89] St Matthew's, built in 1704 and rebuilt in 1878, still retains its original tower.

280

In 1807, their eldest daughter Anne married Lieut General Sir Henry Maghull Mervin Vavasour Bart of Spaldington in Yorkshire. She died in 1845 leaving issue. The family had a lot of property in the area.

Vavasour Square, located off Bath Avenue, was named after W. Vavasour. In 1792, he acquired from Lord Fitzwilliam the marshy area between Beggar's Bush and Ringsend, through which the Dodder flowed to Ringsend Bridge. Vavasour reclaimed this land which was flooded by each tide, by constructing a double embankment on the Dodder. In the *Annals of the Parishes* (1795), it is recorded:

Riding to Ringsend, we were presented with a striking proof of the vast extent of human labour and human genius in the docks building there; and were highly pleased to find Counsellor Vavasour reclaiming the great tract of waste ground near the bridge.... Williamstown is adjoining Blackrock, and has been much improved by Counsellor Vavasour.

This churchyard did not escape the threat of the bodysnatchers. In many of the old Dublin burial grounds, several graves dating back to the early nineteenth century are covered by cumbersome stone slabs placed on equally heavy pillars. This served as a protection as it would deter any potential grave robber from interfering with the grave. On one occasion when this graveyard was being tidied, several of the graves were found to be protected by two such slabs, one on the surface and the other about a foot underground.

By an order of the Lord Justices and Privy Council of Ireland, in July 1872 the burial ground was closed against further interments except for those holding rights.

In *Saunder's News Letter* of 3 July 1872, it stated that the graveyard had existed for one hundred and sixty years and that the number of burials for the ten years ending 1864 was 549 and for the ten years ending 1871 was 585. It also stated that, for the protection of the public health and because the neighbourhood was populous, burials should be wholly discontinued.

This neat and well-kept churchyard is under the care of the Select Vestry of Irishtown.

St Michael and St John (Vaults)

Situation: Lower Exchange Street, Dublin 2

Period in use: 1829–1896

Situated in city centre

The parish church of SS Michael and John, which was designed by J. Taylor, was built in 1815. The church derives its name from the united titles of the old medieval church of St John in Fishamble Street and the penal chapel of St Michael in Rosemary Lane.

The church, which contained the first bell to toll in the city since the Reformation, is on the site of the former Smock Alley Theatre that was built in 1662. In 1701, the gallery of the theatre collapsed during a performance of *The Libertine*, killing and injuring many in the audience. It was rebuilt again a couple of times. In October 1811, Austin Cooper noted in his diary that the old playhouse in Smock Alley was nearly pulled down, the adjoining house ruined and, on the whole site, 'a large Popish Chapel is erecting'. The only remnant of Smock Ally Theatre was a portion of an arched passage on the south-eastern side of the church. The burial vaults originally formed the pit of the theatre.

The church has seven vaults, which originally contained 124 coffins. Perhaps the most noteworthy person here was a priest who contributed a huge amount of his energies to providing education for the people in this area. Father Thomas Betagh, an eighteenth century Jesuit of extraordinary personal qualities, is interred here. He took over the running of the classical school in Saul's Court near Cook Street on the death of the famous Father Austin. Father Betagh gave his time willingly and increased the opportunity for education by including day, evening and Sunday classes for the deprived people in this teeming part of the old city. William Reed, a Baptist minister from Gloucestershire, described Father Betagh in his old age, as

> the most learned and best-informed man in Ireland, and who added to these accomplishments an amenity of manners that was almost enchanting.

Father Betagh, who died at 74 Cook Street, had a crowd of 20,000 at his funeral. In appreciation of his work, the citizens of Dublin paid for a monument to commemorate him. It was fashioned by Turnerelli.

282

Initially Father Betagh was interred in the vaults of the Presentation Convent at George's Hill, but he was later transferred to the Church of SS Michael and John.

Other clergy who were interred here included the Revd Patrick Corr, 16 October 1831 aged forty; the Revd P. Moran, osf, 21 June 1831, aged seventy-nine; the Very Revd Nicholas Roche, Canon and Parish Priest for SS Michael and John, 29 November 1873, aged eighty-three and the Revd John Smyth, CC who was interred on 23 August 1858 aged sixty-eight.

In recent years, the church was used for the celebration of the Tridentine Rite. It ceased to be used as a place of worship when the remains from the crypts were moved elsewhere to accommodate Dublin's Viking Adventure, which contains Viking artefacts discovered in the area and reconstructs life in Viking Dublin of a thousand years ago.

[90] THE CHURCH OF ST MICHAEL AND ST JOHN, BLIND QUAY.

St Michael Le Pole Churchyard (Demolished)

Situation: Great Ship Street, Dublin 8
Period in use: Pre-Christian to c. 1850
Situated in city centre

The pre-Viking parish of St Michael Le Pole was one of the most ancient in Dublin. It is of note as the churchyard contained the only known round tower in Dublin city. It stood close to Great Ship Street.

A schoolhouse was built on the site of the ancient church and granted to Dr John Jones who used it as a Latin school. It was here that Henry Grattan and John Fitzgibbon, Earl of Clare, were educated together. The school, which continued until 1787, was granted to Dr Jones on condition that he preserve the adjacent round tower. In 1737, Dean Swift contributed to its repair, but it was badly damaged in a storm in 1775. Part of it was taken down in part in 1778 and the remainder of it demolished in 1789.

Gabriel Beranger, the Dutch-born Huguenot, made a sketch of the tower, adjacent building and churchyard.

A tablet which gave a thumbnail sketch of the site was written by the Revd William George Carroll and erected over the arched entrance to the site. It read:

Entrance to

S. Michael Le Pole Church Yard.

(Here anciently stood the church and the
Round Tower — adjacent lay the mill pond or
'pool' which gave name to these buildings
And to the old city gate in Bridge Street.)

S. Bride's Widows' Alms House.

(Founded in Bride's Street and Bull Ally, AD
1683, in succession to an older Widows'
House in Bride Street — opened here in 1786)

284

S. Bride's Teacher's Residence.

(School established in Golden Lane and
Arthur's Lane about 1700 AD Move to
Little Ship Street, 1746 — Hither 1796 A.D
Bride Street 1859)

Here in the above named church when
rebuilt, was the famed Latin school of the
Last century, in which Henry Grattan and
John Fitzgibbon, Earl of Clare, were
Educated together.

[91] BERANGER'S SKETCH OF THE OLD TOWER OF MICHAEL OF POLE. (COURTESY OF THE NATIONAL LIBRARY OF IRELAND)

In 1895, there were only ten remaining gravestones in the churchyard. They were stacked against the southern boundary wall close to the old schoolhouse.

Dr Thomas Ball, the celebrated schoolmaster, and his son, the Revd John Ball, were buried in this churchyard, as was the Revd Dawson Crowe.

The Revd R.S. Maffett recorded some of the gravestones of this ancient ecclesiastical site in 1895. According to the caretaker at that time, many of the gravestones were used for wall repairs at the beginning of the century. Some of the local people included a merchant:

> *Here lieth ye Body of Domk M[c]DANIEL Mercht of William | Street in the City of Dublin who Departed this life the 18th Decr | 1761 Aged 84. Here also lieth the Body of his Wife MARY McDANIEL who Departed this life 23 May 1763 Aged 75 | Also their Son MICHL who Departed this life 20 May 1746 | Aged 19 Also Ye Bodys of JANE & MARY MCDANIEL | Grand Daughters of ye Said DOMK & MARY by there (sic) Son FRANCIS.*

and

> *Here Lieth the Body of Mrs ELIZABETH MASON Wife of Mr | JOHN MASON Vicar Choral of St Patricks and Christ Church | Dublin and Also Vicar Choral of Armagh. She Departed this | life on Wednesday the 9th day of March 1774 in the 66 year of | her Age in full hopes of a happy and Joyful Resurrection (sic) | through the Merits of JESUS CHRIST our Most Blessed | Saviour and Redeemer.*

One of the early inscriptions included:

> *[Her]e are Buried [E]LIZ. SERVANT who [d]eparted this | life Augt ye 25th 1701,*
> *& SAMUEL her Son who died july ye | 17th 1701 Aetas fluit.*

The entrance to the churchyard was originally approached by Great Ship Street and existed until 1944. It was then converted for use as a school playground and the memorials were stacked against the wall, after which it was taken over by Messrs Dockrells as a timber stores.

St Michael le Pole parish became part of the union of St Werburgh's, and the parish church which had several monuments in it, was demolished.

St Michan's Church and Churchyard

Situation: Church Street, Dublin 7

Period in use: 1096–1880s

Bus No (from city centre): 134

In 1095, the Danes built St Michan's, which was the first parish church on the north side of the river Liffey. At the time, the surrounding land was wooded by oak trees and was occupied by a few Danes or Ostmen, whose town was Ostmantown or Oxmantown. On 14 May, the Ostmen dedicated the church to St Michan, an old Danish saint and martyr.

At the end of the seventeenth and beginning of the eighteenth centuries, the parishioners of St Michan's increased, both as a result of citizens migrating over the river and the growth in the number of country seats. As a result, the churches of St Paul and St Mary were built in 1697 for the two parishes.

Dr John Pooley, the then rector and subsequently bishop of Raphoe and Cloyne, rebuilt St Michan's church in 1685–86 and the vaults date from this time. It was completely remodelled on the old foundations when it took on the appearance it still has today. It was restored in 1828 when the main body of the church was replaced. The tower remains and it dates from the twelfth century. Dr Pooley, in his will dated 30 January 1710, left the sum of sixty pounds for alterations and a font for the church. It was in this font that Edmund Burke (1729–97), statesman, orator and writer, who was born at 12 Arran Quay, was baptised.

The interior of the church contains much of interest. It has one of the oldest organs still in use in the country, which was built by J. Baptist de Couville of Dublin in 1724. On the front of the gallery there is some fine carving of musical instruments made out of one piece of wood. The pulpit, which dates from the eighteenth century, is unusual in that it was originally on wheels so that it could be moved easily into the required position for the service. The Penitent's Pew, originally a prayer desk, also dates from this period. In 1922, when the Civil War broke out and an explosion severely damaged the Four Courts on Inns Quay, the east stained-glass window of St Michan's was shattered. This contained several panels with the coats of arms of families who had associations with the parish. It was replaced in 1958 by the present plain-glass window, which was rededicated by the Most Revd Dr G.O. Simms, the then Archbishop of Dublin.

The vaults in St Michan's are of special interest and are perhaps the most famous feature of the church. These arched chambers extend under the church from north to south, except under the tower. The descent to the vaults is by stone steps, which lead down to a long passage, with burial chambers on the left and right hand sides. Generally each chamber belonged to a single family. The atmosphere in them is dry and the temperature remains constant. Bodies, which have been here for centuries, are in such a good state of preservation that their features are still discernible. There is a body of a woman with distinct features, which is beautifully preserved. It is said that she was a nun who died at the age of one hundred and eleven years. Another body is said to be that of a Knight Crusader. The vaults attract many visitors. Unfortunately they were broken into by thieves in July 1996 and vandalised, but the coffins were saved and a re-interment service was held.

Among those interred in the vaults is Sir Patrick Dun, who died on 24 May 1713 and was buried in the vaults three days later. An extract from his will expresses his wishes:

> *I desire my body may be privately interred without any Public Noise or ostentation in a vault adjoining to the south-west wall in the inside of the Parish Church of the new St Michan's in Dublin, which vault I purchased from the Minister and church wardens of the said church for my heirs for ever by deed indented & duly perfected for them wherein is a clause excluding any person from being buried therein without leave obtained from me, my heirs or assigns.*

Dun, a celebrated medical figure, was brought to Ireland by the Duke of Ormonde. He was appointed Physician to the army in Ireland and was the first Physician to the Royal Hospital Kilmainham where he attended to the wounded after the battle of the Boyne in 1690. He was present at many of the engagements in the war of 1689–91. A man of great ability, he was considered to be ahead of his time in practical anatomy. In 1696, he was knighted, and with Ormonde, he founded the College of Physicians in Dublin of which he was the first president.

Dun's wife Mary, the daughter of Colonel Jephson, survived him and died on 19 January 1748 and was buried in the same vault. Dun's name was perpetuated by the Dublin hospital named after him, which recently ceased to function as a hospital.

Dr Jonathan Osborne, who was born in Dublin in 1794 and joined the staff of Mercer's Hospital in 1835, is also buried in the vaults but with a difference! A classical scholar, who spoke Latin fluently, he wrote on a wide range of subjects. His book, *On the Nature and Treatment of Dropsical Diseases*, which was published in 1837, was translated into German. An excellent lecturer, he had a great sense of humour. When he developed arthritis in his hips and was forced to use two sticks, he made light of it saying that it was more natural for people to walk with sticks. Thinking ahead to the time of the Resurrection, he stipulated that he wished to be buried standing in an upright position so that he would not be at a disadvantage. When he died, his wishes were carried out and his coffin was placed in an upright position in the family vault of St Michan's.

The vaults contain the remains of Sir Henry Parnell (1776–1842), the granduncle of Charles Stewart Parnell. He was the author of *History of the Penal Laws* (1808) and *Financial Reform* (1830). On 11 October 1891, the remains of Charles Stewart Parnell were brought from Westland Row Station (now Pearse Street) to St Michan's, where a service was held. They were then moved to the City Hall for the lying-in-state, where more than 30,000 filed past the remains.

In the vaults are the remains of the brothers, Henry Sheares (1753–1798) and John Sheares (1766–1798) both barristers who were implicated with the Rising of 1798.

Dr Madden wrote that they were inseparable and were united by an almost unparalleled attachment. They were executed in front of Newgate on the morning of 14 July 1798.

Interred in the churchyard under a large stone are Oliver Bond (1760–1798), who died suddenly in Newgate, on 6 September while under sentence of death and the Reverend William Jackson (1737–1795), who avoided execution when he poisoned himself in the dock. Bond, a prominent United Irishman, had a business in Pill Lane and in 1786 moved to a house in Bridge Street where the meetings of the Leinster Directory were usually held. It was here, on 19 February 1798, that the well-known resolution was passed:

> *We will pay no attention to any measure which the Parliament of this kingdom may adopt, to divert the public mind from the grand object we have in view; as nothing short of the entire and complete regeneration of our country can satisfy us.*

On the wall outside there is a testimonial to the memory of Samuel Rosborough, one of the founders of The Sick and Indigent Roomkeepers Society AD 1790. He was treasurer for many years and died on 3 November 1832 aged seventy-five.

> *'When the ear heard him, then it blessed him, | And when the eye saw him, it gave witness of him, | For he delivered the poor that cried, the fatherless, and | him that none to help him.' | This tablet has been erected by order of the Committee | of the Society, as a mark of respect and esteem for the | deceased.*

Charles Lucas (1713–1771), the patriot and founder of the *Freeman's Journal* and the first physician who ever sat in parliament, is interred in the churchyard. As an apothecary, he had a shop for many years in Charles Street. He then received a medical degree and had a lucrative practice in Dublin. His *Translation of The Great Charter of the City of Dublin* (1749), was a formidable piece of work, which focused on long forgotten rights. He is described in his later years as having an uncommon neatness of dress and grey venerable locks, blending with a pale but interesting countenance, in which an air of beauty was still visible. A stranger never entered the House of Commons without enquiring who he was. He died in his house at Henry Street on 4 November 1771.

A monument to him bears the following inscription:

To the memory of | CHARLES LUCAS, M.D. formerly one of the representatives in Parlia | ment for the City of Dublin; whose incorrupt integrity, unconquered | spirit, just judgment, and glorious perseverance in the great cause of | Liberty, Virtue, and his Country, endeared him to his grateful constituents. | This tomb is placed over his much-respected remains, as a small, yet | sincere tribute of Remembrance, by one of his fellow-citizens and consti | tuents, Sir Edward Newenham, Knight. | Lucas! Hibernia's friend, her joy and pride, | Her powerful bulwark, and her skilful guide, | Firm in the senate, steady to his trust, | Unmoved by fear, and obstinately just | Charles Lucas, born 26th of September 1713. | Died November 4th, 1771.

[92] ST MICHAN'S CHURCH AND CHURCHYARD. THE TOWER SURVIVES FROM THE TWELFTH CENTURY.

The tomb of the Emmet family is behind the church, halfway up the churchyard and beside the central walk, which divides the graveyard. This is one of the many churchyards where it was said Robert Emmet was interred. Others include St Peter's, St Paul's and the little cemetery in Glasnevin, St Mobhi's, beside Delville which is now the grounds of the Bon Secours Hospital.

Many of the memorials date from the 1700s and one of the oldest recorded in the churchyard is inscribed:

HERE. UNDER LYETH. THE | BODY OF JOHN HORE OF | THE CITTIE OF DUBLIN | COOPER WHO DECEASED | THE 29th OF MAY ANNO | DOMINI 1662.

Alderman Richard Tighe, who served as Mayor of the City of Dublin in the years 1651 and 1655 and likewise as High Sheriff in the county of Dublin, is buried here. He died on 20 February 1673. He is commemorated with a memorial slab in St Michan's.

Some other memorials from the 1700s include the following:

This stone & burial place belongeth to Mr Thos | Plunket And his posterity | Here lyeth the Body of the | above who departed this life the 22nd of August 1726 | in the 60th year of his age.

Here lies the body of | Euphemia Gibson | late wife of Mr Robert Gibson | Mathematician who died the 2nd of | August 1712 in the 30th year of her age. | Here also lie 12(?) of their children.

Close to the entrance of the vaults, on the south side of the church, there is a tombstone adorned with a cockerel in a circle over an inscription which reads:

The Burial Ground for Rob. Lawe, Esq | Of the City of Dublin and Cork | Where nine of his children | Lyes buried and Margaret | The wife of George Lawe, Esq

A similar type memorial beside it also relates to the Lawe family:

Also | Were interred here the remains | Of his Eldest Son Robt Lawe, Esq, | of Leixlip on the 18 Jan. 1826 | Aged 80 yeares & his beloved wife | Elizabeth on the 3rd Dec. 1836 | Aged 74 years & his Second son | Alexander on the 27 Jan. 1812, | aged 20 years. This memento of | affection for his beloved parents & | brother is recorded by his eldest son | Lieut Colonel Robt Lawe, K.H.

Robert Lawe of Robertsville in Leixlip was the father of General Robert Lawe, 71st Highlanders, Knight of the Royal Hanoverian Order and a distinguished Peninsular veteran. This family of Lawes belonged to the ancient house of Lawe of Laurieston. In his account of *The Lawes, Marquises of Laurieston*,

291

Grant refers to the Lieutenant Colonel (afterwards General) Robert Lawe, K.H. as 'perhaps the last representative in the United Kingdom' of that ancient and distinguished family.

Another person with military connections interred here was a music master:

Erected to the memory of her beloved husband John | Hayden Crozier Music Master to the 85th Regt. late | King's Light Infantry, who departed this life 27th | March 1848, aged 50 years.

The notorious William Sydney, 3rd Earl of Leitrim, was interred in his family vault following his assassination on 2 April 1878. He was ambushed and killed on his way to an eviction in Donegal. As his cortège approached St Michan's church, an angry mob tried to pull his coffin off the hearse. The mourners entered the church under police protection, and, after the funeral service, his successor, the 4th Earl, made good his escape by a side door in the church!

In the churchyard, there are memorials to many local Dubliners from Camden Street, Greek Street, Bride Street, Ormonde Market, Bachelor's Walk, New Church Street, Upper Coombe, Francis Street and North Anne Street. Also many crafts and trades are represented such as:

This burial ground for Mr Daniel Finn, Of the city of | Dublin, hatter, and family, where 14 of his children lie | interred. here lieth the wife of the above Daniel Finn, | who departed this Life Oct. 15th 1788, in the 46th year of her age.

St Michan's churchyard is under the care of the Select Vestry of Christ Church Cathedral Group.

St Mobhi's Churchyard

Situation: Church Lane, Glasnevin, Dublin 9

Period in use: from 1600s. Closed except to those with burial rights

Bus Nos (from city centre): 19

S t Mobhi's churchyard is situated one and a half miles from the city centre on the northern bank of the river Tolka. Coming along the old Finglas Road past the Bon Secours Hospital turn right up Ballymun Road. Take second turn right which is Church Avenue and the churchyard is at the end of this. The name Glasnevin is derived from *Glas Naedhan* or the Naedhe stream, which now flows mostly underground and passes quite close to the east wall of the churchyard.

St Mobhi, known as 'Cláirineach' or the flat-faced, was the patron saint of Glasnevin, and according to the *Annals of the Four Masters (Annala Rioghacta Éireann)*, died on 12 October 544. Mobhi was head of a religious community, which comprised about fifty scholars who lived in little huts. Amongst his notable students were St Columba, who finished his studies here before founding the Abbey at Durrow, and later left Ireland for Iona, Comhgall of Bangor, Ciaran of Clonmacnoise and Canice of Kilkenny.

Due to events throughout the centuries, the church fell into disrepair, was restored many times and in 1707, it was rebuilt. The church tower dates from the fourteenth century and was restored in the latter half of the seventeenth century. Later, various additions were made, such as the chancel and an aisle on the south side of the church. There was a mural slab in the south wall of the church which is now broken and which bore the inscription:

> *REBUILT ANNO*
> *DOMINI 1707*
> *SR JOHN ROGERSON*
> *[KNI]GHT AND CHARELS*
> *REEVES ESQR*
> *[C]HURCHWARDENS*

It is interesting to note the devotion of the parishioners to St Mobhi's church. Towards the end of the fifteenth century, the wills of some of the parishioners illustrate this as recorded by Elrington Ball from *Crede Mihi*:

Geoffrey Fox's first wife desires to be buried in the nave, before the image of St Mary, and leaves twelve pence to buy a cope for the priest; Nicholas Barrett leaves twelve pence towards works then being executed in the chancel; and Geoffrey Fox's second wife desires to be buried in the nave, and leaves two shillings towards the works and a towel for the use of the clergy.

There are many monuments of note in the churchyard commemorating doctors, poets, lawyers, artists, architects, clergymen, landowners, military men, tradesmen and academics. The oldest legible tombstone located is a slab at the base of the church tower. It reads:

GEORGE CLAYTON DIED | IN MAY 1695 WALTER | FITZSIMONS DIED THE | 10 OF JUNE 1699.

When the south aisle was added to the church, it caused a certain amount of disturbance and memorials that were formerly in this area were transferred to the far boundary wall.

Sir Henry Jebb, who died in 1811, is buried on the north side of the graveyard, though as yet his memorial has not been located. Jebb was a surgeon to Mercer's Hospital and Professor and Head of the Midwifery (now Obstetrics) Department in the Royal College of Surgeons in Ireland from 1793–1794. He was also President of the College in 1800. He built North Frederick Street and named it after his son, Frederick, who was assistant surgeon to Mercer's for a time and Master of the Rotunda Hospital in 1773. He died in 1811.

John Winstanley (1676–1750), the Dublin born poet and son of a lawyer, is interred here. His Poems were published in Dublin in 1742 and his son edited a second volume after his death in 1751.

At the east end of the church is the Barber tomb where Mary Barber (1690–1752), the poetess, and her artist son, Rupert Barber (1736–1772), are interred. Mary, who was married to a woollen draper in Capel Street, was a protégé of Swift. He helped her to publish her work *Poems on Several Occasions* (1734) by raising subscriptions in England and Ireland. He also helped with the publication in 1738 of *Polite Conversations*, the proceeds from which helped her to live out the rest of her life in comfort. Rupert Barber studied art at Bath. He returned to Ireland in 1743 and worked as painter of miniatures in enamel as well as a portrait painter. He did many portraits of eminent people, including Swift and Mrs Delany, who encouraged him and gave him a house at the end of her delightful garden in Delville where he worked on his enamelling.

George Grattan (1787–1819), another Dublin artist of some note, is interred on the south side of the graveyard. His oil on canvas entitled *Beggarwoman and Child*, which he painted in 1807, hangs in the Royal Dublin Society. The RDS purchased it from him for one hundred guineas, declaring that the work 'discovers the highest talents, and deserves the warmest appreciation.' Grattan died aged thirty-two in Cullenswood and was buried on 31 June 1819 in St Mobhi's. His gravestone has the following inscription:

Here lieth George Grattan; He was pre-eminently skill'd as a painter, and was justly considered one of the brightest flowers of Irish Genius; He devoted his short life to the duties of a son and the affections of a brother. His piety was of that retiring kind which hides itself from human scrutiny, and while he saw and admired the beauty of this world, he yet worked and hoped through Christ our Lord to be received into another and better. He died June 18, 1819.

In 1759, the Right Honourable Henry Singleton, Master of the Rolls and former Chief Justice of the Common Pleas in Ireland, was buried here.

Andrew Caldwell (1683–1731), the architect and antiquary who is buried in the church with members of his family, is commemorated by a marble monument on the west wall which reads:

SUBTER IN CRYPTA | REQUIESCANT | ANDREAS GULIELMI CALDWELL FILIUS AMICUS | NAT. 1638 OB. 1731 | ET | HUGO ANDREAE FILIUS NATU MINIMUS | NAT. 1708 OB. 1710 | HOC MONUMENTUM PIETATIS CAUSA | CAROLUS BENJAMIN CALDWELL | ET | SOPHIA FRANCES CUST | UXOR DILECTISSIMA | POSUERUNT | AD 1871.

Glasnevin is inextricably linked with the name of the Revd Dr Patrick Delany (1685–1768), Dean of Down, who lived at Delville, an estate with a magnificent garden which adjoined the churchyard. It was where the Bon Secours Hospital is now sited. In 1732, Dr Delany married Dame Margaret Tenison, a wealthy widow. A genial man, he entertained all the Dublin celebrities and distinguished literary men at Delville, including his friends Dean Swift and Stella. His wife died on 6 December 1741, and two years later he married another widow, Mary Pendarves née Granville (1700–88), diarist, member of the Blue Stocking Circle, gifted artist and one of the most remarkable women of the eighteenth century. The days she spent at Delville were said to be the happiest in her life. Dr Delany, who it appears acted for some years as incumbent of Glasnevin, died in Bath on 6 May 1768 where he had gone to take the waters. He was buried close to his beloved Delville in the adjoining churchyard of St Mobhi's where he is commemorated by a stone in the north-east corner, which bears the inscription:

Here lyeth the Body of Patrick Delany, DD | Formerly Senior Fellow of | Trinity College Dublin | Late Dean of Downe | An orthodox Christian Believer | An early and earnest Defender of Revelation | A constant and zealous preacher of the Divine laws | For more than fifty years, | And an humble penitent | Hoping for mercy in Christ Jesus, | He died the Sixth day of May | MDCCLXVIII | In the Eighty-fourth year of his age.

Thomas Tickell [1686–1740], the poet and contributor to the *Guardian* and *Spectator*, lived in Glasnevin. The magnificent Botanic Gardens, which were founded by the Dublin Society in 1795,

[93] St Mobhi's in Glasnevin showing the church tower which dates from the fourteenth century.

encompass what was formerly Thomas Tickell's property and his house is now the Director's residence. Tickell was a close friend and neighbour of Dr Delany. His ballad *Lucy and Colin* was admired by Goldsmith and Gray, who believed it to be one of the best in the language. He was literary executor to Addison and edited Addison's Works, publishing a very fine elegy on Addison's death in the first volume (1721). Tickell died on 23 April 1740 at Bath in England and his body was brought back to Ireland and buried in St Mobhi's churchyard near his friend Dr Delany. He is commemorated by a tablet, which reads:

> *Sacred to the memory of Thomas Tickell Esq. He was sometime Under Secretary in England, and afterwards for many years, Secretary to the Lords Justices of Ireland: but his highest honour was that of having been the friend of Addison.*

The grave of the Lindsay family, who were prominent landlords in the area in the nineteenth and early twentieth centuries is to the right of Dr Delany's monument. Some roads in Glasnevin are named after members of the family, such as Lindsay Road, Claude Road and Crawford Avenue.

Also buried in St Mobhi's is John Barrett, DD (1753–1821), a loveable eccentric whose life revolved around Trinity College. He studied at Trinity where he was later professor of oriental languages. He was Vice-provost in 1807. He was described as being of low stature, with a huge head and small feet, so that he looked like an equilateral triangle standing on its vertex.

296

Due to the dire poverty experienced in his early life, Barrett was known to be miserly. He was always ready to help others, provided he was not called on to give any money. For the last fifty years of his life, he hardly ever left the precincts of the College. He lived in a garret in Library Square where he had two holes cut out of his door, a large one to let in his big cat and a small one to let out his little cat! He allowed himself no fire and little light. He generally crept down to the college kitchen for warmth, where the servants were a bit wary of him on account of his ragged appearance.

Many stories circulated about Barrett's absent-mindedness. He was observed tentatively regarding an egg in his hand while his watch was boiling away in the saucepan. He was astounded when he discovered that mutton came from sheep. He was equally amazed when he saw a crow in the college park, and his discovery, after some study in the classics, that this was 'a Corvus by Jove'.

Barrett spent most of his latter years reading in seclusion. He had a prodigious memory and could recall almost everything he had seen or read, though he was known to be ignorant of everything that pertained to the most ordinary affairs of life. His literary achievements included the discovery of an old palimpsest manuscript of fragments of the gospel of St Matthew. His main works included an essay on the life of Swift, works concerning the Zodiac and comments on St Matthew. When Barrett died, his estate was worth £80,000, a lot of money in 1821.

A flat stone near the vestry commemorates a former Minister of the parish:

Here lieth the Body of the Revd John | Boyle, who was Minister of this | Parish for 25 years, he died the 4th of | Decr 1779 Aged 72 years.

There are a number of gravestones in the churchyard which have the place name Glasmanogue on them. The lower portion of the road between Broadstone and Glasnevin, once known as the old Finglas Road, was known as Glasmanoge. In 1575, the city Mayors and Sheriffs held their court here during an outbreak of a plague which 'carried off 3,000 persons, depopulating the city to such an extent that grass grew on the streets'.

Some of the older memorials in the churchyard commemorate Dublin tradesmen such as the following:

This stone & Burial Place | Belongeth to John Connor of | St Thomas Street linnen weaver | both for him & his Posterity | Janary ye 27th Anno Domino[sic]1740 | Here Lyeth his father & Mother | & 4 of his children.

People from all over the city, including Meath Street, Smithfield, Bachelor's Walk, New Row, Church Street and Pimlico, were interred in St Mobhi's churchyard.

St Mobhi's is under the care of the Select Vestry of Glasnevin.

297

St Nicholas Within Church and Churchyard

SITUATION: CHRIST CHURCH PLACE, DUBLIN 8

PERIOD IN USE: 1671–1863

SITUATED IN CITY CENTRE

The walls of what remains of the church of St Nicholas Within may be seen at the corner of Christ Church Place and Nicholas Street, which adjoins the Peace Park. This parish dates from the middle of the eleventh century, when Bishop Donat built the church, which formerly was sited in Winetavern Street.

Some time in the twelfth century, a church was built on the present site in Nicholas Street. It was rebuilt in 1573. On the survey directed by Lord Deputy Sir John Perrott in 1585 of the Gates, Towers and Town Walls, St Nicholas Church is marked as is St Nicholas's Gate in the city wall, which originally separated Nicholas Street from Patrick Street.

In 1630, it was stated in a report that 'the church and chancell are in good repair and decencie; the most of the parishioners are Papists; there are many Protestants who frequent that church in the tyme of divine service and sermon; there is only in that parish the greate howse built by the Jesuits, which is seysed upon for his Majesty....' Dr Samuel Winter, who was Provost at Trinity College, preached at this church which was attended by 'Commissioners, city magistrates, and many others, so that he had a very frequent congregation; and to encourage poor people to come to church, he caused some white loaves to be distributed among them always when the sermon was ended'. Dr Winter was said to be 'a man of great zeal, rich in good works, and his faith and patience were very signal both in his life and death'.

Dr Samuel Mather, a Senior Fellow of Trinity College who was ordained in 1656, was appointed co-pastor of this church.

In 1707, St Nicholas Church was again completely rebuilt. Dr Patrick Delany (1685–1768) was among the chaplains appointed. He wrote on religious and biblical subjects and also wrote a defence of Dean Swift (1754). Swift described Dr Delaney to Alexander Pope as 'a man of the easyest and best conversation I ever met with in this Island, a very good list'ner, a right reasoner, neither too silent, nor talkative, and never positive'. Known as a brilliant preacher, Dr Delany resigned his office here in 1746. He married Mary Pendarves and through her influence he was appointed Dean of Down.

In 1835, St Nicholas's Church was unroofed and it was later demolished due to its unsafe condition. However, Sunday service was continued in an adjoining schoolhouse until 1867 when the parish of St Nicholas Within was united with that of St Audoen's.

The cemetery was formerly large enough to cater for the requirements of the parish of St Nicholas Within the walls, which owing to so many other churches in the vicinity, was the smallest in Dublin. In area, the parish comprised only five acres and eleven perches. The Corporation of Dublin purchased the major part of the cemetery to erect the Tholsel, the offices of which were rebuilt in 1683 and later demolished in 1791.

What remained of the graveyard after this purchase of land was merely a passage to the vaults under the church. The vaults contained several persons of importance, but there are no monuments to mark the spot where they were laid. One monument which remained, consisted of a small mural slab in memory of Edward Trotters, Esq, who died in 1769.

[94] TO THE RIGHT ARE THE REMAINS OF THE WALLS OF THE CHURCH OF ST NICHOLAS WITHIN, AT THE CORNER OF CHRIST CHURCH PLACE AND NICHOLAS STREET. CHRISTCHURCH CATHEDRAL IS IN THE BACKGROUND.

The Revd R.S. Maffett, on a visit to what remained of the graveyard in 1903, stated that it was the strip of ground behind the verger's house that constituted the graveyard. The only inscriptions that he came across at that time included one which projected from the inside of the north wall of what was originally the church. It read:

Here Lieth the Body | of Edward Torton Esq | Who Departed this | Life Augt ye 21 1762 | Aged 69

A stone in the graveyard displayed the following inscription:

Here lieth the Body of Mr Thomas | King who Departed this life on | the 15th July 1771. aged 39 Years. | He was a Good Christian | And a Sincere Friend.

The Revd Samuel Mather, the former co-pastor of St Nicholas's parish who died on 29 October 1671 and was interred in St Nicholas's Church.

The parish burial records include a number of people from the immediate area, such as John Murphy, aged seventy-four from Nicholas Street, who was interred on 13 August 1834; Marianne Kirwan from Skinners' Row aged sixteen, interred 22 June 1829 and Alice Kirwan, aged forty-five from Christchurch Place, interred 8 March 1834.

Three members of a family named Reynell from Rutland Square were all buried here. Colonel Reynell, who died aged seventy-six was buried 10 May 1829. His sister, Alice aged seventy-four, was interred on 26 March 1849 and a Miss Catherine Reynell aged ninety-six was interred on 10 July 1850.

At least the walls of this very interesting and historic parish church have been preserved.

St Patrick's Cathedral and Churchyard

Situation: Patrick Street, Dublin 8

Period in use: from the 1400s

Situated near city centre

A church stood on this site since 450 AD. According to tradition and ancient writings, St Patrick baptised converts to the Christian faith in a well close by on one of his visits to Dublin. This well was discovered during excavations on the river Poddle culvert in 1901. A stone slab decorated with the design of a Greek cross in high relief, surmounted with a double ring and a round boss in the centre covered it. This stone is now on view in the northwest end of the cathedral. A small stone in St Patrick's Park, which adjoins the cathedral, marks the site of the well. On it is inscribed:

Near here is the reputed site of the well where St Patrick baptised many of the local inhabitants in the fifth century AD.

St Patrick's Cathedral, founded in 1191 and built between 1220 and 1254, is Ireland's largest cathedral church measuring over 300 feet long and fifty-six feet high at the nave. Sir Thomas Drew restored it in 1864. The choir is the best preserved section of the medieval fabric.

The cathedral embodies within its walls the heritage of the Irish people from the earliest times. It contains many interesting memorials, monuments and family vaults. Some of the memorials dating from medieval times have vanished due to natural causes such as floods, storms, fires and the troubled periods of the sixteenth and seventeenth centuries. A few have been moved from their original positions. The memorials, thirty-four of which are inscribed in Latin, commemorate eminent men of the church, old families, Huguenots, writers, artists, composers, musicians, regiments, and military who fell at various battles. Many distinguished names are associated with the work of the memorials, which are fashioned in marble, stone, brass and glass.

St Patrick's Cathedral is the focal point of Jonathan Swift's Dublin. He was the most famous incumbent of the Cathedral and was Dean here from 1713 to 1745.

In the west end of the nave are the graves of Swift and Stella, Swift's bust and epitaph, and the memorial to Stella.

301

[95] VIEW OF ST PATRICK'S CATHEDRAL.

Stella died on 27 January 1728 in the care of Lady Eustace at Arbour Hill, close to the main entrance of the Phoenix Park, or the Deer Park as it was then known. Swift did not go to her funeral 'which my sickness will not suffer me to attend'. He moved to another room in the Deanery so that he would not see the light of St Patrick's Cathedral as they buried her. Later he wrote about Stella 'This was a person of my own rearing and instructing from childhood; who excelled in every good quality that can possibly accomplish a human creature'.

The inscription on Stella's white marble memorial reads:

Underneath lie interred the mortal remains of Mrs Hester Johnson | better known to the world by the name of Stella under which she | is celebrated in the writings of Dr Jonathan Swift Dean of this | Cathedral.

She was a person of extraordinary endowments and | accomplishments in body, mind and behaviour, justly admired | and respected by all who knew her on account of her many | virtues as well as her great natural and acquired | perfections.

She dyed January the 27th 1728 in the 46th year of her age and | by her will bequeathed one thousand pounds towards the support | of a chaplain to the hospital founded in this city by Doctor | Steevens.

Swift died aged seventy-seven in the autumn of 1745, having survived Stella by seventeen years. Buried beside Stella, his memorial is inscribed with a Latin epitaph which he composed himself, and which translates as: 'He has gone where savage indignation can lacerate his heart no more.'

Swift's Corner is in the North Transept of the cathedral. It contains his death mask, his wooden pulpit, the communion table from Laracor in County Meath, a collection of his works and a scroll which he received as Freeman of the City of Dublin in 1730. Sir Walter Scott visited the Cathedral in 1825 to see Swift's tomb (he had edited *The Works of Swift: with a Life*).

In the South Transept is Swift's memorial to his faithful servant, Alexander McGee which reads:

Here lies the body of Alex McGee, servant to Dr Swift, Dean of St Patrick's. His grateful Master caused this monument to be erected in memory of his discretion, fidelity and diligence in that humble station.

Swift was persuaded with difficulty to omit the words 'and Friend', which he had written after 'Master'.

Gabriel James Maturin succeeded Swift as the Dean of St Patrick's Cathedral in 1745. Gabriel died a year later and was buried in the cathedral. His grandson, Charles Maturin was later curate at St Peter's Parish, a stone's throw away.

In the North Aisle is the marble memorial to Samuel Lover (1797–1868), who died at St Helier in Jersey, and whose body was later interred at Kensal Green, London. The inscription on his memorial reads:

In memory of Samuel Lover, Poet, Painter, Novelist, and Composer, who in the exercise of a genius as distinguished in its versatility as in its power, by the pen and pencil, illustrated so happily the characteristics of the Peasantry of his country that his name will ever be honourably identified with Ireland.

He died July 6, 1868, aged 72, in firm faith that having been comforted by the rod and staff of his Heavenly Father in approaching the dark valley of the shadow of death, he would be, through the tender mercies of his Saviour, gathered among the flock of the Good Shepherd.

Also of interest in the same area is a memorial to the Revd Charles Wolfe (1791–1823), author of the poem, 'The Burial of Sir John Moore'.

The last of the Irish bards, Turlogh Carolan (1670–1738), is commemorated in white marble playing his harp. Lady Morgan, the celebrated nineteenth century novelist, paid for this. Carolan occasionally visited Swift in the deanery.

303

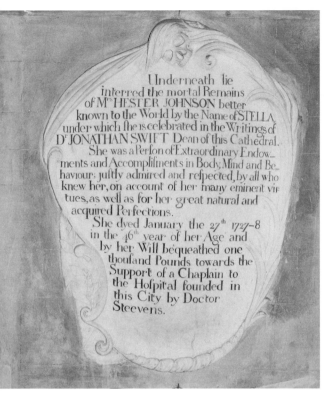

[96] MONUMENT TO STELLA IN ST PATRICK'S CATHEDRAL.

In the South Aisle is a memorial to Douglas Hyde (1860–1949), the first President of Ireland. His inauguration as President was held in the Cathedral in 1938, and his funeral service was held here in 1949 before he was borne back home to the graveyard at Portahard near Frenchpark in County Roscommon. Beside this is a memorial to Sir Samuel Ferguson (1810–86), poet and antiquary, who was President of the Royal Irish Academy and Deputy Keeper of the Public Records in Ireland. Ferguson died in Howth on 9 August 1886, and after a public service in St Patrick's Cathedral, was buried at Donegore in County Antrim.

The North Choir Aisle contains the grave of the Duke of Schomberg (1615–1690), the Huguenot leader killed while in command of the Huguenot cavalry regiment at the Battle of the Boyne in 1690. A marble slab, erected to his memory some forty years later by Dean Swift, can be seen on the wall of the North Choir Aisle with a Latin inscription which bears witness to a row behind the scenes.

Beneath this stone lies the body of Frederick, Duke of Schomberg, who was killed at the Boyne AD 1690. The Dean and Chapter earnestly and repeatedly requested the Duke's heirs to undertake the erection of a monument in memory of their father. Long and often they pressed the request by letter and through friends. It was of no avail. At long last they set up this stone that at least you may know, stranger, where the ashes of Schomberg lie buried. The renown of his valour had greater power among strangers than had the ties of blood among his kith and kin. AD 173.

In the South Transept, there is a large marble memorial to Narcissus Marsh (1638–1713), which was originally in the adjoining cemetery where he is buried. In 1728 Swift had it moved into the cathedral.

Those who fell in both World Wars are commemorated with a Brass plaque:

There is also a Roll of Honour containing the names of the 50,000 Irishmen who lost their lives in the Great War 1914–18.

The quaint old cemetery extends along part of the west side and around the eastern end of the Cathedral. It contains a number of interesting memorials, many of which relate to clergymen and musicians formerly connected with the Cathedral.

Adjoining the land of St Patrick's Cathedral is Marsh's Library in the garden of St Sepulchre's, which was built by Archbishop Marsh between 1701–1704. It is the oldest public library in Ireland. Archbishop Marsh's grave is marked with an inscribed tablet in the boundary wall with the library.

Archbishop Armstrong is commemorated near the east end of the churchyard. His memorial reads:

In Memoriam | John Ward Armstrong | 1915–1987 | Archbishop of Armagh and Primate of all Ireland | 1980–1986 | Dean of StPatrick's | 1958–1968 | I am the resurrection and the Life.

Some of the musicians interred in the churchyard include:

George Henry Phillips Hewson | 19th Nov.1881–21st Nov 1972 | Doctor of Music Organist and Master | of the choiristers of St Patrick's Cathedral | 1920 – 1960

and

In loving memory | of | William Sydney Greig, Mus.B | 19th November 1910 – 6th March 1983 | Organist and Master of the choiristers | 1960–1977.

In loving memory of | Ewart Molesworth Grace | 1905–1989 | Lay Vicar Choral 1928–1968 | And his dear wife | Mary Stanley Grace (nee Brightmore) | 1906–1989

On the west side there is a statue of Sir Benjamin Lee Guinness who restored the Cathedral in 1865.

Nearby are two of Ireland's most distinguished playwrights, Lennox Robinson (1886–1958) and Denis Johnston (1901–84).

Johnston's grave is easy to find as a little unicorn marks the back of the upright gravestone. This is in recognition of his play, *A Bride for the Unicorn*, staged at the Gate Theatre in 1933. Inscribed on his tombstone are the following lines from *The Old Lady Says No!*:

Strumpet city in the sunset
Wilful city of savage dreamers,
So old, so sick with memories
Old Mother;
Some they say are damned,
But you, I know, will walk the streets of Paradise
head high, and unashamed.

There are several horizontal stone memorial slabs which are difficult to decipher due to age and weathering.

Captain J. Boyd, who is commemorated within St Patrick's Cathedral by a statue executed by Sir Thomas Farrell, is buried in the graveyard. A large flat granite plinth marks his grave:

Beneath | Are the remains of | Captain John McNeill Boyd | Commanding H.M.S. AJAX | .....Of Five of his gallant sailors | attempt to rescue from destruction.... crews of 2 vessels wrecked | on the rocks of Kingstown | February 1861 | This brave act of humanity | In which he met his Honourable death | Was in character | With his Christian Virtues | For which he was remarkable in life | He feared in God | And knew no other fear.

The high tribute of a public funeral | At which the representative of Royalty attended | And the erection of a statue in the | Cathedral of St Patrick | Declared the appreciation in which this | Act of self (?) Devotion was held by his countrymen | And their desire that his memory | Should be kept in undying remembrance | Aged 49 years. (See also under Carrickbrennan)

At the east end is a small horizontal stone bearing the inscription:

Here lie | The remains of | Two men and a Little child | buried side by side | Many centuries ago | on the site of | The Palace of St Sepulchre | Thence they were removed | And were interred | In this hallowed ground | 30th October 1928.

Across the street is St Patrick's Cathedral Choir School, which was founded in 1432 and is still in existence today.

St Patrick's Cathedral is under the care of the Select Vestry of Saint Patrick's Cathedral Group.

St Paul's Church and Churchyard

Situation: North King Street, Dublin 7

Period in use: 1697–circa 1860

Situated near city centre

St Paul's, along with St Mary's, was created a parish from part of St Michan's in the year 1697. The church, which was a galleried structure, became ruinous and service was celebrated for the last time in it on Easter Sunday, 1821. St Paul's was rebuilt in gothic style on the same site and completed in 1824. The architect was William Farrell from the adjacent Queen Street and the builder was Abel Bass. A spire enhanced it, but this was removed in 1958 due to deterioration of the stonework.

The church was closed as a place of worship in November 1987 and was converted into a community-based enterprise centre in 1990. Unfortunately, none of the former memorials within the building remain.

The first vaults in the church were allocated around 1702 to the families of Corker, Westenra and Tillson.

A memorial within the church commemorated

THOMAS TILSON ESQ. Who cheerfully resigned this mortal life on 23rd November 1744.

There was a poor list in the parish from the very earliest times and the parish put much effort into trying to help them. In 1740 it is recorded that forty-four large coffins at 4s 4d each and thirty-three small coffins at 1s 7d each were provided for burial of the poor.

St Paul's Church has connections with George Berkeley, the philosopher and master of English prose, as it was here on 19 May 1734 that he was consecrated Bishop of Cloyne. He subsequently gave his name to the Berkeley Library in Trinity College and the Berkeley College in Yale University.

In 1755 the Vestry passed an unusual Resolution. It read:

Whereas there has prevailed of late a practice of bringing corpses to be interred at very unreasonable hours in the morning and nights to the great prejudice of the healths of those who are obliged to attend on such occasions, it is agreed this day and consented to, to prevent that evil custom as far as in them lies, that for the future the Minister,

Clerk and Sexton shall have Double Fees for every corpse that comes to be interred before 6 o'clock in the morning and before 8 o'clock in the winter, and after nine at night.

It was certainly an unusual practice to carry out burials at such odd hours and the reason could possibly have been to avoid grave robbers.

Inside the church, there are a number of interesting wall plaques. The military memorials included one to Lieut Col Browne who was killed by the insurgents under Robert Emmet. It read:

Sacred to the memory of | Lieut. Col. T.D.E. Browne | of His Majesty's Fuzileers | who was barbarously murdered by an armed banditti | in this City | on the 23rd of July 1803 | As a small tribute of respect | to his Memory His Brother Officers | Have erected this stone.

The Trevor family vault in St Paul's Church was considered to be one of the many burial places of Robert Emmet after his execution in 1803.

Other military plaques included:

Near this place lie Interred | the remains of Captn John Minchin | Lieut. Colonel Joseph Ferguson | and | Captn Archibald Rutherford | of the XXVII or Enniskillen Regiment | they departed this life | within a few days of each other | In the year MDCCLXXXVIII | Beloved and lamented by their | Brother Officers and Fellow soldiers | who have | as a Testimony of unfeigned affection | and a small tribute to their numerous virtues erected this stone.

LIEUT. JOHN COCKBURN, Royal Horse Artillery, decd. November 7th, 1837, aged 36.

MAJOR WALTER WHITE, for 26 years Town Major of Dublin, died 7th October, 1849, aged 58.

LIEUT. COL. AUGUSTUS CUYLER, Chief Commissioner of the Metropolitan Police of the City of Dublin, decd., 14th June, 1837, aged 40 years, formerly in the Coldstream Regiment of Foot —

Farewell to him whom youthful valour drew
to seek a soldier's fame at Waterloo.

The churchyard is directly behind the church and is now a car park, except for a small portion which is railed off. There is no entry to this derelict area where a few damaged gravestones are scattered against part of a boundary wall.

The churchyard was described as tolerably spacious and not as crowded as other burial grounds in Dublin. In 1822 an estimate was accepted to build a wall around the churchyard for £107.10.8.

It was almost completely occupied by tombstones dedicated to military men and their families, some of whom were commemorated inside the church by wall plaques. Many of the military interred here were from the vicinity and were based at the nearby Royal Barracks, now Collins' Barracks, which is occupied by the National Museum of Ireland.

There was a gravestone in the churchyard which consisted of a flat stone with an extraordinary mathematically incorrect inscription as regards the age of those interred. It read:

LIEUT WILLM GORDON, AGED 11 YEARS, | DEPARTED THIS LIFE SUDDENLY, BEING | ONLY FOUR HOURS ILL, AUGUST 3RD, 1796 | THE ONLY SON OF LIEUT WM GORDON, | AS ALSO HIS MOTHER, WHO FROM GRIEF | FOLLOWED HIM ON THE 8TH DAY OF FEBRY, | 1797, AGED 16 YEARS.

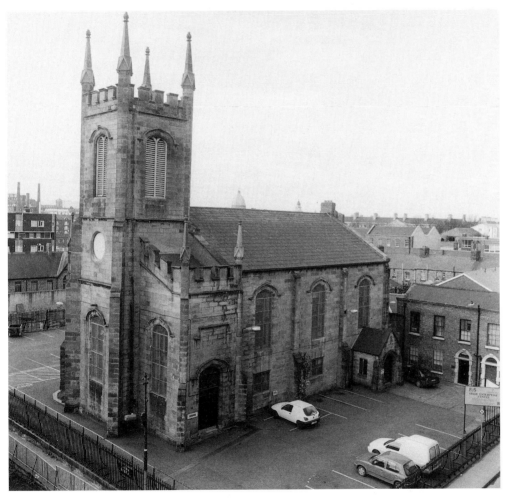

[97] ST PAUL'S CHURCH, NORTH KING STREET.

Near the centre of the churchyard was Col Ormsby's mausoleum. This was a structure of granite stone, one storey in height, entered by a doorway in the western side, and with the family coat of arms affixed to the opposite side. It was from a design of A. Baker and was a square building, with a plain entablature and pilasters of the Tuscan order at the angles. Here also the ancestors of the great senator, Henry Flood (1732–1791), are buried beneath a plain grey stone enclosed by an iron balustrade.

There were also some doctors commemorated at St Paul's. Two nephews, George and Thomas Smyth erected a memorial to their uncle, Dr Edward Smyth, who was born in May 1709 and died on 17 November 1778. Part of the inscription read:

Near this monument with his most dearly beloved wife, REBECCA, lies EDWARD SMYTH, M.D. the tenth son of the Rt Revd Thomas, formerly Bishop of Limerick. His uncommon abilities had received great improvement from an excellent education. His cheerful temper adorned with every branch of elegant learning and a correct taste for the Fine Art made him in Social Life a most agreeable Friend. In his profession his faithful attention, integrity and skill advanced him early to the highest class where he shone with distinguished merit above 30 years. His liberality in conferring favours was only equalled by his graceful and happy manner in bestowing them and his charity was never weary of doing good.

Dr Thomas Torney who died in 1897 and Dr Rudolph Arthur Wolson Byrne who died in 1905 are also commemorated.

The only memorial, which is still intact, is situated on the southern outside wall of the church. It reads:

This monument was erected by the non commissioned | Officers and Privates of his Majesty's 21st Royal North | British Fuzileers in Memory of James Chapman | James Wogdon and Daniel Patton Soldiers in the | Above Regiment the former was most barbarously | and in humanly murdered by a Rebel Banditti on | the Evening of the 23rd July 1803 the two latter | Died of the Wounds they Received on the same night | Erected in Jan 1804 | And patronised by Lieut. Colonel Donald Roberston | Commanding the Regiment.

Restored | by | the 2nd Battalion Royal Scots Fusiliers | AD 1910

St Peter's Church and Churchyard (demolished)

Situation: Aungier Street, Dublin 2 (formerly on site of what is now YMCA Building)

Period in use: c.1670–1883

Situated in city centre

O nce one of the largest parishes in Dublin, St Peter's dates from the time of the Anglo-Norman invasion. It was originally in Stephen Street, but was moved to Aungier Street where the church was built in 1680. Between 1863 and 1867 it was rebuilt in the Gothic manner. The architect was Edward Henry Carson, who lived for a time nearby in York Street. He was the father of Edward Carson.

Sadly, this church with so many interesting and historic associations with the country's heritage, was closed in 1975 and demolished in 1982. The site was redeveloped as the new office for the headquarters of the YMCA.

It was here that the Duke of Wellington and Robert Emmet were baptised. The Emmet family also had a vault here which was uncovered in 1905. Emmet's mother, who died a few days before her son was executed, was buried here. No evidence was found of Robert Emmet's burial here.

Charles Maturin (1782–1824), one of the most important writers of the Gothic novel who lived nearby in York Street, obtained a curacy in St Peter's in 1805 where he remained for the rest of his life. Maturin's masterpiece, the novel *Melmoth the Wanderer*, was published in 1820 and he was buried in the churchyard on 2 November 1824. Of his literary talent Maturin said,

If I possess any talent, it is that of darkening the gloomy, and of deepening the sad; of painting life in extremes, and representing those struggles of passion when the soul trembles on the verge of the unlawful and the unhallowed.

The church had many interesting memorials of military significance such as the tablet to Lieutenant George Westby, who fell in Spain at Fuentes d'Honor on 5 May 1811 aged twenty and his brother Edward, who fell at Waterloo on 18 June 1815 at the same age. The memorial was erected by their father, William Westby of Merrion Square, as a tribute of respect to the memory of his two beloved sons.

There was also a memorial to Lieutenant-General Archibold Hamilton who was interred in St Peter's. He fought at the siege of Derry in 1688. He also served abroad with distinction during all the wars of King William and Queen Anne. He died on the 1st July 1749 aged eighty-two.

Other memorials included one to John Scott, Lord Clonmell (1739–1798). Known as 'Copper-faced Jack' on account of his bronzed appearance, he studied at Trinity College, was called to the Irish Bar in 1765 and built up a good practice. In 1769 he was appointed MP for Mullingar. He turned from the patriotic side when promised office, saying 'My Lord, you have spoiled a good patriot'. He died on 23 May 1798. His family printed his Diary privately after his death. It confirmed that he was 'unscrupulous, passionate and greedy'. His remains were deposited in the chancel of the church.

The Reverend Philip Skelton (1706–1787), the philanthropist and writer, was commemorated with a mural tablet in the south transept. He was born in February 1706 in the parish of Derriaghy, near Lisburn, where his father had a farm. His grandfather, who was an engineer, had been sent over by Charles I to inspect Irish fortifications.

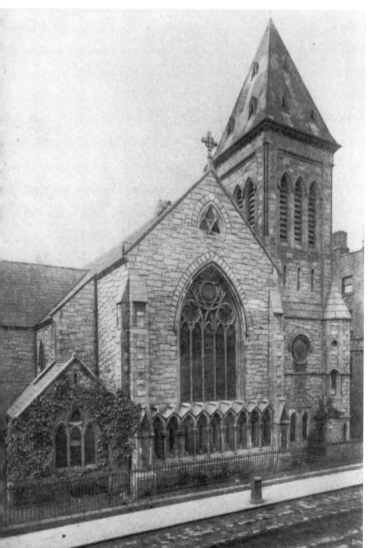

Educated at Trinity College, Skelton held various curacies around the country. Known to be a hypochondriac, he sometimes gathered his parishioners to his deathbed, until one of them remarked: 'Make a day, sir, and keep it, and don't be always disappointing us thus'. It is said that this statement cured him of his hypochondria! He published *Description of Lough Derg* (1759) and a number of theological works. He retired to Dublin in 1780 and died on 4 May 1787.

It is recorded that the Revd Skelton was privately buried at 6.00 a.m. near the west door of the churchyard. His gravestone had one the longest inscriptions in the churchyard and was made up of over forty lines, some of which follow:

With a heart which felt for the distresses of the Indigent, | He had a hand still open to relieve them | Denying himself even moderate gratifications | That he might more liberally provide for the | Necessities of others. | Without ambition he acquired celebrity | And without ostentation he long continued to enjoy it | A friend to the poor.

[98] St Peter's Church. (Courtesy of Peter Costello)

The churchyard contained the remains of a number of bishops and dignitaries, such as the Earl of Roden and the Dunboyne family. The Dunboyne memorial read:

Underneath are interred the remains of ELLEN LADY | Dunboyne, wife of the Right Hon Lord Dunboyne, who | departed this life on the 15th March, 1817, aged 36 years. | She lived an ornament to her rank, and a pattern of every | virtue that distinguishes the affectionate wife, the fond mother, | and the steady and warm friend | Dauter of David O'Connell, Esq, of Cork, and 1st wife | of James Butler, 13th Lord Dunboyne.

James, the first Earl of Clanbrassil, is also interred here and the memorial was inscribed:

To the memory of the Hon George Jocelyn, 2nd son of | ROBERT, 1st EARL OF RODEN, by ANNE, only surviving | child and heiress of JAMES, 1st EARL OF CLANBRASSILL, | He died March 15th, 1796, aged 32 years. Also to the | memory of the Hon THOMASINA COLE JOCELYN, otherwise | BOWEN, his wife, who died Oct. 15th 1818, aged 56 years | dauter of HENRY COLE BOWEN, Esq, of Bowens Court, Co. Cork.

At the south side of the churchyard the remains of John Fitzgibbon, Earl of Clare (1749–1802) and Lord High Chancellor of Ireland were interred. He died on 28 January 1802 and his funeral was followed a by mob of jeering Dubliners.

The remains of a number of people with military connections were interred in St Peter's churchyard. It was the family burial ground of Mr Henry Grey, captain's clerk in the Foot Regiment of the Coldstream Guards, and Master of the Masonic Lodge of the Regiment. He died on the 25 May 1824 aged twenty-eight years. Six of his children, all of whom died young, were buried with him.

In the vault on the south side of the church, the remains of Colonel John Shelton were interred. He died on the 16 May 1845 aged fifty-four. A distinguished soldier, he served in the battles of Rolcia, Vimiera, the retreat to and battle of Corunna and the expedition to Walcheren in 1809, including the siege at Flushing. He afterwards returned to the Peninsula, and was present at the siege and capture of Badajos, the battle of Salamanca, the capture of Madrid, the retreat from Burgos, the battle of Vittoria, and the siege and capture of St Sebastian, where he was severely wounded and lost his right arm. Subsequently, he served the campaign of 1814 in Canada. In 1822 he embarked for the East Indies, where he served twenty-one years. He was engaged in the campaign in Ava, and the taking of Arracan. He served as second in command under General Elphinstone in the disastrous retreat from Cabal in the winter of 1841–42. William Shelton, his nephew, erected a tablet in St Peter's church. He was formerly of the above regiment and captain of the 9th Foot.

Other inscriptions included:

The remains of BENJAMIN DISRAELI, Esqr. are deposited | here. He departed this life on the 9th day of August, in | the year 1814, aged 48.

and

Here lieth the body of GENERAL CHAS.VALLENCY, who died | on the 8th day of August 1812 in the 88th year of his age.

The remains of those who had been interred in the graveyard were removed and re-interred, in the crypt of St Luke's church, The Coombe, in 1980 and 1981. Headstones are stored in the vaults of St Luke's and St Patrick's Cathedral.

The records from St Peter's parish, which date from 1669 and are comprehensively indexed, form one of the most complete and important register collections held in the custody of the Representative Church Body Library.

St Thomas's Church and Churchyard

Situation: Formerly in Marlborough Street, Dublin 1

Period in use: c.1700–1882

Situated in city centre

The churchyard and vaults of St Thomas no longer exist but it deserves mention as it contained the remains of many distinguished families such as the Gardiners, Viscounts Mountjoy and Earl of Blessington.

The parish of St Thomas was created in 1749 when it was separated from that of St Mary's. This was the result of the increase in population and expansion of St Mary's parish when Luke Gardiner (1745–98), 1st Viscount Mountjoy, the banker and entrepreneur, bought some of the property originally owned by St Mary's Abbey on the north side of the river Liffey and developed it. St Mary's Church became too small for the increase in numbers and the work too much for one incumbent.

After acquiring Henry Street, Moore Street and North Earl Street, Gardiner moved a little further north, and in the 1720s, built Henrietta Street, whose magnificent town houses were considered to be the finest in the city and known as 'Primate's Hill'. In 1770, North Great George's Street was constructed and was followed by the residential houses on Mountjoy Square (1780–1798). Streets such as Sackville Street were included among Dublin's most fashionable streets and were inhabited by many rich and titled people. The new Parish of St Thomas encompassed much of these areas.

In 1757, the Rt Hon Charles Gardiner donated a site in Marlborough Street for the new parish church. This was designed by John Smyth after Palladio's Redentore in Venice and built in 1758–62. Charles Cobbe, the Archbishop of Dublin, consecrated it on St Thomas's day, 21 December 1762. It then faced on to open fields.

Being in what was then a fashionable area, many of the parishioners were of the nobility. Included was Lord Charlemont whose house in Rutland Square (now Parnell Square) is now the Municipal Gallery of Modern Art. Sir Marcus Beresford, later the Earl of Tyrone, lived in Tyrone House in Marlborough Street. The wealthy inhabitants of Rutland Square were the patrons of leading artists, sculptors and craftsmen, many of whom came from abroad, such as Charles Thorp the stuccodore and Simon Vierpyl, the English sculptor whom Lord Charlemont had brought from Rome.

Documented in the church records for the period 1750–1791 are the burials of some of the craftsmen and the prominent citizens in the parish. From the records, it would seem that the craftsmen were in the area working on the plaster in the houses of what was then one of the most fashionable areas of Dublin at the end of the eighteenth century. For example:

On 12 January 1767 William Hart, stucco man aged 25 years. Abbey Street.

There were several entries with the name Vierpyl. These included John Vierpyl, a child buried on 17 April 1773, Frances Vierpyl, a child buried on 9 March 1775, Frances Vierpyl, aged forty-six years, buried on the 4 April 1779 and John Vierpyl, aged thirty-five years, buried on the 16 January 1780.

Others from the neighbourhood who were buried in the graveyard included the Right Honble Earl of Tyrone, who was buried on the 5 April 1763 and William Frances Lord Caulfield, the infant son of the Earl and Lady Charlemont, who was buried on 9 May 1770.

[99] ST THOMAS'S CHURCH ON MARLBOROUGH STREET WHICH WAS DAMAGED IN 1922 AND LATER DEMOLISHED. (PHOTO: DAVISON ASSOCIATES)

The Right Honble Charles Gardiner, Esq, was interred aged forty-nine years on 17 Nov 1769. Other members of the Gardiner family interred here included Florinda Gardiner aged twelve, who was buried on 12 March 1786 and Hon Elizabeth Gardiner, aged eight, who was buried on the 1 Feb 1791.

The body of the last Earl of Blessington was removed to St George's in Hardwicke Place when the old church of St Thomas was destroyed. When St George's was sold for other purposes it was then transferred to St Michan's.

John Henry Foley (1818–1874), the sculptor, was born in Montgomery Street and baptised in St Thomas's church on 8 June 1818.

During the Civil War in 1922 St Thomas's Church was extensively damaged, along with a large part of O'Connell Street. The church was demolished and Gloucester Street was extended into O'Connell Street, thereby creating a new street which became Cathal Brugha Street.

The remains of those interred in St Thomas's graveyard were transferred from Marlborough Street in 1925–6 to a plot in Mount Jerome Cemetery in Harold's Cross.

The present St Thomas's Church, designed by Frederick Hicks was built at Findlater's Place (formerly Gregg's Lane) in 1931–32. Some of the monuments from the previous church are just inside the entrance.

St Werburgh's Church and Churchyard

Situation: Werburgh Street, Dublin 8

Period in use: c.1650–1920

Situated near city centre

St Werburgh Street derived its name from a church, which was built towards the end of the twelfth century shortly after the Anglo-Norman settlement. It was dedicated to St Werburgh, the patron of Chester. In earlier times, there was there was a church dedicated to St Martin of Tours which was situated a little south of the present St Werburgh's church.

In 1662, St Werburgh's was enlarged and later, between 1715–1719, it was rebuilt to the design of Thomas Burgh. What remains of the façade dates from this period. A more elaborate form than the present one existed and may be seen on *Brooking's Map of Dublin* [1728]. In November 1754, the roof, dome and part of the interior were destroyed by fire. George II granted £2,000 towards the restoration and it was rebuilt and reopened in 1759. In 1768, a tower and spire were added, but later removed in 1810 when declared unsafe. Another reason given for its removal was that after the Emmet rising of 1803, it would have provided a good vantage point for a revolutionary sniper over the Castle yard. The eminent architect Francis Johnston offered to secure the tower and spire but his offer was rejected.

In the church porch, some of the monuments from the now demolished churches of St John the Evangelist in Fishamble Street and St Bride's in Bride Street are displayed. The beautifully carved pulpit by Richard Stewart came from St John's in 1877 when the congregation united with St Werburgh's. It was originally from the Chapel Royal, Dublin Castle. St Werburgh's was the parish church of the viceroys until the Chapel Royal was built inside Dublin Castle (1814).

There were numerous interesting ministers and curates attached to St Werburgh's. Included amongst them was Nicholas Walsh who was minister from 1571–1577 and was later Bishop of Ossory. He was responsible for introducing Irish typefaces into Ireland with a printing press which Queen Elizabeth had provided.

James Ussher (1581–1656), who was born nearby in Nicholas Street, entered Trinity College aged thirteen, where he was one of the first undergraduates. In 1607 he was appointed to St Michan's and was later Primate of Ireland. He had a valuable library of over 10,000 volumes, which included many valuable Oriental and early Irish manuscripts. A scholar of European renown, he wrote extensively on theology, ecclesiastical history and early Irish history. His *Works*, comprising seventeen volumes, were published in Dublin (1847–1864).

William Chappel was John Milton's tutor at Cambridge and he succeeded Ussher. Chappel later became provost of Trinity College, Dublin, and Bishop of Cork and Ross. The celebrated work, *Whole Duty of Man*, was attributed to him.

Edward Wetenhall, who was curate at St Werburgh's in 1672, was tutor at Trinity College to Thomas Southerne, the dramatist. A distinguished writer, Wetenhall was the author of popular Greek and Latin grammars. Dr Faithful Tate, father of Nahum Tate (1652–1715), the poet laureate, was associated with St Werburgh's during the reign of Charles II.

William King, who was later Archbishop of Dublin, was minister at St Michan's from 1679 to 1688. The Revd Patrick Delany had connections with St Werburgh's from 1730–1734. A genial man, known as one of the best preachers of the day, he entertained Dublin wits and celebrities of the time, including Swift and Stella, at his home in Delville, Glasnevin. Dr Delany was husband of the famous diarist, letter-writer and gifted artist, Mary Delany.

St Werburgh's church was the burial place of many noted Anglo-Irish families in the seventeenth century. Sir James Ware, the antiquary and historian who was born nearby at Castle Street on 26 November 1594, was interred in the family vault in 1666. It bears neither a stone nor monumental inscription. According to his biographer, 'he had taken care in his lifetime to erect a monument for himself by his labours, more lasting than any mouldering materials.' Ware, who collected and studied charters and manuscripts, engaged Dubhaltach McFirbisigh, the Sligo-born antiquary and scribe, to prepare various transcripts and translations for him. Ware was auditor-general for Ireland in 1632 and became MP for Dublin University. He published treatises in Latin on Irish literary and ecclesiastical antiquities. Between 1739 and 1764, *The Whole Works of Sir James Ware* were published in three volumes. Ware's manuscripts are now in the British Museum and Bodleian libraries.

Jonathan Swift's uncle, Godwin Swift, who financed his education, is buried in St Werburgh's church. He died in 1695. A lawyer, he lived nearby at 7 Hoey's Court where Swift was born on 30 November 1667. Nothing now remains of Hoey's Court.

The twenty-seven vaults contain the remains of the courageous Lord Edward Fitzgerald, (1763–1798), the United Irishman and leader. He was arrested by Major Sirr on 19 May 1798 in a house in Thomas Street, and in the ensuing struggle, Fitzgerald killed one of his attackers and was badly wounded himself. He died of his wounds in Newgate gaol on 4 June 1798. Fitzgerald's removal from Newgate Gaol to St Werburgh's was delayed a number of times along the route with the result that his burial directly under the chancel did not take place until the very early hours of the morning.

319

The graveyard, which is behind the church, contains the remains of Major Henry Charles Sirr (1764–1841), the Town Major who arrested Fitzgerald. His remains were buried in the eastern corner under a stone with the following inscription

The family burying ground of Major Sirr and Humphrey Minch, 1790.

This stone, which is now broken was originally placed over Major Sirr's father, who was the Town Major of Dublin before him.

John Edwin, an actor from the Crow Street Theatre, is buried in the churchyard. His death was blamed on a mixture of grief and annoyance after he received a bad review. The following is inscribed on his grave.

[100] The exterior of St Werburgh's Church. The burial ground is to the rear.

320

'Tis strange the mind, that very fiery particle,

Should let itself be snuffed out by an article.

The Roman Catholic Bishop of Down and Connor, Edmund Dungan, who died on 2 November 1628 during his imprisonment in the Castle on a charge of conspiring with foreign powers against the Government, was buried in the churchyard at the unusual hour of 4.00 in the morning.

Built between the lower windows on the outside of the south wall of this church are the remains of a fifteenth century altar-tomb of one of the earls of Kildare. This Fitz-Gerald tomb consists of the covering slab bearing the effigies of a knight in armour and his wife. It has weathered due to long exposure. It bears the Geraldine Arms – a saltire. The Geraldine buried is either John 'the crooked 6th Earl of Kildare' and builder of Maynooth Castle (1176), or possibly Thomas, the 7th Earl, both of whom were buried in the monastery of All Saints, where Dublin University now stands – John in 1427 and Thomas, who was Lord Deputy, in 1478.

Similar to other burial grounds in the area, St Werburgh's contained the remains of a number of aldermen along with merchants and tradespeople, such as woollen drapers, goldsmiths and cutlers. Some extracts from their grave inscriptions include:

Here lieth the remains of John Dawson Esq | formerly an eminent Woollen-draper | in this Parish | he was a good father a sincere friend | and an honest man | he died the 21 Jan 1801 | aged 65 years.

This Stone & Burial place belon | geth to Mr Matthew West of the City | of Dublin, Gold-Smith.

Here lieth the Body of | John Read Esqr | late of College Green, Cutler, who departed this life 28 December 1822 | aged 58 years.

Some doctors included:

Underneath lie interr'd | W. Dobbs Esqr of Dublin Surgn died 28 Aug 1741 | aged 52

and

W. Ruxton Esqr of Dublin Surgn died 29th Dec 1783 | aged 62

There are two stones here, which were removed from St Bride's when it was demolished to make space for the Guinness Trust Buildings.

Interestingly, the accounts of Philip Brentwood and Patrick Burnell of St Werburgh's, which date from the period 1481–84, are the oldest churchwarden's accounts in Ireland.

St Werburgh's is under the care of the Select Vestry of Christ Church Cathedral Group.

STILLORGAN (ST BRIGID'S) CHURCHYARD

SITUATION: STILLORGAN, CO. DUBLIN

PERIOD IN USE: 1600S TO DATE

BUS NOS (FROM CITY CENTRE): 46, 46A AND 63

St Brigid's churchyard in Stillorgan is situated four miles south-east from the city centre to the left off the Bray Road. The original name of the district was *Athnakill*. The present church of St Brigid is on the site of an ancient church, nothing of which now remains except for the churchyard and a well. It is probably connected with the nearby church in Tully, also dedicated to St Brigid. The dedication would suggest a link with the monastery of St Brigid at Kildare. In both these churchyards, similar stone slabs with concentric circles were discovered, which would confirm the early date of the churches. A most interesting Celtic headstone with a carved angel's head is outside the present church at the north west corner.

The name Stillorgan is derived from Teach Lorcan, the House or Church of Lorcan or Laurence. This is possibly derived from Laurence O'Toole, the Archbishop of Dublin in 1161. He is reputed to have built a house near St Brigid's church. As he was descended from the Royal family of the O'Toole's in Kildare, he was closely affiliated with St Brigid as Brigid of Kildare would have been his patron saint.

This church was first mentioned in 1216 when Raymond de Carew, a Norman knight granted it to the Priory of the Holy Trinity, along with some land. The Hacketts, Sir John Cruise, Robert Derpatrick, John Leyhenan, Richard La Cumbe, and the Plunketts of Rathmore succeeded Carew. Following the dissolution of the monasteries and religious houses, it fell into disuse and disrepair. The church fields were then rented out to various people, including Jacques Wingfield, and the Wolverstons who lived nearby in Stillorgan Castle. This is now the Hospital of St John of God. These families were among the first known to be interred in the ruined church with their heraldic honours.

With the rebuilding of the church in the early eighteenth century by Archbishop King and John Allen, many of these former graves unfortunately disappeared. The church was enlarged in 1812 and again in 1833 and was described as a 'neat edifice'.

Lewis described the parish as comprising mainly of demesne lands, with 'numerous handsome seats and pleasing villas beautifully situated and commanding some fine sea views and mountain scenery, with

322

extensive prospects over Dublin bay'. One of the principal seats was Stillorgan House, which was once the home of the Allens.

Many of the well-known families from these large houses and demesnes in the Stillorgan area are interred in this well-kept churchyard which was once surrounded by a wood. There is a gravel path and on either side are a great variety of interesting memorials from table graves to railed-in tombs. Families from the neighbourhood who have graves here include the Darleys of Beaufield, the Georges of Thornhill, the Doynes and Drevars of Newtown Park, the Jamesons of Montrose, the Jollys of Merville who had a large dairy farm, the Scovells from Ferney, the Verschoyles of Stillorgan House, the Leslies, the Lewis-Crosbys and the Cornwalls from Rathmore House in Naas. The latter two families were closely related.

Two young sons from the Scovell family are buried in the family plot, which is enclosed by iron rails. One oval marble tablet commemorates Henry Scovell and his wife Ann Marie who died in 1861 and 1875 respectively and a second tablet has the following inscription:

Sacred to the remains and memory | of | Charley Augustine Scovell | Gentleman Cadet | of the Royal Military College | Sandhurst | who departed this life 16th November 1855 | aged 16 years | also of his brother | Fitzhenry Scovell | Ensign 55th Regiment | who died 2nd April 1854 | aged 21 years.

A number of gravestones date back to the 1700s. Edward Bullor, who lived in a thatched castle at Laughanstown, an area between Carrickmines and Loughlinstown, is commemorated with a gravestone outside the church, which is now badly weathered:

Here lieth the body of Edward Bullor, | who departed this life ye | 1st of April, 16(91). His | wife, Jane Bullor, alias Ferral, caused this | stone to be laid here for them and their posterity.

Other memorials dating from the 1700s include the following:

[101] THE CELTIC HEADSTONE OUTSIDE THE WEST CORNER OF ST BRIGID'S CHURCH, STILLORGAN.

This stone & burial place Belongth to Bryan Kavenagh | who departed this life ye 46 yr of his age in ye yr 1717. | Also his wife Ann & their son Edward & all their | posterity for ever. Here also lieth the body of their | Son-in-law Thomas Riddley late of Black Rock who | Erected this stone to the memory of the above who | departed this life the 16th of May 1786 aged 78 | years.

Here lyeth ye body of | Hugh Burn who depart | ed this life ye 7th day of | July 1722 | aged 55 years.

In Memory of Mrs Ann Bagley Wife of Mr Richd | Bagley of Dublin who Departed this Life the 30th | Day of July 1783 Aged 40 years.

This Stone was erected by Mr W. Weston. Here lieth | the body of Letitia Weston who died 25 May 1768 | Aged 16.

Of military interest is the burial place of Field Marshal Sir Hugh Gough (1779–1869) and other members of the Gough family from St Helen's in Booterstown. Three large coped stone memorials bearing inscriptions are within an iron-railed enclosure which surmounts the vault.

The entrance is under the gravel path at the east end. Sir Hugh Gough's inscription reads:

The Right Honourable Hugh 1st Viscount Gough K.P., GCB, G.C.S.I., KG, S., P.C., Born 3rd Nov 1779 died 2 March 1869.

Born at Woodstown in Co. Limerick, Gough started his military career aged fifteen when he was commissioned into the Limerick City militia. In 1795 he was promoted lieutenant in the 78th Highlanders and was present at the capture of the Cape of Good Hope. He transferred to the 87th Prince of Wales's Irish and was present at the capture of Trinidad. He became a major in 1805 and commanded his battalion when it embarked for Portugal in 1805. At the battle of Talavera on 28 July 1809, he was severely wounded, and had his horse shot under him. In 1811 he fought at the battle of Barossa, when he was involved with the famous charge on the French 8th light infantry. He was with Wellington in 1812 and fought in the battle of Vittoria. The following year he was wounded at the battle of Nivelle.

[102] THE VAULT OF FIELD MARSHALL SIR HUGH GOUGH (1779–1869) AND MEMBERS OF THE GOUGH FAMILY.

In 1815, Gough received the freedom of the city of Dublin. When not engaged in military duties he spent time on his estate in Tipperary. In 1843, he was appointed Commander-in-Chief of the forces in India. After his colourful military career, which involved much travel and many battles, he died on 2 March 1869 in his ninetieth year at his home at St Helen's in Booterstown (now the Radisson Hotel).

After a quiet church service, Gough was buried on the 9 March in St Brigid's churchyard. An equestrian statue in the Phoenix Park sculptured in bronze by John Foley commemorated him. It was cast from the metal guns taken during the Sikh campaign and was unveiled on 21 February 1880. The statue was damaged when blown up in the 1950s. It was removed and lay in storage at the Royal Hospital Kilmainham before being transferred for restoration to an estate in England.

St Brigid's churchyard is under the care of the Select Vestry of Stillorgan.

TANEY (ST NAHI'S) CHURCHYARD

SITUATION: BESIDE DUNDRUM LIBRARY

PERIOD IN USE: 1600S TO DATE EXCEPT FOR THOSE WITH BURIAL RIGHTS

BUS NOS (FROM CITY CENTRE): 44 OR 48A TO DUNDRUM OR 14A TO CHURCHTOWN ROAD UPPER

The area around the village of Dundrum and St Nahi's Church has changed enormously since its description as a favourite place of rest for invalids from Dublin, for whom the mildness of its climate and the purity of the air were particularly favourable. It had been noted too for its numerous herds of goats, which, ambling among the mountain pastures, afforded milk of very excellent quality. Once a haven of quietude, the little churchyard of St Nahi's is now an island completely encircled by busy roads.

A monk named Nahi, who lived in the early part of the seventh century, was attached to the monastery in Tallaght. Nomadic in his ways, he left Tallaght and made his way through the then dense forestation to a clearing on elevated ground, which overlooked a stream. Here Nahi remained for a number of years with his followers and founded his church. Taney derived its name from *Teach Naithí* or *Tigh Naithí*. Eventually Nahi departed for the north-west of the country and here he is commemorated by St Nathy's College at Ballaghadreen. St Nahi's feast day is 7 August.

There has been a church on this site for over a thousand years, but all traces of the monastery have vanished. In 1615 there is mention of Taney when Archbishop Thomas Jones, acting for James I, made a 'Royal Visitation'. He reported back to the King that the Reverend Robert Pont was the curate and that the Church and Chancel were in a good state of repair and that Prayer Books were available.

The present 'old church' was built in 1760 through the action of Dr Isaac Mann, Archdeacon (1757), and the curate Revd Jeremy Walshe (1758). It is marked on *Rocque's Map* as New Church. It has been rebuilt on three occasions. At various times, restoration work has also been carried out. No service was held in the church on the first Sunday in July 1909 because the roof was in such a dangerous state. The kindly Mr Fuller, one of the parishioners, drew up plans for a new roof and another munificent parishioner, Mr Law, paid for the all work which was completed by 1910.

The Revd Canon William Monk Gibbon, the rector of Taney parish gave of his time unstintingly and supervised all the work. He rolled up his sleeves and lent a hand with the manual work. He was also responsible for choosing some of the stained glass windows. It is interesting to note that Evie Hone's first commission, *The Annunciation*, is in St Nahi's, as Evie was a parishioner of Taney.

On the right-hand side of the church door there is a plaque which reads:

The entrance gate to this churchyard | Was erected by the parishioners of Taney Parish | To the memory of | William Monk Gibbon | Canon of Christ Church cathedral. | By whose inspiration and effort the restoration of | This church was accomplished. | 'He repaired the Altar of the Lord.'

There is a small railed-in enclosure directly opposite the church door containing six memorials. Included is the grave of the Revd Canon Gibbon, which is a square marble tablet backed by granite. It reads:

In Loving Memory | Of | William Monk Gibbon | For 34 years Rector of Taney | Who died the 26th March 1935. | Also of | His dearly loved wife | Isabella Agnes | Who died the 24th July 1945 | 'They that turn many to righteousness | Shall shine as stars for ever and ever.' | 'All from the good God comes, | All then is good.'

In the same plot is a memorial to his son, Monk Gibbon, the poet and novelist. This consists of an open book with two pages one of which is inscribed:

William Monk | Gibbon | Poet | 15th Dec 1896- | 29th October 1987.

On the facing pages is inscribed:

Mabel Winifred | Gibbon | (nee Dingwall) | 28th Dec 1904 | 30th March 1989.

The book is placed on a granite support on which is written

Sing in that scented night | invisibly | And, as you always do, | Sing cheerfully

As a child, Monk remembered witnessing his father, the Canon, who was a keen gardener as he interviewed a new curate from the top of an apple tree! The poet had spent much of his childhood in the parish of Taney. He chose to wear his most comfortable outfit, his pyjamas, for the occasion of his burial.

To the left of the church, just beyond Monk Gibbon's grave, is an enclosed area which was formerly used for a number of years by the Central Mental Hospital in Dundrum. It is now used for the burial of ashes and as a Garden of Remembrance.

In the early 1800s Christ Church Taney was built, as the little church of St Nahi's was unable to cope with the increasing numbers. St Nahi's continues as a place of worship.

St Nahi's Church contains some items of great historic and artistic interest. The font in which Arthur Wellesley, the Duke of Wellington, was baptised is now in this church. It was originally in St Peter's Church [now demolished] in Aungier Street.

327

There are four tapestries to the rear of the Communion Table, which are the work of Susan 'Lily' and Elizabeth 'Lollie' Yeats, the sisters of Jack B. and W. B. Yeats. The Yeats sisters had associations with the area from 1902 when they returned from London to help Evelyn Gleeson found the industry known as the Dún Emer Guild at a house named Runnymede [renamed Dún Emer] on the Sandyford Road. The purpose of the industry was 'to find work for Irish hands in the making of beautiful things'. Lily organised the embroidery workshop and Lollie founded the Dún Emer Press as part of the scheme. In 1908, the Yeats sisters moved their side of the business to their house, Gurteen Dhas, in Churchtown where they remained for forty years. Under the name Cuala they worked here for many years. Lily and Lollie now rest in the same grave in St Nahi's churchyard.

During Lollie's funeral ceremony, her coffin, which was slightly misplaced on the trestles, slipped to the ground with a thud. Her amused niece Anne Butler Yeats whispered to her Uncle Jack 'There's Lollie having the last word'. The grave is situated at the end of a steep grassy slope. Go left at the church and follow the gravel path down the slope, at the end of which is a stone with the name McDonnell. The Yeats grave is just opposite this. It reads:

Elizabeth Corbet Yeats | Gurteen Dhas, Churchtown | Daughter of | John Butler Yeats | Born 11th March 1868 | Died 16th January 1940 | And her sister | Susan Mary Yeats | Born 26th August 1866 | Died 5th January 1949

The churchyard at St Nahi's was extended on two occasions in 1872 and 1887. In Ball and Hamilton's *History of Taney Parish* (1895), it states that some idea of the number of interments in this graveyard may be obtained from the fact that between 1814 to 1835, there were 1,044 burials entered in the register.

Of the many memorials recorded by Ball and Hamilton, two date from the seventeenth century, but these are no longer to be found.

In his will, which was proved in 1676, James Nicholson of the parish of 'St Michaell in the Citty of Dublin', directed that his body should be 'enterred in the Church of Churchtowne'. He mentions Mary (als. Nicholson), wife of Edward Archbold, his cousin Richard Archbold of Kilmacud and 'Gerrard Archbold of Newtowne, in the Co. Kildare'.

[103] THE HEADSTONE OVER THE GRAVE OF THE YEATS SISTERS, LILY AND LOLLIE, IN ST NAHI'S CHURCHYARD.

Here under lyes the Body of James Nicholson, | whose fidelity as clerk hath been sufficiently shown | in His Majestie's Treasury Office, in the city of | Dublin, for 36 yeares or thereabouts. Aged sixty | foure, and was here interred 10 September, Anno | Domini 1676.

Quaestor honestus amans solvi tenui reparavi | Credita parta meos sponte labore manu | Funde preces Regi fueram per debita fidus | Fidus pontifici caetera funde preces. | Memento mori.

The will of Gerard Archbold of Eadstown, Co. Kildare, dated 25 March 1694–5 asks that 'My body I pray my friends to see buried in Churchtowne, als.Tanij'.

This burial place belongeth | to Gerrard Archbold of Eadston | Archbold, alias Ball his wife | who departed this life January ye | .... aged 67 years. | Requiescant in pace.

Richard Archbold died on 6 June 1678, and in his will, he directed that his body may have a 'Christian buryall in the Parrish of Churchtowne'.

Counsellor William Ball, known as Index Ball, because he had edited a book of legal indexes, resided in Churchtown for the last twelve years of his life. Descended from a County Fermanagh family, he was the son of the Revd Thomas Ball, a well-known schoolmaster in Dublin in the eighteenth century. William graduated from Trinity College Dublin in 1769, was called to the Bar in 1775 and in 1806 the degree of LL.D. honoris causa was conferred on him.

Sacred to the memory of William Ball, Esq, who | died July 18th, 1824, aged 73 years.

Some military memorials include:

Sacred to the memory of Lieut-Col.Wm. Cowell, | C.B., late of the 42nd Royal highlanders, whose | premature death was occasioned by severe campaigns | and wounds received in the Peninsula | during the war; he died 24th September, 1827, aged | 45 years.

Sacred to the memory of Capt. James Espinasse, | late 1st Royal regt., who died at Dundrum, Co. | Dublin, 1st March, 1874, aged 70 years, Erected | by his sorrowing widow. 'Precious in the sight | of the Lord is the death of his saints.'

Family burial-place of J.L.Verschoyle, eldest son | of the Revd Joseph and Catherine Verschoyle, | Captain, H.M. 66th Regiment, Duoro, Talavera, | Albuhera, Vittoria, Pyrenees, Nivelle, Nive, Orthes, | Peninsula. He departed this life the 28th Sept., | 1875. Erected by his wife and three sons. 'The | Lord gave, and the Lord hath taken away; blessed be the name of the Lord.'

Beneath this stone are deposited the mortal remains | of the late Lieut.-Colonel George Hart, formerly of | His Majesty's 26th Regiment; he served for upwards | of 28 years. He departed this life at his | house on Rathmines Road on Thursday, the 7th | day of April, 1811, in the 78th year of his age, and | is buried here at his own desire.

This stone was erected by Maria to the memory of | her husband William White, of the 61st Regiment, | who departed this life on the 30th April, 1828.

Some local doctors interred here include:

In memory of John L. White, Esq, Surgeon, who | departed this life on the 25th day of June, 1870 | aged 65 years. This monument was erected by a | few personal friends and inhabitants of Dundrum, | in remembrance of his many social qualities, his | care and kindness as a physician, and especially his attention to the poor of the village and surrounding district.

In Loving memory of Michael Charles Bernard, | M.B., T.C.D., & L.R.C.S.I., who for forty years labored | as a Physician in this parish. Died 24th April, | 1881, in his 71st year. 'I know that my Redeemer | liveth.'

And a poignant inscription to another with the Bernard name:

In Loving memory of Henry Hilton Bernard, | medical student, who died on the 11th December | 1887, of scarlatina, caught in the path of duty, in | his 20th year. 'Blessed are the pure of heart: for they shall see God.'

Dr Daniel Haliday is buried alongside his brother William, both of whom are of interest. Dr Daniel Haliday died in Paris and was buried at Père La Chaise. At the time of his demise, he was engaged in researching the memoirs of the Irish Brigades in the French and Spanish services. His surviving brother Charles arranged for his body to be removed from Père La Chaise and re interred at St Nahi's. His inscription reads:

Danielis Haliday, Edinburgensis Parisiensisque, | Medicinae Facultatum Socius: Academiae Regiae | Hiberniae Sodalis. Natus Dublinii, 19 October, | 1798, Ibiit Die nono Maii, 1836, Aetatis 38. | Requiescat in Pace.

William Halliday [1788–1812], who was one of the most promising Irish scholars of that time, died at the age of twenty-four. He studied to be a solicitor but his consuming interest was the Irish language, which three Munstermen who lived in Dublin taught him. He assumed the name William O'Hara and in 1801 he published in Dublin *Uraicecht na Gaedhilge*, a grammar of the Irish language. This appeared under the pseudonym of Edmond O'Connell. In 1807 he was one of the founders of the Gaelic Society of Dublin established for the investigation and revival of ancient Irish literature. He had started work on an Irish dictionary just before his death.

His epitaph reads:

Beneath this stone are deposited the remains of | William Haliday, Junior, cut off by a lingering | disease in the early bloom of life. He anticipated | the progress of years in the maturity of under | standing, in the acquisition of knowledge, and the successful cultivation of a mind gifted by providence | with endowments of the highest order.

At a period of life when the severe studies have | scarcely commenced, he had acquired an accurate | knowledge of most of the European languages, of Latin, Greek, Hebrew and Arabic. But of his | own, the Hiberno-Celtic, so little, Oh! shame to the | youth of this once lettered Island, an object of | attainment and study, he had fathomed all the | depths, explored the beauties, and unravelled the | intricacies. He possessed whatever was calculated | to exalt, to ennoble, to endear: great talents, social | virtues, sincere religion, a good son, and an | affectionate husband, a steadfast friend. Carried | off in the 24th year of his age, his worth will be long | remembered, and his death lamented.

Obiit 26th October, AD 1812. Requiescat in Pace.

The noted scientist, George Johnstone Stoney (1826–1911), is buried here. On entering the main gate, his memorial is enclosed by rails and is the third on the right-hand side. It reads:

Righteousness exalteth a Nation | G. Johnstone Stoney | M.A. Hon Sc.D. T.C.Dub. F.R.S. | Died July 1911, aged 85 years. | 'Felix Qui Potuit Rerum Cognoscere Causas.'

Stoney, who was born at Oakley Park, King's County, worked as assistant to Lord Rosse at Parsonstown observatory from 1848–52. He introduced the word 'electron' into scientific writings. From 1852–57 he was Professor of Natural Philosophy in Queen's College Galway, from 1857–82 he was secretary to Queen's University and he was also secretary of the Royal Dublin Society for twenty years. Stoney was the first recipient of the Boyle Medal in 1899, an award for outstanding contribution to science. He went to live in London in 1903 where he lived the last eight years of his life. A fine portrait of Stoney by Sir Thomas A. Jones (1883) adorns the Council Chamber of the Royal Dublin Society.

[104] THE GIBBON BURIAL PLOT INCORPORATING THE HEADSTONES OF THE REVEREND CANON WILLIAM MONK GIBBON, RECTOR OF TANEY PARISH FOR 34 YEARS, AND THAT OF HIS SON, THE POET WILLIAM MONK GIBBON, AND HIS WIFE, IN ST NAHI'S CHURCHYARD.

331

Isaac William Usher, who is commemorated by a monument in Dundrum village, is buried in St Nahi's, as is Canon William Hamilton who was Rector from 1867–1895.

St Nahi's did not escape the grave robbers or the 'sack 'em up' men as they were called. A bullet in a confrontation with these resurrectionists damaged one gravestone, that of Mary Kenney, who died on 16 November 1815, whose grave was described by Dalton as a 'very handsome sarcophagus'.

Garret English, who had connections with Rathfarnham at the end of the eighteenth century, is buried in St Nahi's. He was described as being an upright and active magistrate. When he was the victim of an assault in 1790, his attacker was whipped from one end of the town to the next.

In Walker's *Hibernian Magazine* dated February 1791 there is a report of an occurrence which must have proved of great interest and excitement to the residents in the Dundrum and Churchtown area:

A night or two ago, at a very late hour, two persons, seemingly gentlemen, drove themselves out in a post-chaise to Churchtown, where there is a burial-place, with a dead body coffined up in the carriage. They rapped up the grave-digger, and told him that they had, under the disguise of night, brought out a corpse to be interred, which in the day time they were apprehensive might be arrested for debt, and for the burial of which he should have a guinea. The grave-digger alleged he was unequal to the business himself; upon which these persons said they would give him half a guinea for an assistant; which was agreed to, and the corpse was accordingly left with the grave-digger. The latter immediately called up an assistant; but upon an agreement they determined postponing the business until daylight. When they arose in the morning, curiosity urged them to open the coffin, which on so doing -O! shocking to mention – they found the body of a man in his clothes, with his boots on, and his throat cut in a most frightful manner. In his pockets were found six guineas and a watch; for the property of which these two persons differed, or else the transaction would probably never have come to light. The body remains at the place to be owned, which as yet has not taken place, nor has anything occurred which can lead to a discovery!

St Nahi's is under the care of the Select Vestry of Taney.

Tully Church and Churchyard (National Monument)

Situation: Lehauntstown, Cabinteely, Co. Dublin

Period in use: Early Christian times until c. 1967

Bus Nos (from city centre): 46, 84 and 86 to Cabinteely

The simplest way to get to Tully churchyard is from Cabinteely village. From there take the Carrickmines Road for half a mile then turn left where the signpost indicates. Follow the narrow winding road, and just before reaching the churchyard, there is a high modern base on the left-hand side of the road on which there is an undecorated Celtic granite cross within a circle. Under it is an inscription to the memory of James F. Grehan who saved this cross in 1897.

In the field on the opposite side of the road, there is another cross, which is tall and narrow with an arm missing. On this cross there is a full-length figure in high relief on one side and a head on the other. Interestingly, G. V. Du Noyer (1817–1869) illustrated both crosses, which date from about the eighth or ninth century. He was a young topographical draughtsman who, through George Petrie's influence, worked for a few years on the Ordnance Survey where he developed a great love of archaeology and art for which he was later noted.

The ruined church at Tully, which was possibly the site of a monastery, dates from the twelfth or thirteenth century. Situated on a height sloping eastwards, it is dedicated to St Bridget. From an early date, the place was known as *Tullagh na Nespuc*, or the Hill of the Bishops. It is recounted in the *Book of Lismore* that seven Bishops set out from Tully to visit St Bridget in County Kildare.

The ruined church comprises an imposing archway leading to the chancel, where two round-headed east windows remain as well as windows on both the north and south sides. The chancel is unusual in that it is wider than the nave.

After the Norman conquest, Tully was assigned to the Priory of the Holy Trinity and was attached to Kill o'the Grange. During the fourteenth century, it was a prominent religious centre. However, following the dissolution of the monasteries, it was little used. Francis Grose (1731–1791), the antiquary. included an illustration of Tully church in his *Antiquities*.

333

Two very early Christian grave slabs were discovered in the churchyard and were placed in the chancel. They appear to be absent at present. One is described as being inscribed with a concentric circle and the other as a carved cross which is surrounded by a circle.

There are a number of memorials dating to the 1700s. Some of these have clear and deep inscriptions which seem to have weathered much better than later inscriptions. In the chancel of the church is an upright stone decorated with an hourglass on either side of the top.

IHS This Burial place belongeth to | the WALSH'S of Carrick-mines | of the County of Dublin | Here lyeth the Body of Willm | WALSH who Departed this life | the 20th of June 1755 Aged 50 | Here also lyeth the Body of | JANE WALSH his Daughter who | Departed this life the 1st Novbr | 1755 Aged 25 years.

The Hutchisson memorial has the most beautifully carved lettering and reads:

Here lyeth ye | body of Mrs Kathrn | Hutchisson wife | of Mr Josua. | Hutchisson of ye City of Dublin | Joyner who depated ye life ye 14 of Septembr & in ye 85th | year of her age | Anno Domini 1712.

Some others dating to the 1700s include:

Here lyeth the body of Shusana Potts Deceased the | 12th of September 1731 aged 49 years.

This stone is the property of Mary Ball (alias GREVILLE) | in memory of her beloved Husband JONATHAN BALL who | died 21 March 1795.

This stone | was erected by John Robinson | of Kevan Street in the memory of his Father | and Mother. Here lieth ye | Body of his mother Mrs Anny | Robinson who Departed this | Life 26th March 1760 Aged 47 | Here lieth the Body of his Father | Mr Ant Robinson who Departed | this Life ye 30th of Octr 1766 Aged 60 | & 2 of their Daughters Mrs Grey & Mrs Morgan.

In the south side of the churchyard near the hedge is an upright memorial to Mr Joseph Farrell from Killiney who died on 24 December 1837 in his 102nd year.

[105] TULLY CHURCH AND GRAVEYARD, LEHAUNSTOWN, CABINTEELY, COUNTY DUBLIN.

334

There is a railed-in enclosure, which contains a yew tree and two memorials to the Field family.

Other families here include Byrne, Staunton, Grehan, McCabe, Brady, Deehan, Greene, Ryan, Kearney, Reilly, Fleming, and Kirwan.

The views in all directions from this churchyard are splendid.

As the church and early Christian crosses are national monuments, they are under the care of the Office of Public Works.

[106] THE TALL, NARROW CROSS DATING FROM ABOUT THE EIGHTH OR NINTH CENTURY IN THE FIELD OPPOSITE TULLY CHURCH.

WHITECHURCH CHURCHYARD (OLD)

SITUATION: WHITECHURCH, DUBLIN 16

PERIOD IN USE: UNKNOWN. IT IS NOW CLOSED

BUS NOS (FROM CITY CENTRE): 15C

On the right-hand side of Whitechurch Road coming from Rathfarnham direction is the remains of an early church perched on a height. It has been called various names such as *Alba, The church of Balgeeth* (windy town) and *The church in the Marches*, the name applied to the hinterland or borderlands of the Pale. The barrier of the Pale ran across the northern side of Kilmashogue Hill where remains of it were to be seen in the eighteenth century. Dublin County Council did some work on partially restoring the framework of the church, which consists of a nave with a chancel. The walls are almost three feet thick.

The landscape in just part of the immediate vicinity has altered considerably with the new housing development of Grangebrook, which borders almost up to one side of the churchyard. The churchyard, which is completely walled-in, may be reached via a narrow lane, which is a cul de sac to the right off Whitechurch Road. The churchyard is not sign posted but the turning is near a bend.

Most of the gravestones in this churchyard, which number circa ninety-three, appear to be made of limestone. The oldest recorded legible stone, which is located near to the top left outer wall of the church, dates from 1710 and is dedicated to Jackson:

This | stone and bur(ial) | place belonge(th to) | William Jackson | Ticknock | Here lieth ye bo)dy of) | Joseph Jackson (son?) | of William Jack(son) | who departed ye ..... | Febry Anno 1710 | 11.

A former Pastor of the parish rests also near the left outer wall. His gravestone unfortunately has been vandalised with paint:

IHS | here lieth the body of the | Revd Robert Bethel, | formerly Pastor of this Parish, | but lately of St Audoens Dublin. | He departed this life the 21st day | of January in the year 1791, | and 60th year of his age. | Pray for him.

This churchyard contains many people from areas such as Arran Quay, Townsend Street, New Street, Black Pitts and Cuffe Street.

This stone & burial place | belongs to John Sally of | the City of Dublin Silk | Weaver & his posterity | 1762.

And a bit of advice and gentle reminder from Edward Costello from Summerhill which reads:

IHS | Stop | pray as you pass by | So as you are now so once was I | As I am now so you will be | Prepare yourself and pray for me | This stone and burial ground belongs to Edward | Costello of Summerhill in | the City of Dublin May 16th 1823 | Requiescant in Pace.

Not too often is the cause of death included on an inscription:

IHS | In memory of | Elizabeth the (be) loved daughter of | Richard & Catherine Murray, | Roundtown, | who died of consumption, which she bore | with patience and resignation to the will of God | 14th, March 1871, aged 16 years. May she rest in peace. | Also of Peter Murray, died 29th March 1861 | and Patrick Byrne, died 18th April 1857 | R.I.P.

A visiting priest from Australia had a memorial erected to his parents consisting of a tall cross:

I.N.R.I. | Thy Will be Done | Erected 1910 | by | Revd Joseph O'Brien P.P. | Warracknabeal, Victoria, Australia | (on visiting his native town, Rathfarnham) | to the memory of his beloved parents, | John and Elizabeth O'Brien, | and sister Margt. Footweingler, | and cousins, Peter & Harry Lennon | whose remains are interred in this grave | Requiescant in Pace | Vere Langudres nostros ipse tulit.

Slightly further up this laneway which is now enclosed by high stone walls is another smaller private burial ground or annexe. It is on the left-hand side and contains the remains of mainly related families such as the Hartys and the Porters, of which there are quite a few.

The burial ground is small and oblong. The majority of the memorials are flat stones on the ground. In the summer it is difficult to see them, as the grass is high and unkempt. There is one large palm tree.

There are six memorials with the name Davis, three of which are to children aged seventeen and under.

[107] THE GRAVESTONE IN OLD WHITECHURCH CHURCHYARD OF THE REVEREND ROBERT BETHEL, A FORMER PASTOR OF THE PARISH WHO DIED ON 21 JANUARY 1791.

A limestone block marks the grave of:

Mrs Mary Davis | wife of Charles Davis of Cloragh | died 16th August 1836, aged 32 years | Also their children James Moore Davis | died 8th Jan y 1839, aged 9 years. And Charles Davis, | died 6th August 1845, aged 11 years.

There are nine memorials with the name Porter, two of which include:

In | Loving memory | of | Sir George Hornidge Porter, Baronet | Surgeon-in-Ordinary to the Queen | in Ireland, | who died 16th June 1895, | in his 73rd year. | Also of George Bond his son | who died 12th June 1870, | aged 6 years and 10 months. | 'All live unto God.'

A small limestone tablet on the ground marks the resting-place of:

Captain | James Porter | of the 11th Regt. of Foot | died June 12, 1818 | aged 49 years.

There are fourteen memorials with the name Harty. A limestone slab on the ground commemorates,

Sir Robert Way Harty, Bart | died 10th Octobr 1832 | aged 52 years.

His wife is also commemorated with a flat limestone slab,

Elizabeth Lady Harty | wife of Sir Robert Way Harty Bart | born 10th Feby 1789 | died 9th June 1875 | in her 87th year.

Five of the fourteen memorials are to children and are marked by small limestone tablets on the ground.

One with a military connection is:

John Locn Harty. | Major in the 33rd | Regt of Foot. | Died June 28th 1814 | aged 36 years.

The churchyard is under the care of Dublin County Council.

WHITECHURCH CHURCHYARD (NEW)

SITUATION: WHITECHURCH ROAD, DUBLIN 16

PERIOD IN USE: C 1827

BUS NOS (FROM CITY CENTRE): 15C

Formerly part of Tallaght, the new parish of Whitechurch was created and the church built in 1825 at a cost of £2,000. The Reverend Lundy Foot who had been appointed Perpetual Curate, was offered the land on the Marlay Estate, which was bought from John David La Touche. Marlay derived its name from the Rt Revd George Marlay, Bishop of Dromore, whose daughter was married to the Rt Hon David La Touche, by whom the house was built.

John Semple designed the church and it has his trademark pointed features of deep-set lancet windows, pinnacles and a towering spire. It was built entirely of local granite and was consecrated on 3 June 1827.

The churchyard is on a grassy knoll which is sheltered by a grove of trees and is extremely picturesque and well kept. It is encircled by the Grange Golf Club to the rear. A look around the gravestones here provides a remarkable glimpse into the past of Whitechurch parish, the local teachers, people involved in military careers and the various families who lived in the lovely country houses from Marlay to Killakee.

There is a large enclosed area in the churchyard comprising of four memorials for members of the La Touche family. The earliest is to John La Touche from Marlay and it reads:

Sacred to the memory | of | John David La Touche Esqr | of Marlay | born 2nd January 1772 | died 20th August 1838. | 'O Thou that hearest the prayers, | unto Thee shall all flesh come.' | Psalm LXV-Ver 2.

Nearby is St Columba's College, which was founded in 1843 at Stackallan, Co. Meath and relocated in 1849 to its present location at Hollypark, at the base of Staghill, the former residence of Jeffrey Foot, a Dublin merchant. He was the father of Lundy Foot mentioned above.

Some pupils of the College commemorated a former matron who is buried in the churchyard:

To | the memory of | Sarah Louisa Callen, widow of Thomas Callen, Esqr | of Ballinasloe. | Matron of St Columba's College | who died 20th March 1861 | This stone is erected by the pupils of the College.

Another with connections with St Columba's College is:

William Blackburn | Warden St Columba's College | died 17th Nov 1919 aged 41.

Some teachers from the area interred here include:

'Till | He | Come.' | In memory of | James Wiseman Bourke | died 27th November 1877, | aged 50 years. | And Susanna his wife | died 15th February 1884, | aged 55 years | Clerk & School Teachers | of this parish | from 1862 to 1877.

Companions and helpers who worked in local houses are also commemorated:

In | memory | of | Justine Carcin | of Lausanne, Switzerland. | For 34 years in the service of | W.R. Swifte Esq | of Whitechurch Lodge | died 28th August 1873 | aged 74 years | Sois fidele jusqu a la mort et | Je te donnerai la coronne de vis.

also Erected | to the memory of | Susanna Way, | of Butterliegh, Devonshire, | and for 10 years Cook and Housekeeper | to Mrs White of Killakee | who died on the 19th day of April, 1870 | aged 60 years

and:

Mina Brown | of Cluny, Aberdeen, | faithful nurse to | the Phibbs family. | born 26th July 1888 | died 7th November 1953.

The parishioners presented a memorial in the church for the Revd Canon James A. Carr who is interred in the churchyard. For twenty-two years he was the editor of the *Irish Ecclesiastical Gazette.* The father of thirteen children, he was married to Anna-Maria Fry from Clyde Road in Ballsbridge. His gravestone is inscribed:

'Forever with the Lord' | In | fond remembrance of my dear husband | James Anderson Carr LLd. | Canon of Christ Church Cathedral | Dublin, and for nearly 30 years | Vicar of Whitechurch. | He fell asleep Oct 26th 1900 aged 65 | 'Until the day dawn' | Also in fond remembrance of | Anna Maria, wife of the above | She fell asleep Jany 11th 1909 aged 71.

Members of the Hughes family from Hazelbrook in Rathfarnham are buried here.

In loving memory | of | William Hughes of Hazlebrook | who died 24th July 1906, aged 66.

[108] WHITECHURCH CHURCH AND CHURCHYARD.

They were famous in their time for the Hazelbrook Dairy and anyone who lived within some miles radius of it will remember the shiny, well-groomed, beautiful horses that pulled the milk drays. The hammer of their hooves on the road could be heard early each morning as they left the dairy at Hazelbrook to deliver their rounds.

Similar to Old Whitechurch cemetery, there are many here with the family name of Davis. There are five memorials within the church, and in the churchyard, there are two gravestones.

There are a few graves with military associations, as well as a stained-glass window within the church to commemorate those who gave their lives in the First World War:

To the Glory of God | and | in memory of the following | members of the congregation | who gave their lives in the | Great War | Capt. W.J. Davis, 60th Rifles 1915 | 2nd Lieut. E. Farran Black Watch, 1915 | Private Robert McFadzean Cameron Highlanders 1915 | Lieut. H.G. Killingley R.D.F. 1916 | Private G. Baldwin Tank Corps, 1917 | 2nd Lieut. W.C. Tosdevon. | Northamptonshire Fusiliers 1917.

There is also a tablet in the church commemorating General Sir John Davis, KCB, and Colonel of the Royal Sussex Regiment. He was the second son of John Davis of the Park, Rathfarnham. He died aged sixty-nine on 5 October 1901. He was active during the Indian Mutiny (1858–59), the Soudan (1884–85) and at El Tel and Temai.

Some others with military connections include:

In | loving memory of | George Augustus Frederick De Rinzy | Major General Royal Artillery, | Willbrook House, | died October 30, 1895 aged, 81.

And a gravestone which includes a fallen soldier of the Great War:

To the sacred memory of | Annie | the dearly loved wife of | John H. Coard | who departed this life on the 8th Dec. 1909 | aged 42 years. | Also in memory of their two dear sons | Alexander Rupert | who fell asleep 18th Dec. 1898 | agd 11 years & 9 months. | And | Henry Harold | 1st K.O.Y.L .I | Killed in action near Ypres, Flanders | 8th May 1915, aged 26 years. | He answered his country's call | He 'fought a good fight.' | 'The Lord is my strength and song, and | is become my salvation.'

Another casualty of the Great War:

[109] THE HEADSTONE OF ANNIE M.P. SMITHSON (1873–1948). SOME OF HER NOVELS ARE SET IN THE LOCALITY OF WHITECHURCH.

341

In ever loving memory of | Edith Jane Burton | Who passed peacefully away | at Rathfarnham | on 3rd February 1954, in her 90th year | and of | Major Louis Burton R.F.A. | died 9th June 1917 | and buried at Freunt Cemetery France | 'He that believeth in Me though he were | dead, yet shall he live.'

In the area opposite the church door is the simple grave of Sir Frederick Moore (1857–1949), DSc, MA, VMH of Willbrook House who was keeper of the Royal Botanic Gardens in Glasnevin. In 1875, Moore attended the Ghent Botanic School of Horticulture and developed a special interest in budding, grafting and pruning. A year later he worked and studied in a botanical garden attached to the University of Leiden. He then worked as Curator of Trinity College Garden in Ballsbridge. He succeeded his father, David Moore as Curator of the Botanic Gardens in Glasnevin at a young age in 1879 and worked there until his retirement in 1922.

[110] THE GRAVESTONE OF ARTIST MAY GUINNESS (1863–1955).

During these years, Moore initiated many improvements and developments in the garden, such as setting up a new rock garden, extending the arboretum and constructing weirs on the river Tolka. He remade the paths in the original part of the garden with stones and gravel. During the early 1900s, many honours were bestowed on him for his work, and in 1911, King George V conferred him with a knighthood. Moore, who had a special interest in tropical orchids, died aged ninety-two on 23 August 1949.

Nearby is the grave of Colonel Samuel White

Underneath | lie the remains of | Lieut. Colonel Samuel White | of Killakee | died May 29th 1854 | aged 70 years | Also | Anne Salisbury | his wife | died November the 27th | 1880 | aged 79 years.

Col Samuel White was the second son of Luke White, the millionaire financier and bookseller who had land around Killakee towards the end of the eighteenth century. He also owned Luttrellstown Estate at Lucan. On Luke White's demise in 1824, the house and 2,900 acres at Killakee passed on to Samuel White, who was MP for County Leitrim. He lived well and had a beautiful terraced garden laid out containing many unusual plants. It was later the seat of Lord Massy who married Samuel's youngest sister. The Massy heirs did not have the same aptitude in financial matters and were forced to leave their fine house, which was eventually demolished in 1941. Killakee was then taken over by the Department of Forestry

Another house no longer remaining is that of John O'Neill of Larchill. O'Neill was a Dublin merchant with a residence in the city. He used Larchill just for the summer months. He erected a large monument with high railings in the churchyard to his wife:

Erected by | John O'Neill Esqr | of Fitwilliam Sq & Larchill, | J.P. for Co. Dublin & consul de S.M.C. | To the memory of his good and beloved wife | Caroline, | only daughter of Thos Billings | of Silliothill Co. Kildare | She lived in the fear and love of God | and possessed the prayers of the poor. | Died 24th February 1835 | aged 67 years. | Pro fide rege et patria pugno
By the side of his beloved wife | are deposited the remains of | John O'Neill Esqr | Alderman of the City of Dublin. | Aged 74 years.

The Guinness family has a large area which is kerbed and chained. In total there are five Guinness memorials.

This includes one which is inscribed:

In loving memory | of | Mary Catherine Guinness | Croix de Guerre | of St Thomas | Born 11th of March 1863 | Died 16th July 1955.

343

May Guinness was quite a remarkable woman. An artist, she was the daughter of Thomas Hosea Guinness, a solicitor, and Mary Davis, only daughter of Charles Davis of Tibradden. Like Evie Hone and Mainie Jellett with whom she was closely associated, she studied under André Lhote. She spent a number of winters in Paris painting and in 1914 she joined the French Army as a military nurse for which she was awarded the Croix de Guerre. On the death of her mother in 1925 she left Tibradden House for the annexe at Marlay and later moved to St Thomas, a large house near Kilmashogue Bridge.

Another remarkable woman was Annie M.P. Smithson (1873–1948), the best-selling Irish romantic novelist of her era. Her paternal grandfather, John Smithson, who had a business in the chandlery line in Capel Street, lived in a house named Cloragh where Annie often stayed. Cloragh Road lies between Whitechurch, Rathfarnham and Tibradden. At that time there were no buses or trains in the area and each day he set off for work in his carriage. He and the house feature in Annie's novel *The Weldons of Tibradden*. She wrote lovingly about Whitechurch and the area in her novels *Nora Connor* and *Paid in Full*. Several of her novels are still in print. Her grave is in a quiet secluded corner to the left at the rear of the church.

Whitechurch is under the care of the Select Vestry of Whitechurch Parish.

FURTHER BURIAL GROUNDS

Burial Grounds in the Dublin suburbs and county, which have not been included in this book, are listed below. Religious houses, institutions, demesnes and private family burial grounds and vaults have been excluded.

ABBOTSTOWN, Castleknock, Co. Dublin

ADERRIG near Lucan

ARLAGH, Milverton, Skerries, Co. Dublin

ARTANE, Kilmore Road, Dublin 5

BALBRIGGAN (ST GEORGE'S), Church Street, Balbriggan, Co. Dublin

BALBRIGGAN (ST PETER'S AND PAUL'S), Balbriggan, Co. Dublin

BALDONGAN, Skerries, Co. Dublin

BALGRIFFIN, Dublin 17

BALLYBOGHILL, Co. Dublin

BALLYFERMOT (ST LAWRENCE'S), Le Fanu Road, Ballyfermot, Dublin 10

BALLYMADROUGH, Donabate, Co. Dublin

BALLYMADUN, Ballymadun, Co. Dublin

BALROTHERY, Balrothery, Co. Dublin

BALSCADDEN, Balscaddan, Co. Dublin

BALSCADDEN, Church of the Assumption, Balscadden, Co. Dublin

BETH OLAM, Aughavanagh Road, Crumlin, Dublin 12

BOHERNABREENA (ST ANNE'S), Bohernabreena, Co. Dublin

BOHERNABREENA (ST JOSEPH'S), Bohernabreena, Co. Dublin

BREMORE, Balbriggan, Co. Dublin

CASTLEKNOCK (ST BRIGID'S), Castleknock, Dublin 15

CHAPELIZOD, St Lawrence's, Main St, Chapelizod, Co. Dublin

CHAPELMIDWAY, Kilsallaghan, Co. Dublin

CLOGHRAN, Swords, Co. Dublin

CLONDALKIN (ST JOHN'S), Tower Road, Clondalkin, D. 22

CLONMETHON, Oldtown, Co. Dublin

CLONSILLA (ST MARY'S), Clonsilla, Dublin 15

COLMANSTOWN, Athgoe, Castlewarden, Co. Dublin.

COOLOCK (St John the Evangelist), Tonlegee Road, Coolock, Dublin 17

DARDISTOWN, Collinstown Cross, Swords, Co. Dublin

DONABATE (BALLALEASE), Portrane Road, Donabate, Co. Dublin

DONABATE (St Patrick's), The Square, Donabate, Co. Dublin

DONABATE (St Patrick's), Donabate, Co. Dublin

DRIMNAGH (BLUEBELL), old Naas Road, Dublin 12

ESKER OLD AND NEW, Lucan, Co. Dublin

ESKER (St Mary's), Lucan, Co. Dublin

FINGAL, Balgriffin, Malahide Road, Dublin 13

FINGLAS (St Canice's), Church Street, Finglas, Dublin 11

FINGLAS (St Margaret's), St Margaret's, Finglas, Dublin 11

GARRISTOWN, Garristown, Co. Dublin

GLENCULLEN (St Patrick's), Glencullen, Co. Dublin

GRALLAGH, Naul, Co. Dublin

GRANGE ABBEY, Grange Road, Donaghmede, Dublin 13

HOLLYWOOD, Naul, Co. Dublin

HOLMPATRICK, Skerries, Co. Dublin

KENURE OLD CHURCH, Rush, Co. Dublin

KILBRIDE, Co. Dublin

KILCREAGH, Kilcreagh Road, Donabate, Co. Dublin

KILLEEK, Swords, Co. Dublin

KILLOSSERY, Rowlestown, Co. Dublin

KILMACTAWLAY, Newcastle, Co. Dublin

KILMAHUDDRICK (St Cuthbert's), Deansrath, Bawnogue, Clondalkin, Dublin 22

KILSALLAGHAN, Kilsallaghan, Co. Dublin

KINSEALY (St Nicholas), Kinsealy, Malahide, Co. Dublin

LOUGHTOWN, Newcastle, Co. Dublin

LUCAN CHAPEL HILL (St Mary's), Lucan, Co. Dublin

LUSK (St Macculind's), Lusk Village, Co. Dublin

MALAHIDE (St Andrew's), Church Road, Malahide, Co. Dublin

MALAHIDE (St Sylvester's), Main Street, Malahide, Co. Dublin

MALAHIDE (YELLOW WALLS), Malahide, Co. Dublin

MULHUDDART, LADYSWELL, Mulhuddart, Dublin 15

MULHUDDART (ST THOMAS'), Mulhuddart, Dublin 15

NAUL, Naul, Co. Dublin

NEWCASTLE, Newcastle, Co. Dublin

NEWCASTLE-LYONS (ST FINIAN'S), The Glebe, Main Street, Newcastle, Co. Dublin

NEWLANDS CROSS, Clondalkin, Co. Dublin

OLD CONNAUGHT, Little Bray, Co. Dublin

PALMERSTOWN, Kennelsfort Road, Palmerstown, Dublin 20

PALMERSTOWN, Dublin 20 (behind Stewart's Hospital)

PALMERSTOWN, OLDTOWN, Co. Dublin

PORTMARNOCK, Strand Road, Co. Dublin

PORTMARNOCK (ST MARNOCK'S), Old Portmarnock, Co. Dublin

PORTRANE (ST CATHERINE'S), Langstone, Portrane, Co. Dublin

RATHCOOLE, Main Street, Rathcoole, Co. Dublin

SAGGART, Main Street, Saggart, Co. Dublin

ST DOOLAGH'S, Kinsealy, Co. Dublin

SANTRY (ST PAPPIN'S), Santry, Dublin 9

SHANGANAGH, Bray Road, Shankill, Co. Dublin

SKERRIES (ST MOBHI'S), Grange Road, Milverton, Skerries, Co. Dublin

SKERRIES (ST PATRICK'S), Skerries, Co. Dublin

SWORDS (ST COLUMBA'S), Church Road, Swords, Co. Dublin

SWORDS (ST COLUMCILLE'S), Chapel Lane, Swords, Co. Dublin

TALLAGHT (ST MAELRUAN'S), Tallaght Village, Dublin 24

TEMPLEOGUE, Willington Lane, Dublin 12

TEMPLEOGUE (OLD), Willington Lane, Dublin 12

WARD, THE, Co. Dublin

WESTPALSTOWN, Naul, Co. Dublin

WHITESTOWN (ST MAUR'S), Rush, Co. Dublin

WOODTOWN, Rathfarnham, Co. Dublin

Maps

The following maps are from the 1838 survey of Dublin. Based on Ordnance Survey Ireland by permission of the Government. © Government of Ireland Permit No. MP009201

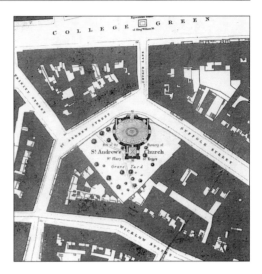

St Andrew's Church

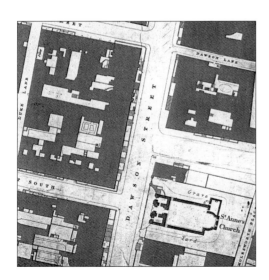

St Anne's Church

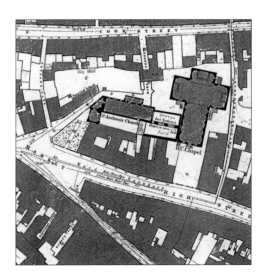

St Audoen's Church

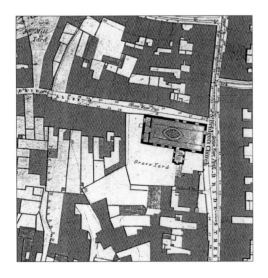

St Bride's Church

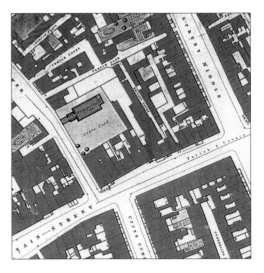

St George's Church (Little)

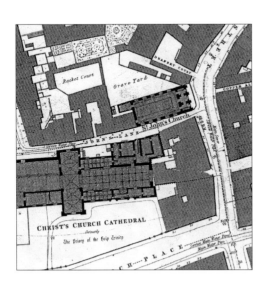

St John's Church

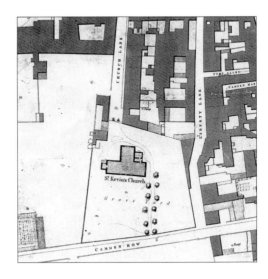

St Kevin's Church

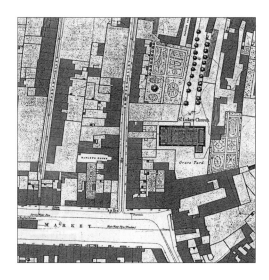

St Luke and St Nicholas Without

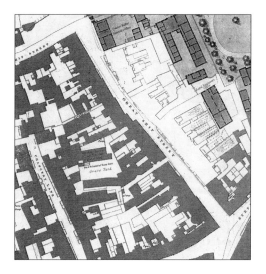

St Michael le Pole

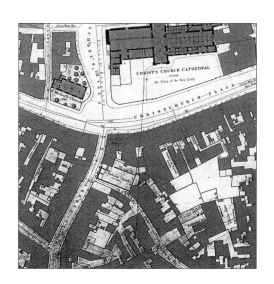

St Nicholas Within

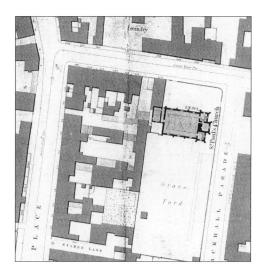

St Paul's Church

351

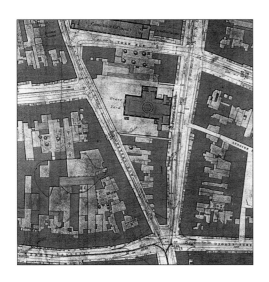

ST PETER'S CHURCH

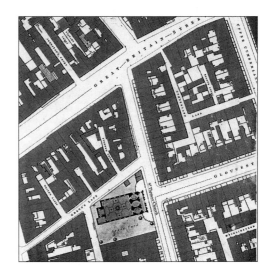

ST THOMAS'S CHURCH

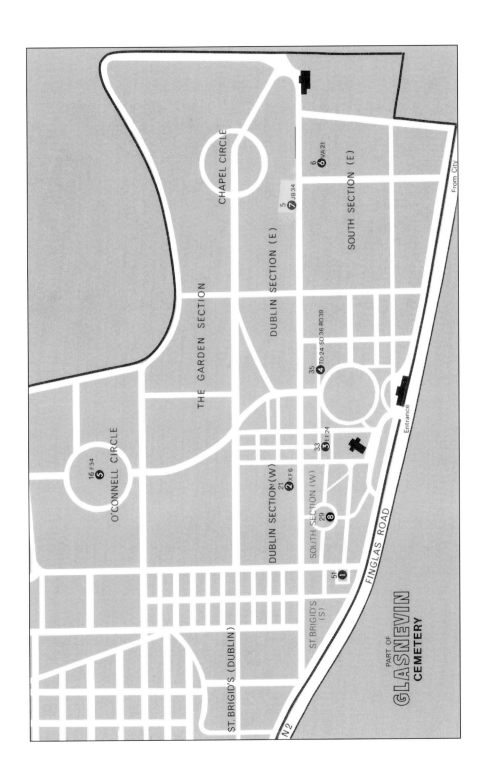

CHAPEL CIRCLE

6 ❻ VA 21

SOUTH SECTION (E)

5 ❼ JB 34

DUBLIN SECTION (E)

THE GARDEN SECTION

35 ❹ TD 24 SD 36 RD 39

O'CONNELL CIRCLE

16 F 34 ❺

33 ❸ EF 24

DUBLIN SECTION (W)
21 ❷ X F 6

SOUTH SECTION (W)
29 ❽

ST. BRIGID'S (DUBLIN)

ST BRIGID'S (S)
51 ❶

FINGLAS ROAD

Entrance

From City

N 2

PART OF
GLASNEVIN
CEMETERY

GLASNEVIN CEMETERY

(** after name denotes that grave is marked on map. The number refers to location on map.)

Daniel O'Connell	[O'Connell Tower Circle]
Rev. John Spratt	[AI O'Connell Tower Circle]
Barry Sullivan	[RE 32 st & 33]
Thomas Farrell	[Vault B26]
John Hogan	[E25, 26]
Christopher Moore	[Ja 62 Garden]
John Philpot Curran	[LMN 51-57]
Roger Casement	[A 1 6 7 & 17]
Augustinian Order	[AH+Bh, 5-8]
Christian Brothers	[MH-OH, 4-9]
Dominican Order	[AH-CH, 15-21 1/2]
Franciscan Order	[AH-CH, 9ST-15 1/2]
Carmelite Order	[Oc & Pc, 48-51]
Society of Jesus ** [1]	[AH-GH, 30-40 1/2]
John Keegan	[Zg 248 Old Poor Ground]
James Clarence Mangan ** [7]	[Jb 34]
John Keegan Casey	[Nc 7]
Brendan Behan ** [6]	[VA 21]
Edward Martyn	Unmarked grave, NE near Violet Hill
Dora Sigerson** [5]	[F34 all, O'Connell Circle]
Maura Laverty** [3]	[EF 24 all Dnc]
Seamus O'Kelly	[NB 48 St. Paul's Section]
Christy Brown	[IF 50, St. Paul's Section]
Luke Kelly	[LE 39 St. Paul's Section]
Charles Stewart Parnell** [8]	Parnell Circle
John Stanislaus Joyce** [2]	
and Mary Jane Murray	[XF6 1/2 & 7 Dublin Sect. W]
Matthew F. Kane	[11 238 1/2]
Joseph Patrick Nannetti MP	[HF 25 South Section]
Timothy Harrington	[Ug 4 Dublin]

John Henry Menton	[Zg 148 Garden]
Alderman John Hooper	[Zg 178 & 1/2]
Canon John O'Hanlon	[EH - 19]
Michael Cusack	[Dg - 163.5]
James FitzHarris	[UH 159 all]
Thomas H. Burke	[ZB 74 South Section E]
Michael Collins	[Gd 82 all South New Chapel]
Kitty Kiernan	[FD 68.5 South Section E]
Anne Devlin	[Vc 45 all South]
Republican Plot	[TD24 all 25 1/2 South]
John O'Leary** [4]	[RD 39 all, SNC]
James Stephens	[RD 40 South New Chapel]
Eamon De Valera & Sinéad De Valera	[Yd 11 & 12, Snc]
Sean T. O'Ceallaigh	[AH64 & 65, St. Brigid]
James Larkin	[VD 25 South New Chapel]
Frank Ryan	[TD RD 22 all south]
William Dargan	[TD 40 South Section E]
Frank Duff	[HA 23 all South]
Thomas Bodkin	[FD 46 South]
Sir Alfred Chester Beatty	[SD 53 South Section E]
Francis & Hanna Sheehy Skeffington	[LA 18, South]
Margaret Burke Sheridan	[XD 16 17 1/2 South]
Peadar Kearney	Republican Plot
James Devlin	[AC 74 South Section E]
Major John Dyke	[B60 - 194] Unmarked
Zozimus (Michael Moran)	[AG 30 Dublin Section W]

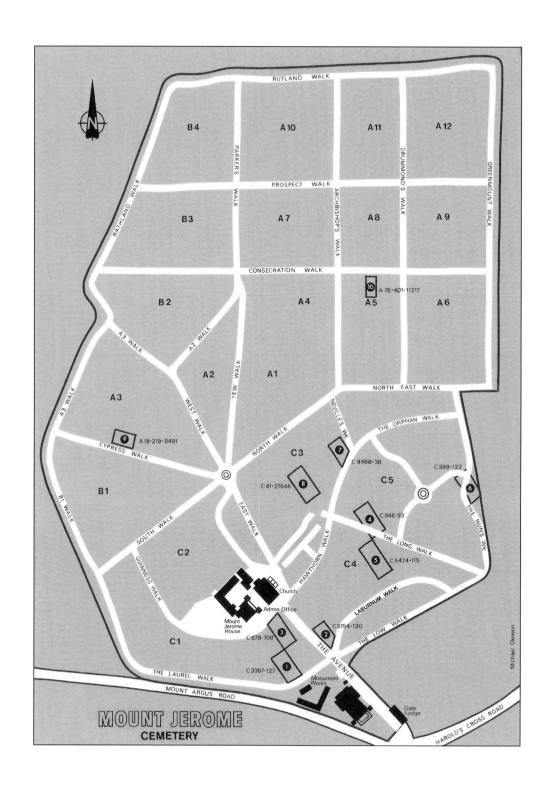

MOUNT JEROME

(** after name denotes that grave is marked on map. The number refers to location on map.)

Reverend William Conygham Plunkett	[C91 - 145 Vault]
William Carleton** [2]	[C3754-130]
John Kells Ingram** [1]	[C3367-127]
Sir William Wilde ** [3	[C678-108]
Thomas Caulfield Irwin** [4]	[C946-93]
Thomas Davis** [5]	[C5474-115]
Joseph Sheridan Le Fanu ** [6]	[C399-122]
John Millington Synge** [8]	[C9468-38]
George FitzMaurice	[C19 - 29414]
George Russell (AE)** [10]	[10] [A76 - 401-11-217]
Mairtin O'Cadhain	[CRB+4 - 465 - 37 967]
Edward Packenham, 6th Earl of Longford	[C53 355 38]
Edward Dowden	[C5 -14017]
Paul Smith	[C8 48145]
Colonel Fritz Brase	[C25 462 - 62 -67]
Thomas Kirk	[C130 - 843]
George Papworth	[B68 - 179 - 7673]
John Skipton Mulvany	[C134 - 511]
Sir Richard & William Vitruvius Morrison	[63 - 199 Vault]
Jacob Owen	[B 210]
Jerome Connor	[A98 497 25947]
Sarah Purser	[C121 -19521]
Jack B. Yeats** [7]	[C4 - 27646]
Walter Osborne	[C24 -11 11 3]
Cusack Memorial	[C89 -29 56]
Harvie Memorial	[C88 Vault]
Gresham Tomb	[C90 Vault]
John Bernard Logier	[C88 -287]
John Brown	[C25 -12120]
Col. Hans Garrett Moore	[C25 & 26 - 7903]

Robert Graves	[C19 - 1698]
Robert Adams	[C27 - 1509 Vault]
Abraham Colles	[92 - 744]
William Hartpole Lecky	[C136 - 1183]
George Petrie	[C110 - 2603]
Sir William Rowan Hamilton	[C116 - 3489]
George Francis Fitzgerald	[20/21 - 7953]
John Joly	[C17 - 20221]
Alexander Thom	[C115 - 5372]
Sir Richard Griffith	[C87 - 2276 Vault]
Henry Hutchin Stewart	[C11 - 5395]
Ninian Niven	[C106 -177]

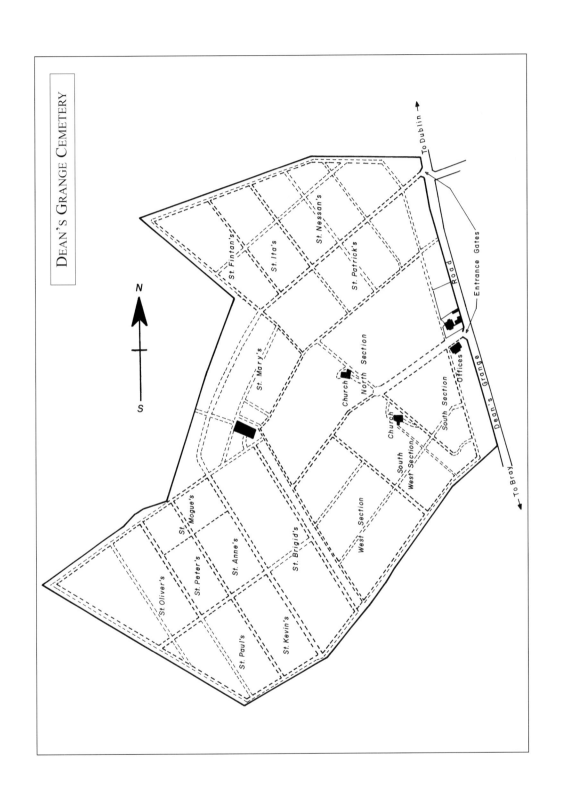

DEAN'S GRANGE CEMETERY

N
S

To Dublin

Entrance Gates

Road

Dean's Grange

To Bray

Offices

Church

Church

North Section

South Section

South West Section

South West Section

West Section

St. Fintan's

St. Ita's

St. Nessan's

St. Patrick's

St. Mary's

St. Mogue's

St. Peter's

St. Anne's

St. Brigid's

St. Oliver's

St. Paul's

St. Kevin's

DEAN'S GRANGE CEMETERY

Anastasia Carey	[31/32 K North]
John Howard Parnell	[S.W. Section Row O]
Dr. Augustine Henry	[56 14 North]
Constantine Curran	[121 K St Patrick]
Frank O'Connor	[Sect. N. St Patrick 79/80]
Donagh MacDonagh	[Sect. N. AO 137]
Brian O'Nolan	[20 A West]
Michael Farrell,	[15 G2 St Mary]
Padraig O'Siochfhradha	[83 Q St Patrick]
Richard Irvine Best	[66 H SW]
John McCormack	[119-120 E. & F. St. Patrick]
John Boyd Dunlop	[72 & 73 C & D SW]
John Costello	[119, 120 M St Patrick]
Sean Lemass	[38.39.R. St Patrick]
Barry FitzGerald	[55, 59 A St Nessan]
Anew McMaster	[N 210 St Patrick]
F. J. McCormick	[121, 122 GH St Patrick]
Noel Purcell	[85 E St Oliver]
Joseph Edward Woodall	[H 173 St Patrick]
Coleman, Mary Edith	[30 S2 South]
Vaughan, Capt. James	[36 Section B North]
Republic Plot	[Section A West]
Fionn Connolly Edwards	[18 A West]
John Gardiner Nutting	[76, 77, 78, M7N -SW]
Solway/Palme Shipwrecks	[87-88, H. North - 86, 87, 88, 89-1, - North] and [15, 16, 17 N2 - South - 17 02 South]
Sir John Talbot Power	[3 D2 North]
Joe McGrath	[26-27-28/E&F St Patrick]

BIBLIOGRAPHY

Ball, F.E., *A History of the County Dublin*, Dublin: Alex Thom, 1903.

Ball, F.E and E. Hamilton, *The Parish of Taney: A History of Dundrum near Dublin, and its Neighbourhood*, Dublin: Hodges Figgis, 1895.

Blacker, the Revd. Beaver H., *Brief Sketches of the Parishes of Booterstown and Donnybrook in the county of Dublin*, Dublin: George Herbert, 1874.

Boyer, Marie-France, *Tree-Talk. Memories, Myths and Timeless Customs*, London: Thames & Hudson.

Burton, Revd Nathanael, *History of the Royal Hospital, Kilmainham*, Dublin: William Curry & Co., 1843.

Carroll, W.G., *Succession of Clergy in the Parishes of St Bride, St Michael-le-Pole and St Stephen*, Dublin: J. Charles & Son, 1884.

Centenary Year 1989, Select Vestry of All Saints' Church, Raheny, Dublin 5.

Childers, Major E.S.E and R.E. Childers, *The Story of the Royal Hospital Kilmainham*, London: Hutchinson & Co., 1921.

Commonwealth War Graves Commission Cemetery Registers for Co. Dublin.

Cosantóir, An, (April, 1991) 'An Irish Soldier remembered by Corporal Liam Byrne'.

Cosgrave, D., *North Dublin: City and Environs*, Dublin: Four Courts Press, 1909.

Costello, Peter, *Dublin Churches*, Dublin: Gill & Macmillan, 1989.

Craig, Maurice, *Dublin 1660–1860*, Dublin: Hodges Figgis, 1952.

Crawford, John, *Within the Walls. The Story of St Audoen's Church, Cornmarket, Dublin*, Dublin, 1986.

Crawford, John, *Among the Graves. Inscriptions in St Audoen's Church, Cornmarket, Dublin*.

Crone, John S. A., *Concise Dictionary of Irish Biography*, Dublin: Talbot Press, 1937.

D'Alton, John, *The History of County Dublin*, Dublin: Hodges and Smith, 1838.

Dictionary of National Biography.

Directory of Graveyards in the Dublin Area. An index and guide to burial records. Dublin Public Libraries, 1990.

Dublin Historical Record, Vols xii, xiv.

Egan, M.J.S and Flatman, R.M., *Memorials of the Dead: Dublin City and County. Number 1: Golden Bridge Cemetery Inchicore, Dublin*. Dublin: Irish Genealogical Research Society, 1988.

Egan, M.J.S. and Flatman, R.M., *Memorials of the Dead: Dublin City and County. Number 2. Dublin City and County Graveyards*. Dublin: Irish Genealogical Research Society, 1989.

Egan, M.J.S and Flatman, R.M., *Memorials of the Dead: Dublin City and County. Number 3: Dublin City and County Graveyards*. Dublin: Irish Genealogical Research Society, 1990.

Egan, Michael J.S., *Dublin City and Country Graveyards,* edited and transcribed by Michael J.S. Egan, Vol. 4.

Finlayson, Revd J., *Inscriptions on the monuments, mural tablets etc. at present existing in Christ Church Cathedral,* Dublin: Hodges, Foster & Figgis 1878.

FitzPatrick, William J., *History of the Dublin Catholic Cemeteries*, Dublin: Catholic Cemeteries Committee, 1900.

Fleetwood, John A., *The Irish Body Snatchers. A History of body snatching in Ireland*. Dublin: Tomar Publishing Ltd, 1988.

Fitz-Simon, Christopher, *The Boys. A Biography of Micheál MacLiammóir and Hilton Edwards*, London: Heinemann, 1994.

Garrett, Arthur, *From Age to Age: History of the Parish of Drumcondra, North Strand and St Barnabas*, Dublin: Blackrock Printers, 1970.

Garrett, Arthur, *Down through the ages. The history of Killester Church and Parish*, Dublin: Church of St Brigid Killester, 1996.

Garrett, Arthur, *Through Countless Ages. The Story of the church and parish of All Saints, Raheny,* Dublin: Church of All Saints, Raheny, 1989.

Gilbert, Sir J.T.A., A *History of the City of Dublin*, 3 vols, Vol. 1, Dublin: James McGlashan, 1854; Vols 2 & 3, Dublin: McGlashan & Gill, 1859.

Harbison, Peter, *Guide to the National Monuments in the Republic of Ireland*, Dublin: Gill & Macmillan, 1970.

Hughes, Revd S.C., *The Church of St John the Evangelist Dublin*, Hodges Figgis and Co., 1889.

Hyman, L., *The Jews in Ireland from earliest times to 1910*, Irish University Press, 1972.

Igoe, Vivien, *A Literary Guide to Dublin*, London: Methuen, 1994.

Ingram, John A, *The Cure of Souls. A History of St Brigid's Church of Ireland, Stillorgan*, Dublin: 1997.

Irish Builder, Vol. 28

Irish Genealogist 5(1) 1974, 'Names on coffin-plates in the vaults of St Andrew's Church Westland Row', transcribed by E.J. McAuliffe and Julian C. Walton.

Irish Genealogist 7(2), 'Monumental Inscriptions from Rathfarnham Graveyard, Dublin', transcribed by Seán Murphy.

Irish Genealogist 4(6) 1973, 'Monumental Inscriptions from Killiney old churchyard, Co. Dublin', transcribed by E.J. McAuliffe and R.J. O'Kelly-Lynch.

Irish Genealogist 4(5) 1972.

Irish Sword, Vol. XVI, 1985, No. 63, 'Imperial Yeomanry Notes' by F. Glenn Thompson.

Jackson, Victor, *The Monuments in St Patrick's Cathedral, Dublin*, Dublin: 1987.

Journal of the Association for the Preservation of the Memorials of the Dead in Ireland, Vols i, ii, iii, iv, v, vi, vii, viii, xi, xii.

Journal of the Royal Society of Antiquaries of Ireland, 104, 1974, 'St Paul's Parish, Dublin', by Edith M. Best.

Joyce, Weston St John, *The Neighbourhood of Dublin*, M.H. Gill & Son, Ltd., 1939

Langtry, J and N. Carter (Eds), *Mount Jerome – A Victorian Cemetery*, Dublin, 1997 [Mount Jerome Historical Project]

Lyons, J.B., *The Quality of Mercer's. The story of Mercer's Hospital 1734–1991*, Dublin: Glendale Publishing, Ltd., 1991.

Lewis, Samuel, *A Topographical Dictionary of Ireland*, 1837.

MacCarthy, R.B., *St Mark's – the history of a Dublin parish*, Dublin, 1971.

McCready, C.T., *Dublin Street Names*, Dublin: Hodges Figgis, 1892

Mac Giolla Phádraig, Brian, *History of Terenure*, Dublin: Veritas Company Ltd., 1954.

McRedmond, Louis, *To the Greater Glory – A History of the Irish Jesuits*, Dublin: Gill & Macmillan, 1991.

Madden, Richard R., *The United Irishmen, their lives and times*, Dublin: Mullany, 1860.

Murphy, Seán, *Bully's Acre and the Royal Hospital Kilmainham graveyards: history and inscriptions*, Dublin: Divelina Publications, 1989.

Murphy, Seán, *Memorial Inscriptions from St Catherine's Church and Graveyard, Dublin*, Dublin: Divelina Publications, 1987.

Nelson, E.C. and E.M. McCracken, *The Brightest Jewel: A History of the National Botanic Gardens, Glasnevin, Dublin*, Kilkenny: Boethius Press, 1987.

Northridge, Revd R., *St Andrew's Church Dublin, 1171–1916. A Short Review*. Dublin: Hely's, 1916.

O'Connor, Kevin (ed), *Thou shalt not kill. True-life stories of Irish Murders*, Dublin: Gill & Macmillan, 1994.

O'Dwyer, Frederick, *Lost Dublin*, Dublin: Gill & Macmillan, 1981.

O'Hanlon, Canon John, *Lives of the Irish Saints, Dublin 1875–1903*. 10 vols.

Parkinson, Danny, *Huguenot cemetery 1693*, Dublin Family History Society, 1988.

Parkinson, Danny, *Donnybrook Graveyard c800–1993*, Dublin Family History Society 1988.

Refausse, Raymond (Ed), *The Register of the Parish of St Thomas, Dublin 1750–1791*, Representative Church Body, 1994.

Sadie, Stanley (Ed), *The New Grove Dictionary of Music and Musicians*, 1980.

St James's Graveyard Project/FÁS, *St James's Graveyard, Dublin. History and Associations,* Dublin: FÁS and St James's Development Association, 1988.

Shepherd, Ernie, *Behind the Scenes. The Story of Whitechurch district in South County Dublin*, Dublin: Whitechurch Publications, 1983.

Shillman, Bernard, *A Short History of the Jews in Ireland*, Dublin: Eason & Son, Ltd., 1945.

Snoddy, Theo, *Dictionary of Irish Artists 20th Century*, Dublin: Wolfhound Press, 1996.

Spencer, Paul Francis C.P., *To Heal the Broken Hearted. The Life of Blessed Charles of Mount Argus*, Dublin: Gill and Macmillan, 1988.

Strickland, Walter G., *A Dictionary of Irish Artists*, Dublin: Maunsel & Company, 1913.

Watchorn, Finola, *Crumlin and the way it was*, Dublin: 1985.

Widdess, J.D.H., *The Royal College of Surgeons in Ireland and its Medical School 1784–1984*, Dublin: Royal College of Surgeons in Ireland, 1984.

Webb, Alfred, *A Compendium of Irish Biography*, Dublin: M.H. Gill & Son, mdcccxxviii

Wheeler, H.A. and M.J. Craig, *The Dublin City Churches of the Church of Ireland*, Dublin: A.P.C.K. 1948.

Whiteside, Lesley, *The Chapel of Trinity College Dublin*, Dublin: Chapel Committee, Trinity College Dublin, 1998.

Wright, G.N., *An Historical Guide to the City of Dublin*, London: Baldwin, Cradock and Joy, 1825.

INDEX